FREE-LANCER AND STAFF WRITER

Newspaper Features and Magazine Articles

Third Edition

William L. Rivers,
  Stanford University

Shelley Smolkin,
  Free-Lance Writer

Wadsworth Publishing Company
Belmont, California
A Division of Wadsworth, Inc.

ISBN 0-534-00873-9

Senior Editor: Rebecca Hayden
Production Editor: Diane Sipes
Designer: Janet Wood
Copy Editor: Stephen McElroy
Cover Illustration: Andra Rudolph

Printed in the United States of America

 2 3 4 5 6 7 8 9 10 — 85 84 83

Library of Congress Cataloging in Publication Data

Rivers, William L
  Free-lancer and staff writer.

  Includes index.
  1. Authorship.   I. Smolkin, Shelley, joint author.   II. Title.
PN147.R59 1981   808'.02   80-14865
ISBN 0-534-00873-9

PREFACE

The third edition of *Free-Lancer and Staff Writer* has been updated and thoroughly revised to reflect the changes in the world of journalism. For example, during the past five years many newspapers have become more like daily magazines. We feel that newspapers will continue to change in this direction, and this textbook emphasizes that change. The book has also been adapted to the needs and interests of the increasing number of college students who are turning to journalism classes for vocational instruction.

This emphasis is evident in the reordering of chapters and the addition of new material. Chapter Three, "Breaking into Journalism," was, in the second edition, the last chapter of the book. It has been revised and moved to the front of the book because students want to know what the job market is like before they begin to develop their skills as writers. Chapter Eleven, "The Free-Lance Writer," has been added because of the increasing interest students have shown in pursuing the independent life. It is a frank and practical discussion of the day-to-day realities of free-lancing. Both this chapter and Chapter Thirteen, "Generating and Developing Ideas for Magazine Articles," include tips on how to market magazine articles successfully. The overall message of these chapters is that there is much more to free-lancing than writing good articles. Writers are increasingly faced with the necessity of working with photographers, so Chapter Twelve, "Working with Photographers," has also been added.

The chapters on writing different kinds of newspaper features and magazine articles have been revised in response to students' requests for more and shorter examples. These chapters have been reorganized to make them more concise. For example, the material from former Chapters Eight and Fifteen on how-to-do-its has been combined in Chapter Eighteen. A chapter on writing humorous articles has also been added, Chapter Twenty.

Exercises relevant to the material in all the chapters have been added at the end of each chapter. Their purpose is to illustrate the main points made in the textbook and to provide students with clear examples of how these ideas can be put to use in writing.

We wish to thank the following people whose comments have been very helpful in reviewing this book in the manuscript stage: Holly Arpan of Indiana University; Elizabeth Fraas of Eastern Kentucky University; Dean M. Gottehrer of the University of Alaska; Susan K. Harris of Queens College; and William McReynolds of the University of Colorado at Boulder.

William L. Rivers
Shelley Smolkin

CONTENTS

PART ONE
The World of the Journalist

CHAPTER 1
Changing Times

A 1979 Sunday edition of the *Seattle Post-Intelligencer* ran a front-page headline that clearly illustrates the changes taking place in newspapers today: "FOUR SUNDAY MAGAZINES IN TODAY'S *P-I*." The presence of the magazines in the newspaper and its use of them to attract readers is evidence that newspapers and magazines are becoming more alike. Newspaper editors are running longer stories while magazine editors are relying on shorter ones. The writing style in newspaper feature stories is moving away from a straight-news tone toward the more lively style found in magazines. At the same time, magazines are offering the detailed guides to local services and events that formerly were the exclusive domain of newspapers.

This change has taken place because television, having established a solid base in news reporting, is now encroaching on the news feature territory of both newspapers and magazines, and they have had to find new ways of competing. The success of CBS's "60 Minutes," which it refers to as a news weekly magazine, exemplifies television's newest challenge to print journalism and magazines and has prompted network executives and local programmers to create similar series. This style of television reporting creates a kind of visual magazine article that relieves the viewers of the necessity of reading. They need only to sit back and have the story presented to them. "60 Minutes" even introduces its stories with graphics similar to those found in magazine articles! Since 1971 when the Federal Communications Commission turned over a half hour of evening prime time to local programming under the Prime Time Access Rule, many television stations have installed local versions of the national television news magazine. This trend began at San Francisco station KPIX when Bill Hillier realized that he could produce a local show for less money than it cost to buy a game show, and could also control the budget. The result was "The Evening Magazine," a program shot entirely on location around the Bay Area. The show was so successful that it later served as a model to other locally produced television magazines.

HOW NEWSPAPERS AND MAGAZINES
COMPETE WITH TELEVISION

Yet the public's desire for printed news has not been diminished by the success of television's incursions into territory once claimed by newspapers and magazines. Some observers claim that television actually whets the viewers' appetites for more news. Since 1950, the number of daily newspapers published in the United States has remained virtually unchanged. At the same time, the number of weekly periodicals has increased 22 percent and the number of monthly periodicals has increased 4 percent. They try to do in their pages what television cannot do—that is, they offer readers tightly written stories that cover subjects in depth, using formats that enable readers to choose from among many different kinds of stories in the order of their interest and at the time of their choosing. No matter how it tries, television will never be able to duplicate these functions. Viewers will always have to watch news stories in the order the program presents them, and until every home has a video recorder, they will have to watch the programs at times chosen by the stations.

THE NEWSPAPERS CHANGE

To compete with television, the metropolitan newspapers find it essential to put hard-digging reporters on stories. Moreover, reporters must write more smoothly than they were required to in the past. The editors of these metropolitan newspapers are less inclined to honor the old, straight reporting, looking instead for a bright feature touch on anything that deserves more time than the short items. The long stories are often a blend of reporting and feature writing.

Suburban papers had been less competitive with television than the metropolitan papers because news programs generally did not cover suburban events, but even this has changed somewhat with the advent of the television magazines.

But even so, television cannot compete with suburban newspapers' focus on their own cities. San Francisco's six television stations, for example, focus almost entirely on San Francisco news. The stations could not hold their many viewers if they reported the routine happenings of a dozen nearby cities. Much the same is true of television news programs in other metropolitan areas. The suburban papers rely on the papers of their metropolitan areas to cover the national and international news, and they tackle the local news.

The Rise of the Feature Story

Both suburban and metropolitan newspapers have upgraded the feature story as they attempt to keep up with the television magazines.

What is the difference between a news reporter and a feature writer? One anecdote illustrates the point. A young woman who planned to leave a small newspaper asked her managing editor for a reference. He wrote one praising her intelligence, diligence, and warmth, and added this sentence: "She has a wonderful flair for feature writing, and she has been working hard on her news reporting and writing." Obviously, the managing editor was also saying that she had a long way to go before her ability to gather and report news would match her feature-writing ability.

Like a good many who work for newspapers, this young woman was a natural feature writer, although editors normally seek the writer who can blend a feature touch with reportorial ability. Feature writers are becoming more prominent with time, particularly as a result of the great interest among young newspaper staffers in investigative reporting, which got a new impetus during the reporting of the Watergate scandal. As Jim Reed of the *Topeka Daily Capital* said: "Any news story—fires, automobile accidents in which there are fatalities, acts of heroism—is used regularly. Good feature stories are *always* wanted. Unusual hobbies, success stories, inventions, interviews, personality stories, human interest stories—all can be used." This statement keynotes the trend among newspapers.

Another change in newspapers that has fostered feature writing is the demise of the "Women's Page" or "Society" sections. In their place have risen sections with names like "Style," "Living," and "View." These pages are generally filled with feature stories that are of interest to both sexes. As a result, one newspaper features editor noted that more of her readers are men, and that men today are more interested in feature writing. Features are no longer regarded by newspaper professionals as the "soft" news stories.

Journalists are also finding feature writing more attractive because it provides greater freedom of style than is found in straight-news reporting. The distinction between the two is obvious, as illustrated by this excerpt from a feature article:

> When Herman O. Tolson first came to town, the restrooms at the fairgrounds were marked "white" and "colored."
>
> That was in the mid-1960s. The signs are gone now. Mexico, Missouri, has changed quite a bit since then, especially for a town that calls itself the capital of "Little Dixie"—a band of counties through the heart of central Missouri that traditionally have considered themselves a part of the South.
>
> The biggest sign of change is Tolson himself. The forty-four-year-old assistant high school principal and ordained Baptist minister became the town's first black mayor this month. . . .

If this same story had been written in straight-news style, it might have begun like this: Herman O. Tolson, 44, this month became the first black mayor of Mexico, Missouri. A former assistant high school principal and ordained Baptist minister, Tolson has been a resident since the mid-1960s. . . .

Even when the news is sad, writers may often lure their readers with a quiet note instead of straight reportage:

> The Post Office manager sat in his cubicle munching on a sandwich, a solitary figure behind a row of wickets marked "closed."
>
> Where is everybody? he was asked.
>
> "They're all sick—again," he said.
>
> When will they get well?
>
> "They're all supposed to recover tomorrow," he said. "But who knows how long they'll stay well."
>
> The illness that periodically infects this city's 4,000 residents. . . .

Certainly, the writer who has a feature touch can see the distinction between this kind of writing and the kind that opens most news stories.

THE MAGAZINES CHANGE

First, we must recognize *how* the magazine world has changed during the past twenty-five years. The fact that it *has* changed is indicated by the laments of some veteran writers who say that the article market has shrunk dangerously. They maintain that the deaths of some leading magazines and the trend among others to hire staff writers who work full-time for a magazine rather than relying on independent free-lancers has reduced opportunities for the independent writer.

They argue persuasively, and in a sense they are right. But to consider only their lamentations is to misunderstand what has happened, and is happening, in the world of magazines. In his valuable history of American magazines, John Tebbel points out that during the decade of the 1960s, a total of 162 periodicals disappeared through sale, merger, or suspension, but 676 new magazines appeared.*

This growth does not mean that there has been an increase in free-lance opportunities. The article market is quite different today.

---

*John Tebbel, *The American Magazine: A Compact History* (New York: Hawthorn Books, 1969), p. 249.

The key difference is that the number of general magazines has decreased significantly and the number of special-interest publications has increased significantly. Most of the special-interest magazines that have long been published pay writers more than they once did, and many of the new ones pay more than the most openhanded publications in their fields paid ten or twenty years ago. But the old-time freelancers were accustomed to dealing with a dozen *general* magazines, and they were often able to work up an article that might be published in any one of half a dozen of them if their first choices turned them down. Now they find so few general magazines left that their range is restricted and their margin for error is slender to the point of invisibility.

To understand what has happened in the magazine world, it is necessary to look again at the role of television. To the extent that it is an *information* medium, television is primarily useful in reporting spot events, but as we have seen television magazines are usurping functions that once belonged almost exclusively to the newspaper. This usurpation has pushed many newspapers into pirating part of a function that was once almost exclusively the magazine's—reporting at length and sometimes in depth. Although most newspapers continue to provide a startling range of information on many subjects, mostly in short items, many are giving at least a few reporters the leisure to pursue stories in depth and to write in the fluid style of magazines. The result has been turbulence in the magazine world.

Since radio, television, and newspapers are primarily general media that aim at the broadest possible audience, the magazines most affected by them are the general magazines. It is not at all surprising, then, that the mass-circulation general magazines suffered first, and most, from the change in the roles of the mass media brought on by television. *Collier's,* long one of the most popular weeklies, moved to fortnightly, then died. Several monthlies—notably *American Magazine, Woman's Home Companion,* and *Liberty*—also died. *The Saturday Evening Post* moved from weekly to fortnightly publication and hung on for years through financial crisis after crisis before it died. It was revived as a quarterly in 1971, but as a weekly it had supported so many free-lancers so handsomely that the new publication seemed only a silhouette of the old *Post.*

Magazines for Special Interests

In contrast to the general nature of the magazines that have died during the past two decades, the successful magazines that grew up during this period emphasize special interests and seek particular audiences—*Sports Illustrated, American Heritage, Horizon, TV Guide,* and others, including dozens of "city" magazines like *New Orleans, San Francisco, Dallas, Atlanta, Milwaukee,* and *New York.*

One of the most convincing illustrations of the need to address a special audience was provided by *Rolling Stone.* Created with a borrowed $7,000 by twenty-one-year-old Jann Wenner, it began as a rock magazine in 1967. Dozens of magazines had discovered rock and were covering it then. But Wenner and his young staff soon proved that their belief that music *was* the youthful counterculture, combined with their ability to speak to a youthful audience in familiar and convincing terms, could make *Rolling Stone* a success. By 1976, *Rolling Stone*'s circulation was approaching 400,000.

And, of course, hundreds of religious, occupational, fraternal, farming, business, and professional magazines were born during the same period. In his excellent *Magazines for Millions*, James L. Ford complains that the consumer publications are given so much attention when the thousands of specialized publications are "produced by an enthusiastic army of 100,000 men and women."* He points out that there are nearly 1,700 magazines in religious publishing alone, and perhaps as many as 17,000 company publications.

A more recent example of a new magazine that addresses a particular audience is provided by *Mainstream*, which celebrated its third anniversary in 1979. *Mainstream* is a monthly magazine for the able-disabled. It was started by Jim Hammitt with seed money provided under the Comprehensive Employment and Training Act (CETA). Now financially self-sufficient, *Mainstream* serves as a training center for disabled people who are interested in learning journalism-related skills. It is the only independent magazine in this country whose publishers, staff and audience are people with nearly every kind of disability. Obviously, like the magazines mentioned above, *Mainstream* fills a special need.

Of course every generalization is undermined by at least one glaring exception. In this case, it's *People* magazine, begun by Time-Life, Inc. in 1974. If *People* specializes in anything, it has to be "celebrity journalism," but it also devotes half of its pages to stories about interesting but unknown personalities. Its stories are superficial, but the magazine's success is not. It began with a remarkable starting circulation of one million, and in five years boosted that figure to a total circulation of 18.3 million. Its audience is 42 percent male and 58 percent female, a rare distribution in magazine readerships that usually are dominated by one sex or the other.

Part of the key to *People*'s success has been its marketing strategy. About 85 percent of its circulation is single-copy sales through grocery stores, drug stores, or convenience chains. The shift away from reliance on mail circulation was a deliberate strategy developed to combat the 400-percent increase in second class postage rates that occurred between 1970 and 1974. (It was this increase that shrank the size of many magazines and forced others such as *Look* and *Life* to

---

*James L. Ford, *Magazines for Millions: The Story of Specialized Publications* (Carbondale, Ill.: Southern Illinois University Press, 1969), p. 4.

fold. Now both these picture magazines have been revived, though their future appears uncertain.)

In conclusion, it is clear that both magazines and newspapers are responding to external forces that are beyond their control. Yet they are surviving through a long process of adaptation that is changing both their appearance and content. How these changes affect the people who write the newspapers and magazines is a subject this book will discuss in detail in subsequent sections.

FREE-LANCERS AND STAFF WRITERS ON THE MODERN MAGAZINE

Many of the magazines that survived the realignment of the roles of the mass media began to make new demands on writers and editors. The most notable aspect of the new magazine became its tailor-made quality. To shape precisely the image they thought they needed and to provide the service they thought their readers should have, some publishers moved to staff-written products, in part because many had learned from the example of the news magazines that a tailor-made quality is most evident when a closely knit staff produces a magazine. The move toward staff writing was not designed to cut costs. In fact, staff-written articles are usually much more expensive to produce than free-lance articles. *National Geographic* usually pays $2,500 to $3,500 for a free-lance article, but Associate Editor Franc Shor has estimated that a staff-written article of the same length costs $15,000. This is because a staff writer who is capable of writing long articles for the magazine makes at least $25,000 a year, has a secretary, and writes only about three pieces a year.

Although later chapters will deal extensively with staff writing, it might be helpful here to suggest some of the reasons for the trend. When one considers the flaws of the free-lancer from the editor's point of view, the reasons become clear. Not long after he became managing editor of *World View,* a prestigious magazine that reprints serious articles from leading newspapers and magazines around the world, Barry Golson, then twenty-five years old, wrote to an author of this book:

One of the more amazing things I've found about free-lancers, to judge by the letters and queries we receive here, is their lack of discrimination. They seem to whip off queries without pausing to consider the nature of the publication. Some guy sent us an unsolicited manuscript on beauty aids for children. Others deluge us with constant hot tips, ambitious projects, political essays, revolutionary tracts—none of which have the slightest bearing on "Best from the World Press," our clearly marked subtitle.

Rather than devote hours to considering unsolicited articles and letters from free-lancers, many editors prefer to spend their energies on staff writers who have a clear notion of the needs of the magazine and possess the ability to write for it. This does not mean that the editor dictates the form and substance of an article to his writers. Clay Felker, the former editor of the highly successful *New York* magazine, has said of his role, "I can't tell intelligent and accomplished writers how to think." Rather than prescribing subjects and guiding the writing, Felker challenged his writers' ideas when they discussed an assignment. One of his ablest writers, Gloria Steinem, says of Felker, "Clay is a walking test area for ideas. He grasps them, makes them grow—and doesn't care where they come from." *New York* magazine became a success in a period of economic recession—its advertising revenues in 1975 were nearly 200 percent higher than in 1969, and its circulation doubled during the same period—largely because Felker and the other editors shaped their magazine to inform and entertain New Yorkers, but especially to teach them how to survive in the world's most unlivable city.

Tailoring publications to audiences has taken over much of the magazine world, and editors have adapted staff systems to conditions and needs. *Harper's,* for example, is a high-quality magazine that has about 300,000 subscribers. It often loses money, and it cannot pay for the large staff that would be required to produce a major magazine every month. But when Willie Morris became the editor in 1967, one of his first major decisions was to hire as regular contributors Larry L. King and David Halberstam, both of whom had written excellent free-lance articles for the magazine. They were not staff writers in the strictest sense, and much of the income of each derived from books that grew largely from articles they wrote for *Harper's.* But even after Morris and his writers left, the principle of hiring regular contributors was continued at *Harper's.*

Some of the current arrangements editors make with writers resemble the system developed by Harold Ross. Shortly after his *New Yorker* was established in 1925, Ross put a few free-lancers on generous "drawing accounts" that paid them regularly. In effect, they owed the magazine, but the debt was erased when their articles were published. They were not quite staff writers, but they were certainly not free-lancers in the conventional sense.

Such arrangements suggest where many of the free-lancers have gone. Although some are still free-lancing and others have become full-fledged staff writers, still others are in the ill-defined area between free-lancing and staff writing. They are likely to work at home, and they are tied to magazines by contracts that call for a few articles a year, with some time left for conventional free-lancing. Only successful free-lancers are likely to be offered writing contracts of the sort described here, but one need not be successful as a free-lancer to become a staff writer. Indeed, it is likely that a majority of the magazines that are now published in the United States employ staff writers (and editors) who have never sold a free-lance article. As a later chapter will indicate, free-lancing (even with only moderate success) is a good avenue to a job as a staff writer or editor.

Some free-lancers, of course, remain free-lancers. Some publications still rely largely on their work, and a great many editors believe that at least part of their magazines must be produced by free-lancers, because magazines produced solely by staff and contract writers often seem stale and lacking the freshness of view that outsiders can provide. Due to the special demands of modern magazines, free-lancers are likely to write for fewer publications than they did in the past. Further, the writer must keep in close touch with editors, usually by visiting magazine offices for story conferences, rather than merely reading and analyzing magazines from a distance.

WRITER-EDITOR RELATIONSHIPS:
TWO CASE STUDIES

Generalizing about writer-editor relationships is nearly always misleading. Instead, let us look at two quite different cases that illustrate what happens. The first can be depicted best by tracing the development of an article by Paul E. Deutschman that appeared in *Better Homes and Gardens*, "A GI Returns to the Great Battle Areas of Europe." (The fact that such an article appeared in such a magazine suggests that the titles of magazines sometimes have little to do with their content.)

The idea for the article was developed by Gordon Greer, associate editor for special features, who described it in a memo to the magazine's Issue Planning Committee:

> . . . A return to the scene by a man who fought there and remembers it well; who has naturally changed in the intervening years; who comes back with memories both pleasant and unpleasant; and who, as a writer, has the unusual ability to carry armchair veterans through time and space, and to hold them in Europe for roughly 5,000 words.

The committee approved the idea and decided to assign it to Deutschman, a former GI and a veteran writer. But Deutschman was living in Paris, so the magazine editors worked through his agent, Sterling Lord. The terms of payment were set in advance: a minimum of $2,500 plus reasonable expenses for a publishable article; $1,000 plus expenses in case the article was rejected.

Deutschman did not simply begin typing. He outlined his concept of the article in a long letter to the editors, arguing that he could explore the experience of a return to the battlefields more fully and meaningfully in 10,000 words, which would require publishing the article as a two-parter in consecutive issues of the magazine. The editors agreed, but they told Deutschman that the time element could not be changed. The first draft of the article would have to reach the editorial offices in Des Moines by December 15. That would give the Special Features Department time to prepare the piece for publication in the April issue—just in time for the many American readers of *Better Homes and Gardens* who would be planning summer trips to Europe. Deutschman promised to meet this deadline. He began traveling through the battlegrounds of Europe early in November.

The events of the next two-and-a-half months ultimately involved feverish communications from Des Moines to New York—where Deutschman's agent and the magazine's eastern representative, George Bush, had their offices—and to Rome, where, late in December, Deutschman holed up in a hotel room to work on the article.

The first wire went from Special Features Editor Neil Kuehnl in Des Moines to Sterling Lord. It was December 21, six days after the article was to have arrived, and Kuehnl was edgy: STERLING LORD: WHERE ARE PAUL DEUTSCHMAN AND HIS MANUSCRIPT? WE ARE VERY CLOSE TO DEADLINE. On December 26, Deutschman cabled: PIECE SHAPING BEST IVE DONE HOPE YOU FIND IT VERY WORTHWHILE BUT WORKING FULLBLAST HOLIDAYS DONT FEEL IT READY MY SATISFACTION ARRIVE DES MOINES BEFORE MONDAY PLEASE ADVISE DEUTSCHMAN LEGATION HOTEL ROME.

Knowing that Deutschman was a conscientious and skillful writer, Kuehnl was mollified. He reported that he was willing to stretch the deadline but that the article must arrive in Des Moines by January 2 or shortly thereafter. It didn't. On January 6, Kuehnl wired Bush: GEORGE, STILL NO MANUSCRIPT FROM DEUTSCHMAN, WOULD YOU ASK STERLING LORD IF HE STILL HAS A CLIENT BY THAT NAME?

But Lord was unable to reach Deutschman, who had dropped out of touch again to complete the manuscript. When the manuscript finally reached Des Moines, more than a month after the original deadline, Kuehnl wired Bush: DEUTSCHMAN MANUSCRIPT FINALLY ARRIVED FROM ITALY, ASTOUNDING 87 PAGES LONG. EDITING TASK WILL BE MONUMENTAL. GOD HELP US ALL.

It was a captivating piece of writing, but it ran more than 25,000 words; the magazine had room for only 10,000. Fortunately, although Deutschman prized his work to the point that he could not bring himself to delete a word (a fairly common failing among writers), he had marked many paragraphs that might be deleted by the editors without paining him severely. That still left fifty pages.

Associate Feaures Editor Gordon Greer devoted a weekend to boiling the mass down to manageable size. Then, as often happens, the editors decided that more material was needed. Off went a cable to Deutschman. It was followed a few days later by a preliminary edited manuscript—a checking procedure that enables the writer to correct errors and to take some part in the editing process. Deutschman found several minor errors and one that he described as a "whopper."

Meanwhile, the editors arranged for material to support Deutschman's article. The Special Features Department bought information on European travel (transportation costs, what to wear, and the like) and shaped it into a sidebar article to be published with Deutschman's. Then the editors arranged to reprint (at $50 each) five cartoons from Bill Mauldin's *Up Front*, a best seller about World War II.

By the middle of February, everything for the April issue was in type and corrected, which cut the production process much too close for anyone's comfort. The editors paid Deutschman $4,000 plus his expenses, which had been itemized across eleven pages.

This relationship turned out well for both Deutschman and the magazine, and yet it must be obvious that this is an unusual case. Magazines cannot be published unless, month after month, the editors are able to count on their authors meeting deadlines with articles coming in at the prescribed length. A much more typical case is described by a series of letters from an editor to an author who had suggested writing an article on how bombers are used to fight fires. The first letter ran:

> Thank you for your outline, "Here Come the Flying Fire Engines." This sounds like an interesting story, but I wonder if you could give me a little information about it? Do you suppose you could arrange to ride in one of the bombers fighting an actual fire, or at least on a trial run? I have an idea that an actual experience such as this would provide you with usable color and details. Could you also spend some time with a group of the pilots at their base, in an effort to dig up anecdotal material about actual fire fighting? Could you get a quote for me, either on or off the record, from the top fire authority in California, attesting to the efficacy of this new method of fighting fires? Before we go all out in saying that this is the most effective method of forest fire fighting yet developed, I should like to be sure that top authorities agree with us. If you can provide this extra information, I feel there is a good chance that I can give you a go-ahead with the piece.

The author replied by letter that he could provide the kind of reportage and detail the editor wanted. The next letter from the editor ran:

> Our Washington Office has obtained permission for you to fly on one of the fire-fighting jobs. Now that this has been

cleared, I hope you will go ahead with the story. We are glad to guarantee you $250 for submitting a manuscript; and we shall of course pay your expenses. The piece seems to be shaping up in most promising fashion. I hope you will set yourself to producing the most complete and definitive article that could possibly be done. Please feel free to travel to any places where you think you can dig up additional material. I would concentrate on California until you had everything available there, and by that time you ought to know where else you should go. Remember that it is anecdotal material which we must have—little stories of action, drama and characterization. There can't be too many of them.

The author plunged into the research and writing, submitted the article, and received this letter:

You have certainly done a big and careful research job on this subject, amassing an impressive amount of material. I am sure it is the most comprehensive job that has ever been done on the subject. In its present form, however, the manuscript is too long. And you need to be more selective. A good deal should be cut out of the piece; much of what remains should be sharpened up, made more dramatic. You have got to keep the reader keenly interested in every paragraph from beginning to end.

I have taken the liberty of making a number of suggested deletions and changes on the manuscript—in a very rough way—which may be useful to you in rewriting. I feel sure that, when you read the article over again in the light of these suggestions, you will see how much it can be improved by general tightening and specific heightening of effect. My pencil markings, of course, are meant as suggestions for revision, not as hard-and-fast editing changes. Their main purpose is to help the piece move faster from your opening lead up to your dramatic conclusion.

In that conclusion, incidentally, would it not be possible for you to introduce yourself as a passenger in the scout plane? Or is that not for publication? If you could describe your own emotions when flying over a fire, as well as the conversation of the fire boss, I am sure the reader would get a greater sense of participation. This section must be dramatic and memorable—it is what the whole article builds up to. I hope you will make it just as vivid as possible.

Back to the typewriter went the author. He revised the article along the lines suggested by the editor, submitted the revision, and got this response:

Your adding the first-person material to this article makes all the difference. It shows exactly what is needed. Until I read this section, I was puzzled by the piece, feeling that it did not come off. Now I realize that the approach was wrong. You should start out with this first-person stuff, and then weave the technical information into the story as you go along.

I suggest that you start with a lead something like this (roughly):

> The fire broke out in crackling dry brush below Angeles Crest Highway and soon became a yellow hurricane roaring uncontrolled on three fronts, fanned by a strong wind off the desert. State foresters, county firemen, and city fire forces hit the fire like Marines smacking a big beachhead. They threw in 145 fire trucks, 23 bulldozers, long convoys of jeeps and trucks laden with axes, shovels and backpumps, as well as 23 tanker planes, 5 bird-dog planes and 10 helicopters.
>
> "This is the kind of fire the boys will talk about for the rest of their lives!" said a pilot, who was getting a view of an exploding forest which few other people have ever lived to describe.

Something like that ought to catch the attention of the reader—you can easily heighten its effect. Later on bring in the chemical business and, when you have finished describing this fire, tell the rest of your story.

As the piece stands, we are told more about borax and the other chemicals than we really need to know. The most interesting parts of the piece are, I should say, the first-person stuff, the sections about pilots, and the other airplane material. See if you don't feel easier in revising this piece when you have changed the accent.

A professional, the writer reacted as professionals do. He went back to the typewriter and hammered out still another revision. A few days later, he received a telegram of acceptance, then this letter:

As I wired you yesterday, we are glad to accept the fire-fighting article. Check has been sent to your agent. It is really a pleasure to work with you, because you do so expertly what an editor asks!

THE FREE-LANCER AS A PROFESSIONAL

The extent to which the editor shaped this article may suggest that a "professional writer" must be a kind of literary prostitute. And it is certainly true that some professionals are willing prostitutes. At least a few are so intent on writing successfully that their first and only interest is pleasing an editor. A young man who worked briefly as an editor said, "The pros I talked to were reluctant to write at all unless they were sure what the editor had in mind; they had little or nothing in mind themselves."

But there is much more to say on this point, for there is a sharp difference between a professional and a hack. The professional writer who deserves the name listens carefully to suggestions about the *way* he shapes his article. If he can be persuaded that a different structure or approach will make his piece clearer or more vivid or more provocative, he will take the suggestions—and with no fear that he has sacrificed a principle. It is the writer who can be persuaded that he should change his *attitude* toward the substance of his article who is the literary prostitute and who deserves to be called a hack.

The letters excerpted above can be used to sharpen this distinction. Note that the editor *never* suggests that the writer should adopt this attitude or that one. In fact, the next-to-last sentence in the first letter ("Before we go all out in saying this is the most effective method of forest fire fighting yet developed . . . ") suggests that the writer's attitude was made clear in *his* letter to the editor. Throughout, the editor is trying to persuade the writer only that he can make the article more readable and evocative by using different techniques. Had the editor argued that the article should try to prove that this method of fire fighting is a costly farce, and had the writer bent his work to that end, the mark of the hack would be clear on the writer.

The distinction between the true professional and the hack can, of course, be subtler and more complex. One can imagine a case in which an editor argues only techniques, not attitudes, and in so doing persuades the writer to cheapen his work. This, too, may be considered a kind of hack work. Writers who churn out assignments in which they have no interest are dangerously close to performing as hacks.

The basic structure of magazine free-lancing creates other problems. Joseph Bell, who has been a writer for nearly twenty years, has described two incidents during which he thought he had sold articles to magazines, only to have them rejected for capricious reasons. He philosophized about free-lancing:

> It's the only business I know where the worker is compensated totally at the caprice of the customer, whether or not the customer ordered the merchandise and whether or not it was delivered in good faith and in reasonably good con-

dition. In free-lance writing, the risks that beset any contractual arrangement between two fallible human beings are borne almost entirely by the writer.

It is true that, although threshing around considerably, the free-lance does tend to accept these rules of the game—which, of course, perpetuates them. No purchaser is going to give up voluntarily a working relationship in which he can order a piece of custom-built merchandise and, if he doesn't like it for any one of a myriad of reasons, simply return it and forget the entire matter. This is the buyer's market de luxe, one reflecting remarkable philosophical ambivalence. While editors cry out in anguish that free-lances never bring fresh or imaginative ideas to them, they refuse to underwrite the sort of research and investigation that would enable a free-lance to live while pursuing these fresh—and palpably risky—ideas.

This is a persistent complaint from free-lancers, most of whom do not have the contractual arrangement mentioned above.

Free-lancing articles is usually far more rewarding than writing and trying to sell short fiction, if only because most magazines have discovered in recent decades that most readers are far more interested in fact vividly reported than in fiction. But the beginner should be aware that free-lancing articles is not the most profitable work a talented and industrious person can pursue. Nothing is more essential, perhaps, than conditioning the mind for disappointment. Of sixty-four members of the American Society of Journalists and Authors who participated in a survey, eight made more than $30,000 a year, but eleven made less than $10,000.

Free-lancing should first be thought of as a game the writer plays. He is pitting his wits and resourcefulness against a hundred other writers who may have hit on the same idea on the same day, or perhaps the week before. So he plays it as a game, knowing that he cannot win all the time. Many beginners cannot stand the defeats and disappointments—some veteran writers are eventually crushed by them—and they should not play the game. Those who are sensitive and easily hurt by rejections discover that it is a cruel contest.

But if a beginner is to become successful, he must also think of free-lancing as a business. He has no employment security. He must make his own provisions for the lean month, for the lean year, and for his retirement. Some successful writers fail ultimately simply because they are unable to work at peak efficiency while they are worrying about the arrival of the next check—which points up the importance of developing a system for building a savings account. One of the most successful free-lancers began early in his career to save 10 percent of every check and invest it in stocks.

The necessity for businesslike procedures envelops the free-lancer's life. He must make himself write regularly and during the same hours every day. "It's a brutal discipline," one holds, "and you have to stick to it. If you make the mistake of trying to write fiction in your spare time or fix light bulbs around the house, you're finished."

What does the writer derive from the hard work and discipline he must require of himself? Most free-lancers focus on the importance of the other rewards. Joseph Bell, who deals so incisively with the disappointments of free-lancing, writes:

> The freedom, once it is put into proper perspective, is very attractive. The free-lance doesn't really have freedom of subject matter, since he must write what editors are willing to buy, and he must often compromise his own convictions in order to save an article in which he has already invested a considerable amount of money and time. But once those restrictions—which are not unlike those facing anyone else in publishing—on freedom are accepted, the free-lance can set his own hours, function from any place his fancy sends him, and meet a fascinating assortment of people. After fifteen years of this kind of life, I consider myself unemployable. The regimen of regular hours and corporate policy is simply unthinkable.

Nearly every free-lancer agrees with Bell, especially about the fascinating assortment of people the writer meets. Free-lancing is a license to butt in, almost anywhere, and to become a part of the contemporary scene. It is an opportunity to make many different kinds of friends, and at least a few enemies. It allows travel, not as a tourist but as a purposeful traveler who is likely to see more and learn more than almost any tourist could. There are few dull moments in free-lancing, and it culminates in one of the most rewarding of human experiences—to see one's writing in print. Many veteran male writers maintain, though, that the definition of "free-lancer" is "a man with a typewriter and a working wife."

How should talented beginners view free-lancing? If they are fully aware that it can be a cruel game for the sensitive, if they will discipline themselves for businesslike writing, if they will work toward the many kinds of rewards, then free-lancing is an opportunity. Certainly, there is room for talented beginners—provided they will work at their craft.

In any case, it is becoming more difficult to distinguish between the various kinds of articles published in newspapers and magazines. For example, the differences between a newspaper personality sketch and a magazine profile are often negligible, as are the differences between a color story and a descriptive. Following sections of this book will make these distinctions because beginners should be aware that some differences do still exist, and that they can greatly influence the way an article should be written. It is still too soon to discard the rule that writing for newspapers is definitely not the same as writing for magazines.

If writers yearn to write for national magazines, they must study them carefully. The worst of it is that some of the most talented writers fail. Paradoxically, this is *because* they are so talented. Knowing that they can put one word after another attractively, they stint on research and lean much too heavily on writing, which makes it mere writing. Some of their plodding contemporaries, who recognize the limits of their own talents, are more likely to succeed because they dig for facts, insights, and ideas.

CHAPTER ONE EXERCISES

1. To investigate for yourself whether the large newspapers are becoming more like magazines, read the features in the nearest metropolitan newspaper and the articles in the national magazines *People* or *Cosmopolitan*. After reading one of the newspaper features and one of the magazine articles, choose which you prefer. Be prepared to defend your choice at the next class session.

2. See the next episode of "60 Minutes," and choose one of the "magazine" chapters. Then read a magazine article that will take you about twenty minutes to read. An hour after you've seen "60 Minutes," write what you remember of the "magazine" chapter. Then, an hour after reading the magazine article, write what you remember of that article. Finally, match what you remember of each of those with your fellow students in the next class session.

3. Choose a topic for a feature story, then describe how the story might be handled by a newspaper, a magazine, and a television news show. Who would be interviewed and how would quotes be presented? How would the story be handled visually? How would the information presented differ among the three media?

CHAPTER 2
The New Journalism

SOME DEFINITIONS

Ronald Weber has written of the new journalism that it "whips together a mixture of feature-story journalism, true confessions, mass magazine fiction, the middlebrow novel, and narrative history . . . " (from *The Reporter as Artist: A Look at the New Journalism Controversy*, Hastings House, New York: 1974, p. 11). Perhaps this is as close as it is possible to come to describing a style of writing for which no one has found a succinct definition and that many deny exists at all. Numerous phrases have been constructed to package the elements into one neat box. They include "personal journalism," "documentary narrative," and even "parajournalism."

Like the blind men examining the elephant, writers inspecting the new journalism find it easier to describe its distinguishing characteristics than to comprehend the whole beast. This is partly because the work of writers who have been called new journalists is so diverse. The group includes Tom Wolfe, Jimmy Breslin, Gloria Steinem, Norman Mailer, Joan Didion, Rex Reed, Truman Capote, and many others with equally divergent styles. Some writers whose work has been classified as new journalism by other practitioners adamantly refuse the label because they do not believe that their writing should be lumped together with that of others whose styles differ from their own.

One of the most vocal advocates of the new journalism is Tom Wolfe. He has defined it as the use in "nonfiction of techniques which had been thought of as confined to the novel or the short story, to create in one form both the kind of objective reality of journalism and the subjective reality that people have always gone to the novel for."

It may be misleading to speak of the new journalism as a "form"; it certainly is misleading if that is taken to mean a formula like the who-what-when-where-why of the news story. Rather, the new journalism can appear in many forms. Tom Wolfe developed his particular form by accident. Assigned to write an article for *Esquire* on custom cars, he did the research but then developed a writer's block and found that he was unable to complete the article. One of the editors of *Esquire*, Byron Dobell, told Wolfe to type his notes and hand them in so another writer could turn them into an article. Wolfe obliged him, but he wrote the notes in the form of a memo to the editor. Dobell was so pleased with it that he simply removed the "Dear Byron" salutation and published the memo as an article.

There is more to Wolfe's method, of course, than writing articles as memos, but this incident suggests the *kind* of subjective involvement and the kind of form that he often favors. It is informal writing that owes part of its appeal to the simple fact that it is different from the relatively formal, relatively detached writing of the past.

SOME TECHNIQUES

New journalists use many conventional reporting and writing techniques. Beyond these, Wolfe singles out four central devices:

1. Scenic construction, moving from scene to scene and resorting as little as possible to sheer historical narrative.

2. Recording dialogue in full.

3. Presenting scenes through the eyes of a character by interviewing him about his thoughts and emotions at the time of the event the writer describes (also known as *interior monologue*).

4. Recording everyday gestures, habits, manners, customs, styles of clothing, decorations, styles of traveling, eating, keeping house—everything, Wolfe says, "symbolic, generally, of peoples' *status life.*"

New journalism also relies on interior monologue and that is one of its most controversial aspects—the journalist cannot possibly have observed or listened to the inner thoughts of another person. Yet many writers can and do write very effectively about what an individual was thinking at a certain time.

SOME PRACTITIONERS

Gay Talese, a former feature writer for the *New York Times* and a writer for *Esquire,* is regarded as one of the more adept new journalists—especially with interior monologue. Consider this excerpt from an article he wrote about Joshua Logan and the star of one of Logan's plays, Claudia McNeil. In it he records dialogue, a perfectly acceptable old-style journalistic technique, but at the end he switches to interior monologue.

"Don't raise your voice, Claudia," Logan repeated.
She again ignored him.

"CLAUDIA!" Logan yelled, "don't you give me that actor's vengeance, Claudia!"

"Yes, Mr. Logan."

"And stop Yes-Mr.-Logan-ing me."

"Yes, Mr. Logan."

"You're a shockingly rude woman!"

"Yes, Mr. Logan."

"You're being a beast."

"Yes, Mr. Logan."

"Yes, Miss Beast."

"Yes, Mr. Logan."

"Yes, Miss Beast."

Suddenly Claudia McNeil stopped. It dawned on her that he was calling her a beast; now her face was grey and her eyes were cold, and her voice almost solemn as she said, "You . . . called . . . me . . . out . . . of . . . my . . . name!"

"Oh, God!" Logan smacked his forehead with his hand.

"You . . . called . . . me . . . out . . . of . . . my . . . name."

She stood there, rocklike, big and angry, waiting for him to do something.

"Oliver!" Logan said, turning toward his coproducer, who had lowered his wiry, long body into his chair as if he were in a foxhole. He did not want to be cornered into saying something that might offend Logan, his old friend, but neither did he want Claudia McNeil to come barreling down the aisle and possibly snap his thin form in half. . . .*

Recalling his work on this article, Talese said, "They got into an argument that not only was more dramatic than the play itself, but revealed something of the character of Logan and Miss McNeil in a way that I could never have done had I approached the subject from the more conventional form of reporting." Talese was simply an observer at the time the confrontation took place, so he was able to record the dialogue in full. But by talking to Oliver, and by observing him, Talese was also able to write about what Oliver was thinking when Logan turned to him.

Despite criticism of his techniques, Talese continued to use them when the situation seemed appropriate. Whether an obscure, old bridge tender was being left jobless by the construction of a modern

---

*Quotations from Gay Talese's works are reprinted with his permission.

bridge in Brooklyn or the uncommunicative Joe DiMaggio was refusing to grant an interview, Talese tried to report what each was thinking. Talese explained that in interviewing a subject, he would "ask him what he thought in every situation where I might have asked him in the past what he said. I'm not so interested in what he did and said . . . as in what he thought. And I would quote him in the way I was writing that he thought something."

In *The Kingdom and the Power,* the human history of the *New York Times,* Talese made effective use of the interior monologue. This and a rich descriptive narrative based on his perceptions during his years as a *Times*-man enabled him to capture the interpersonal drama of the great liberal-establishment newspaper. Instead of the usual dull press-history approach, Talese wrote about the pettiness, bickering, and self-doubts of *Times* executives. He showed how management wielded power and controlled the lives of some of America's most talented journalists. The book offended some of his subjects, but it was his frequent use of interior monologue that brought the most intense criticism. Here, for instance, Talese probes the mind of Frank Sinatra in a piece that was published in *Fame and Obscurity:*

Sinatra had been working in a film that he now disliked, could not wait to finish; he was tired of all the publicity attached to his dating the twenty-one-year-old Mia Farrow, who was not in sight tonight; he was angry that a CBS television documentary of his life, to be shown in two weeks, was reportedly prying into his privacy, even speculating on his possible friendship with Mafia leaders; he was worried about his starring role in an hour-long NBC show entitled *Sinatra—A Man and His Music,* which would require that he sing eighteen songs with a voice that at this particular moment, just a few nights before the taping was to begin, was weak and sore and uncertain. Sinatra was ill. He was the victim of an ailment so common that most people would consider it trivial. But when it gets to Sinatra it can plunge him into a state of anguish, deep depression, panic, even rage. Frank Sinatra had a cold.

Talese keyed his entire article on Sinatra's cold, which he explained later: "Frank Sinatra was not feeling well and everyone was very nervous—'everyone' meaning those people who worked for Sinatra, like the publicity man and a dozen other people who have various roles. And Sinatra had a cold. Because he had a cold, he was very irritable. . . . He was not able to sing with the ease and perfection that he might otherwise be able to do. That was interesting. The cold afflicted not only him—it affected his whole group, his whole organization."

Both Wolfe and Talese have said that they admire the journalism of Norman Mailer, who is generally considered the most skilled of the new journalists. The form of Mailer's work is deceptively simple: He uses himself as a character in his own journalism. In *The Armies of the Night*, Mailer wrote interior monologue—his own:

> "You know, Norman," said Lowell in his fondest voice, "Elizabeth and I really think you're the finest journalist in America."
>
> Mailer knew Lowell thought this—Lowell had even sent him a postcard once to state the enthusiasm. But the novelist had been shrewd enough to judge that Lowell sent many postcards to many people—it did not matter that Lowell was by overwhelming consensus judged to be the best, most talented, and most distinguished poet in America—it was still necessary to keep the defense lines in good working order. A good word on a card could keep many a dangerous recalcitrant in the ranks. Therefore, this practice annoyed Mailer.

SOME IMITATORS

The legions of young writers who try to imitate Mailer soon find that his method is not nearly as easy as it looks. This is largely because they are not as talented as Mailer, but their failures also spring from the fact that they write about themselves rather than about events. In opposition to this trend, Herbert Gold wrote, "The first-person arias of the Wolfettes and Mailerlings center the whole world in the self of the writer. They don't do their job of telling and sharing experience. Instead, they sacrifice knowledge for a parading of personality. . . . " There is a subtle difference in Mailer's work; the reader does not get just a view of how events affect Mailer but how Mailer viewed events. The reader may learn much about the writer, but the primary message is about the events in which the writer participated.

Beginners often mistakenly believe that writing in the style of new journalism requires less discipline than writing conventional style articles. They do not realize that new journalists have mastered the techniques of basic news and feature writing before experimenting with innovative forms. Tennis players need to learn basic ground strokes before trying to put spin on the ball. If they don't, it's unlikely that they'll be able to control their shots. The same applies to naive writers who want to use the techniques of new journalism.

Despite the emphasis many new journalists place on truth as opposed to facts, new journalism does not relieve the writer of responsibility for accurate reporting. Dan Wakefield explained in his article "The Personal Voice and the Impersonal Eye," that *"Esquire's* editorial attitude seems to be anything goes as long as it is interesting and true. The magazine has a research department, and every fact in every nonfiction piece is checked and verified. The license they offer writers is not for distortion of facts but experimentation in style."

EMPLOYING THE NEW TECHNIQUES

Beginners who want to try to use new journalism techniques can start right away, but slowly. Writers may try it first by putting themselves in the place of the person they are presenting. Here is a short example from *Time* magazine of the writer's putting himself in the shoes of Lawrence O'Brien, chairman of the 1972 Democratic National Convention:*

> . . . O'Brien picked up the huge gavel. Too heavy, he thought. Why not get an electric buzzer next time? He whacked it down, and the great spectacle of Miami Beach was on. He made an early decision. The noisy mass below him had to be managed, somehow led through four days of business, but more important were the millions and millions of Americans who were watching through those blinking red eyes directly in front of him. Talk to them, he told himself, wondering what the man in San Clemente would be seeing in a few hours.

> The convention was already behind time when O'Brien started his speech. That was deliberate. Don't harass or push. Stay loose, he kept telling himself. The noise on the floor hardly subsided as he talked—the old Irish rasp, the square sentences full of platitudes, annoyingly interspersed with film clips. Yet here and there people began to listen. It was not the familiar polemic against Richard Nixon. It was not the extravagant praise of the Democratic past. He talked about "the crisis of truth," of the Democrats being "on trial." He did not avoid blame for problems, and he tried to warn his youthful audience that the world is not remade by "a stroke of the pen."

Saturation Research

Another aspect of the work of the new journalists that beginners can adopt immediately might be called saturation research. This re-

---

*Reprinted by permission from *Time,* The Weekly Newsmagazine; copyright Time Inc.

quires that researchers do much more than ask a few people a few questions. It requires that they become involved in their subjects the way Mailer became involved in the march on Washington so that he could write *The Armies of the Night* or the way Wolfe and Talese became involved with subjects by staying with them for long periods. Wolfe pointed out, "You start following somebody or a group around, and you really have to end up staying with them for a day, sometimes weeks, sometimes months even. And you are waiting for things to happen in front of your eyes, because it's really the scene that brings the whole thing to life."

This kind of research is essential in producing the new journalism, but it is also important in producing imaginative articles of any kind. Some successful articles are written without this whole-souled approach to research, of course. But it must be obvious that this kind of exploration enables the writers to understand their subjects fully, and thus enables them to help their readers understand. Whether they are free-lancers or staff writers, promoting understanding should be their goal.

THE CONTROVERSY: OBJECTIVITY VERSUS WRITER INVOLVEMENT

Even though leading practitioners like Tom Wolfe and Gay Talese began as newspaper writers, a strong controversy rages over the propriety of the new journalism.* This is largely an argument between the old and the young, many of the older journalists holding that established standards of objectivity and verifiable fact must be observed. Many young journalists argue that since everyone agrees that absolute objectivity is impossible, and since the established standards rarely enable one to report more than mere facts—thus ignoring the *truth about facts,* freer forms are essential. This controversy is not the old argument over objectivity versus interpretation— certainly not if one defines interpretation as no more than clarifying, explaining, or analyzing problems, issues, or controversies. The new journalism goes far beyond interpretation because it calls for the direct involvement of the writer in his article.

Sometimes this involvement creates the impression that the writer of an article is more important than the subject he or she is writing about. The temptation to insert the writer's presence into the story is very strong. Such stories often begin with sentences like "When I first decided to interview _____, I thought . . ." or "When I walked into _____'s house, I felt . . ." This autobiographical approach can be successful when the subject of the story is an intriguing situation in which readers would like to find themselves, or a person they would like to meet. In those cases, the writer can share his or her first-hand experience with readers by writing about his or her own thoughts and feelings. The same technique applied to an article about an unknown subject is often less effective. There is no inherent interest in the subject among readers, so their need to share the writer's experience is not as great as their need to learn about the subject itself and why it is being discussed in an article. Tom Wolfe has suggested that autobiographical journalism is most appropriate when the author is a leading character in the event being written about. When this is not the case, personal point of view merely distracts the reader from the story.

Yet it is this personal aspect of the new journalism that appeals to many writers and readers. Ronald Weber explained its popularity by writing that new journalism is " 'I' writing for an 'I' time, personal writing for an age of personalism. All about us ego seems loosed into the cultural air as never before. Notions of detachment, objectivity, and neutrality conflict in every sphere with a passion for uninhibited individual expression. Both one's first and last duty now belong to oneself." Whether or not one agrees that new journalism is a reflection of the times, it is clear that this style of newswriting is much more subjective than its predecessor.

Tom Wolfe has written resignedly of the new journalism, "Any movement, group, party, program, philosophy or theory that goes under a name with 'new' in it is just begging for trouble, of course. But it is the term that eventually caught on." It *is* the term that caught on. Much of the criticism of the new journalism springs from adverse reactions to many who practice it. It has its unobtrusive personalities—Lillian Ross, who writes for the *New Yorker,* and Gay Talese, for example—but it has more than its share of practitioners who range from the irritating to the insufferable. Norman Mailer seems to ask to be disliked, in person and in print. Some of the young who model themselves after him—and think they model their writing on his—blend bad manners and bad prose. But it may be that Wolfe, who is personally engaging and has done more than any other writer of the new journalism to promote that form, is responsible for more adverse reaction than any. other new journalist.

IS THE "NEW JOURNALISM" REALLY "NEW"

If the devices used in new journalism sound familiar, it is because they have long been used in various forms by feature writers. This compels some writers to deny that anything about the so-called new journalism is actually new. The four devices add up to a strong dose of descriptive writing, perhaps a stronger dose than writers dished up to their audiences in the past. Long before the term "new journalism" was coined, newsman A. J. Liebling wrote, "A police reporter sees more than he can set down; a feature writer sets down more than he can possibly have seen." "New journalist" can easily be substituted for the subject in the second clause.

In the March 13, 1971, issue of *Saturday Review,* another critic of the new journalism, John Tebbel, deplored as "dismaying" the arrival "of an action-reaction pattern between older and younger writers that has revived subjectivity as the accepted journalistic writing style, and condemned objectivity as a hoary icon of the past with no meaning for the present and no substance in fact in any case." He titled his article "The New Old Journalism" to point up his belief that the proponents of the new are simply reviving eighteenth-century journalism, "when activist propaganda of the most scurrilous kind filled the pages of newspapers."

The point must be made instantly that Tebbel is arguing against the new journalism in *newspapers.* He mentions magazines only once, and then to protest that young writers "see subjectivity deified in the best magazines" and carry it to extremes in their campus newspapers. (Among the best magazines publishing new journalism are *Esquire, New York, The Atlantic, Mother Jones,* and *New West.*) Indeed, it would have been difficult for Tebbel to argue against subjectivity in magazines; his own magazine article is highly subjective.

This points up an important distinction between the new journalism controversy as it is argued among newspaper journalists and as it is argued quite differently among magazine writers and editors. The magazine world has never been tied to a form like the newspaper formula for the straight news story. And because magazines are published less frequently and carry many fewer items than daily newspapers, magazine writers have always had more time and space than newspaper reporters to develop their articles. As a consequence, magazine writing has been more innovative and varied, and the reaction to the new journalism much less feverish. The question among newspaper reporters is, "Does this form violate our standards?" The question among magazine journalists is, "Does this form help to present the truth?"

ITS PLACE IN THE FUTURE

In the end, however, what matters is not the bickering over definitions and the clashing of personalities but the future of journalism. Whatever the critics' motivations, their effect has been positive because they have helped provide visibility for the new journalism during its formative period. Gay Talese says, "It is, or should be, as reliable as the most reliable reportage, although it seeks a larger truth than is possible through the mere compilation of verifiable facts, the use of direct quotations, and adherence to the rigid organizational style of the old form." To Talese, it "allows, demands in fact, a more imaginative approach to reporting, and it permits the writer to inject himself into the narrative, if he wishes, as many writers do, or to assume the role of detached observer, as other writers do, including myself."

This is a demanding form, and it is nonsense to imagine that most journalists will be able to master it. But neither is it attainable by only a few. Harold Hayes, former editor of *Esquire*, wrote in 1972: "It must be hell these days for the poor news reporter in Topeka, sitting there punching out his one-sentence, monosyllabic news leads, wondering how many light years he must travel to get with it."

Ironically, at about the time that issue of *Esquire* appeared on the newsstands, members of the Topeka Press Club spent an evening discussing the new journalism, and many of the Midwesterners proved to be restless indeed and ready for change. Of course, the straight news report will not disappear. It serves a valuable purpose, both in Topeka and in New York, for most events simply do not deserve the time and attention that the new nonfiction demands. Many are reported more appropriately in a terse, bare-bones form.

But touches of the new journalism are appearing in newspaper features, where it belongs, and the degree to which it becomes dominant in feature writing may depend largely on the amount of time writers are given to develop their assignments and the amount of space available in the already crowded columns. The new journalism has by now won a secure place, and will win a larger one, for the simplest of reasons: For many journalistic reports, there is no better form.

CHAPTER TWO EXERCISES

1. Find someone who has recently had an unusual experience (a fight, a job interview, an odd conversation with a stranger, an athletic contest, a stressful encounter, or something similar) and interview the person about it. Then write two one-page stories—the first in conventional third-person reporting style, and the second using the first-person interior monologue style of new journalism. Which is more effective? Which was easier to write, and why?

2. Do you agree with Raymond Mungo's assertion that "truth is more important than facts"? How does journalists' reliance on facts affect their style of writing?

3. Discuss which kinds of stories you think are most suitable to the techniques of new journalism. Which are not, and why?

---

*Those who have a special interest in the new journalism may want to read Gay Talese's *The Kingdom and the Power* (New York: World, 1969) and *Thy Neighbor's Wife* (New York: Doubleday, 1980); Tom Wolfe's *Radical Chic and Mau-Mauing the Flak-Catchers* (New York: Farrar, Straus & Giroux, 1970); and *The Armies of the Night* (New York: New American Library, 1968), and *Miami and the Siege of Chicago* (New York: World, 1968), both by Norman Mailer.

CHAPTER 3
Breaking into Journalism

JOB OPPORTUNITIES

A pamphlet published in 1969 by the American Newspaper Publishers Association Foundation contained a caption that read: "Reporter at work—all it takes is concentration, speed, accuracy—and talent." Ten years later most journalists would still agree with that prescription, but many would add an additional item—luck. Today the number of journalists seeking jobs far exceeds the openings in the field.

Despite the overcrowding, journalism's popularity among college students continues to increase. In 1978 there were 70,601 journalism students studying in U. S. colleges. This figure represents a 156.9 percent increase over the 1968 enrollment level and a 562 percent increase over the 1958 figure. At a time when enrollment in humanities courses is declining, students are turning to journalism because of its vocational possibilities. This movement is the logical outcome of the increased presence and importance of the media in American life.

There was a time when newspapers couldn't find enough qualified staff members. In the early 1960s, *Editor and Publisher* estimated that there were three positions open for every graduating journalism major. A study undertaken for The Newspaper Fund indicated that two-thirds of all the daily newspapers in the United States regarded manpower as their major problem. According to this survey, newspapers had to attract 3,500 new employees every year to fill news and editorial positions alone. But colleges and departments of journalism were graduating fewer than 3,000 journalism majors a year, some of whom did not go to work for daily newspapers.

By 1978, the number of journalism graduates had increased to 51,924. Their job-hunting endeavors have resulted in a flood of applications both at newspapers and magazines. It is not unusual for a publication advertising a single job opening to receive hundreds of applications. Even when no openings are announced, applicants submit their resumes and clippings. An associate editor at *Women's Sports* estimated that he had accumulated a file of over 500 unsolicited applications for staff jobs, and that he received an average of two per week. A Seattle newspaper features editor said that her paper received over 2,000 applications annually.

Edwin Haroldsen summed up the situation this way:

> Over the country, news executives are being flooded with job applications. This is shown by the responses of 30 representative U. S. daily newspaper and broadcast news executives recently surveyed for the *Quill.* The *Chicago Sun-Times* alone receives 1,000 a year, approximately 700 of them from young persons fresh out of school.
>
> The *New York Times* gets approximately 40 applications a week, but has had only two or three reporting positions open so far this year. And another report tells us the *Philadelphia Inquirer,* with 1,800 applications on file, sends a monthly list of candidates to other papers. A promising applicant to the *Washington Post* might be referred to a paper as far away as Colorado.
>
> Meanwhile, the journalism schools are getting more applications than they know what to do with. Eight hundred bids for 133 slots at Columbia. Northwestern graduate applications are 672, compared to 550 a year ago. Some schools feel the need to hire more J-teachers.

These may be gloomy figures, but other statistics should give journalism students reason to be optimistic about their chances of finding jobs. A 1978 survey conducted by the Newspaper Fund indicated that over 60 percent of the journalism graduates polled that year had found media-related jobs within six months of graduating. About 3,600 of them were hired by daily newspapers. The Department of Labor has forecasted that there will be 2,200 job openings each year for newspaper reporters. Most of these are expected to occur as the result of promotions or retirements rather than expansion of the industry.

The Qualified Applicant—Newspapers and Magazines

Here are a few comments managing editors have made about the qualifications they seek in applicants who would like to fill openings on their staffs:

> Preferably experience on another newspaper, or at least internship on papers of comparable size. Where a person comes to us directly from school, the minimum requirement is nearly always good campus publication experience, part-time work on a newspaper, or sum-

mer interning elsewhere. Solid educational background, not limited to journalism schools or departments, demonstrated writing talent and reportorial experience, a strong commitment to newspaper journalism.
—Ralph Otwell, managing editor, *Chicago Sun-Times*.

Deep dedication to daily newspaper work, intelligence, wide range of interests, ambition to advance, skills, thoroughness, accuracy, ability to meet deadlines, excellence in grammar and spelling.
—Paul McKalip, editor, *Tucson Citizen*.

Must be able to type, spell, show a talent for writing . . . should indicate he/she can get along with other staffers and contacts. . . .
—Jerald A. Finch, managing editor, *Richmond News-Leader*.

A person who is well-grounded in liberal arts, insatiably curious, well-mannered in person and on the telephone, a skilled researcher on the street and in the library, and with a basic knowledge about back-shop operations.
—Harvey Jacobs, editor, *Indianapolis News*.

Must have a strong interest in one of our subject areas, which are food, travel, gardening and home building projects. We do occasionally hire people right out of school and train them. The gardening and building areas are the most difficult to staff because of the lack of qualified people with knowledge about those subjects.
—Bill Marken, Managing Editor, *Sunset* Magazine.

A CASE HISTORY

Peter Sandman's experience describes the adventure of breaking into journalism. While he was a freshman at Princeton, Sandman began working as a general assignment reporter for the *Daily Princetonian*. He proved himself so conscientious that when the senior board of the *Princetonian* decided the following year to publish a guide to the women's colleges in the vicinity of Princeton, Sandman was assigned to gather the prosaic data on distances to the colleges, curfews, and the like. A senior was given the more interesting task of writing the breezy judgments of the schools and the girls. Months later, Sandman had finished his assignment, but the senior had not even started. So Sandman did his work as well. *Where the Girls Are* became so popular in the edition published by the *Princetonian* that the editors arranged for a commercial publishing house to bring out an expanded edition, which Sandman also wrote.*

---

*Peter M. Sandman and The Staff of the *Daily Princetonian*, *Where the Girls Are* (New York: Dell, 1967).

The book gave him an instant reputation and helped him start free-lancing articles. During his junior year, he sold pieces to the *Princeton Alumni Weekly,* earning from $25 to $150 an article depending on length and difficulty. When he became a senior, Sandman wrote the column "On the Campus," a news-and-views roundup of the undergraduate perspective, for the alumni magazine and also worked as a campus stringer for *Time.*

Like most college stringers for *Time* (and for *Newsweek*), Sandman covered the campus—"everything," he said, "from what students are watching on TV to trends in curriculum"—and was paid by the assignment. Most of his reports were parts of much larger articles; he provided the Princeton angle on national articles, while other college stringers fed the same kind of information in to *Time* headquarters.

Covering Princeton for the *Princetonian,* the *Princeton Alumni Weekly,* and *Time* made Sandman one of the best-informed undergraduates on the campus. One thing he learned was that startling numbers of students work their way through college in quite unconventional ways, some of them by starting their own businesses. A survey of other campuses turned up so many student-run enterprises that Sandman and Goldenson compiled their findings in a book titled *How to Succeed in Business Before Graduating.** When that was published during his first year as a graduate student, Sandman sent a copy to *Reader's Digest* with a query asking whether the editors would be interested in an article based on the book. They liked the idea. They also liked the article he wrote, by and large, but suggested a few changes. He revised to the editors' specifications, mailed the revised article, and received a check for $1,750.

During his next three years as a graduate student, Sandman sold articles to *Look, Playboy, Careers Today, Moderator, Family Health,* and *Rapport,* among others. "But," he said, "I have never yet matched the ease of that first sale to the *Digest.*" At the other extreme was his experience in writing an article on baby foods for *Family Health.* It went through seven drafts before he could satisfy both the sources and his editors. He was paid $1,000, and described it as "hard-earned."

Sandman also sold four articles to the Meredith Corporation (publishers of *Better Homes and Gardens* and other magazines) for a prospective magazine for college students that was to be called *The Magazine.* The editors liked his work; Sandman was hired as West Coast editor to search for writers. He performed well and was made senior editor. In all, he worked for nearly a year for a magazine that was never published. It was the recession period of 1970–71, and Meredith decided that it would not be possible to sell enough advertising to make *The Magazine* profitable.

---

*Peter M. Sandman and Daniel R. Goldenson, *How to Succeed in Business Before Graduating* (New York: Macmillan, 1968).

The experience was valuable; Sandman was well paid; he learned how publications work in a way that few free-lancers ever do; and he developed new contacts for free-lancing, some of them with Meredith publications. Not long after the Meredith Corporation decided not to publish *The Magazine*, Sandman wrote eight short articles for the company's *Apartment Ideas*. All were based on the legal rights of those who own and rent apartments, all were researched in a law library during one period, and all eight were written in the equivalent of a week's time. He was paid $2,000 for the articles.

BREAKING IN AS A FREE-LANCER

There are a few other lessons for the beginning free-lancer in the example of Peter Sandman. The most important lesson that Sandman's experiences teach is that one should aim at reasonable targets. The impatient novice is likely to focus on the fact that Sandman sold an article to *Reader's Digest* for $1,750 while he was still a student—and to forget that the sale was founded on *years* of writing for the *Princetonian*, the *Princeton Alumni Weekly*, and *Time*, not to mention his two books. Sandman learned to write for many diverse audiences. The typical student is accustomed to writing for himself or for a professor and hasn't yet had the chance to master the knack of writing for a large audience. Ill-equipped to aim for a high-paying national magazine, he or she may nonetheless do exactly that. Success is doubtful at best. The more effective course is to write for the college newspaper or magazine, then for a publication with a larger and more varied readership—if not the alumni journal, perhaps the Sunday magazine of a nearby metropolitan newspaper.

Such work not only gives the beginner the experience of writing for an audience but also emphasizes the value of *reporting*—gathering facts through interviewing and observing as well as reading and thinking. The typical undergraduate term paper is based on library research and thought. It is therefore no surprise that many students rely almost exclusively on these techniques in free-lancing. A small percentage of magazine articles are based on library research, but most are more demanding.

This does not mean that a student must always compete with professional writers on *their* terms. In fact, the alert student may use a course assignment as the basis for an article, as we have seen earlier. Unfortunately, students often assume that an "A" term paper can become an article with no more effort than retyping. Two experiences of Frank Allen Philpot, who was then a graduate student in communications at Stanford, are instructive. Philpot had been editor of the campus newspaper at Vanderbilt and had later worked briefly for a professional daily and a television station. In a course at Stanford he studied the changing technology of mass communication and decided that the subject was valuable not only for a term paper but also for a magazine article. He queried *San Francisco* magazine, and the editor was interested. But Philpot tried to make one piece do double duty, both as an article *and* as a term paper. His work pleased the professor but not the editor. The article was rejected—a fairly predictable fate for a piece that attempts to appeal to two such different audiences.

In another course, Philpot learned that three new UHF television stations would soon begin operations in San Francisco. He wrote a term paper on the potential economic impact of the stations. Later, he queried *San Francisco* magazine and received a go-ahead. Then he interviewed the general manager of each station and fashioned a manuscript that borrowed something from the term paper, a bit from his own experience with a UHF station, and a great deal from the interviews. The article, which was published, can serve as a model for using course work in free-lancing.

Leonard Sellers had a similar experience with a student piece that led to a published article. When he was editor of the campus daily at San Francisco State College (now State University), a campus confrontation was at its height. Sellers was asked by the editor of *Seminar*, which assesses the mass media, to describe how a student newspaper handles a student strike. Using his own experiences and interviews with strike leaders and faculty members, Sellers put together a piece that touched on staff dissension, newspaper production under stress, the importance of objective information, the background of the strike, and the founding of a new campus newspaper. The editor deleted the strike background and published the rest of the article.

On another occasion, Sellers wrote a long memo of observations and advice to the student who was to succeed him as editor of the campus paper. He pinned it to the board behind the editor's desk so that his successor would see it. Professor Bud Liebes saw it first and sent a copy to *Quill*, the magazine of the journalism fraternity Sigma Delta Chi. Sellers's memo was published.

The successes of Philpot and Sellers suggest how young writers can use college experiences and emphasize the value of writing for a publication that is certain to be interested in the subject.

Developing Writing Skills as a Free-Lancer

Writers who aim at reasonable targets usually develop their talents faster than those who aim too high at the beginning. Impatient novices who shoot for riches receive rejection slips. What they learn from *that* experience is only that their writing has been rejected. They are not likely to be told why their articles were unacceptable, what the shortcomings were, or how they might have improved them. Even if a long shot is published, the writer learns little—which helps explain why a writer may sell an article to a respected magazine, count on hitting it regularly, then go for years without selling again to the same magazine. Perhaps only then will writers become aware that their early successes were happy accidents. Patient writers who move from one attainable target to another, however, learn with each upward movement. The mere fact of changing from one magazine to another will teach them about varying audiences. More important, writing for local publications will give them ready access to criticism. And criticism, whether it comes from editors or readers, helps writers learn self-criticism, which is the central necessity of all writing. All writers need the views of others because they are always too close to their own work to see it with the proper detachment. But they must develop a self-critical attitude or they will never be able to improve even their first drafts. It does not matter whether self-criticism takes the form of setting aside a period for measuring what has been written against a checklist of writing techniques and devices or whether it is in the form of a vague dissatisfaction that pushes writers into tinkering with this paragraph, rewriting that one, or discarding two others. In either case, the writers have learned to be critical. If they have listened carefully to informed critics, their dissatisfaction will result in effective action.

It is difficult for everyone to accept criticism, and especially difficult for writers because they are likely to be so personally involved in their work. But learning to accept criticism is pivotal, and it may be the chief value of courses in writing. Thoughtful novices learn to *weigh* the critical comments of their teachers and classmates rather than react defensively. Having learned that important lesson, writers are ready to learn from editors, which makes it vital that they submit their work to editors who will offer criticism and advice.

The chief danger in aiming at reasonable targets is that the talented writer soon finds that they are easy to hit. The alumni magazine, the local Sunday supplement, the little political or literary journal with a scattered national readership—each may, in time, become a wide-open market for talented writers who work their way up through them. The more receptive they become, the greater the hazard. For writers are likely to dash off a piece with a left-handed flourish for magazines that are eager for their work. Instead of exercising their talent and requiring it to grow by making new demands on themselves, writers may allow their talent to atrophy by calling on it to do only what it can do easily. One way to avoid this trap is not to write for a magazine that has become too easy to hit. But a better rule is that one should rewrite and reshape and polish everything, no matter what the market. It is all very well for writers to tell themselves that a minor magazine will publish their second-rate stuff. The return on left-handed writing does not match the cost to the writer.

BREAKING IN AS A MAGAZINE STAFF MEMBER

The techniques and devices of the free-lancer are also those of the staff writer. Many magazine staffers work with and sometimes guide free-lancers. Before seeking a staff job, one should first try free-lancing, not only because the experience will give the staffer a firsthand view of free-lancing but also because writing successfully for the magazine whose staff one wants to join is persuasive proof that one understands the magazine's purpose and can reach its audience. Further, prospective staff members who have been published elsewhere—the more respected the magazines, the more respected the writer will be—have demonstrated at least that they are at home in the world of magazines. In either case, applicants who have free-lanced have a significant advantage over most of those seeking staff positions: they need not begin in a flunky job and spend months or years proving that they deserve important assignments; they have already proved themselves, and they will begin higher on the ladder.

The value of free-lancing first is suggested by the hiring practices of a little magazine called *Plane and Pilot.* June Chase, assistant editor, said that most of the staffers are college graduates with majors in journalism and English. "After learning to fly, they free-lanced for us and other aviation magazines and then moved in as staffers."

National Geographic also looks for those who have proved that they can write for magazines. Associate Editor John Scofield says:

> After screening by our Personnel Office to assure at least minimal professional qualifications, the applicant is interviewed by at least three Assistant Editors. In their evaluation they weigh heavily the applicant's previous writing—preferably magazine articles in fields we normally cover. In the past few years no staffer has been hired without undertaking a trial assignment, usually a short to medium-length article often on a subject suggested by the candidate himself, and often on a "minimum-guarantee" basis.

Thomas Griffith, editor of *Time,* said that several of his staff writers began by "writing pieces for us, having a track record, and then being signed on. We often see something people write elsewhere, and begin by asking them to do a book review for us, where we get the first measurement of their talents, and adaptability to length, tone, frequency, and speed."

Another important path to staff writing offered by *Time, Newsweek,* and many other weeklies calls for working part-time as a stringer. Needing coverage of campuses, state capitals, and large metropolitan areas that full-time correspondents cannot always provide, many weeklies and not a few monthlies retain students and young newspaper reporters. Griffith points out that most *Time* staffers "rose to the top by the same method: They began perhaps as stringers in our Time-Life News Service, or on the way up from office boys and summer fill-ins, proved reliable, fresh, talented, and got better and better assignments. The final stage—doing signed text pieces—is a very difficult last hurdle, for we have few available spots, and here writing talent, reportorial quality, judgment are decisive."

Moving from Newspaper to Magazine

Newspapers represent another important path to high-level magazine work. John Adams, managing editor of *U.S. News & World Report,* said, "As a general rule we require five years or more of prior experience on a press association or metropolitan newspaper." Few other magazines are so stringent, even in setting general rules, but newspaper experience is prized in the magazine world, and not only by news magazine executives. Bryon Scott, first editor of *Today's Health* and then executive editor of *Medical Opinion,* said, "Of the eight members of the *Today's Health* staff who held editorial posts, only two had not 'served time' on a daily newspaper. Over many a beer we agreed that newspaper experience imparts to the magazine writer a sense for accuracy, conciseness, and speed. These become an excellent base for the qualities of style, depth-reporting, and creativity required of a magazine type."

Direct Application and Internships

For varied reasons, not all those who become staff writers have either the opportunity or the inclination to work their way onto magazine staffs by beginning as free-lancers, as stringers, or as newspaper reporters. Indeed, so many are impatient for staff positions that they simply apply, and perhaps more staff writers are trained and developed on the job than in any other way. For a long time, the process of working up to important assignments was frustrating. Beginners did secretarial work and simple clipping, filing, and research. A full opportunity to demonstrate reporting, writing, and editing ability was often agonizingly slow in arriving. Such frustrations still exist on many magazines, and novices should consider the possibility that getting a few writing credits through free-lancing may enable them to bypass the tedium of low-level staff work. But in recent years, many magazines have recognized that personnel policies must be revamped. Some companies, especially those like McGraw-Hill, which publish many magazines, have set up training programs that make use of beginners' talents and also help to develop them. The Magazine Publishers Association has established a summer internship program that gives about fifty journalism students a ten-week taste of magazine staff work. Accredited schools and departments of journalism are invited to nominate an outstanding junior every year. In many cases, the interns prove their talents so well they are given responsible positions on graduation.

Students who work as interns are generally regarded as trainees. They sometimes receive minimal wages for their work, but more often, they work for free in exchange for the knowledge and experience they acquire. Many journalism departments award college credits for internships because they recognize their educational value. An author of this book was hired as an editorial assistant after a three-month internship at *Women's Sports,* and many other young staff writers and editors find jobs this way.

Internships need not be at national magazines to be valuable. In fact, it is often easier to find them at local publications because the competition is less keen. A small publication can actually be a better place for a beginner to learn because it is less likely to limit an intern's activities to filing and typing letters. But even those chores can be instructive because they help a novice gain insight into the way a magazine operates. Interns are often asked to perform clerical tasks that may seem unrelated to the business of becoming a journalist, but it is important to realize that beginners are expected to start at the bottom. Those who are willing to do so usually are offered more challenging assignments sooner than are those who complain about their work.

Unorthodox Beginnings

Occasionally, too, editors use unorthodox methods for hiring. When he was an editor for *Esquire,* Harold Hayes announced in his "Editor's Notes" column that he was looking for a junior editor:

> We would like for him to be resourceful, intelligent, and committed to high purpose. But mostly what we need is somebody with a sense of humor. No rush. We can wait until the right man comes along. If you are under twenty-five and interested, just give a try at rewriting the titles and subtitles in this issue. Where you see an opportunity to be funny, seize it. No phone calls or personal appearances, please. Just send in the stuff with your name and address. If you make us laugh, you can come tell us a joke and see how you like us.

Two years later, in a letter to an author of this text, Hayes said that he had written that invitation in some despair of finding a suitable applicant, but "the wife of one young writer saw the column and persuaded him to apply. He proved to be the best of some 75 to 100 applicants, and is today thriving as an Associate Editor here at *Esquire.* His name is Lee Eisenberg."

Two Magazine Staffs

A rough notion of how some magazine staffs are formed can be gleaned from reports by two editors. First, Associate Editor John

Scofield of *National Geographic* magazine, which is published by the National Geographic Society, writes:

> In pondering how our writers and editors joined the staff, I am somewhat surprised at the random pattern that emerges. The most consistent thread seems to be that writers *apply* to the National Geographic Society for employment rather than being actively recruited from other publications. Only rarely have we resorted to advertising in the trade press. In general we have tended to hire talented young (under thirty-five) writers, some of whom have demonstrated considerable editing talent and have moved up the ladder. Thus all of our editors are capable of undertaking writing assignments, and they frequently do.
>
> Of some forty people actively engaged in the writing, editing, and production of *National Geographic*, the majority have had staff experience on other publications. Thirteen came directly from newspapers, wire or feature services, public relations, or related enterprises. Nine left the staffs of other magazines (among them, *Life, Holiday, U.S. News & World Report, Changing Times,* and *Pathfinder*). Nine have transferred from the Society's other departments or publications, although most of these, too, have had newspaper or magazine experience. Seven came from other fields— government, science, or directly from college, for example. Only two present-staffers were full-time free-lance writers when we hired them. (Several others in this category are no longer with us.)
>
> Thus one might fairly conclude that the applicant with the best chance for a staff position at *National Geographic* is currently holding down a writing job with another magazine or newspaper; has an impressive scrap-book to show us; and is willing to undertake a trial assignment, on speculation if necessary.
>
> I think, understandably, staff openings on the magazine itself do not occur frequently. Thus an applicant might have a better chance if he aimed first at one of the Society's other publishing activities: our Book Service, Special Publications, News Service, or School Service. As I have indicated, a number of our magazine staffers have moved up (or over) from other departments.

Assistant Managing Editor John Tibby of *Sports Illustrated* reports:

> *Sports Illustrated* began publication in August 1954 under the assumption that about one-third of the magazine would be produced by staff writers, the remainder by free-lance and contract writers. But it was soon judged that a pattern quite suitable to many monthlies was inadvisable in a weekly that undertakes to be as timely as any other

newsweekly. *Sports Illustrated* began the gradual development of a "senior editor" system, with departmentalized responsibilities in certain clusters of sports assigned to such editors. In addition, the title senior editor was awarded in a number of cases to persons who did not prefer to specialize in story-planning and editing; these are in effect senior writers.

Today about 80 percent of *Sports Illustrated* is staff-written, and of the remainder about half comes from contract writers (e.g., Jack Olsen) and the other half from usually well-established writers not under contract.

In addition to the managing group, we have forty-one staff editors and writers ranging in masthead designation from senior editor through associate editor to staff writer. These are supported by an auxiliary group with masthead designations ranging through writer-reporter and senior reporter to reporter. These individuals help research stories, help check them, and often accompany writers on story locations. All are encouraged to show writing ability, and a good many in the senior and intermediate writing groups have risen from the reporter divisions.

MANAGEMENT GROUP

Managing Editor André Laguerre: from London Bureau Chief of Time *in 1956. Appointed managing editor 1960.*

Executive Editor Roy Terrell: hired in the '50s from a daily in Corpus Christi, Texas, where he had been a sports columnist.

Assistant ME John Tibby: transferred from Time, *where he had been a senior editor for subjects including sports.*

Assistant ME Ray Cave: hired from the Baltimore Evening Sun, *where he had been assistant city editor and SI's regional correspondent.*

Assistant ME Jeremiah Tax: hired in the '50s after tryout writing.

SENIOR EDITORS

Approximately half are senior writers who do no editing. In the group as a whole, where the median age is in the mid-forties, one finds that they come to SI as follows:

By transfer from other Time, Inc. magazines (4)

Newspaper or magazine writer with five years or more of significant experience, who made direct application to Sports Illustrated *(8)*

Same with at least one to two years of experience with effective exhibits of their work, who were hired to the reporter division or other junior staff (6)

Started as a secretary (a woman who grew up in a family of horse trainers) (1)

ASSOCIATE EDITORS

By transfer, as above   (2)
With five years or more of experience   (5)
With one to two years   (2)

STAFF WRITERS

By transfer   (2)
With five years or more   (5)
With one to two years   (5)
Started as a secretary   (1)

In general, appointments to junior staff (reporters) go to men and women in their early to mid-twenties. The competition for the relatively few openings in any year is especially severe for men, since the largest number of applications or inquiries reach us from men (up to 100 a year). As a result *Sports Illustrated* is inclined to choose from among those with the best writing samples of their professional work. One or two years of professional writing is not an absolute requirement, but such experience helps to show something more than latent talent.

We use no form letters in correspondence with people inquiring about staff opportunities. We are always glad to have such men and women introduce themselves to us in person. We regret that we have no means of conducting job interviews except in New York City.

To summarize, the clearest paths to magazine staff work are free-lancing, working as a stringer, working as a newspaper reporter, and simply applying for a job. Some have followed *all* these paths, and many have reached high-level magazine positions by combining newspaper reporting and free-lancing.

CHAPTER THREE EXERCISES

1. Make out a resumé of what you've done as if you were a graduate applying for a newspaper or magazine job. Match that with the resumés done by the other class members at the next session.

2. Because of the specialized nature of many magazines, more journalists are beginning to specialize in particular fields. Using *Writer's Market*, choose three magazines devoted to specific audiences and decide how you might prepare yourself to write for them. What courses might you consider taking in college that would help you develop expertise in a given subject?

3. Discuss the differences between working as a writer for a magazine and working for a newspaper. How do these differences suit your particular interests, style of writing or goals? Do you think a good writer should be able to write well for any publication?

CHAPTER 4
How to Find Facts

Research is the raw material from which articles are made. Skimpy research leads to equally thin articles. Novelist John Cheever once claimed that he could detect a single glass of sherry in a writer's prose; insufficient research is as easy to spot.

Whether you choose to write in the style of new journalism or to stick with conventional forms of feature and magazine writing, you need to develop strong research skills, and you must know where to look for the information you need. That usually means consulting many different sources, such as library reference materials, as well as interviewing subjects, writing letters, and observing and recording events. Every story benefits from information that comes from such research, but it is a rare writer who can produce a top-rate story based entirely on any one of these elements alone—library work or interviews or observation.

Professionals always wonder whether they have covered all the bases, whether there might still be some important element to the story that they have overlooked. Lesser writers look instead for only enough sources to provide sufficient information on which to base the story. Beginners often carry both these tendencies to the extreme. They either become so preoccupied with doing thorough research jobs that they miss their deadlines, or even worse, never get to their typewriters at all, or they do so little research that writing their stories is like trying to fill a balloon with a hole in it. The best approach lies somewhere in between.

LIBRARY RESEARCH AND STANDARD REFERENCES

Anyone schooled in the old newspaper form is likely to think of the interview as the primary means of gathering information. That will sometimes suffice. But as newspapers and magazines become more sophisticated, the feature writer and the magazine writer must learn how to use the library.

Readers' Guide to Periodical Literature is the first volume to consult on almost any article assignment. Some writers consider it such an important reference that they subscribe to it, paying about $30 a year.

The writer must know what else has been written on a subject or on related subjects, and *Readers' Guide* approaches being an exhaustive listing. Reading what has appeared on a subject may persuade a writer that it has already been covered too heavily to warrant another article—at least for a time. But the writer will usually discover that other articles have covered only some aspects of the subject. The writer will learn which angles have been explored and will turn up leads to sources of information for a different approach.

In some cases, much of the information for a story must be dug out of a public library or a newspaper library, and in some instances serious research in libraries can yield startling results. For example, during World War II, a German spy in the United States shunned cloak and dagger in favor of libraries. Government officials learned after the war that by analyzing newspapers, magazines, and technical journals, he was able to predict American war production more accurately than the United States government.

Many veteran writers build their own libraries as well as being familiar figures in the reference room of the public library and in that of the nearest metropolitan newspaper office. They keep on their own shelves the books they are likely to use again and again. *Readers' Guide*, a standard encyclopedia, an almanac, a desk dictionary and an unabridged dictionary, a thesaurus, and probably a dictionary of quotations. Personal libraries may contain thousands of books. Many writers also build extensive files of newspaper and magazine clippings. Because they cannot hope to collect all the reference books or clippings they may need to use some day, writers eventually establish first-name relationships with reference and newspaper librarians.

Some writers occasionally boast that they have written articles "from the clips," which means that they have used only newspaper and magazine clippings. But for every such article that succeeds, fifty fail. A common complaint among editors is that some writers simply rehash material that has already been printed. Magazines with large research staffs sometimes look carefully at articles that seem stale, and a writer who develops a reputation for rehashing is in trouble. The chief point to remember about library research is that it is only a supplement, if a valuable one, to the other kinds of research that enliven writing.

The following annotated list is a sampling of a few standard reference works frequently useful to the newspaper and magazine writer (publishers are noted in parentheses)*:

Bartlett's Familiar Quotations (Little, Brown). This famous

Famous First Facts (Wilson). The first occurrence of nearly

---

*For further information see William L. Rivers, *Finding Facts: Interviewing, Observing, Using Reference Sources* (Englewood Cliffs, N.J.: Prentice-Hall, 1975).

source lists sayings and writings from 2000 B.C. to the present. A valuable reference tool.

Book Review Digest (Wilson). This publication condenses published reviews of books.

Columbia Encyclopedia (Columbia University Press). This one-volume edition is an excellent research tool, containing a wide range of information. It is far from a replacement for the thirty-volume *Encyclopaedia Britannica* or the thirty-volume *Encyclopedia Americana,* but its most recent fourth edition is an excellent handbook.

Contemporary Authors (Gale Research). Restricted to living authors, it includes those who have written relatively little and also those who have written in obscure fields.

Current Biography (Wilson). Prominent persons in the news of the day are sketched in informal word portraits. Published monthly, the issues are accumulated in annual volumes.

Facts on File (Facts on File, Inc.). Published weekly, this is a valuable encyclopedia that culls the news of the day from metropolitan daily newspapers.

anything can be found here: athletic feats, discoveries, inventions, and bizarre incidents.

The Guinness Book of World Records (Guinness Superlatives). This book is the final authority on who has the world record in almost any undertaking.

The New York Times Index (New York Times). This is a valuable semimonthly subject index to the *Times.*

Statistical Abstract of the United States (U.S. Government Printing Office). This is a digest of data collected by all the statistical agencies of the United States government and some private agencies.

Television News Index and Abstracts (Vanderbilt University). Published since 1972, this monthly volume is a summary of the evening news broadcasts of the three major television networks.

Who's Who in America (Marquis). This biennial is considered the standard source on notable living Americans. It consists of brief, fact-packed biographies and current addresses.

LEGWORK: INTERVIEWING AND OBSERVATION

Many beginning writers who have written only compositions, essays, and term papers are likely to lean too heavily on library research and their own ideas as they begin a career in journalism. And the more seasoned writer who has worked for a small paper is accustomed to the usual hectic newspaper pace and is likely to clip an old story or two, conduct a one-hour review, and then try to stretch 2,000 or 3,000 words out of these scraps. Neither method alone will work very often.

Both the beginning newspaper writer and the newspaper staffer trying to switch from conventional newspaper style to the longer, more-demanding feature or in-depth article must accustom themselves to a new pace. They must learn the background that goes into writing lengthy articles. Legwork is the touch that adds to initial, thorough library research the extra dimension achieved from multiple or repeated interviews, and enhanced whenever possible by direct personal observation.

The rule for writers, beginner or professional, is that they must simply gather at least twice as much information as they can use. Writers who have collected more information than they need are freed of the necessity of using everything they have. They can *select*, which is the key to all successful writing. Instead of recounting both a tasteless anecdote and one that actually reveals character, they can choose seven revealing anecdotes from a stock of twelve. Instead of attempting to describe a political convention that someone has described to them, probably ineptly, they can draw on the experience of hours of watching the maneuvering on the convention floor.

Consider how Maurice Zolotow, a veteran free-lancer, researched an article on Salvatore Baccaloni, a Metropolitan Opera singer. Zolotow began by reading eight books on opera (from *Opera, Front and Back* to *Caruso's Method of Voice Production*). Not one of the books said anything about Baccaloni; Zolotow was merely educating himself on opera in general. Next, he went backstage at the Metropolitan to get the feel of the place. Only after completing this "atmospheric research" did he begin with Baccaloni—and he began by reading everything on the singer in the clipping files of the *New York Times*.

Finally, Zolotow got around to Baccaloni himself, interviewing him six times and traveling from New York to Boston to watch him perform. Then he interviewed ten people who knew Baccaloni. Still, Zolotow did not consider himself ready to write. As usual, he devoted several days to brooding about the article, then spent a week organizing it mentally. At last, he was ready. He wrote the twenty-page first draft in three days.

Such legwork is central in writing 99 percent of all articles, and it is fun. Writers open doors that are closed to others; they meet interesting people and learn interesting things. James Thurber viewed legwork this way:

If an astonished botanist produced a black evening primrose, or thought he had produced one, I spent the morning prowling his gardens. When a lady sent in word that she was getting messages from the late Walter Savage Landor in heaven, I was sent up to see what the importunate poet had on his mind. On the occasion of the arrival in town of Major Monroe of Jacksonville, Florida, who claimed to be a hundred and seventeen years old, I walked up Broadway with him while he roundly cursed the Northern dogs who jostled him, bewailing the while the passing of Bob Lee and Tom Jackson and Joe Johnston. I studied gypsies in Canarsie and generals in the Waldorf, listened to a man talk backward, and watched a blindfolded boy play ping-pong. Put it all together and I don't know what it comes to, but it wasn't drudgery.*

Those who dread legwork, or think they do, probably need only implement a few guidelines to simplify it.

Interviewing   *How* one interviews is the critical point. Sometimes a writer who has never conducted a formal interview and knows little about conventional techniques may be a better interviewer than one who has conducted many interviews and has carefully studied the insights and experiences of professional interviewers. Interviewing has a highly personal character, and curiosity, intelligence, and warmth are all valuable assets. Studying interviewing techniques, however, can certainly help improve one's interviewing style. For example, study Benjamin Franklin on the technique of the argumentative interview:

> I made it a rule to forebear all direct contradiction to the sentiments of others, and all positive assertions of my own. I even forbid myself the use of every word in the language that imported a fixed opinion, such as *certainly, undoubtedly,* etc., and I adopted instead of them, *I conceive, I apprehend, I imagine a thing to be so and so,* or *so it appears to me at the present.* When another asserted something that I thought to be an error, I denied myself the pleasure of contradicting him abruptly, and of showing immediately some absurdity in his proposition; and in answering I began by observing that in certain cases or circumstances his opinion would be right, but in the present case there appeared or seemed to me some difference, etc. I soon found the advantage of this change in my manners; the conversations I engaged in went on more pleasantly. The modest way in which I proposed my opinions procured them a readier reception and less contradiction; I had less mortification when I was found to be in the wrong; and I more easily prevailed with others to give up their mistakes and join with me when I happened to be right.

This is valuable advice, and it suggests the atmosphere of the kind of interview the authors of this book use—easygoing, conversational. Interviewees are usually so disarmed by the conversational

*James Thurber, *The Thurber Carnival* (New York: Harper & Row, 1945), pp. 22–23.

mode that they talk more freely than they might have had the interviewer been either more formal or more aggressive.

For example, it was important in writing "Airports: Our Newest Billion-Dollar Business" to know the annual earnings of Kennedy International Airport. But the New York Port Authority, which runs the airports as well as the docks and bus terminals, did not want the earnings of any unit of its operations revealed. The authority juggles funds from one unit to another as the directors see fit. The figure for Kennedy International could not be drawn out of any official. But during the friendly, conversational interviews with many officials, enough manipulations were revealed to enable the writer to add two and two from annual reports and come up with a close estimate of Kennedy's earnings. After the story was published, the New York City Corporation Commissioner called to ask how the earnings figure was derived and admitted, *"We've* been trying to get it for more than a year."

An entirely different interview atmosphere is created by the tough, aggressive reporter who bores in with rifle-shot questions, sometimes upsetting the interviewee to the point that he defensively says much more than he intends to say. This method is especially effective in researching hard-hitting exposés and some political articles. But it is almost always dangerous. It usually results in the interviewee's bringing up his guard and revealing as little as possible—even about matters that he would not have minded discussing under more relaxed circumstances.

Sooner or later, however, even during the friendliest interviews, a writer is likely to find that he must ask a hard-boiled question, one that may make both parties uncomfortable. It is wise to ask this question late in the interview after the conversational method has done its work.

Similarly, a writer may find it easy to acquiesce when an interviewee begins to offer information "off the record," or "confidentially." It is almost always wise to respond, "Don't tell me anything that can't be printed." There are exceptional cases, of course, but closing off "confidential" information enables a writer to pursue the same facts elsewhere—for publication.

These suggestions and the guidelines below are only rules of thumb for conducting interviews. Interviewers, interviewees, and interview situations are so varied that nothing like a formula can be devised.

Prepare for the Interview   Always learn as much as possible about your subject before the appointment. Those who are not actually incensed by an interviewer's ignorance will almost surely be uncomfortable with one who demonstrates that he has not done his homework. Doing the homework—learning at least the basic facts about the interviewee—is a compliment to the subject and will encourage response. John Gunther, the famous author of the *Inside* books, warned: "One thing is never, never, never to ask a man about his own first name, job, or title. These the interviewer should know beforehand.''* And, of course, much more.

Prepare questions, but remember that an interview is a human, not a bookkeeping situation. Most professional journalists have a few questions ready—in mind or jotted in a notebook—but not many of them prepare long lists of questions. Growth and continuity in an interview stem from conversation. Transitions should be natural. Questions should grow logically from the discussion, one answer suggesting another question. The reporter who knows, 1–2–3–4–5, what he is going to ask misses the opportunity to improvise during the course of the interview—to pursue new ideas, perspectives, facts that come out in asking the set questions. Nonetheless, it is wise for the beginner to list the more important questions and leave spaces to record answers. The smooth, natural discourse of the professional takes time to develop.

Take Notes   Professionals disagree on when and how to take notes. Some interviewees may become self-conscious when they see their words being recorded. Some freeze. These are also sound arguments against tape-recording interviews, but many writers are turning to the recorders anyway. Other interviewees are uneasy when notes are *not* taken, fearing that the interviewer (especially an obvious beginner) will later try, ineptly, to remember what was said. At least a few journalists follow this rule: Take notes freely—or use a recorder—in talking with those who are accustomed to speaking for publication: politicians, civic leaders, entertainers, and the like. Be wary with those who are not in public life. Few of these people can avoid tightening up in the presence of a notebook or tape recorder, and that dilutes the natural flavor the interviewer wants. One writer says:

> Flipping out the notebook the minute you flush the quarry has never worked too well for me. It scares some subjects. The best excuse I find for breaking out the pad is a bit of blue-eyed admiration for some happy observation they've just made. I may try, "Say, that's good. I want to be sure I get that down just right." And write. The notebook now spells reassurance.

As for the mechanics of note taking, most journalists devise their own shorthand: *imp.* for *important, w/* for *with, w/o* for *without,* and the like. One reporter's technique for winning time to record an important answer is to ask another, unimportant question immediately. While the interviewee is responding to the second, the reporter records the answer to the first.

---

*John Gunther, ''Writing the Inside Books,'' *Harper's* (April 1961), p. 73.

Encourage a Response   Only with the busiest people—and those who are merely suffering the interview—should questions begin abruptly. Usually, small talk at the beginning will oil the later conversation. This does not mean that the interviewer should make an obvious and awkward effort to chitchat, which requires a stumbling leap to the real subject. It means, for example, that the prelude to questioning a politician about his candidacy is not the weather but politics in general.

More important, the ideal interview should mark the halfway point between monologue and dialogue. If the interviewee talks in an endless monologue, leading points are likely to be missed. Most interviewees must be steered. But if the interview is a real dialogue, the interviewer is doing half the talking and, as a result, showing off and probably irritating his subject. This is the most delicate point in interviewing—the balance between the interviewer's commenting appropriately on an answer in developing the next question and not seeming to dominate the interview. A comment is effective in connection with at least a few questions, for an interviewer is never more likely to draw a full response than when he makes it clear, modestly, that he is knowledgeable. In this manner the interviewee develops confidence that his responses will be reported in a meaningful context and speaks more freely. It is a cardinal error, however, for an interviewer to fail to ask questions because he fears exposing his ignorance of particular points. If he knew *everything*, there would be no reason for an interview.

This point is worth elaborating because admitting ignorance can become a valuable tool in conducting interviews. Although one should prepare for an interview and encourage responses by commenting appropriately, it is also important to confess ignorance at appropriate points so that the interviewee will spell out his meaning. Too often, beginners put on a facade of understanding and are afraid to ask questions that reveal their ignorance. This can become a dangerous habit.

Inevitable in the life of every journalist is the awful occasion when a bored interviewee answers in monosyllables: "Yes." "No." "Who knows?" Transforming these deadly situations is difficult, but it can sometimes be accomplished with a simple question: "Why?" Although an interviewee can answer most direct questions with a simple positive or negative, it is quite another thing for him to explore the *why* of his answer in one syllable. The real aim, of course, is to inspire interest, to ask the interviewee to explore his point of view. Few can resist the temptation. Gunther has commented on a related matter: "One thing I have found out is that almost any person will talk freely—such is human frailty—if you will ask him the measure of his own accomplishment."*

---

*Gunther, p. 74.

Gunther's advice is sound and can be used to turn a poor interview around. Another veteran writer has said on getting people to talk about themselves and their work:

> I've found that as soon as I've discovered a man's obsession or enthusiasm and have got him started talking about it, I've opened the gate. All I have to do is nudge him now and then with a question to keep him talking. If I have any curves to throw at him, I save them until the end of the interview, when we're on pretty good terms; and then I don't throw spitballs, just curves.
>
> Once, a union boss hit me with a spitball before I could begin questioning him. He asked, "How much did Joe Sevier (an opponent of the boss) pay you for writing that story about him in *Nation's Business*?" I thought about it a minute, to keep from replying angrily, then told him, "Well, he paid me exactly what you're going to pay me for doing this story about you." He grinned, and then we had a long and congenial interview that ended with an invitation for me to attend a meeting of his union that night— an unheard-of invitation because reporters were usually excluded.

Ending an Interview   It usually pays to wind up an interview with something like, "My hindsight is better than my foresight. When I check over my notes, I'll undoubtedly find that there are questions I'll wish I had asked. May I come back with another question or two?" This keeps the door open and suggests to the interviewee that he is dealing with a careful writer. Peter Sandman closes his interviews in another fashion:

> I make it a habit to ask the source a broad leading question toward the end of the interview—something like, "Is there anything I haven't asked you that you think I ought to ask or that you are anxious to answer?" It sometimes opens up whole new fields of exploration that I didn't even know existed.

Respect Confidences   Finally, it is important to remember that often those who conduct interviews are asked to keep some information confidential. This request occurs when the subject suddenly decides that he or she has been indiscreet or has been so lured by the interviewer that more had been revealed than should have been. In ideal circumstances, the interviewer and interviewee determine at the beginning what kind of, and how much, information will be disclosed.

But in this matter every writer must decide whether informants are serving private or public interests, although most people usually serve both, to some degree. Seldom will a public official, for example, arrange or submit to an interview unless he can see *some* advantage for himself or his policies. Writers must learn to recognize whether they are being used in a way that does not serve the public interest.

The area of confidential information is thus sometimes complicated, and developing guidelines may be difficult. However, there are two clear necessities: (1) ground rules must be established—preferably before the interview, and (2) an agreement to keep confidences must be respected. And of course, adaptations to the particular interview situation must be made as well.

Observation   Observation is vital to a true report. Like interviewing, direct observation yields liveliness—paragraphs that lend a lift and freshness. And woebetide the journalist who can't observe. Early in his career, Bruce Bliven had the good fortune to work under Fremont Older, a demanding San Francisco editor with "a personality so vigorous that you could feel his presence through a brick wall." Deciding that one dull reporter could write compellingly only by immersing himself in his subject, Older assigned him to write about the Salvation Army and gave him all the time he needed to research and write captivatingly. But after three weeks with the "Army," the reporter turned in his usual flavorless stuff. "Didn't you observe *anything?*" Older bellowed. "At night, for instance, *where did they hang the bass drum?*" The reporter did not know. He was fired. Older repeated the story for decades to push young reporters into becoming sensitive observers. The lesson stuck so well with Bliven that, fifty years after his own experiences with Older, Bliven said, "After I meet someone, I ask myself questions about his personal appearance, to make sure I really *saw* him."

Focused concentration is essential to good writing largely because we become too accustomed to our environment. Familiarity breeds indifference. This was demonstrated strikingly in a series of studies during which students proved themselves incapable of describing the entrance hall of their university. They had seen the entrance countless times, but it had never registered clearly in their minds.

Concentration is necessary too because vision is so complex. Unlike spoken words that present themselves to us successively, visual forms appear simultaneously. Everything in our field of vision registers in one vague mass. Focusing on the shape, the color, the dimensions, and the movement of a single object requires conscious effort.

There are other variables associated with observation. Imagine two reporters covering an emotional event—for example, a campus protest rally. One reporter is only a few feet from the principal speaker, the leader of the movement, and thus is likely to rub elbows with the speaker's most vocal supporters. The other is twenty-five feet away, in a good position to hear every word of the speech but ringed about by the speaker's detractors, who fill every pause in the speech with phrases like "that Communist." Obviously, the reports of the crowd's reaction to the speech will be conditioned by the perspectives of the two reporters—and may differ markedly.

The variations on this problem are almost endless. It is one thing, for example, to tour the construction area of a dam in the company of the architect, quite another to make the same tour with a congressman who is a bitter opponent of the project. And, of course, the writer himself is not an objective machine. His own attitudes toward what he observes are likely to condition what he writes.

Beginning reporters can best train themselves to see sharply by recognizing the common pitfalls of observation.

The process of distortion All writers attempting to be observers should remind themselves that human perception is not infallible, and that habits, interests, and sentiments are deeply embedded and likely to affect the way one takes on new information. Thus, we are forced to shorten and select—or distort—what we observe. Remembering this tendency should cause one to go slowly to guard against the effects of distortion.

Emotional states Most of us learn to discount some unfounded impressions, and later to dismiss them with, "Well, I guess I was pretty emotional then." It is true that the most accurate observations are normally recalled immediately after an event. But if the event places emotional stress on the observer, he or she is more subject to distortion caused by emotions. This problem can often be resolved by recording impressions of an event immediately after it occurs to capture details that might be forgotten. Later, at a more tranquil time, the writer can assess his first account and evaluate any possible distortion arising from his earlier emotional state.

Significant details As mentioned before, concentrating on the important visual details is a difficult job. You as observer must decide beforehand which forms, events, or details are worth your attention. Your task as an observer attending a political convention, for example, would be hopeless if you did not have in mind or on paper what you expected to focus on. You must train yourself to concentrate on what is significant for you. The ability, or the will, to concentrate varies, which is the reason that some football coaches are better than others at scouting upcoming opponents and picking out small, but crucial, details of interior line play while nearly everyone else in the stadium is watching the ball. But everyone with vision can learn to focus it.

Distortions of perspective The most obvious method of avoiding this pitfall is to recognize that any single perspective is necessarily limited and must be supplemented with others. Careful researchers are usually quick to recognize that they must consider other perspectives when they are weighing another observer's report, but they may not be so quick to supplement their own observations. Nearly all observers are too ready to trust the evidence they have seen. Wilbur Schramm, a thorough investigator, says that whenever possible he arranges to have another researcher accompany him for observing and interviewing. He has learned that checking one impression against another often yields surprising and useful results.

It is easier to isolate these enemies of valid observation than it is to conquer them. But isolating them and recognizing their power is the first step in countering their effects. Observers who know that they are subject to the vagueness of vision and to personal perspective and attitudes are at least on guard against most obvious distortions.

CORRESPONDENCE

On some occasions, much of an article may be researched through correspondence. In one instance, a writer was gathering information on an international scholarship program that brought highly placed officials and businessmen in mid-career to the United States. The writer had an opportunity to interview the director of the program, who had large files of reports written by the foreign visitors, but the visitors themselves had returned to their homes. There was nothing easily at hand that would help bring the article to life.

The only solution short of traveling to many countries for interviews, which would have made the article prohibitively expensive, was correspondence. It worked. Most of the visitors described in detailed letters how study and travel in the United States had enhanced their skills and their opportunities back home. Interviews with the foreigners would have improved the article, but with the director's help, the writer was able to stitch together their correspondence and his notes on interviews into a readable report.

Perhaps writers should use correspondence more often than they do, but it is seldom central to research. Most writers have found that they can set up interview appointments and gather a few facts by letter, but the color, the flavor, the anecdotes, and the incidents that enliven writing are difficult to collect through correspondence. Most often, letters are valuable at the beginning and at the end of research. That is, a writer who has developed the idea for an article can write letters to ask for interviews and, in some instances, ask for return letters that will help establish whether there is a sound basis for the piece. He or she can also write to ask for an opportunity to telephone, and this is usually wise; phoning out of the blue—without writing a letter first—often catches a source unprepared and busy, with thoughts on other matters. At the other end of the writing process, letters may be written to ask for facts that were not gathered during the interviewing and observing period. No matter how carefully a writer plans an article, he or she is likely to find an overlooked item or two. A letter and sometimes a phone call usually help. They may even bring a response that adds a dimension the subject failed to mention during interviews.

PUTTING IT ALL TOGETHER

How library research, interviewing, observation, and correspondence fit together to produce an article is illustrated by the researching and writing of "What the World Owes to the Gardens at Kew." Much of the research went into determining whether Kew Gardens would actually make a story. The notion that it was more than a horticultural showplace came from a passage in a travel book that mentioned as an aside that King George III, who had provoked the American colonies to revolution, could at least be credited with having helped to establish the gardens. The king had supported British horticulturists who hoped to start a vast glass conservatory for acclimating and upgrading plants from Britain's tropical colonies. They had invented a miniature portable greenhouse that enabled them to keep plants and cuttings from dehydrating during long voyages. Thus, Kew became the incubator of great new industries: the rubber saplings transplanted from South America to Kew to Malaysia; the pineapple plantings of Ceylon; the "horticultural booty," as it was known, that launched sisal, cinchona for quinine, oil palms, ginger, allspice, and numerous trees prized for their beauty.

After the editors approved the idea, the writer studied Kew Gardens in encyclopedias, horticultural books, and in botanical articles located through *Readers' Guide*. When he arrived at Kew Gardens, he was amused to discover that neither the director nor his staff could answer some of the key questions. They sent him to Kew's botanical library to rummage through scrapbooks and records going back more than a century. This yielded the gist of the story—Kew's great usefulness to mankind during its first half-century.

Then the writer toured the extensive greenhouses, some more than a century old, to observe how Kew created artificial climates suitable for cultivating plants from all over the world. He thought he had everything for his article when he left England to return home to the United States. But after the editors worked over the manuscript, a few more questions came up. Back the writer went to correspondence to wrap up the assignment.

All writers develop their own research methods, of course, and alter them with the varying demands of different pieces. But it is especially important to you as a beginner to practice all these research techniques so that you can call on any or all of them.

CHAPTER FOUR EXERCISES

1. Because interviewing is central to almost any journalist's job, you must first prepare yourself to interview—and this is much more than

knowing the interviewee's name and job. Practice your first interview by learning everything you can about the interviewee. For this exercise, choose an interviewee whose name is all you know. Before talking to him or her, see how much you can learn without speaking to the interviewee. Bring what you have learned to the next class session.

2. To learn to observe, do the following exercise. Go to a football game (basketball game, baseball game) and concentrate on the crowd. Write what you have observed in about 500 words, making it as interesting as you can. Then match that with the story written by one of your classmates who went to the same game. Which is more accurate? Which is more interesting?

3. Tape record an interview with someone you plan to write a story about. Then listen carefully to the tape in order to discuss which of your questions were most effective in eliciting the kind of information you wanted. Which questions were not, and why? Discuss how you might have improved the interview. Did you miss any opportunities for follow-up questions or phrase your questions so that the subject could easily respond with single-word answers and in the process subvert the interview?

PART TWO
Writing for Newspapers

CHAPTER 5
Some Journalistic Forms

Because of the specialized nature of most magazines, magazine writers usually know exactly what kinds of persons will read their articles. Readership surveys indicating the sex, age, education, income, and interests of the magazine's average reader enable them to write as though they are addressing particular individuals. In contrast, newspaper writers usually must aim their articles at the broadest possible audience. Their paper's readership surveys may tell them who reads certain sections of the newspaper, but it won't tell them to write with only those people in mind.

The problem of trying to offer something for everyone, while making each reader feel that his particular interests are being covered, is one that is especially important for newspaper feature writers and editors. To a certain extent, the straight news content of a paper is dictated by its editorial policy of covering international, national, or local news. But there are no easy rules for creating feature coverage. Feature articles are often linked to news stories, but they may also exist independently on the basis of interesting subject matter. This is where writers and editors exercise their leeway to choose subjects that will interest the range of people in their audience.

Depending on the size of the newspaper, reporters may do much more than write articles. At a large metropolitan daily, their only task may be to cover a certain beat, but at a small weekly paper, reporters may have other roles to fill. Here is how Jeanette Germain, a reporter at the *Mountain Express* in Ketchum, Idaho, described her job:

I'll start with our television view of big city journalism. My editor and I love to watch the "Lou Grant" show. We marvel at the time everyone has to stand around and talk about the nuances of their work. They spend hours on ethics, days on stories, weeks on personalities. Can it really be like that on daily newspapers? we ask.

It's not like that here in Ketchum, Idaho. We don't have that kind of time. We've got too much to cover and too few people to spread around. The woman who takes classifieds also answers the phone. The photographer works on sports pages and does subscriptions. Everyone, from the office help to the editor, takes turns cleaning the bathrooms, driving the paper 100 miles to the printer, and collating for delivery at 6 A.M. on Thursday mornings. Collating is about the only time we have to chat with one another. Every other day of the week, we are running.

Deadline fever starts Monday mornings. I wake up before the alarm rings and immediately start setting priorities. Within the next two and a half days, I will have to gather the information, write and illustrate at least a dozen stories. I have to decide which stories deserve some time and which do not. I must produce a few hard news stories, a few pieces of fluff, some tidbit fillers, and visuals or photos to accompany them. I can't hesitate to dispatch a routine story. I have to know how to locate a source or information without delay. The editor won't give me assignments or babysit me through the upcoming edition. She has other things to do. I know I must fill, fill, fill.

By Wednesday afternoon, the writing is done. I pitch in to help with proofreading, layout and the opaquing of page negatives. A 64-page tabloid is complete by 4 or 5 P.M. We sweep up and go home for one short evening of rest before the weekly schedule starts all over again.

People ask me why I work like this, in a pokey little town where the pay is low and the winters long. They ask me if I'm hiding from the real world of competitive journalism. Am I afraid that I won't measure up? Am I wasting my training and talent?

I don't think so. The response to my work here is direct and immediate. The phone rings every Thursday morning as soon as the paper is on the streets. People call with compliments, complaints, additional information, or another question. When I've made a mistake, I hear about it. When I've touched someone's life, he stops me on the street to tell me. Petitions appear when the community as a whole responds to something I've written. I love the feedback. I don't think it would come as easily in a bigger community.

Feature writing is just one of many tasks Germain completes in her weekly schedule. She usually writes features on Thursday or Friday, because on those days she has more time to devote to them. Like Germain, most reporters must decide for themselves which stories are suitable for feature slants, then take enough time to both research and write the stories carefully.

In discussing how they do this, we should consider why newspaper feature articles exist in the first place. Without them, newspapers would be quite dull! Feature articles are published to liven up the papers, and to provide relief from the somewhat dry tone of most news stories. They fill our need to know more about the world than the standard formula for news stories provides. This chapter discusses how feature articles differ from other types of newspaper stories, and how they fill the information gap in news coverage.

JOURNALISTIC FORMS

Most newspaper staff writers are primarily reporters. Often, they must be facile at writing in many journalistic forms. First, let us review briefly the various types of news writing.

Straight News Report

The straight news report—also known as the objective report—is a timely account of an event. A newspaper report of a speech is usually straight news. Because it covers only what happened during a brief period, straight news provides a valuable focus. It is valuable also because it makes such limited demands on reporters that they can come close to presenting an objective report of verifiable fact. Straight news is written by a formula that requires the first few sentences (in some cases, the first sentence alone) to report at least the who-what-when-where-why of an event, with the details strung out in descending order of importance. Because this formula gives reporters little leeway for self-expression, and especially because reporters are instructed neither to editorialize nor to use words that even hint at an opinion, the report usually lives up to its name— "straight." For example, here is the lead from a straight news report:

> The Washington Teachers' Union yesterday agreed not to strike the District of Columbia schools following an agreement worked out in a four-hour meeting in the office of Mayor Walter E. Washington.
>
> The union had threatened to begin its walkout Tuesday, but after yesterday's session, William Simons, president of the teachers' union, said, "School will be open on Tuesday and every day. . . ."

But if writing according to the formula prevents reporters from editorializing, it also prevents them from helping readers understand events. Because straight news isolates a small slice of life at a particular time and reports none of the surrounding facts that might provide meaning, it is usually superficial. For that reason, many reporters argue that nothing like the full truth can emerge from such reports. They are aware, of course, that some events are not *worth* more time and attention than a straight news report offers, but their arguments for more complete reports on important events are the principal reason that other forms of news writing have emerged.

Depth Report

The depth report takes a step beyond straight news. Instead of merely trying to mirror the highlights of an event, the reporter gathers additional information that is independent of the event but related to it. A reporter who covers a speech on medical practices in China may consult experts and reference sources, then present the speaker's words in a larger framework. In some cases, additional information is placed in the report on the speech; in others, it is reported separately. In either case, depth reporting calls for transmitting information, not the reporter's opinion. Verifiable fact is as pivotal in depth reporting as it is in straight news reporting.

Here are a few paragraphs in which the writer gathers other information that enables him to put an event in perspective:

> President Ford is coming to grips, for his first time as president, with gun control. His proposals come in time for a crime message, due any day now.
>
> Interviews with administration officials working on the message, congressional sources, and interested outsiders suggest that the presidential proposals may:
>
> • Ban "Saturday-night specials." The present embargo on importation of these handguns may be extended to their production and sale anywhere in this country—an industry now channeling an estimated 1 million nonsporting guns a year into U.S. streets.
>
> • Tighten licensing on gun dealers. The present simple license—granted to anyone paying a $10 fee. . . .

Although a writer's opinions have no place in a depth report, the facts gathered may rebut or refute the speaker—in which case the speaker or his supporters may charge that a report is slanted. Perhaps it is. The crucial decision has been *which* of the many available facts a reporter uses to build the larger framework, and this may create bias.

Interpretive Reports

Interpretive reports—also known as *news analyses*—are another step beyond straight news. These usually focus on an issue, problem, or controversy. Here, too, the substance is verifiable fact, not opinion. But instead of presenting facts as straight news or depth report and hoping that the facts will speak for themselves, the interpretive reporter clarifies, explains, analyzes. The interpretive report usually focuses on *why:* Why did the president take that trip, appoint that man, make that statement? What is the real meaning of the event?

In this interpretive report, the writer explains why small investors are suffering:

> Negotiated commission rates, begun on Wall Street on May 1, have resulted in almost no savings whatsoever for the ordinary investor buying or selling stock.
>
> There are some special plans offered to the investor, such as Merrill Lynch's "Share-Builder Plan" or Paine Webber's "Alpha Account." But over all, the brokerage industry has preferred not to negotiate with small investors.
>
> There are several reasons for this reluctance. For one thing, small investors have little negotiating clout. . . .

Whatever their intentions, reporters who are given the freedom to interpret events may inadvertently offer their opinions; they are always in danger of using words that steer their readers toward their particular impressions and beliefs. Because clarification, explanation, and analysis require that reporters weigh and filter facts, the interpreter approaches the reporting process much more personally than do other reporters. And because an interpretation is not written by formula, reporters have latitude that makes it easier for them to disguise personal opinions.

Investigative Reporting

Investigative reporting, which some call "muckraking," is the practice of opening closed doors and closed mouths. As in interpretive reporting, the focus is on problems, issues, and controversies. In fact, interpretive and investigative reports are the same in cases in which the reporter must unearth hidden information in order to clarify, explain, and analyze. Normally, though, interpretive reporters have relatively little trouble finding facts because they are endeavoring to explain public events, and they can usually find many sources who are happy to help them. (In fact, the danger in all reporting is that a source may want to provide information that will serve its own private interests.) In contrast, the investigative reporter must try to discover facts that have been hidden for a purpose—often an illegal or unethical purpose.

In this excerpt from an investigative piece, the writer sifts many reports, talks to many government investigators, then writes:

> Federal agents, conducting a sweeping investigation here and in other ports, are piecing together a picture of corruption in the handling, grading, and weighing of grain that

raises questions about the quality of grain shipments to foreign buyers.

Seven privately employed grain inspectors who are licensed by the Department of Agriculture have been indicted thus far in an investigation with charges of bribery for certification of ships for fitness to carry grain. Five of the inspectors pleaded guilty to accepting bribes.

Agents conducting a continuing investigation have been taking secret testimony. . . .

Features

Features differ from news reports primarily in their intent. Whereas a news report ordinarily presents information that is likely to concern readers, a feature is usually designed to capture their interest. The feature reporter casts a wide net in search for facts, sometimes pulling in and using things a news reporter would consider frivolous. The feature writer's report provides a reading experience that depends more on style, grace, and humor than on the importance of the information. This difference is reflected in the fact that those who produce features exclusively are called "feature writers," not "reporters." Slowly, though, features are becoming less distinguishable from some of the other forms of news writing.

Here is the lead of a feature:

> Tens of thousands of black and Puerto Rican teenagers in New York City are "piling up at the bottom" of the recession. With no jobs and no prospect of jobs, they are abandoning their dreams of education, and the belief in the institutions of a civilized society, and are slipping back toward the drugs and hustling of "the street."
>
> "I'm up at 5:00, going places, getting rejected," said one South Bronx teenager who has a small daughter. "I'm not a moron, but it feels degrading."
>
> "Once they know I never worked and have no skills—no job," said Migdalia Colon, 20 years old, also of the South Bronx. "That's not right. We need a chance."
>
> "Best that you can do is hang out, get out," said a young black woman. "All that's out there is reefer. Either smoke it or sell it, or both."
>
> Anger, frustration, hopelessness. Such is the picture. . . .

This is different from the usual feature that appears in many small newspapers. In metropolitan newspapers, journalistic forms overlap. Traces of depth or investigative reporting may appear in a feature, sometimes quite strongly. An interpretive report may have both feature and investigative elements. Often, a feature may seem to be weighted as heavily with matters of concern as with matters of light interest.

USING THESE JOURNALISTIC FORMS

Consider this description of how the same subject matter could be approached for an article in a campus daily, using any of several different journalistic forms.

Imagine that university administrators, discovering that too little dormitory space is available for all the students who want to live on the campus, have leased 100 trailer homes and have parked them on the edge of the dormitory area to house 400 students.

Assigned by the editor of the campus paper to write a straight news report, you as reporter would quote the speech or the press release in which the administration announced the establishment of "Trailer Dorm." If student leaders spoke for or against the conditions of trailer living, you would quote them as well. If students held a protest rally, you would report its highlights dispassionately.

Assigned to write a depth report, you might gather opinions by questioning students, comparing home campus housing to that at a nearby university, or you might report the results of any or all of a dozen quests related to student housing. The limit is marked only by the imagination you bring to the research.

Assigned to write an interpretive report, you might interview administrators to determine why they decided to lease trailers rather than make other arrangements and interview student leaders to determine why they support or oppose the trailer park. Again, you as reporter can use many approaches to gathering information to help you clarify, explain, and analyze.

Assigned to write an investigative report by an editor who suspects that the administration was lax in not planning for more dormitory space, or that an administrator's brother owns the trailers, you must interview widely and adroitly and check financial records. The most difficult kind of journalism, investigative reporting requires a researcher who is imaginative, industrious, patient, and aggressive. You must write a hard-fact report, not speculation.

Assigned to write a feature, you look for the color and flavor of trailer life. Do trailer residents live differently from other students? How? Have they painted their homes in wild colors? Are they planting gardens? Who does the cooking—and with what results?

THE FEATURE SLANT

There is much work to writing features. A reader said: "Entertain me while you educate me. Make me laugh. Make me cry. I want to escape from the narrow confines of my life, while deriving moral satisfaction from the hope that I am learning at the same time."

There is one rule for all features: The story must be endlessly interesting. The feature is as important in the middle as it was at the beginning, as important at the end as it was in the middle and at the beginning. You must tell your story clearly and simply. It must be readable. The following guidelines for feature writing should help make all of your writing clear and readable.

Sentence Structure   This is the basis of readability in nearly all sentences. Usually, sentences should be constructed: subject, verb, object. That may sound simple, but many sentences begin with clauses or adjectives. Beginning writers often like to twist their sentences. They should do this rarely, for effect. The overarching rule is that nearly all sentences should be as simple and direct as possible.

Sentence Length   Generally, the shorter, the more readable the sentences will be. It is true, of course, that if you write for *Harper's*, for example, you can write in a more complicated form—as long as you can control it. But if you write for newspapers or for widely circulated magazines, as a rule you must keep your sentences short.

Concreteness   Wherever possible, you should use concrete words instead of abstract words. The following excerpt of the abstractions of James M. Landis, who was an assistant to President Franklin Roosevelt, and the revision made by the president is a good illustration. Landis wrote:

> Such preparations shall be made as will completely obscure all Federal buildings and non-Federal buildings occupied by the Federal Government during an air raid for any period of time from visibility by reason of internal or external illumination. Such obscuration may be obtained either by blackout construction or by termination of the illumination. This will, of course, require that in building areas in which production must continue during the blackout, construction must be provided that internal illumination may continue.

President Roosevelt said to rewrite it this way:

> Tell them that in buildings where they have to keep the work going to put something across the window. In buildings where they can afford to let the work stop for a while, turn out the lights.

Verbs   Making the verb do the work of adjectives is always preferable. The verb expresses action, and if it is carefully chosen, it can even describe personality. For example, "The four men were on hand in the office." All the reader learns from this is the number and location of the men. But if you say, "The four men sprawled in the office," you have conveyed a great more about the personalities of these men.

Adjectives   The fewer adjectives a writer uses, the more readable the style. For example, "The sharp-eyed, gray-haired general's sharp eyes flashed as he got up and shook his head," could be better put this way: "The general's sharp eyes flashed as he rose and shook his gray head."

Story structure   All beginning writers are told that a lead must catch and hold their readers. If possible, the lead should be a startling, witty, or pithy statement. It is usually a mistake to devote the beginning to summing up a story, much as a straight news story often does. That is the death of the feature.

Transitions   Learning to link the paragraphs in a way that pulls the reader on is a skill that distinguishes the professional from the amateur. After the first paragraph, what comes next? A beginning writer can learn much by studying *Time* and *Newsweek,* both of which place transitions in first importance.

CHAPTER FIVE EXERCISES

1. Because you may want to be convinced of the difference between features and news stories, you should do the following: Clip five features and five news stories from a newspaper. Are the features more interesting at the end than the news stories at the end? In the aggregate, which are more interesting, the features or the news stories?

2. Interview a veteran reporter or editor at the nearest daily newspaper. Ask him or her whether the mission of any reporter is different than it was ten years ago. Ask whether the term "reporter" applies to everyone or whether "feature writer" describes some of the employees. Are the reporters also feature writers? Ask him or her which three are considered best at writing (not at reporting).

3. Go through an edition of a daily newspaper in your area and determine how much space the paper devotes to straight news stories and how much it devotes to feature articles. Do the same for another newspaper, then compare the two. How does the use of feature articles affect the overall tone of the newspaper?

CHAPTER 6
Leads, Transitions, and Endings

Few objects are quite as intimidating to novice writers as a pile of blank paper. A symbol of the writers' unwritten stories, blank paper is a reminder that they must solve one very important problem before completing their articles—how to begin. Yet waiting for them at the other end of their journey is another certainty; they must write a good last sentence or closing paragraph. And along the way they must travel smoothly and easily from idea to idea, and from paragraph to paragraph, with transitions as inconspicuous as editing splices in a movie.

THE LEAD

Journalists writing straight news stories generally rely on a formula to produce their leads. The ingredients are familiar—who, what, when, where, and why. Once the writer has composed the lead, the rest of the story follows naturally from an elaboration of each of these elements, in order of importance.

There is no formula for writing feature stories or magazine articles, nor is there a rule for how to write their leads. The possibilities are infinite, and this is what confounds many beginners. If ten journalists were writing from the same material, perhaps no two would choose the same lead. However, if all ten were professionals, each different lead would accomplish the same objectives—

1. To attract the reader.

2. To give the reader the central idea.

3. To lead him into the story.

If you are writing newspaper features, you must try to establish your central idea from the beginning. You do not have as much freedom to establish your lead as the magazine writer does, who may sometimes take up to 500 words. You need not, however, jump into the central idea in the first sentence, as do most straight news stories. For example, you might introduce your piece this way:

> In Florida, they tell it this way: A new arrival in heaven was well pleased with the place. He found everything to his liking, deciding that it was all it had been cracked up to be.
>
> Then one day he came upon another who had been admitted to the heavenly portals; this man sat in the corner with a ball and chain attached to his ankle. The new citizen, puzzled, went to St. Peter and asked: "How come this man has to wear a ball and chain?"
>
> "Well," St. Peter replied, "that man's from Florida and every time we turn him loose he tries to go back."
>
> The people who live along the 100-mile stretch of that curve along the Gulf of Mexico from Pensacola to Panama City vow that the man was from Northwest Florida. . . .

This is an entertaining lead, a natural beginning for your story—light, airy, and boastful. It does not matter that it runs five sentences to tell the apocryphal story. If the reader begins the story, he is hooked. Although he may not finish the story, the reader must at least go to the end of the lead. Remember, however, that if you have used this as a means of getting the reader into the story, you must see to it that the tone of the rest matches the lighthearted tone you have established.

A grim story would not, of course, lend itself to a cheerful beginning. For example, consider this lead:

> February 12, 1974: "Mom, dad, I'm okay . . . I'm not being starved or beaten or unnecessarily frightened . . . I know that Steve is okay . . . I heard that mom is really upset and that everybody is at home . . . I hope this puts you a little bit at ease . . . I just hope I can get back to everybody real soon."
>
> April 24, 1974: "To the pig Hearsts . . . I am a soldier in the people's army . . . I have chosen to stay and fight . . . as for my ex-fiancé I don't care if I ever see him again. . . ."
>
> After Patricia Hearst was kidnapped February 4 from an apartment in Berkeley a few blocks from the University of California campus, the gossip of San Francisco was that she was in on it from the start.

This story was published June 3, 1974, months after the kidnapping of Patricia Hearst. The writer, Jack Fox of United Press International, had been mulling over what would be the appropriate lead to a story that had broken months before. It suddenly came to him to use the two direct quotes that pointed up the dramatic change in the kidnapped young woman's attitude.

Developing Leads

Clarence Schoenfeld, a veteran writer, has outlined these suggestions for those who have trouble writing leads.

1. *Link.* This lead is an integral part of the feature and supports a natural flow of thought from the beginning to the development.

2. *Exposition.* Before writing a single word, it's always helpful to spell out your article in a few sentences. What is the heart of the article? Its central idea?

3. *Appeal.* Explore anecdotes, try for narrative hooks, or use a striking statement.

4. *Direct connection.* You must try to establish a direct connection with your readers.

5. *Slant.* Try always to slant your writing to the interests of the readers of a particular newspaper.

Kinds of Leads

There are many different kinds of leads from which to choose. Consider the following classifications and their appropriateness for various types of stories:

Summary   This is the standard straight news lead that literally summarizes all the key elements of the story in a single sentence. Because it conveys the tone of a breaking news story, the summary lead is usually unsuitable for a feature article. Columnist Herb Caen of the *San Francisco Chronicle* once called this example of a summary lead "The all-time All-Timer":

> Communist-led terrorists on a hashish-crazed rampage through Kwilu province shot down a United Nations helicopter with a bow and arrow yesterday as it was flying eight Congolese nuns to safety.

Description   Writing a descriptive lead is often difficult for a beginner because the language must be vivid and colorful. Even the comic strip character Snoopy of "Peanuts" finds it challenging. He sits atop his dog house writing again and again, "It was a dark and stormy night." Writers searching for strong descriptive phrases often go astray, as Herb Caen pointed out in another example involving a young reporter sent to cover a flood. The reporter, wiring in his article, began this way: GOD SITS ON THE HILLS OVERLOOKING JOHNS-TOWN TONIGHT. According to Caen, the editor wired right back: TO HELL WITH THE FLOOD, INTERVIEW GOD.

A good descriptive lead can sometimes create dramatic impact, as in this lead from a sports story:

> Running a marathon in 95-degree heat is like walking into a death trap, and that's how hot it was in Hopkinton, Massachusetts, the Monday of the Boston Marathon.

But a descriptive lead need not be dramatic to be effective, as this lead illustrates:

> Louisiana has been the moon-dipped, myth-draped strange sister among Southern states since its Acadian beginnings, but its political upheavals during the past three decades have been unusual even by Louisiana standards.

Descriptive leads are often useful in profiles of interesting or colorful characters. The description can be of the subject's appearance or personality, but it can also focus on his accomplishments, as in this lead by George Dobbins, managing editor of *Peninsula:*

> He stands at the pinnacle of American culinary success. The more than 20 worldwide restaurants bearing his name gross over 36 million dollars annually. And if you have never eaten at one of those, it is still likely he has influenced your eating habits. For he is not only a restaurateur but an innovator. He created the Mai Tai. Professionals consider his bartending guides classic. He has fostered dishes so unique that his cookbooks are sought by the kitchen dilettante as well as the discerning chef. This is Hillsborough resident Victor Bergeron, better known as the internationally famous Trader Vic.

Direct Address   This kind of lead can be used to involve the reader in the story immediately. It is often written in the form of a question, such as "Where were you when . . . " The following lead from an article titled, "Fear of Figuring" shows how it works:

> Do numbers make you uneasy? Would you prefer to do almost anything rather than solve a math problem? Do you

consider the hand calculator a menace? If your answer to any of these questions is "yes," you may have a handicap that afflicts thousands of Americans—women especially: math anxiety. It can keep you out of a job you want, or from progressing in the job you have.

Travel writers often use direct address to entice their readers into the setting they are writing about. Such leads can combine descriptive elements as well, as illustrated in this example:

> Imagine yourself on a mountaintop in the morning, sailing in the afternoon and at the theater that night. Imagine a day of rafting through white water, followed by an evening at a four-star restaurant. Imagine that snowcapped mountains are only an hour's drive from your hotel, and that from your room you can see their peaks silhouetted against the evening sky. Now picture yourself in Seattle, one of the few cities in the United States where this fantasy can be a reality.

Striking Statement   This kind of lead makes the reader ask, "Is that true?" It may refute some commonly held belief, as in "Drinking alcohol is good for you." Or it may present a startling statistic, such as "Seven million women in this country have had their jobs canceled and find themselves without financial support." It may even make a surprising assertion, such as "If a basketball game is ever held on the moon, Geese Ausbie will surely play it." But regardless of the form, the intent is the same—to get the reader's attention quickly by making a statement that is so striking that he will feel compelled to read on in order to discover why the statement is true.

Narrative   The narrative lead is often like a short story. It may be an anecdote or description of a scene that creates the setting for the article. Consider this example from a profile of skier Katie Morning:

> The sky was clear at the Mammoth Mountain ski area in California that winter day. Spectators watching the giant slalom race from the bottom of the snow-covered slope could just about discern a brightly colored shape at the top of the mountain. As the spot of color zigzagged down the course, onlookers anticipated a good run. The unrecognizable dot had just taken human form when suddenly the figure slipped, transformed from a speeding skier into a tangled mass of flailing arms, legs, and skis, careened downhill with horrifying velocity, and finally landed in a motionless, crumpled mass. For a frightening moment, no

one moved. Then, as though by some invisible cue, there was a rush toward the still body.

"Cut!" screamed the director.

Katie Morning picked herself up from the snow, brushed off her parka, and inquired, "How'd I do?"

It was the final day of filming "The Other Side of the Mountain," the story of champion 18-year-old skier Jill Kinmont who was paralyzed from the shoulders down in a tragic fall on the slopes.

As shown in these examples, leads come in many lengths. And just as obviously, writers of feature stories are not bound by the same restrictions that guide the work of straight news reporters. Nor must they listen to newspaper editors complain like the one in this story recalled by Herb Caen:

And then there was the city editor who roared that his reporters' leads were too long. "Short, keep 'em SHORT!" he hollered, and one of his heroes promptly turned in a story that began:

Dead.

That's what John Doe was yesterday after an auto accident at—."

WRITING TRANSITIONS

A film editor makes transitions from one shot in a movie to another by deftly splicing together hundreds of separate pieces of film. When a splice is poorly made, so that people or objects seem to leap from one position to another, the jarring result is called a "jump cut." A writer avoids jump cuts and tries to join the units of a story (sentences and paragraphs) so smoothly that the reader is unaware of the progression from beginning to end. This is what is meant by "flow."

Beginners sometimes err on the side of too much transition in their efforts to create a cohesive story. It is important not only to use transitions but to use them inconspicuously. Consider these examples of too much transition:

. . . labels are pinned to cognitive cues. Cognitive cues in this case could be. . . .

. . . degree he would eventually like to go into some form of education.

But before education, Terry's first goal is the pros. His coach. . . .

. . . increased ability to score has added a new dimension of respect from opposing guards. "I guess I improved most during the summer," he said.

During the summer months he worked on his quickness and driving ability while playing basketball in Australia and New Zealand for a. . . .

. . . played a guard, although he was 6′ 4″ by his senior year. Surprisingly, John's first goal upon entering high school was to play baseball.

"Before I went to high school my dream was to become a pro baseball player." Davis was a pitcher, with excellent control, more. . . .

In each case, the writer has been much too concerned with the need for transition: "cognitive cues. Cognitive cues . . . ," "some form of education. But before education . . . ," and so on. Now consider some closely knit excerpts about Margaux Hemingway.* Note that the end of each paragraph is tied strongly to the beginning of the next paragraph by an echo, but the writer does not obviously repeat words, as in the examples above.

Says Designer Halston: "She has all the components to become a modern young superstar—openness, infectiousness, beauty, and the ambition to follow through."

Openness and a boggling spontaneity have made Margaux something more than a model, a pop personality. . . .

Says Scavullo: "She talks a mile a minute. She chews gum until she gets in front of the camera; then we carry a silver spoon and platter to her and take the gum."

Margaux did pine for the great outdoors. "I saw *The Four Musketeers* and I wanted to fence," she said wistfully. . . .

"I felt so energized," she beamed.

"That's how I like to feel—healthy and energized."

That is how Margaux grew up in Idaho's spectacular Sun Valley, where her father, Jack, Ernest's eldest son, settled down in 1967 after throwing over a career as a stockbroker. . . .

"Margaux never did like competition," says Jack, "and I think that's why she wasn't too interested in school."

---

*Reprinted by permission from *Time,* The Weekly Newsmagazine; copyright Time Inc.

Her parents encouraged her to try art school, but Margaux was too energized to buckle down and took off after a year for Europe. . . .

Her younger sister, Mariel, is not so sure: "I don't know —Margaux is kinda crazy."
Crazy like Napoleon. Margaux has. . . .

Not many writers are so attentive to their transitions, although they should be. The article should flow from beginning to end. For example, here is one that limps to a close:

> . . . In a recent class, Marti remarked, "Music today is written for you—if you can't listen to it, the music shouldn't be written." Emphasis is on construction of the musical idea, no matter what historical period it is from. Marti's intent is that any well-structured part is capable of being a legitimate esthetic whole, without judgments of "good and bad" music.
>
> Students' enthusiasm for this thoroughness was reflected by awarding him the Gores award for excellence in teaching, which cited him for "elegance in both lectures and performance" and his "multifarious contributions" to education as Faculty Resident of Twain House. Marti's comment, "It's nice to know they felt as warmly about me as I feel about them," carries because of his sincerity.
>
> His family? It's pending any day now. For at least a month, Barbara and he have considered names—Igor, Percy, and Bliss are definitely out. "I really don't care what the baby is," he admitted somewhat abashedly. "Just nervous." They are currently Faculty Residents at Lagunita.
>
> A fascination with the state of the world has long honed Marti's political intellect, but he also confesses a fascination with the state of the sandlots. "If I had more time, I'd be a jock," he laughed. "I'm a New York City boy, it'd be fun to play ball." It's the kid that makes him fun as a professor.

When one begins a paragraph with a question ("His family?"), that's usually a sign that the unity is breaking down. In effect, the writer is saying, "Now, how do I work his family into this?" Such a transition weakens the cohesion. But the writer has an unusual opportunity to make all this cohesive by considering the preceding paragraph. The teacher in question is a "Faculty Resident." In such cases, the family is usually almost as involved as the teacher, which would have made it easy to talk about the family without having to leap to make the transition.

To have made the transition neatly, the writer should have had information that she didn't think she needed when she began the article, since she probably didn't realize that she would have trouble working the teacher's family into this. The writer should have asked questions about the subject's residency at Twain and his residency at Lagunita well before beginning to write, on the chance that any notes taken will turn out to be useful later. Then, when the time came to tie the family into the article, the writer would not have to stumble from Twain to Lagunita by disjointedly saying that he was once at Twain and is now at Lagunita with his family. Instead, the writer would have had the information to enable her to move pleasingly from other matters to the subject's family by talking about the family in the context of their house residency.

The larger point and one that we have made earlier is that a writer should have much more information than can possibly be used. The essence of good writing is being selective. You must have a range of alternatives so that you can choose the best material. You need to ask yourself what has gone before. In the article cited, the last paragraph is about politics and athletics. What does that have to do with the subject's family and his work as a resident? Perhaps he talks politics with the students at Lagunita (perhaps with his wife included in the group), and perhaps he plays volleyball or other games with the students. If so, your problem is how to make all this neatly transitional.

ENDINGS

A writer who has been a straight news reporter may often have problems with endings since news stories gradually taper down to almost nothing. They begin with the most important elements and then let the story run out. The style of straight news writing may become habitual. Such reporters need to remember that the form of the feature is different; its ending is as important as its beginning.

For example, consider this ending to the earlier-quoted lead of the Patricia Hearst kidnapping (first, the lead again):

> February 12, 1974: "Mom, dad, I'm okay. . . . I just hope I can get back to everybody real soon."
>
> April 24, 1974: "To the pig Hearsts . . . I am a soldier in the people's army. . . . as for my ex-fiancé I don't care if I ever see him again. . . ."
>
> After Patricia Hearst was kidnapped February 4 . . . the gossip of San Francisco was that she was in on it from the start. . . .

And now the ending:

> Randolph Hearst said he had not given up hope but he now felt Patricia believes in what she is doing.
>
> "I think it happened as a result of duress," he said. "This apparently can happen when a victim has no hope, when the only salvation for the victim is the oppressor."

Using the direct quotation from Randolph Hearst is highly appropriate. A thousand words later, it raises the point made in the first lead, knitting the story together nicely.

Completing an Analogy

Sometimes a writer can use an analogy in his lead, carry it through in the development of the story, and go back to it for the ending. In the following excerpt from an article on racquetball, the writer used a combination descriptive/narrative lead to begin the article, set up an analogy using the "family" theme, then returned to it to tie the piece together at the end.

> **Lead:** Two players enter a white handball court carrying rackets that look like the broken remnants of a tennis tantrum, strings intact but handles only a few inches long. They warm up, whacking a black rubber ball that rebounds off two, even three walls before hitting the floor. A spectator assessing the scene through a Plexiglass window notes the knee pads of one player and predicts knowingly, "She's a diver." Bruises the size of coffee cups cover the arms and legs of the other player, and as the ball streaks like a riotous comet through this small galaxy, it's not hard to guess where they came from.
>
> The game is racquetball, stepchild to squash and cousin to handball, tennis, and paddleball. The racket sports family doesn't quite know what to think of its new relative, but racquetball's popularity quiets any objections to the game's pedigree.
>
> **Ending:** New courts are designed with spectators in mind, and an all-plexiglass portable court that can be erected in auditoriums or gymnasiums is available. Television coverage is the goal, but no sponsor has yet appeared to make racquetball a media star. Tennis needn't worry yet about losing its backers to racquetball; the sport has a long way to go before that happens. But the racquet sports family had better start setting another place at the table—its new relative has come to stay.

A Summary Ending

The ending need not always refer back to the lead, of course. It may be a summarizing statement, a revealing or insightful quotation, or a striking statement that stands on its own as a kind of culmination to the build-up of the article. It may even be an anecdote, as in this illustration from Rex Reed's "Ava: Life in the Afternoon," a profile of a fading star:

> Outside, Ava is inside the taxi flanked by the N.Y.U. student and Larry, blowing kisses to the new chum, who will never grow to be an old one. They are already turning the corner into Fifty-seventh Street, fading into the kind of night, the color of tomato juice in the headlights, that only exists in New York when it rains.
>
> "Who was it?" asks a woman walking a poodle.
>
> "Jackie Kennedy," answers a man from his bus window.

Experienced writers can often spot the ending to an article among the interviews, notes, and other material they have gathered before even writing the lead. A good ending can even suggest a lead, or give the writer a sense of the direction in which the article is heading. There is a pitfall, however, in saving an item that appears to be a good ending—sometimes a good ending is really a good beginning in disguise. Writers must learn to tell the difference.

CHAPTER SIX EXERCISES

1. You are writing an article about the rate of heart disease among working women and have assembled the facts listed below. Write three different leads for the story based on your reading in this chapter.

Dr. Suzanne Haynes at the National Heart, Lung and Blood Institute conducted a study in which she found that working women did not have a significantly higher rate of heart disease than did housewives.

American women live an average of almost eight years longer than American men do.

Scientists have identified a number of cornary risk factors, individual characteristics of health and behavior, that when taken together predict the likelihood that a person will develop heart disease. Among them are cigarette smoking, excess body weight, salt intake, saturated fat and cholesterol intake, level of physical activity, and level of stress and tension.

Type A women (those who are hard-driving, aggressive, and competitive) have a much greater chance of developing heart disease than do more relaxed Type B women.

The rate of smoking among young women has nearly doubled in the past 14 years. It has declined slightly among women over 30.

2. Choose a magazine article that you think is particularly well written. Identify the transitions in the article and discuss how the writer used them to change topics or to change ideas. Then choose an article that you think is poorly written and do the same thing. To what extent do you think the transitions in the poorly written article contribute to its low quality?

3. Read several articles in the same magazine, giving particular attention to the leads and endings. Compare those that you like with those you consider ineffective and explain why. Can you detect any similarities in style that may have come from the magazine's editors instead of from the article writers?

CHAPTER 7
News Features and
Color Stories

If a dozen reporters were assigned to cover the same event and write a straight news story about it, they would probably produce articles that were quite similar. But if the same reporters were assigned to write a news feature or color story, it is likely that no two would choose exactly the same angle.

Just as witnesses to an accident rarely remember the same details, feature writers select different elements of a scene to report. One might discover an interesting individual; another might observe a revealing exchange between several people; a third might focus on the overall scene without choosing any particular element in it. Such choices are largely subjective, but a reporter learns how to make them with an eye toward the best story material.

News features and color stories are often, but not always, keyed to news events. When they are, the writer must assume both the roles of factual reporter and keen observer. Then he or she must write the article as a smooth blend of news and description.

THE NEWS FEATURE

Beginning feature writers are often captivated by their own graceful writing, letting their skill overshadow the fact that they are linked closely to the news. They must learn to recognize that their proper position is halfway between the news story and the feature. In the following excerpts, a student has written the article that appears at the left. A professional writer, whose story appears at the right, has struck the proper balance between news story and feature.

Article

The sky is falling. Or so say the international mélange of soothsayers who met this month to deliberate the destiny of 1975. Crystal balls in hand, they

Article

In oil-rich Saudi Arabia, an absolute monarchy where royalty payments are more than just a figure of speech, King Faisal has argued for years that his nation emerged from their traditional meeting spot—a devilish Druid cave—to decree a significant upswing in air crashes for the coming fiscal year. But one need not be a Merlin or Mephistopheles to notice the trend towards tragedies in the heavens. As the price tags on aircraft soared to $25 million with the advent of the 747, one is led to wonder who picks up the tab for such aerial disasters. These risks royale must be underwritten, and the princely premiums must be paid. But how?

should own part of the production facilities and operations of the Western-owned oil company that has a concession in his realm. This week Saudi Arabia agreed to pay an amount estimated to top $500 million for a one-fourth interest in the oil and gas producing operations of Arabian-American Oil Co. in Saudi Arabia.

The lead at the left was written by a talented writer, but he is trying too hard, making it difficult for a casual reader to grasp the point of his article. The professional writer, in contrast, is quick to recognize that his first responsibility is to the news.

We turn now to part of an article written by a student who is following up a controversy at the Hoover Institution. He begins with a reference to the controversy, neatly dips into the beginning of the institution, then brings it up to date. Note that the aim here is *not* to try to imitate the kind of scholarly writing common to many universities. There are no footnotes, no weighty tone, and this should be the case even when a news feature is lengthy and serious. The feature writer's goal is to produce a clear, logical story—neither primly formal nor chatty. However, it is often essential for the foundation of the story to be formal: What is the significance of this institution? How can I present the story to make it widely readable? The resulting news feature is interesting to anyone concerned with the subject. Note that many stylistic matters are given attention in the comments to the left of the story.

Comment

This news-peg lead is an excellent entry into the subject.

If you don't call something by its right name (Hoover Institution), readers who know its name will be

News Feature

"The Iranian conference is our latest excursion in controversy," said Jim Hobson, public relations officer for the Hoover Institute. "We don't knowingly get into these situations; they just occur."

distracted from what you're saying by the oddity. It's also likely that a reader who is irritated by what you're saying may dismiss the entire article with, "He doesn't even know the name of the thing he's writing about." This is why the little mechanical elements are important—not merely because you want to be correct for the sake of being correct.

Since the preceding sentence put a focus on the conference, the next need not include "of the conference." Look for opportunities to be concise.

This is a wise development of the subject. The author is weaving interview material and written material into a coherent picture of the current controversy.

Although there are relatively few deletions and substitutions on this page, if you read the page aloud in both original and revised versions, you'll agree that the deleted words aren't needed and that the substitutions help relieve the institute-institute-institute (which began in the last sentence).

It might have been valuable here to indicate *when* these quotations

Hobson was speaking of the conference "Iran: 25 Centuries of Achievement," sponsored by the Hoover Institut~ion~ to celebrate the 2,500th anniversary of the Persian monarchy. Speakers at the conference were heckled by a small group of Iranian students.

The students charged the Institut~ion~ with providing a one-sided view of the monarchy's achievements. The charges reopened a dispute about the role of the Institut~ion~ and led a student to write in the business school paper, *The Reporter*, "It is untenable for the Institut~ion~, a renowned symbol of reaction, to remain on the University campus."

Such criticism is not new ~~to the Institute.~~ The *Wall Street Journal* called Hoover "a haven for Goldwater men," and the *Washington Monthly* described it as "a cold-war college think tank." A radical said at a rally that the Institut~ion~ is "one of the world's main centers of counterinsurgency research."

appeared in the *Wall Street Journal* and *Washington Monthly*. Note that the preceding page is all about a recent event. Some readers may assume that these quotations are current.

This is a nice transition. Note especially that the author is moving back into history neatly, tying history to recent events.

Changing the sentence makes for smoother reading. Note that the preceding sentences run subject-verb, subject-verb, subject-verb. Variation is often effective.

Considering that the Hoover quotation refers to the war, it seems doubtful that "from the war period" has any value here.

"Supplied" suggests that an order was filled.

It's probably overinforming the reader with "to include documents on," but the reader *could* think that the original phrasing means that the collection itself expanded into these areas physically.

~~The Institute's~~ Its role has not always been so controversial. ~~It was~~ founded in 1919 when Herbert Hoover gave university President Ray Wilbur $50,000 "for an historical collection on the Great War," it ~~The collection~~ grew rapidly as young scholars searched Europe for books, documents, and newspapers, ~~from the war period.~~

In 1927 the Rockefeller Foundation provided ~~supplied~~ a grant to support research projects on Russia and Germany. After ~~the second~~ World War II the scope of the collection expanded to include documents on ~~into~~ Asia, Latin America, Africa, and the Middle East. . . .

THE COLOR STORY

The color story is a feature that plays up the descriptive elements of a news event. Color stories must occasionally strike a serious tone: the report of a disaster that must be accompanied by a color sidebar or the death of a prominent figure that calls for a color story that sounds a sad note. In this case, the writer is tracing a danger that hounds a young woman:

It has the elements of a chilling Hitchcock thriller: A young woman believes she is being stalked by a stranger. The police don't take it seriously. Her boyfriend is trying to protect her.

Except it isn't a movie. It appears to be real, and it's happening in Chicago. . . .

The writer then narrates the happenings very simply and starkly. First, the writer describes the many calls the stranger makes to the woman's apartment, the night he throws the switch in the building's fuse box and turns out the lights in the apartment house, the calls increasing in number, and finally, a young man's knocking at the door—only to be confronted by the boyfriend. The man says that he is a repairman looking for an address, gets the information, then leaves. When she calls the repairman's alleged employer, she finds that a much older man works as their repairman. The writer closes his story simply:

> She has locked up her apartment and is living somewhere else for awhile, with a friend.
> So far, the friend's phone hasn't rung.

Much more commonly, though, the feature writer is assigned to cover the color, flavor, and excitement of large crowds. Assigned a sports color story, instead of focusing his attention on the players, the focal points of the writer's story are likely to be the spectators, the cheering sections, the yell leaders, the half-time performance, and the mascots. The feature writer covers the election sidebar in much the same way. While the election reporter is concentrating on results, the color story writer describes the manner and the mood of the voters as they enter the election booths. He looks for quotable signs that herald the voters, listens to the sound trucks making last-minute appeals, and records the candidates' reactions on the last day.

Sometimes a color story focuses on individual reactions to an event, as illustrated by this excerpt from a story written by Jeanette Germain (reprinted with permission of the *Ketchum* (Idaho) *Mountain Express*):

> Passersby were scandalized. They were delighted. They couldn't believe their eyes.
> The setting was a Hotel Grande motel room, with static flickering across a television screen and red satin sheets on the bed. A bondage book and sexual fantasies magazines were strewn across the covers with an empty box of amyl nitrate tablets and silk pajamas. The cardboard maniken wore black lace corset, bra, and garter belt.

Avventura clothing store, known for provocative, innovative display windows, had gone borderline this time. The response at the Sun Valley mall was immediate and emotional.

Salespeople were plagued by questions, compliments, and criticism. More men started browsing through the store.

An anonymous critic wrote across the window in red lipstick. "This window is 'disgusting. I hope you do something about it soon." A similar comment was slipped under the door on a frayed cocktail napkin.

Window designer Sherl Seggerman thought the lipstick comment, scrawled across the top of the window, added to the overall design. But store owners Connie Maricich and Millie Wiggins decided it should probably be washed off. The cocktail napkin could more discretely be incorporated in the display. It was laid on the satin sheets with the other props.

By the time the window was changed last week, the good comments had actually outnumbered the bad, Seggerman said. Shoppers loved the detail. They stood and looked and pointed things out to one another as they rounded the corner of the mall. The television set, dating from the 1930's, was especially popular.

Note how the writer uses adjectives sparingly and tellingly in describing the window scene and people's reactions to it. She simply presents a picture of what the scene looked like and records what various people wrote and said about it. The material itself tells the story, but it is the writer's selection and ordering of it that make the story effective.

Writing Good Color Stories

Although writing can be improved by editing, the editor, after all, hasn't covered the story. He is at the mercy of the writer. Here are a few suggestions for writing good color stories:

Make the Story Continuingly Interesting   One sentence should grow out of another; one paragraph should grow out of another. The middle and end should be as interesting as the beginning. Although a color story has no standard structure, the "hard news" should usually be somewhere near the beginning.

Use Imaginative Description   Although you may be covering an event, try to avoid the dryness of straight news writing by creating vivid images.

One of the challenges in writing color stories is to use vivid, visual descriptions without relying on worn-out clichés to do the job for you. Successful writers do this by creating fresh new images such as these:

a woman who could have danced cheek-to-cheek with Wilt Chamberlain

searching for another fix of fast food

arguing beard to beard

a game that gives everyone a chance to read all the ads in the program

Do Not Editorialize   Your goal in writing a color story is to create the flavor and feeling of a scene, not to judge it.

Provide Sufficient Information   Don't become so preoccupied with description that you neglect the essential details of the story necessary for the reader to understand what you are writing about.

Use Dialogue to Augment or Replace Description   Occasionally, reproducing dialogue relieves the writer of the burden of description (and of the hunt for fresh images) as in the following excerpt from an article by Paul Butler.

Leon Bacon had just finished a set of pulldowns when the phone rang. Letting the weight drop with a thud, he walked over and picked up the receiver.

"Barry's Musclehouse."

"Uh . . . hello," said a whiny voice. "What are your rates?"

"Cheap," said Leon, reaching up to reduce the volume on the wall-mounted stereo.

"I was thinking about joining your health club. Do you have a sauna?"

"This place is into serious weightlifting; we don't play around." There was a pause.

"I see. Well, can I talk to Barry?"

Leon began to get impatient. Barry wasn't within sight and he didn't want to interrupt his workout for some Pillsbury Doughboy.

"We buried Barry yesterday."

"Oh, I . . . uh . . . I'm sorry."

"Barry left everything in his will to the new manager."

"Who's he?"

"Wino."

"Wino?"

"His dog."

There was a short moment of silence, then a click. Leon broke into a broad grin as he realized the whole gym had stopped to listen in. He put down the receiver.

"Do you have a sauna?" he mimicked, in a high feminine voice. His training partner laughed.

"You're rude, man." Leon turned up the stereo again.

"Why should I waste my time with him. He'd never benefit from this place. He doesn't know what it's all about." He grabbed the pulldown bar to assist his partner.

"C'mon, last set. We're gonna make your back so wide your lats are gonna flap in the wind."

In this example, the dialogue tells more about the characters than any description could. The writer knew that and realized that he should let the two speak for themselves.

The Seasonal Color Story

Color stories are often linked to holidays and other seasonal events. Though some reporters dread writing these articles, others use them as opportunities to exercise their imaginations and descriptive abilities. Here is a story that shows how both can be used to create a fresh approach to an old subject:

Comment

The anecdotal beginning is useful in many kinds of writing (especially profiles). This lead seems to pull the reader into this story effectively.

Note especially that the writer uses adjectives and adverbs here and there, but the writing is not so obviously visual that it calls attention to itself. There is no piling up of adjectives and adverbs, no reaching for similes.

The worst flaw in most seasonal stories is that the writer tries too hard to be overpoweringly descriptive. Instead, the writer should be content with touches of

Seasonal Story

Count Dracula removed his fangs and leaned over the table toward a green martian with blinking antennae. "Frankly," the count said, "those lights are beginning to annoy me."

The martian reached for a switch somewhere under the table and—surprise!—his nose lit up. The count drew back, startled. He quickly installed his fangs, got up and hunkered over to the bar where he spent the rest of the evening nursing Bloody Marys.

"Some party," the martian said, his nose and antennae blinking in happy harmony.

It was a one-of-a-kind party. Radio station KNEW had hired Oakland's Goodman Hall, provided an incessant background of "golden-oldies" music and 800 of the Bay Area's most bizarre citizens. It was KNEW's Night-Before-Halloween Party.

description: a few visual verbs, an unpredictable adjective or two, an adverb that is allowed to do its work because it's in a crisp sentence rather than in a sentence burdened with other adverbs.

On the dance floor, jitterbugging to Bill Haley's "Rock around the Clock" were a Playboy Bunny with lumps where they shouldn't have been and a young woman swaddled in just a diaper. Two chocolate M&M's covered the floor in a snappy tango to the same tune. And a young man in a brown, nylon jump suit performed a solo, prancing unpredictably with his hands in the air.

This went on for some time, perhaps an hour, until the thrill of seeing the Hunchback of Notre Dame dance arm-in-arm with a girl in a fliptop Marlboro box wore off.

This seems an effective use of a fragment.

The writer resisted the temptation to strain for effects. He's quite content to describe the bizarre scene simply.

Then the entertainment.

Four men stepped from a time warp and took their place behind various musical instruments on the stage. They stood there for a moment waiting for the visual impact to register.

At the organ stood a man with long, silver hair slicked straight back to the nape of his neck, where a black, leather motorcycle jacket started. At the drums, in shades, was a greasy-looking character with a black Sam-the-Sham goatee. Behind the lead guitar was another leather jacket, Sam-the-Sham goatee and a stocking cap. And shouldering the bass! He swaggered to the edge of the stage, resplendent in his foot-high, pomaded D.A., shifted his gum and spoke into the microphone. "Hi," he said, "We're Big Art and the Trashmasters."

Here, the fragments intrude. First, the writer's use of fragments makes the reader too conscious of the device. Second, the fragments would be more effective as one sentence.

And with that they broke into the Ventures' version of "Walk, Don't Run." Proceeded to "Teen Angel," "Hound Dog." Then lit into "The Swim."

At the break Art paused before the microphone and said, "We have a dedication. From Laurie to Ed. Who used to be around." They played "Chicken Guts."

The writer obviously intends this to be an attention-compelling (ironic?) conclusion. "It was a . . . gas" is intended to mean much more than the trite expression imparts. Then it came to me: The phrase is in keeping with Big Art's campy announcement in the preceding paragraph.

Then Big Art stepped forth for another announcement. "We have some fine machines outside, I'm told," he said, "A '55 Buick and a '51 Cadillac." He held up his hands as if to still the crowd. "Pearl-dust white," he said.

It was a . . . gas.

CHAPTER SEVEN EXERCISES

1. Rewrite the following trite phrases using fresh imagery:

at a tender age   in no uncertain terms

too numerous to mention   clear as crystal

green with envy

2. Fill in the blanks:

His face was like _____.   He was so tall _____.

Talking to her was like _____.   Each minute felt like _____.

Walking into class, I felt _____.

3. You have been assigned to write a news feature for each of the following events. Suggest two news feature angles for each.

a rock concert

opening night of a new play at the local theater

a conference of student body presidents

a debate between two candidates running for governor of your state

a ceremony in honor of the 100th anniversary of the founding of your school

CHAPTER 8
Personality Sketches and Human Interest Stories

No one would argue that personality sketches and human interest stories constitute "hard news," but newspaper audiences like to read them as much as reporters like to write them. There are no formulas for writing these articles; they offer reporters considerable freedom of style and content. Though newspapers are running longer stories in both categories, a feature writer usually has less space available than a magazine writer would for a similar piece. The challenge for the feature writer is to create a complete characterization or tell the entire story in the space allotted. Every word, every sentence must contribute to development of the article.

THE PERSONALITY SKETCH

Personality sketches are growing closer to the size of magazine profiles. The stories must be longer and must spell out the significance of the subject. How does the subject talk, move, walk, think, look? How does he or she relate to others and to surroundings? Most important, how do others relate to the subject? What do they say about him or her?

This is not the kind of information one can gather in an hour-long interview. It may take several interviews, hours of observation, and numerous phone calls to compile details of this nature. Yet newspaper feature writers often don't have the time to study their profile subjects in depth. Often their territory is the realm of what can be accomplished in half a day's work, sometimes less. Given this constraint, it is especially important for the writer to become a keen observer and recorder of significant details.

In this opening paragraph from his article "Ava: Life in the Afternoon," writer Rex Reed shows how a good eye for images and a flair for descriptive writing can combine to create a stunning profile:

> She stands there, without benefit of a filter lens against a room melting under the heat of lemony sofas and lavender walls and cream-and-peppermint-striped movie-star chairs, lost in the middle of that gilt-edge birthday-cake

hotel of cupids and cupolas called the Regency. There is no script. No Minnelli to adjust the CinemaScope lens. Ice-blue rain beats against the windows and peppers Park Avenue below as Ava Gardner stalks her pink malted-milk cage like an elegant cheetah. She wears a baby-blue cashmere turtleneck sweater pushed up to her Ava elbows and a little plaid mini-skirt and enormous black horn-rimmed glasses and she is gloriously, divinely barefoot.*

Few beginning writers could create such lavish imagery as effectively as Reed does, but all should practice the kind of observation that enabled him to record these details.

The following article written by a beginner illustrates some common problems in writing personality sketches, as well as some effective techniques others should emulate:

Comments

Perhaps the subject's full name should have come a bit earlier than the end of the third paragraph because readers may confuse "he," not knowing at some points whether "he" refers to the subject or the speaker. But this is certainly an engaging beginning, especially because a trait is mentioned, then illustrated. The deleted words seem to be unnecessary.

So much is made of Smither's wit that another example of it somewhere in the fourth or fifth paragraph would make the point.

Personality Sketch

"Linus is a pleasure to be around because he amuses you," commented a young instructor who has been his straight man more than once.

He picked up a miniature green flag. Musing over it, he recalled that he had worn it in his lapel last St. Patrick's Day. ~~Upon noting the occasion, he continued,~~ Linus had eyed the decoration and punned, "I dreamed I was St. Patrick in my Eringobragh."

Some associates credit this humor to instinctive dry wit; others claim it is a cleverly acquired coverup for more revealing emotion. Whichever it is, it delineates Professor Linus Smither's personality and delimits his relationships with others.

Those who maintain that Smither's wit is a natural gift readily admit he lacks the normal kaleidoscope of moods. "He doesn't seem to show excitement or boredom," his roommate, Allen Ginsberg, noted.

*Tom Wolfe, *The New Journalism* (New York: Harper & Row, 1973), p. 56.

An important bit of editing. The colon after "disagreed" pulls the reader and allows a deletion.

However, Ginsberg ventured that Smither has the potential for warmth and anger, whereas another contemporary disagreed: "Basically, he's kind of antiseptic," Smither's friend explained. Theorizing that his dearth of moods stems from intense emotional control, he lamented that Smither "doesn't like you, but he'll laugh with you. Humor is his only emotion."

This is a deft transition. The writer *uses* the preceding paragraph to dip into history.

Note especially that the historical tracing is *not* grafted on in a series of dull facts. The history is made an integral part of a thematic story.

Smither's background could lend support to either claim. Born in 1940, he is the youngest in a Midwest dairy farmer's family of four daughters and two sons. The older children may have stifled outbursts from the "baby" of the family. On the other hand, a large family is rarely subdued: parental discipline may favor even-temperedness, but there is usually an undercurrent of warmth and excitement.

His former office-mate, another Midwesterner, expressed puzzlement about Smither's "closeness," which is alien to the Midwest. Having shared an office with Smither, acquainted him with the area, associated with him socially, and travelled with him, he was surprised at how little he knew about Smither.

Again, history is tied into the running story.

He suggested that the transition from a small friendly farming community to the urbanity of Cornell, where Smither earned both Master of Science and Doctor of Philosophy degrees in industrial engineering, may have effected his inwardness. Fellow students can have an "intimidating" effect upon someone unaccustomed to their sophistication, he commented.

The basic difficulty is that the first sentence here doesn't seem to follow from the preceding graph. It follows from the graph above the preceding. Perhaps a better sentence: "Ginsberg, too, must speculate."

Ginsberg knew remarkably little, too. He was unaware of Smither's Midwest upbringing or of his academic performance, although both majored in industrial engineering at Cornell. "Linus doesn't volunteer information," Ginsberg explained, "but he seems willing to be prodded."

All this seems extraordinarily valuable, giving the reader a rounded view of the subject. Note especially that this kind of description is not negated by accompanying photographs. *Never* **assume that pictures will describe. Few do. Only a long picture story, for example, could show how a subject walks, talks, moves, the sound of his voice, his mannerisms, and so on. Pictures are barely supplementary. And one picture is almost useless except to offer a general impression. The** *writer* **must describe.**

Equally as puzzling are Smither's immediately apparent inconsistencies. The quiet, young teacher owns a white Sting Ray and, according to Ginsberg, he "drives it in character—hard, fast, and very surely." Neither a smoker nor a drinker, he enjoys stag poker parties and has been spotted in Nero's Nook, the dimly lit nightclub in the gaudy Cabana Motor Hotel.

Tall (about 5' 11") and slender, his tan has only lately begun to fade. The blond streak in his light brown, slightly thinning hair attests to his daily afternoon swims and extensive outdoor activity. As a young bachelor, Smither enjoys a pleasantly varied social life. Girls will call him often, bachelor Ginsberg noted ruefully, and he will talk to them at length. He seems to be at ease among women, noted Ginsberg.

However, Smither teaches male engineers. Does his personality hinder his effectiveness? Apparently not.

English teachers once snorted at "enthused." And the writer should make the case with an example. *Show* **Smither being enthused.**

By the time the reader finishes this, he feels that he has been given views from a number of perspectives. And the ending, which ties back to the beginning, unifies the whole deftly.

He is faced with depressing odds—numbed, upperclass engineers; a room with carved, musty wooden chairs, nausea green walls, linoleum like grey amoebae, and half-hearted fluorescent lights. Yet he is enthused about the class, and the class is enthused about him.

Smither firmly believes in the values of humor and receptivity in teaching. It pays off, for his students perk up at his witticisms, and they ponder what he teaches. They agree that Smither is demanding but helpful. One who had difficulty keeping up at first despaired, "He takes off like a race horse out of the stocks." Yet among others word is spreading that Smither is attuned to the program and its problems.

Missing: quotations from Smither himself. The two puns are effective, but the reader never really *confronts* **Smither in conversation.**

Smither's personality may be an enigma, but his facility for punning is clearly irresistible. Everyone has his favorite Smither pun. The department secretary recalled a conversation between a professor and another secretary, a young mother. Questioning the desirability of being a working wife, they commented to Smither that his bachelorhood precluded such conflicts. Smither shot back: "You mean I'd have to live by the sweat of my frau?"

This is basically well written. Note especially that this writer is showing rather than telling. For example, if she had said that Smither is very funny—a person who causes those near him to dissolve in laughter—the reader may or may not believe this, depending on whether he trusts the writer's judgment. But *merely* telling the reader that Smither is funny won't make him remember this for more than a few minutes. However, since the writer has given examples of Smither's jokes, the likelihood that the reader will be impressed, that he will remember, is much greater.

The writer could have improved this story by observing Smither at work. Moreover, the subject should have been interviewed again after the observation. It is very important for the writer to observe Smither. Sharp descriptions require observation reporting that would almost surely pose other questions.

Anecdotes Round Out the Personality Sketch

Journalists must recognize the value and power of anecdotes. They enliven articles. They need not be funny to be effective. Light or serious, anecdotes illustrate points and bring them to life. To write an effective anecdote, it is usually necessary for the writer to see the subject in action and to be able to quote him at length.

Consider this passage from a long feature about Joseph Papp, who controls the stages at both Lincoln Center and his fabulously successful Public Theater. This article appeared in the *New York Times*.* The writer has introduced him, then observes him at length:

Comments

Note especially how much detail this writer gives: "read over the phone (which has been equipped with a loudspeaker)," "he reads without feeling," and so on. The writer almost takes the readers to this scene.

Personality Sketch

ABC's Kevin Sander's reaction is mixed. Then comes Clive Barnes's critique in the *Times,* read over the phone (which has been equipped with a loudspeaker so everyone can hear). The words are read by a man in the *Times*'s composing room. He reads without feeling: *"Boom Boom Room* is full of chic filth and a desperate Archie Bunker style of racism . . . an empty and poorly crafted play . . . It is said to be di-

---

*Reprinted by permission of the author, Patricia Bosworth.

rected by Mr. Papp himself . . . Mr. Papp must take the rap . . . let us hope the Shakespeare Festival will have better luck next time. There is nowhere to go but up.''

As soon as the review is finished, Papp leaps to his feet, enraged, and lets loose a torrent of four-letter words. "That s.o.b.! That—! What's Clive's number?"

Debuskey gives it to him and Papp charges across the room to the phone. Although it is 11:30 P.M., he dials Barnes at home. Everyone is deathly silent.

"Hello, Clive? This is Joe Papp. I just heard your review. And you are a ————. You think you're going to get me? Well, I'm going to get you. I am going to get you." He slams down the receiver and glares at us. Nobody speaks.

"You know why Clive did this?" he demands. "It's his personal vendetta. Because he doesn't think new American plays should be done at the Lincoln Center. He's mad because I wouldn't listen to him." He pauses. "If the *Daily News* pans *Boom Boom Room*, I'll know I've gone crazy."

Minutes later the *News* review is phoned in. Doug Watt calls *Boom Boom Room* "long, tedious and bleak."

But after listening to this review, Papp grows strangely calmer. "Doug was objective about the play," he says. "Clive was not. Somebody must be crazy but I don't think it's me. I've been involved with a helluva lot of plays in my time and I happen to think *Boom Boom Room* is the most American play, the best, most significant play around. It was the only play I wanted to open Lincoln Center with. I feel very close to this play. This play is about sexual identity and resolving one's sexual identity and it's a raw emotional examination.

Instead of merely telling the readers that Papp was outraged, the writer quotes him, which helps make this scene vivid. Note again how much the writer shows his readers: "Debuskey gives it to him and Papp charges across the room to the phone."

As Papp grows calmer after Watt's review is quoted, the readers can see it. Only after the writer has established Papp's mood does he go on quoting Papp.

Here, the writer quotes Papp at length, which gives the readers a full view of the subject of this piece.

"You gotta see beyond the artifice, the bad jokes. Everything is there for a purpose, for Christ's sake. But the play either turns you on or turns you off. If Clive totally rejects the play on personal grounds, he should say so."

This is typical of the kind of anecdotal writing that is appearing frequently in large newspapers. A beginner can learn a great deal about crafting such pieces by studying magazine profiles and by becoming a good observer of people.

THE HUMAN INTEREST STORY

A human interest story may be a personality sketch, but it has a different aim. A human interest story should engage the reader emotionally, stimulating or depressing him, angering or amusing him, awakening sympathy or distaste. There was a time, several decades ago, when the human interest story was the worst variety of writing. Often, it was called a "sob story," an obvious appeal for sympathy. A few elements of the newspaper industry still produce human interest writing whose only design is to wring tears. Generally, however, they are much more restrained. It would be difficult to find stories today that are like this one of three decades ago:

> Dry your eyes, Mother Hubner. Choke back the tears, Father Hubner. Little Alice of the golden smile. . . .

Today's feature writer is more sophisticated. In this long story, Jerry Flemmons of the *Fort Worth Star-Telegram* knows well the line he must take, even though his story is close to wringing tears.*

Comment

Consider the easy way Flemmons decided to knit the story together. He starts with Roy, the drunkard, then fills in the background, paragraph after paragraph.

Note especially that Flemmons does not try to

Human Interest Story

Roy has been dead almost a dozen winters now and no one remembers him. He had no friends and Roy was not the type of man to cause those who knew him to reminisce.

People in the small East Texas town said only of Roy that he was "the most useless man in the county" and I guess he was. Roy—his com-

---

*Reprinted by permission of the author.

make bright phrases. Instead, he has a story that he tells simply.

plete name was Roy William Simpson—never held a job or did anything that could be considered steady work.

Roy's only pastime was drinking. He consumed whiskey and cheap wine in awesome amounts if he could obtain either but usually he could not. More often he drank after-shave lotion, hair oil, various cooking extracts and other everyday, ordinary liquids no one but Roy considered alcoholic.

Roy existed by stealing. He stole vegetables from gardens and nearby farms. Regularly he stole from old man Otis Williams' egg farm. He never swiped chickens, which would have made Otis angry enough to call the sheriff.

He took only eggs and Old Man Williams would tell about Roy's thievery to the men at the filling station and laugh. "Roy can steal an egg before it's laid," Otis claimed.

Once, between vegetable seasons and when Otis' chickens stopped laying for some reason, Roy was forced to steal Mrs. Truax's registered Poodle. He apparently intended selling the dog for funds with which to buy his distilled liquors or vanilla extract. The sheriff caught him and returned the poodle. He did not arrest Roy. Roy never was arrested for his thefts. Townspeople, in fact, rarely complained about Roy's stealing. Roy was just an irritating cross they bore, like mosquitoes in the spring or a faulty sewer system.

No Alcohol in Prison

Consider how easily the transitions come, even those that come after subheads. The preceding sentence read, in part: "Roy was just an irritating cross they bore." That sentence led him to the sentence that begins, "Somewhere in Roy's background was a prison sentence." A neat transition.

Somewhere in Roy's background was a prison sentence, probably endured for theft of something more costly than vegetables, eggs or poodles. He rarely spoke of his jail days but once told me prison for him was not oppressive except that he suffered from lack of alcohol. He had worked for a time in the penitentiary in the license plate shop and, later, transferred to the laundry where he washed sheets and stitched up rips in mattress ticking.

In addition to stealing, Roy's source of income was curious. He was an object of ridicule to the local teenagers and station loafers.

The kids would say to Roy, "Bet you a quarter you can't run to the cafe and back in 30 seconds." Roy knew he could not but he always tried. He also knew the quarter was his for trying, and he would start off in a sort of shuffling trot, pumping his arms in an awkward rhythm, like a man going nowhere. Or one of the loafers would call, "Roy, can you dance a jig? Betcha four bits you can't." He attempted that, too. Or he would pat his head and rub his stomach for a dime.

The loafers and teen-agers never tired of the cruel game and it may have been their unconscious way of supporting a frail, liquor-ruined old man.

No Variety in Wardrobe

I never saw him when he was not wearing the same clothes. His wardrobe did not change, winter or summer. Roy wore dark green, dirty corduroy pants, once-brown shoes with thin heels, a bluish work shirt and the Eisenhower jacket. The scarf given him by Mr. Ferris, red and green scotch plaid, either hung straight under his jacket or was crossed over in the Continental style.

The jacket's regular buttons had been lost or removed and Roy had replaced them with bright, yellow plastic buttons. The yellow buttons only made Roy seem more of a clown.

Roy slept for years on a dirty old rug in the tool shed behind the cotton gin. When the area's cotton crop declined and the gin was torn down he moved to an ancient sharecropper's shack, a couple of miles south of town, on land owned by the bank. He boarded up windows and stuffed wadded newspaper into cracks. For a stove he used a rickety ice box lined with asbestos shingles. Roy took the rug, his only possession, and continued sleeping on it.

The September before the winter in which Roy died the community suffered a tragedy. Tragedy is the soul of small communities because one man's misfortune becomes public property. Tragedy assumes a collective face and the sorrow is borne by all.

Margaret Lee was not a pretty child. She was 5, perhaps 6, with straight blonde hair, the color of cobwebs, and watery blue, almost icy, eyes. She was thin and her skin was sickly white.

The only time I saw her she wore a print little-girl's dress and carried a battered rag doll, lying across the crook of her left arm. She and her mother lived a block south of the filling station in a three-room frame house. The mother was plain, too, and big-boned. She came from Austria and spoke English with a lowkeyed accent.

Policy, Baking Only Income

Margaret's father had met and married the woman while stationed in Europe as an Army corporal. Margaret was 4 when her father was burned to death in a gasoline truck accident on a lonely Kansas road. Mother and daughter lived on the little insurance money left by the father's death. For additional income, the mother baked and sold pies and cakes.

Note that this is not a first-person story. "I" appears infrequently. As this is written, it is as though the narrator calls on many who knew of Roy and pieces out the story from the information he gathered.

This is an important bridging paragraph. Flemmons must bring into the story another leading character, Margaret Lee, and still seem not to desert Roy. He writes the paragraph about Roy in a way that enables him to talk about the tragedy, Margaret.

See how honestly Flemmons writes: "Margaret Lee was not a pretty child." And, "The mother was plain, too." Many writers would somehow see these as beautiful people. But Flemmons tells it starkly.

In September doctors confirmed Margaret had leukemia. Unable to save Margaret's life, they set about the tedious work of prolonging it. The mother almost was insane with grief and cried hysterically when neighbors came to visit.

Flemmons tells of the gradual death very plainly. He does not attempt to wring tears from his readers. He tells the story matter-of-factly.

Margaret was weaker and sicker. Her mother argued with doctors who wanted to hospitalize the child. The mother asked to keep Margaret home until the grandfather arrived. So the Methodist women continued their weekly drives to the county seat hospital for Margaret's treatments. More than a week before Christmas the letter containing air fare and expense money was sent to the small Austrian village.

The next day Margaret lost her rag doll.

The Methodist lady whose turn it was to drive Margaret to the hospital thought the doll had been left in the waiting room. Perhaps it was, but the doll could not be found when they returned. There began another round of contributions by the church women. Dozens of rag dolls were delivered to Margaret, some store-bought, some home-made, but the child rejected all. None, she cried, was her rag doll.

Her father had given her the doll. That was the difference, explained the mother. Margaret, pale and nervous and weak, announced that Santa Claus would return her doll.

Christmas approached and the town prepared to make the holiday the happiest ever for the little girl. They bought most of the smaller toys in Mr. Ferris' store and made trips to the county seat for larger games and mechanical contraptions to please the little girl.

Last Journey across Fields

To appreciate this transition, consider the preceding paragraph. Note that the first sentence begins, "Christmas approached and the town prepared. . . ." This shows how the writer mentions others, then deals with Roy: "On the 23rd Roy . . ." Then Flemmons goes back to Margaret in the next paragraph. This is a neat device to have the readers consider Roy again.

On the 23rd Roy received one of his $10 envelopes and immediately purchased the extract and bottle of whiskey. He struck out across the blackland fields and no one saw him alive again.

That Christmas for Margaret, although she was cranky and whiney about the loss of the doll, brought the town together as nothing before. There was a moment of concern, the day before Christmas, when Margaret was rushed to the hospital for more blood but she returned and was put to bed.

A Lions Club member volunteered his pickup truck and toys were collected from homes and delivered to Margaret's house about 10 P.M. Christmas Eve.

Before she slept that night she talked about the doll Santa would return and her grandfather who was expected on the 28th. Christmas morning there were rag dolls but not her ragged doll, the one she missed and cried over. She opened each package and hoped, and when it was not there she wept. Later she played listlessly with her toys as she lay in bed.

Christmas Day the snow began, huge uncommon flakes for that season in East Texas. Margaret and her mother watched the snow from a front window and they talked about the grandfather.

Snow continued to fall as darkness arrived.

Her grandfather came. I never saw him but people said he was a small man with a gray mustache and that he spoke no English. The grandfather and Margaret visited for a day. Then an ambulance came and took the child to the hospital.

Here, Roy comes back into the picture.

Snow stayed on the ground for two days before melting but the weather remained unseasonably cold early in January and snow came again, not as heavily, but the ground disappeared again under the layer of white. Late in January two rabbit hunters found Roy's body.

Empty Bottle as Monument

He was stretched out under a small oak tree, in the center of a field midway between the town and his shack. An empty whisky bottle was beside Roy. Roy had not worn his Army jacket or scarf but the corduroy pants were his, so the sheriff identified the body that way. Roy, the sheriff reasoned, had wandered into the field with his whisky and passed out. The snow had covered him.

With the mention of Roy's death, Margaret again comes into the story, as she dies. Thus, the reader makes the connection between Roy and Margaret at the end.

Roy was buried in the cemetery behind the Methodist Church, off in a corner, with the county paying funeral expenses for its most useless citizen. Sober folk saw Roy's cold death as retribution for a wasted whisky-filled life and no one seemed to care very much that he was gone.

Margaret died in early March with her grandfather at the bedside. The funeral brought out most of the town's population. Mr. Ferris closed his store and even the loafers left the station long enough to watch Margaret buried on a bright spring day beneath a cordial blue sky. The mother sold the frame house and she and the grandfather left the little town and returned to Austria.

Almost a month passed before I heard about Margaret's rag doll.

Mr. Ferris said she had the doll when the ambulance came to take her to the hospital and he thought it was the doll she lost. Later when he noticed it closely he knew and he asked the mother. Margaret thought Santa had brought it to her, she said.

Flemmons is subtly leading the readers to ask, "Was that Roy?" If that is your question, the answer can be read in the last paragraph. It seems essential that you recall how Flemmons had given the stress of an entire paragraph to describing "regular buttons," "bright, yellow plastic buttons," and finally "yellow buttons."

Christmas Day, an hour after dark when the snow had stopped, the mother heard a noise on the porch and opened the door. The rag doll lay in the snow, next to the steps. She saw no one.

Margaret loved the doll on sight. It was a pitiful thing, ugly and poorly made, but Margaret said if Santa could not find her doll he knew the kind of doll she wanted. She loved the doll and she was happy.

Mr. Ferris recalled that the doll was much like the old one, ragged and worn and lumpy. But it had, he said, red and green scotch plaid skin and, for eyes, two bright yellow plastic buttons.

This story is the epitome of simplicity. Flemmons has not tried for phrases. He does not try to coax tears for the dead Margaret Lee or even for dead Roy Simpson. He tells the story straightforwardly— first describing the old alcoholic, then weaving in the story of Margaret, then blending Roy into that story. At the end, Roy and Margaret are brought together through the rag doll episode. Flemmons's method is highly effective.

But it is also the story itself that makes this article a good one. Finding equally effective material can be a difficult task for writers. There is no simple solution to the problem of where to look for human interest stories because they can be found everywhere. The best approach is to become a keen observer of humanity and a good listener. As you learn to think in terms of article ideas, your skill in both these areas will improve.

Offhand comments made by people you encounter are often a productive source of ideas. For instance, a woman conducting a tour of a children's hospital said, "Often the person most in touch with a dying patient's feelings is the cleaning lady who comes at night. She's often the only one with the time and inclination to listen." Any writer who fails to hear the human interest story behind that remark had better change careers.

One former reporter recalled that his best source of ideas was the evening edition of the previous day's paper. He scanned the articles looking for the angle that was overlooked, or the story behind the story that was already written. It was a rare day when the search did not prove fruitful. Whether you choose to look in the newspaper or to explore your own environment, the important thing is that you do look, and that you practice ferreting out the human interest stories in the world around you.

CHAPTER EIGHT EXERCISES

1. Describe a person without relying on any physical characteristics.

2. Describe a person using four personality traits (kind, funny, serious, thoughtful, and so on), then rewrite the description using quotes, anecdotes, and descriptions of actions in place of the adjectives. Which is more effective?

3. Find a human interest story from your daily environment. Don't go anywhere you don't usually go or do anything you don't normally do. Your task is to discover a human interest story that has been right in front of you all along.

CHAPTER 9
Research Stories

All articles require research, but those that depend entirely on it to answer a question or explain something are known as research stories. The question may be as simple as "How do colleges decide which students to admit?" or as complicated as "How do people's votes in an election reflect their income, race, religion, and social class?" In attempting to answer such questions, writers must use many different research sources. The writer must know where to look for information and must go beyond the minimum research required to write the story.

Consider this excerpt from an article by Terry Anzur on how young people find jobs today. Note that she combined interviews, observation, and library research to produce the article. At the end of the excerpt, you will find a list of some of the sources she used.

Comment

Although this story is about thousands of unemployed students, the writer realized that she needed to focus on one person at the beginning of the article. Jon Levin was interesting, so she went into his case in detail.

Note that the writer describes Jon's garb minutely, knowing that it was interesting. It would have been a mistake had she written something

Research Article

Jon Levin started out tracking wild cats and ended up tracking subatomic particles.

During fall quarter of his sophomore year, he checked the part-time employment listings in the financial aids office. He discovered that the Health and Safety Department was looking for a student to trap wild cats that have been breeding for generations in the steam tunnels under university buildings.

Jon met all the prerequisites—he was reliable, honest, and had a driver's license. He could earn $2.50 an hour and schedule work hours around his classes. He was interviewed and hired.

Armored with a helmet, heavy work gloves, and coveralls, and armed with a flashlight, a $3\frac{1}{2}' \times 1'$ trap, and a can of cat food for bait, he entered the tunnel labyrinth through a manhole. He had to crouch to avoid bumping his head against the 4' ceiling. And he knew he shared the passageway with 400 to 1,000 wild cats.

like: "Jon was dressed like a wild cat hunter," and been content with that.

He'll never forget the first one he caught: "It shook me up to suddenly realize that it wasn't a normal housecat. It was scrawny. It was vicious. It would just as soon have eaten my arm. And it would have, if it had been clever enough."

After three weeks of outsmarting wild cats, Jon quit the job to spend more time studying for final exams. His next job would be less dangerous, but just as challenging.

The Stanford Linear Accelerator Center (SLAC) advertised in the Physics Department for students who could help analyze data. Jon, a physics major, was hired. For the past year and a half he has been working 15–20 hours weekly, usually between 8 P.M. and 3 A.M. He traces the path of charged protons and electrons across a bath of cold, liquid hydrogen in a bubble chamber. He earns $3 an hour.

By giving herself the space to describe Jon's predicament and success, the writer presents the case of many of those who have succeeded despite the difficulty.

Jon was hired because of his interest and competence, not his financial need. "The experience is the most important thing," he says. "The job helps me understand what I want to do after I graduate and why I want to do it." Now a senior, he plans to do graduate work in physics.

Here the writer is beginning to introduce all the students who need jobs, which meshes Jon's case with many others'.

Jon is one of 2,300 undergraduates who held jobs on campus during the academic year 1973–74. Students with demonstrated financial need are eligible to apply for on-campus jobs listed in the financial aids student employment office. This year 1,100 jobs are listed, representing about $800,000 in earning potential.

The writer deals deftly with these numbers by guarding against the piling of number upon number. Note that this paragraph starts with one number, then there's a space, then a dash separates the next number from three numbers, then there are many words before she uses the last two.

An estimated $1 million was earned in 1973–74 by students who found part-time work through the Student Employment Office of the Career Planning and Placement Center. The Student Employment Office has listings of all on-campus jobs not filled through the financial aids office, but its primary responsibility is off-campus employment. Last year 4,954 people—3,105 undergraduates, 1,548 graduate students, and 301 student spouses—indicated an interest in part-time work by registering at the Placement Center. According to Pam Evans, director of the Student Employment Office, they filled 3,314 jobs off campus and 924 on campus.

Although students who need jobs to meet the self-help requirements of their financial aid packages are given preference for on-campus jobs, it would be impossible for university departments to hire all students who need to work. Jobs account for only about 7.5 percent of the university's financial aid budget. About three-fourths of the total reaches students in the form of scholarships and grants. Gift aid to undergraduates has grown from $6.6 million in 1973–74 to $7.1 million this year.

But tuition is growing too. The Board of Trustees has approved a tuition increase from $3375 to $3810, effective next fall. Partly as a consequence of the 12.9 percent hike, the largest in the university's history, gift aid to students will pass the $8 million mark next year, not including $2 million in student jobs and loans.

It is important that such an article present the university's problem as well as the students' difficulties. Too often, undergraduates write of this kind of problem from the viewpoint only of students. Terry Anzur manages to balance the sides admirably.

During the past decade, the university has met all the demonstrated need of entering freshmen, based on a parents' confidential statement of financial resources. Aid packages usually are a combination of gift aid and self-help. According to Kenneth Kaufman, assistant director of financial aids in charge of loans, a typical freshman is asked to meet half of his or her self-help requirement with income from jobs. The rest may be taken out in interest-free or low-interest loans.

Lynne Mason, assistant director of financial aids in charge of student employment, estimates that the typical undergraduate works 8–10 hours per week at about $2.50 an hour to fulfill a self-help require-ment. Aid packages are periodically reviewed and adjusted to align with changes in student family income and increases in the cost of their education. The aim is to assess the gap between the cost of an education and the student's ability to pay for it, and to fill the gap with an optimum combination of gift aid and self-help. "We will do our best to maintain the same level of financial aid support for a student throughout the undergraduate years," Kaufman says.

Note especially the many quotations used in this excerpt. Quotations interest the reader.

But it won't be easy.

"There's a limit to how much we can increase gift aid and the number of on-campus jobs," Ms. Mason points out. "More students will have to take out loans."

Kaufman predicts a large increase in the number of low-interest federally insured loans to students from middle-income families. "Tuition has risen to a point where it is impossible for a student to completely work his way through this university," he says. . . .

RESEARCH SOURCES FOR THE ARTICLE

Job Descriptions and Employment Listings, Placement Center and Financial Aids Office.

Undergraduate Student Job Wage Scale Descriptions, Financial Aids Office.

University News Release, 1/13/75, on placement center peer counseling.

Internship Descriptions, City of Palo Alto Personnel Department.

Intramural Handbook by W. P. Fehring, director of intramurals.

Campus Report, 11/13/74, "Summer conferences here provide jobs, income—and some laughs" by Pat Black (p. 9).

Memo from Delmer Daves, '26, "History of Stanford Period: Jobs" (to be published in full in *Stanford Magazine's* fall issue).

The Innocents at Cedro by R. L. Duffus.

The Making of a Reporter by Will Irwin.

The Memoirs of Ray Lyman Wilbur.

This excerpt from the beginning of her piece and the partial list of a research report, which included more than thirty interviews, suggest the range of avenues she explored. What this writer had to do before she could begin to write her article is the same process any successful writer for the modern newspaper has learned to follow.

WRITING THE RESEARCH STORY

Here are a few tips on writing good research stories:

Use Authoritative Sources   To have credibility, your article must include information from sources that everyone would regard as authorities on the subject. If the source is a person, be sure to state his or her credentials (president of an organization, leading researcher in the field, and so on). The "man on the street" approach may be useful for providing examples, but the article must include information from a source that has an overall picture of the subject. If the source is a document, be sure that it contains the most current information available.

Present the Information Clearly   The more complicated your subject is, the more attention you need to give to clear, direct writing. That doesn't mean you sacrifice smooth, flowing prose; it does mean that you need to be concise in constructing sentences and precise in choosing words. In addition, the article must be well organized. One way to approach the problem of organization is to first jot down the basic elements of the story in no particular order. Next, group those that are related to each other. Finally, rank the groups and their individual elements in order of importance. The result is an outline that will help you organize the material.

Include Only Interesting Quotations   Direct quotations make the article more lively and readable, but don't use a dull quotation for the sake of having it in the story. "That's very interesting" is an example of a dull quotation. It adds nothing. When you use a direct quotation, subject it to a test of justification. You should have a reason for including it. Perhaps it is an insightful comment on the subject. It may explain something better than you could by paraphrasing. It may reveal something about the speaker. Or it may be interesting, witty, or eloquent. If the quotation doesn't pass one of these tests, discard it or paraphrase.

Write in an Authoritative Tone   Don't hide behind qualifiers such as "in some instances" and "it seems to be." Too many of these make your article weak and uncertain. Although you shouldn't make absolute statements about facts you are unsure of, many qualifiers in an article are usually a sign that you didn't do enough research. Confidence in your own grasp of the subject is the key to an authoritative tone.

Here is an excerpt from an article by Madeline Camisa about an initiative to limit the construction of high-rise buildings in San Francisco. Originally written during a course in magazine writing, the article was published in *San Francisco* magazine. It gives a detailed account of the history of the initiative, the political elements that are for and against it, how its passage or failure is likely to affect the city's future, an explanation of the various provisions of the initiative, and similar laws and trends in other cities. But even in the few paragraphs presented here, it is clear that the author has done considerable research and that she has a good command of the subject.

> The famous French architect, Le Corbusier, designed an ideal city for the twentieth century. Above all, his utopia was a city of administration: "From its offices come the commands that put the world in order. In fact, the skyscrapers are the brain of the city, the brain of the whole country. Everything is concentrated there: the tools that conquer time and space—telephones, telegraphs, radios; the banks, trading houses, the organs of decision for the factories: finance, technology, commerce." The city was composed of glass and steel skyscrapers set in parks.
>
> But one man's dream is another man's nightmare. The dense, centralized city may receive accolades from corporate leaders or clerical workers, but not from some environmentalists and urban dwellers. Certainly not from some San Franciscans. To a growing number of inhabitants of the City by the Bay, the "ills" of high-rises far outweigh their economic benefits. According to these urban dwellers, the negative impacts of the giant slabs on the environment are clearly visible: disruption of the sky-

line, increased traffic, less open space, loss of older buildings, greater density and congestion, and environmental pollution.

Recently this anti-high-rise sentiment led to an initiative that would limit height and density of buildings in the city's financial center. The initiative is slated for the November ballot.

Though some Eastern cities have limited the density and height of their downtown buildings through various means, San Francisco is the only American city that has used this ballot-box approach to urban design controls. It's little wonder then, that Kenneth Halpern, director of the Mayor's Office of Midtown Planning and Development in New York City, wrote in his study of urban design in nine American cities, *Downtown USA:*

> *Concern with the special quality of San Francisco has led citizens to focus more seriously than any other American city on the question of height limitations.*

With its natural and man-made beauties, San Francisco can truly be called a unique city. But some shudder at what has happened to its visual character in the last 30 years. John Elberling, one of the sponsors of the initiative, said:

> *San Francisco has turned into an office city. It's still the Bay in the hills, but it's become less distinctive and that kind of special feeling has been lost.*

Perhaps local columnist Herb Caen best summed up the feeling of San Franciscans about the changing skyline when he addressed the American Institute of Architects, which met in San Francisco in early May 1973. Caen wrote:

> *You architects who have visited San Francisco before may wonder where the city has gone. It's here somewhere, cowering behind hills and down alleys that form the new skyline that is almost indistinguishable from Pittsburgh's, Houston's or Atlanta's.*

This article leaves the reader feeling that the author knew much more than she wrote, but that she selected the most important and informative material for her story. Any good research story should create a similar impression.

CHAPTER NINE EXERCISES

1. You are assigned a story on how inflation has affected the ability of young couples to buy houses. List the sources of information you would consult in order to research the article.

2. Find a research article from a daily or weekly newspaper and analyze it according to the following criteria: (1) sources of information, (2) organization, (3) clarity, and (4) completeness. How do you think the article could have been improved?

3. You have three days in which to produce a 1200-word research article. Choose a topic, then discuss how you would proceed and do a thorough job within these time limitations. What problems might you encounter and how would you solve them?

PART THREE
Writing for Magazines

CHAPTER 10
The Magazine Staff Writer

Landing a job as a magazine staff writer is a bit like trying to hop aboard a moving merry-go-round; the real problem is in getting on, but once you do, it is easy to change horses. In particular, the New York publishing world is a place in which staff members move frequently from one publication to another. The same names appear over and over again on different mastheads and in different combinations. As in many other fields, the key to landing these jobs is experience.

Acquiring that experience has lately meant starting at the bottom of the magazine staff heap. College students and even some nonstudents who work as interns on magazine staffs get the best chance to demonstrate their abilities. They often perform research tasks or even clerical assignments for little or no pay, but in exchange they may learn a great deal about how magazines operate. They may also be given opportunities to write short articles or to take responsibility for magazine departments like "Letters to the Editor." The lucky ones may be offered staff jobs as editorial assistants based on their experiences as interns. Such jobs are usually the first rung of the editorial ladder and are followed by positions like assistant editor, department editor, associate editor, and so on. *Newsweek* even has a position called "senior editorial assistant."

The specific responsibilities of people in these positions vary among magazines. Perhaps the most significant difference between a magazine staff job and a feature-writing job at a newspaper is that the former usually involves many tasks in addition to article writing. This chapter describes magazine systems for handling editorial material, reviews the activities of people in different kinds of magazine staff writing jobs, and then discusses the general role of the staff member.

MAGAZINE SYSTEMS

Every magazine develops its own system for handling articles that are submitted for publication. Usually one or more people are assigned the task of reading unsolicited manuscripts and deciding whether or not they merit consideration by an editor. Commonly known as "the slush pile" in New York editing circles, these articles rarely pass beyond this initial review. Most are not written by professionals, who rely primarily on query letters to pave the way for articles they want to write.

An assigned story usually goes directly to the editor with whom the writer has corresponded. Often this will be the person in charge of a particular department of the magazine, such as profiles, how-to's, and so on. The procedure from this point varies greatly from magazine to magazine, depending on the size of the editorial staff. The department editor may read the article first and decide whether or not it is publishable material. If not, it will probably be sent back to the writer either with a rejection slip or a request for revisions. If the piece passes the first editorial review, it may then be given to other editors for their comments or to the editor-in-chief for a final decision. However, the person with final authority for accepting articles may sometimes be a department editor.

Once the article has been accepted, it is then edited by one or more people. If major changes are made, an editor may contact the writer for approval, but the writer cannot assume that this will happen. Also during this stage a person called a fact checker may be assigned the task of verifying all of the objective facts and direct quotations contained in the article. To facilitate this process, some magazines ask writers to provide a list of their sources of information, including the telephone numbers of the people they interviewed. Most writers welcome the services of a fact checker because they ensure that no easily correctable errors will appear in the published version.

While the article is being edited it may also be under consideration by the art department. If photos were provided with the manuscript, the art director will decide whether or not they are adequate. If an illustration is to be used, the art director will either assign it to an assistant or commission a free-lance artist to do the job. Sometimes the editors consult with the art director concerning the visual appearance of an article. This is especially likely to occur when the article will be featured as a cover story.

An article that has been edited for content and length may then be passed to a copy editor. This person performs a variety of tasks to prepare the manuscript for typesetting by a printer. Among them are checking grammar, spelling, and punctuation and making sure that when there are options for correct usage, the article conforms to the magazine's style. (For example, the magazine may print all book titles in italics or always give a person's middle initial as part of the first mention in an article.) Depending on the magazine's printing arrangements, the copy editor may then hold the article until others are ready to be typeset or send it directly on to the printer.

After the article has been typeset, it is returned to the magazine as a galley, or proof. The editor in charge of it may review the article again, and someone will be assigned the task of proofreading it. Because the editor probably can recite the piece from memory at this stage, most magazines prefer to delegate the task of proofreading to someone who is less familiar with the story. This is often the last chance to make major changes in the article so particular care is taken to ensure that everything is in order. The art department may use a copy of the galley to make a dummy layout of the way the article will appear in the magazine. It is not unusual for slight cuts to be made at this stage if the text is a few lines too long.

The corrected galley then goes back to the printer. Some magazines may get a second or even a third galley before the final stage is reached. As changes ordered by the magazine that necessitate new typesetting can be very expensive, most magazines try to finalize copy as early in the process as possible. However, typographical errors are corrected free by the printer so there is no reason to let those slide by.

The final copy returned by the printer generally goes straight to the art department where it is cut and pasted on the "boards" in the exact form for reproduction. The completed boards with the copy and appropriate spaces left for art work may then be circulated among the editors for final approval. Only very serious errors may be corrected at this stage. When an entire issue is completed, it goes to the printer. Although the art director may check several proofs during the printing process, editors are not likely to see it again until the magazine arrives printed and bound.

SOME UNUSUAL STAFF WRITING JOBS

Sunset   At the home of *Sunset* in Menlo Park, thirty-five miles south of San Francisco, are many staff writers serving a diversified clientele. By any estimate, *Sunset* is the most successful magazine in the West, with more than one million subscribers. *Sunset* magazine serves the entire nine-state region of the western United States and has several writers working in other cities. All *Sunset* workers have a mission—to concentrate on food, travel, outdoor recreation, gardening, and home building or decorating projects. One of the staff writers, Mary Ord, has drawn a sharp picture of the work of the staff writer.

> At *Sunset* a staff writer functions somewhat like an in-house free-lancer. His job may bear little relation to "staff" except that he uses the magazine's resources and conveniences (files, photographers, art staff, darkroom, checking facilities, etc.). Like a free-lancer, he attempts to put his prose into the magazine's style—that is, he writes to serve the magazine's avowed purpose to the reader, in

our case—how to make it, bake it, build it, grow it, visit it. People in *Sunset*'s "outer" offices—Seattle, Los Angeles, Honolulu—sometimes work at home, checking in by phone.

Like a free-lancer, a staff writer proposes article ideas to the editors. He should have done enough research into the topic (and perhaps have scouting photography in hand) to determine if the subject can be handled in such a way as to be interesting to the magazine's specific audience. He must have enough information on the subject and a clear enough idea of a suitable approach so he can "sell" it to the editors. He must convince them that *he*, not another staffer, is the one to do such a story. I once had the go-ahead to do a story on shopping in Los Angeles museums for Christmas gifts. A writer in the Los Angeles office suggested a different way to handle it—covering just three museums and keying gift ideas to their current shows. He got the nod and I lost out. The writer should be able to suggest timing (perhaps tying the story to a news event) and photographic possibilities.

Then there is the same sort of give-and-take that might happen between editor and free-lancer, with editor possibly suggesting different timing, other aspects to consider, other photo possibilities. The editor might also bring up other story ideas he has had in mind along the same lines and ask the writer to help research them or take them over completely for future stories.

The writer then goes out to get scouting photography (if he doesn't already have it and if the story calls for pictures). He does more in-depth research, reporting in as things develop. The story may change shape or focus as research or photos turn out better or worse than expected.

For a staff writer, like a free-lancer, ideas are the stock in trade and he is *always* looking for new ones. Anywhere I go for a weekend, I think, "Would this make a good travel story?" When I eat in a restaurant, I think about the recipes; when I go for a walk, I look carefully at people's gardens and houses; in stores I look for things that could be duplicated by the home craftsman or carpenter. Nearly every *Sunset* writer brings back *at least* one story from his own vacation. *Sunset* writers subscribe to periodicals that might give leads to stories in their fields of interest and clip anything that might be worth following for a future story.

Among free-lancers and staff writers there is competition for stories, and you win some, lose some. Unlike a free-lancer, a staff writer must learn to have a give-and-take relationship with other staffers—face to face, day to day. Free-lancers, I think, are more removed, having only to hear over the phone or by letter, "We already have someone working on that."

On our staff there is an element of looking over each other's shoulder to see if someone got an idea in presentable shape before you did. On a magazine that puts so much stock in fresh ideas, the battle to come up with a good idea first is something you live with every day.

One way to "get above the battle" is to carve out an area of reporting for your own—to stay so much on top of a subject that it is recognized that you have the best background to handle it. For some, it happens inadvertently—over the years, a writer has done several stories on a certain topic and has built up the contacts and files. One writer became the recognized expert on the Bay Area Rapid Transit and Montreal's Expo '74 this way. Or sometimes a writer might decide to make a little-reported topic his own and start making contacts and files, and wait for a story to happen.

Writers tend to try to keep ideas they are working on to themselves until they are sure what the real story possibilities are. This results in some duplication of efforts. Here is an example. A year ago I got hold of a press release about the Pacific Coast Kayaking Championships to be held on the Truckee River with the best in the West competing. I mentioned to one editor that I would like to go up and look into it, doing my own photography (to save the $100+ per day for a photographer—there might have been nothing to photograph). With a go-ahead, I went, got some photography, met several kayakers to get in touch with later, and came back feeling I had a good base for a story on a sport that is largely unreported but has been gaining enthusiasts since the last Olympics. I did some reading on the sport and put the story aside until spring. Meanwhile, another writer had lit upon the idea of a kayaking story and began by writing to all the kayaking clubs around the West. When he presented his story idea to the editors, it was felt that I had the more "tangible" research, and he was asked to bow out.

Fortune   At *Fortune*, the staff writers are so independent of office routine that a man who was once managing editor described the system as "subsidized free-lancing." The subsidies can be substantial, including comfortable salaries and expense accounts as well as the help of capable researchers. The freedom is equally substantial. In fact, few *Fortune* writers visit the office very often, preferring to write at home. Between assignments, a staff writer may be given other chores, such as helping produce the magazine's regular sections and departments. But the limited demands imposed by such supplementary work are suggested by the fact that one *Fortune* writer was in the office only sixty days one year. He described this as typical. (The office is not deserted, of course. Editors, artists, and writers who produce special departments are routinely on hand.)

Gene Bylinsky, who was once a free-lancer and is now one of the best *Fortune* writers, described the operation.

> You do have deadlines, of course. They come maybe six or eight weeks apart. But once you have started on a story you are on your own. *Fortune* is unusual in its researcher help, especially in serving as another reporter on the story. That's how the researcher and I worked on the computer peripherals story in the June issue. We started by interviewing sources in Boston together. Then I went on to upstate New York while she flew to Dallas to interview companies there. We then met in San Francisco, where we interviewed a large number of people, separately. Later, even as I was writing the story, she continued interviewing, in Philadelphia, Washington, and other cities. (In addition, by the way, a great service provided by researchers is that they transcribe notes for the writers.)
>
> I get a much faster response to stories as a staff writer than I got as a free-lancer. The editors have to respond quickly because the way things are organized at *Fortune* a writer's story *has* to work out—it's scheduled for an issue.
>
> A number of people at *Fortune* act as "story editors" (from time to time), although the managing editor actually runs the magazine. After a writer turns in his manuscript to the typing room, it is mimeographed and distributed to the editors. That's the first draft. The managing editor reads it, scribbles comments on it, talks to the story editor, then the story editor talks to the writer. There's usually at least one rewrite. Interestingly enough, when one managing editor voluntarily stepped down to become a writer again, *he* had to rewrite *his* stuff. This probably illustrates the subjective nature of writing. This system certainly isn't a bad idea. I know that most second drafts turn out a lot better.
>
> Assuming that the second draft gets by the managing editor, the "closing" starts. It's almost like publishing a book, but on a smaller scale. The manuscript is checked by the researcher, who calls sources to check on quotations, figures, etc. Then the manuscript goes to the proof room and is set in type. We get one proof of "the front of the book"—the major part of the article that runs near the beginning of the issue. The checking and double-checking results in a magazine that has very few errors—typos or otherwise.
>
> After the staff writer is finished with the story, he goes on to the next one. It can be his idea or the editors' idea.

Regardless of how many staff writers work like those at *Fortune*, Bylinsky's work for *Fortune* and Mary Ord's work for *Sunset* are representative of only a small percentage of the sorts of staff writing jobs that are available on American magazines. What might be termed the more conventional staff writing work is quite different. But there are too many varieties of the "conventional" to describe all of them.

Indeed, the staff writing task on a single magazine often varies. Keith Wheeler has vividly described the fluctuating pace by telling of the staff writer who once locked into combat with his typewriter, "eyeball-to-eyeball," and turned out a finished, organized, and publishable article in only seven hours. Wheeler himself participated in one unforgettable *Life* marathon: "The Bay of Pigs idiocy left us with about forty hours to put together a reasonable understanding of what had taken place, then get it written, edited, checked and into the magazine. Nobody sleeps on nights like that." But Wheeler also recalls spending five months doing the research for a piece on Arab nationalism and another two months writing the article.

The best way to understand all the varieties of staff writing is to consider a few that are fairly common.

TRADITIONAL STAFF WRITING JOBS

The News Magazines   Hal Bruno, the news editor of *Newsweek*, has said that "a news magazine is a place where reporters report, writers write, and a person contemplating a career in this field should have some idea as to which of these skills he or she does best and enjoys most." In the sense in which we are considering the term, "staff writing" refers to both reporting and writing. But it certainly is necessary to be aware of the distinction Bruno makes. One aspect of that distinction is that *Newsweek* writers (and editors) work in New York; almost all the reporters work in twenty-two foreign and domestic bureaus. Basically, the writers fashion most of the stories that appear in news magazines by using the research pieces that are sent to New York by the reporters. Very rarely do free-lancers provide any of the material that goes into news magazines.

In recent years, news magazines have begun to quote long passages from their reporters. It has thus become possible for news magazine reporters to consider themselves writers as well.

How the work of news magazine bureaus is carried out is described by Peter Sinton, who was a reporter in the San Francisco bureau of *Time:*

> The bureaus, national and international, are tied very closely with New York; a teletype-telephone umbilicus ties the bureau with the great mother organization in New York. In the case of *Time*, and I suppose *Newsweek*, the umbilicus is never broken, and New York is sort of the revered and hated parent. Relationships with New York

tended to be rather impersonal, quite businesslike, terse and efficient. Telephone calls are brief, not by edict from New York, but by understanding of the big news magazine process and how things operate. If you can't grasp this, you can't very well work for the magazine.

On Wednesday and Thursday, suggestions for the next week's publication are sent on the teletype to the East. Back-of-the-book suggestions are filed from all of the bureaus on Wednesdays, front-of-the-book story suggestions follow the next day. Perhaps half the stories worked on during the typical week originate in New York during the story conference held there. Often "round-up" stories are called for by the different sections in New York, and these are usually dreaded by the bureaus. For one thing, they mean a hell of a lot of scavenging for little results. So much is filed from the scattered bureaus that the correspondent will be lucky to find one line of his work in the finished story. . . .

There were usually enough exciting stories to go around, many times even more than we could handle, and this made the job especially interesting. No obituaries or fires or gossipy trash that is the staple of many dailies. The stories at *Time* were of a higher level, of national importance or interest. It was especially satisfying suggesting a story to New York, having it accepted, working on it alone, and having it published in brief, but still intact. . . .

As for sources, we didn't have enough writers and researchers to spread around the city or our territory. We had some stringers on campuses but we couldn't cover a beat like a newspaper reporter could. We didn't have men stationed at the Federal Building or the Police headquarters. So we depended a lot on the newspapers and the leads they offered. The *Examiner* and *Chronicle* and *Palo Alto Times*, and the *New York Times* and *Wall Street Journal*, were all searched for important news leads. Our minds were programmed to scan the papers, the daily flack mail, etc., with the sections of the magazine turning over in our minds like IBM cards. Would the story have appeal for its oddity, for its national news value, etc.? We'd send the idea off to New York and the maze of hallways and offices and the final judgment, the word from above. Sometimes we could argue a certain story was worthwhile, but we couldn't press it too far. We were outflanked and outnumbered by the huge New York operation.

Thinking was also useful for dreaming up stories, things that the papers hadn't touched. Things of wider scope, thought pieces. One had to raise his mind above the day-to-day repetition of events. It was drummed into us that we should read widely, get out and talk with sources, and develop sort of an individual think tank. Sometimes this was difficult, for after living in an area for a long while, one loses depth perception and good stories blend in with the well-known environment. That's one of the reasons, I suppose, that *Time* correspondents are frequently pitched from bureau to bureau. . . .

In free time we could tour the galleries, go to movies and theaters, department stores, anything to dream up story ideas that would catch New York's attention—fads, festivals, flops—anything. Sometimes it would be hard to forget about work, and at parties, on weekends, all the time in fact, one would be searching and quizzing people and asking questions.

Groups of Magazines   The trend toward grouping many publications under one ownership is noticeable throughout the magazine world, but it is especially strong among business and industrial publications. One of the most successful groups is McGraw-Hill, which publishes nearly fifty business and scientific magazines. Like the news magazines, all McGraw-Hill publications are produced almost entirely by staff writers (who are known as editorial assistants, correspondents, assistant editors, and the like). Some of the most prestigious magazines in the McGraw-Hill group—most notably, *Business Week*—maintain their own bureaus, but most are served by bureaus that service many other McGraw-Hill magazines.

How this system works is indicated by the organization of the Los Angeles bureau, one of the largest in the McGraw-Hill World News Service. It has six correspondents and one editorial assistant who divide responsibilities for covering much of California for more than thirty magazines. As a rule, each staff writer in the bureau is designated as the local correspondent for five or six magazines. There are two exceptions. If a correspondent who is busy with important assignments receives still another assignment from one of his magazines, it may be passed on by the bureau chief to another correspondent. Second, most correspondents become specialists—one has become expert in air and water pollution, for example—and handle most of the assignments in their special areas regardless of which magazine the story is slated for.

For the most part, this is an excellent system. One former staffer commented: "Work for McGraw-Hill was remarkably pleasant, and was excellent training for a young journalist. Work conditions were, and apparently still are, very interesting and rewarding."

There are inevitable problems, however, in any system. McGraw-Hill may be on the way to solving one that irked staffers— the "inch-count system" that measured bureau performance. The memories of it nurtured by one former Los Angeles bureau correspondent, Jerilyn Sue McIntyre, are worth recounting because they reveal the difficulty in determining efficiency in a large organization that encompasses many magazines and many writers.

The mechanics are simple: Each month we tabulated the number of inches-in-print contributed by members of our bureau to each of the magazines covered by the bureau. At the end of the year, statistics were sent to each bureau chief, indicating the inch-count total for all bureaus in the World News organization, and comparing the totals with previous performances. Apparently, each magazine is assessed for the amount of coverage done by the bureaus; and eventually, or so we were led to believe, these totals probably have some effect on budget allotments for individual bureaus. . . .

While it *is* true that a reporter might *send* more to the "garbage cans"—a term used by one of my friends to describe a magazine which uses anything sent to them—it is also true that the same reporter might *do* more for a magazine he respects, even though it might not give him as high an inch count as the others. Magazines like *Business Week* (not covered by the News Bureau), *Scientific Research, Medical World News* and others are well known in their fields and are respected publications. A correspondent appreciates this, and will probably spend a lot of time on assignments and features, simply because he is proud to be associated with these publications; and, of course, the work for these publications is usually more interesting and more worthwhile for the average reporter. Correspondents also tend to work harder for those editors who bother to keep in touch with them, either through assignments or simply through occasional interoffice memos. News Bureau staffers tend to be somewhat paranoid about editorial indifference; when you're out in the field, you appreciate the editors who make you feel a part of the magazine's staff, and you tend to reward their efforts to maintain communication with a little extra effort of your own.

Occasionally, there may be larger issues than economics involved in publishing groups of magazines. Among physicians and others who know it well, *The Journal* of the American Medical Association (familiarly known as the *AMA Journal* or *JAMA*) is a prestigious publication. It is sometimes criticized because of the policies of the association itself, and, as one staffer has said of all AMA publications, "It isn't always easy to practice freedom of the press in an institutional setting."

Steve Murata, a former *JAMA* staffer who later switched to *Medical World News,* has described the work of the "Medical News" section of *The Journal.*

The Journal of the AMA contains scientific articles written by the doctors themselves. These original contributions are handled by an editorial staff which is completely separate from ours. Looked at another way, we in the Medical News Section are completely separate from them in terms of our day-to-day work. We are assigned a certain number of pages each week to fill and go about the business of doing this with relatively little contact with outside *JAMA* staff members. The only exceptions occur with the senior editors who read our material. Dr. Hugh Hussey, the editor of *The Journal,* as well as Dr. Therese Southgate, read all of our material for scientific accuracy. Although outright kills on stories are infrequent, they are able to catch many small errors in using the medical lingo. I am slowly learning to handle the terminology with some ease and to judge when physicians are used to handling certain types of information and when the readers will probably be in the dark along with me because the material comes from a highly specialized scientific area. In this age of specialization, many physicians are "very well-informed laymen" when it comes to recording and understanding developments outside their immediate area of practice. Thus, we try to present things to a reader with a generalized interest and generalized clinical or experimental background, taking care to explain or define some of the more technical terms.

As an associate editor in the Medical News Section, I am able to spend my time writing rather than editing. Occasionally I will write a headline for someone's story or briefly glance over some of the material of my colleagues. However, at the present time, I am functioning almost exclusively as a reporter and writer and enjoying it a great deal. It's fun to be able to be just a writer and to poke your nose into everyone's scientific business, without having to deal too much with the nuts and bolts of production that require so much painstaking detail.

Small Magazines   A young journalist who has worked for newspapers and for large and small magazines makes this observation: "There seems to be an inverse relationship between the size of the magazine and the staff relations with editors. The bigger and better known the magazine, the less likely it is that the top editors are going to be close to the staff." Although there are certainly exceptions, a moment's reflection should suggest that this observation is almost certainly accurate. Few sizable organizations are noted for close relations between executives and workers.

But if the observation is a truism, it may also suggest to one who yearns to work for a big magazine that a few years on smaller publications may be better training. Just as one who begins work for a giant manufacturing firm is likely to find that his experiences are specialized and limited, the young magazine staffer who takes a job with a giant publication is likely to find the spectrum of his tasks quite narrow.

Normally, the reverse is true for those who work for small magazines. Indeed, if the magazine is small enough—and hundreds are published with staffs consisting only of an editor, an assistant editor, and a secretary—a staffer may find that he is getting a good bit more experience than he can absorb comfortably in a short time.

A young writer described the operation of *Ski* magazine:

> An unbelievable amount of time is spent on researching stories and checking on facts. Many writers at *Ski* seem to spend most of their time on the phone—tracking people down, conducting interviews, confirming details, etc. Actual time spent writing is much less than time spent researching.
>
> There is a big emphasis on coming up with the unique ideas that appeal to many people. With the speedy competition from radio, TV, and newspapers, magazines have to come up with things these other media can't do.
>
> The story is the responsibility of the writer right up to the time it is "closed" in page proof, but a lot of other people share the responsibility. At *Ski*, the managing editor reads everything and goes over it with the writer. The writer writes the head for the story as well as the 2- or 3-line display lead-in. Though these are subject to change by the managing editor, more often than not they're left alone.
>
> At some magazines, checking copies of articles are sent to all sources and to all people involved in the article. At *Ski*, showing copy to any outsider is strictly forbidden. Bill Berry, the executive editor, commented, "Nothing can compromise the integrity of a magazine more quickly than this."
>
> Each monthly issue is kind of the baby of everyone involved. There is a freshness with each copy of the magazine that's lacking in the newspaper world. If you make an error which slips through, there is rarely a tomorrow to rectify it. The entire staff seems dedicated to making every story on every page as appealing, accurate, and original as possible.

THE STAFFER AS JACK-OF-ALL-TRADES

For no clear reason, magazines have never developed titles that adequately describe staff duties. On a newspaper, the work of the editor, the managing editor, the city editor, the political reporter, and the other news and editorial employees is fairly well defined. The work of a city editor for a large newspaper may differ from the work of the city editor for a small paper—the former is likely to be more an executive in the sense of leading and directing operations; the latter probably spends much more time with pencil poised over news stories—but their tasks are at least similar. In the news departments of radio and television broadcasters, the work of the news director, the assignment editor, and the reporters may vary with the size of the station and other factors, but again the similarities are more apparent than the differences. But in the magazine world, anyone hoping to find the kind of order represented by titles and duties neatly defined is likely to be disappointed. On one publication, a "contributing editor" may do no editing; he is actually a staff writer who ranges over the world and writes at home. On another, a "contributing editor" may be a contract writer who gives only half his time to the magazine—and that time is devoted to writing rather than editing—while the other half is given to free-lancing. "Associate editor" may be similarly misleading because one who holds such a title may write articles, article titles, and picture captions, and may edit or supervise production.

All this would be inconsequential if it simply meant that the duties of a staffer on one magazine differ from the duties of a staffer holding the same title on another magazine. These differences are important, however, because they indicate the immense diversity of staff work. Many who are considering magazine careers may think of staff writing jobs as being limited to those outlined in the first section of this chapter. It is doubtful, for example, that beginners ever wonder who writes the captions for the illustrations in picture magazines, and even more doubtful that they consider caption writing important training for the kind of writing represented by 4,000-word articles. One staff writer described caption writing as:

> . . . Fitting headlines, text blocks and captions to the spirit and content of pictures—"writing square sentences," as we sometimes called it in times of desperation. Writing for pictures—with the words meant to illumine the picture rather than the other way around—enforces a special set of disciplines: economy for one (you don't waste many words when you are working within a framework of two lines precisely forty-three characters long—no more, no less). And you acquire a deep respect for the narrative power of the photograph or illustration . . . they are there as an integral part of what the piece has to say—heart and guts rather than mere decoration.

Nor would a beginner be likely to think of a magazine researcher as a writer. It is certainly true that few *are* writers in the sense of producing by-lined pieces. Many researchers do little more than check manuscripts for accuracy. But some who have earned the confidence of writers and editors contribute measurably to the final product that carries the by-line of one whose label is "staff writer." How this works has been described by Ann Scott, a former *Fortune* researcher who became a writer for *Newsweek*.

> Sometimes the writer-researcher team splits up, dividing parts of the story to cover more ground. This can be most useful, especially for the lengthy, in-depth story that *Fortune* should be doing. The better researchers contribute a great deal to the thesis of their stories, too, and this can include writing memos to writers and editors about positions that should be taken, points that should be included, and the like. Sometimes, too, a researcher does a full written report on some aspect of a story, as I did once on the European chemical industry for a piece on big business in Europe.

In 1971, the more than fifty *Time* researchers became "reporter-researchers." As Publisher Henry Luce III pointed out, the new title describes more fully and precisely what they do. Every week they help shape articles and send queries to more than four hundred *Time* correspondents and stringers around the world. They cull the magazine's extensive reference library. Some routinely search for information in Manhattan's offices and institutions. Several have traveled far afield to interview and observe.

These tasks suggest other dimensions of staff writing. When one of the authors of this book was a staff writer and Washington correspondent for *The Reporter* magazine, most of the work was writing. But about 15 percent of it consisted of discussing article ideas with other correspondents who wanted to write for *The Reporter;* editing and rewriting some articles, and considering, accepting, and rejecting others; and providing information for other *Reporter* writers who were based elsewhere.

Editorial Functions

To obtain a broad view of the many possible tasks of the staff writer, it might help to consider the functions of the editor, for staff writers on many publications are assigned some of these functions or are assigned to help with them:

1. Creating the formula or pattern for a new magazine or reconsidering the formula or pattern for an existing one

2. Long-range planning and planning individual issues

3. Procuring and selecting articles

4. Editing articles

5. Preparing layouts and dummies

6. Selecting, sizing, and cropping pictures

7. Coordinating the work of specialists

Planning Major Articles   One function that staff writers often perform for an editor is planning a major article. An editor of a national magazine said:

> It used to be that we could cover almost any subject in a popular magazine by assigning a very good writer to go to a number of obvious sources, get the necessary facts and figures and dramatize them with a few anecdotes or individual experiences, then put it all together in a neat, well-rounded way. The result would be that the reader would be superficially informed, would quite possibly be entertained, but would be left with very little of real value to him.
>
> Now, on some of the most serious subjects, we find that we are investing as much as two years of time; that we're using not only writers, but (often) teams of researchers to help them. In some cases we're working with research organizations to do basic research which goes far beyond reporting, simply to find out what the reality of the situation is before we can figure out what we're going to say about it, how we're going to treat it in a magazine.

The staffer assigned a major article often finds that he can develop some of his best information through public relations specialists. In fact, these people usually have files of stock articles complete with pictures and captions. They can also provide ideas, fact sheets, and histories. The more alert the PR specialist, the more likely he is to be able to offer exclusive information suited exactly to a writer's needs. Douglas Ann Newsom of Texas Christian University has described how Liz Carpenter, who was press secretary to Lady Bird Johnson when Lyndon Johnson was president, could find an emphasis or slant: "She had something different for every reporter or magazine correspondent. I expressed my amazement, and she said she hadn't even realized she was doing it. But, I promise you, she didn't repeat herself. It was quite a performance." Writers prize the public relations specialist who provides exclusive information.

The Editor Makes Assignments   Staff writers often succeed in winning assignments over free-lancers, for reasons suggested by Joe Anderson, editor of *The Reflector*.

From an editor's point of view, the time and trouble of using a free-lancer legislates against employing him when deadlines are tight—even if it means overloading the staff writer.

Consider the directive, "Go see *Henderson* and turn out a *promotional article* on the *new incentive program*." The sentence is complete for the staff writer and he's off to see Henderson. The [stressed] words require introductions, backgrounds, explanations and—in many cases, examples—for the free-lancer.

What happens when the two get to see Henderson is also worthy of some consideration. My guess is that Henderson will spend from 25 to 50 percent more time with the free-lancer, assuming that he doesn't throw him out of the office in exasperation. In industry, with considerations of proprietary information, outside regulation, and office politics, the free-lancer starts out at a decided disadvantage.

Having been on both sides of the free-lance/staff writer fence, and presently balancing precariously on the pickets as an editor, I would make some highly subjective observations colored by a limited amount of experience: I trust the staff writer fourfold over the free-lancer; I have to, he's mine. I am queasy about sending a free-lancer to a "sensitive" source.

In some cases, of course, staff writers work side by side with free-lancers. And when an editor learns to trust the work of a free-lancer, the difference in making assignments is usually slight. Here, for example, Lucille Enix, editor of *Dallas* magazine, has written one assignment memo to a trusted free-lancer, Carolyn Barta, and another to the magazine's associate editor, Jenny Haynes.

Carolyn Barta

Cover article for the September *Dallas* magazine

Subject: What makes Dallas a top convention city?

Length: Approx. 4,000 words

Deadline: August 1

At this time the city of Dallas is ranked as 8th largest in population in the U.S. Yet, according to the book "World Convention Dates," Dallas ranks something like 4th in conventions. You'll need to get the exact rating and sources from Wes Young of the Convention Bureau on convention ratings. The question is, why does Dallas seem to draw a larger share of conventions as compared to the size of the city?

Part of the answer is in the sales force now working with the Dallas Convention Bureau. Ray Bennison, manager, will introduce you to the sales staff and they will explain their responsibilities.

Another part of the answer is the services available in Dallas to groups holding conventions here—air transportation, hotel and motel rooms available, persons to run registration desks, services of decorators to set up booths and lay out exhibit space, audiovisual equipment rentals, transfer companies to move and store equipment, printers for daily house organs, newsletters, reports that come out of conventions, security guards, business machines and office furniture to run convention business, special telephone services, catering services, special Dallas bus services, florists—Bennison can name more.

The city itself draws some conventions, the climate, citizens, and the convention center and market hall complex.

In sketching what the city has to offer for conventions, describe some of the personalities, inside looks at how the services work immediately on the scene and future planning.

How many persons attended conventions in Dallas last year, what's projected for this year? How much money was spent by persons attending conventions? Both for services and personally? How much business becomes repeat business from conventions held here?

What is the city's potential in the convention business?

Jenny Haynes

Article for the September Visitor's Guide

Subject: Exploring the Dallas Health and Science Museum, Planetarium, and Aquarium

Length: Approx. 3,000 words

Deadline: July 27

This is the visitor's exploration through three museums that illustrate and explain the wonder of life and the universe. It is primarily a descriptive piece with anecdotes of exhibits, objects and events within each museum. It is not a history of how the museums came to be.

What can the visitor find when he visits? Can he participate with the content in the museums? How? Where are the museums located—the highway number, not the local name of the highway, helps get the visitor there.

H. D. Carmichael is in charge of the Health and Science museum and the Planetarium. The Dallas Park Department is in charge of the Aquarium.

In the Aquarium, you might describe some of the sea life, why certain species were selected for Dallas and how they live.

These memos are rich in lessons. First, they represent the kind of work that staffers do on some magazines. That is, one who devotes much of his time to writing or editing manuscripts may also be assigned to write memos of this kind to free-lancers and to other staff writers.

Second, although one memo is to a free-lancer and the other to a staff writer, it is obvious that the editor has confidence in both writers. Because Carolyn Barta, the free-lancer, had already written perceptive articles for *Dallas*, the editor knew that she could handle the convention article capably. Perhaps, though, if Editor Lucille Enix had been assigning the article to an untried free-lancer, she would have written in much greater detail. Or, like the editor of *The Reflector*, who was quoted above, the staff editor might have experienced doubt that the untried free-lancer could bring the article off with the competence, dispatch, and knowledge of the magazine's readers that a staff writer would exhibit.

Third, note that both memos focus on the length and substance of the articles. Carolyn Barta's article should carry this fact about Dallas conventions and answer that question for the readers. The article by Jenny Haynes should cover this aspect of the museums and describe these features. In neither case is the editor attempting to dictate writing style or technique. The writers are professionals; and, although the editor's perspective is likely to aid them in revising before their articles are published, the writers decide the approach and the treatment.

The Editor as Critic   All these are important lessons for the staff editor. The care and feeding of free-lance writers may be his most important duty. This does *not* mean that the staffer must pamper the writer. Often, in fact, the staff editor who is considering a manuscript can help a writer by offering a caustic critique. When and *with whom* to be harsh is, of course, a nice matter of balance and psychology.

This aspect of the work of the staffer can be illustrated graphically by citing the experience of Peter Sandman. A talented writer who began to free-lance while he was an undergraduate at Princeton, Sandman became an editor of a new publication called *The Magazine* while he was a graduate student at Stanford. When one of his good friends submitted an article on college athletes, Sandman wrote this critique:

> The information is here. There are three main problems with the piece as it stands: (1) it isn't focused enough; (2) it is top heavy with general quotations instead of specific cases; and (3) it is a bit too involuted, and hence a little dull. Let me take these one at a time.
>
> 1. If I read you right, your thesis is as follows: College athletes have their existence on campus defined for them

as *athlete* and nothing else. For the man who *wants* to be athlete and nothing else, that's fine; but for the man who considers himself a student or a person as well, it leads to tensions and frustrations. The pressure comes from all sides. Faculty and "intellectual" classmates believe (often correctly) that admission standards have been relaxed for the athlete, and conclude (often incorrectly) that he is a dumb bunny with no interests or capabilities beyond athletics—hence, they despise, resent, and patronize him. The athletic department, meanwhile, aided by alumni, administrators, and other boosters, prefer that the athlete stick to his own kind and concentrate on the game. The result is a kind of isolation—social, academic, political, and in all other ways. Some of the campus may worship an athlete, and some may scorn him, but nobody knows him beyond the stereotype except his fellow athletes. Yet athletes, more and more, are real people with intellectual and political interests; and there aren't too many dumb jocks left.

This is essentially a simple enough thesis. It can be expressed in syllogism pretty easily: (a) Athletes are more and more like other students; (b) athletes are under great pressure to keep to themselves; (c) therefore, athletes are increasingly unhappy with their lot. Despite the fact that this is clearly a thesis article, you have written it more like a rambling exploration of the college athlete—it is never clear to the reader if you know what you are trying to prove. I don't, of course, want an article that begins "I am trying to prove that . . ." and goes on to say "Point one is . . . ," "Point two is . . . ," etc. Nevertheless, the structure should be there; we have a right to hear your hypothesis before we see your evidence and to see your evidence in some kind of order. I should never read a paragraph and think, "That's interesting, but so what? What's he trying to prove with this paragraph?" Nor should I have to react, as I did a few times, that "He made that point already," or "He's going around in circles." I think it might be helpful if you set the piece up in syllogistic form and wrote it in that order, marshalling all evidence for and comment on Point One before moving on to Point Two, etc. Keep the presentation smooth and light, of course, not like a debater's outline—but make it orderly as well.

2. Your conclusions about college athletes are neither difficult to understand nor difficult to accept. There is little reason, therefore, for extensive quotations reexplaining and reasserting the same points. Some of your paragraphs seem to have the following structure: "*A* is true. *X* says *A* is true. *Y* says *A* is true. *Z* says *A* is true. Therefore, *A* is true." This is more or less justifiable to the extent that *A* is a complicated and arguable statement, *X*, *Y*, and *Z* are certified experts, and what they say is unusually well ex-

pressed. Often, however, *A* is a simple, well-accepted proposition, *X*, *Y*, and *Z* are unknowns, and their prose is unimpressively identical with each other and with your own. Such paragraphs become incredibly tedious.

What you need, I think, is fewer quotations and more examples—specific anecdotes, in your words or the words of the athletes who experienced them. Especially desirable would be one *long* anecdote which exemplifies as much of your hypothesis as possible—the high school hero wined and dined, finally picking a school for mixed athletic and other reasons, arriving on campus to find that freshman place-kickers are not heroes, but that they are required to live in athletic dorms and major in health, discovering that many classmates and most profs ("Professor McGillicuddy in the English Dept. said . . .") don't think too much of jocks, learning that he has been invited to the college as an athlete and he damn well better stay an athlete period, and finally giving up, or revolting, or whatever. This story should be told in good quasi-fictional narrative style; its purpose should be to give flesh and blood and color to your theories. Similarly, a number of shorter anecdotes should be added at various points to make it clearer (and more interesting) what really goes on. Quotes do not do the job, I think. They add a little authenticity and prove that you've done your homework, but they don't give the verisimilitude and sense of reality that narrative accounts do.

3. I think the problem of too complex, involuted, academic, and dull a style will be very much minimized when the structure is clearer and some of the quotes have been replaced with anecdotes. Still, you should try to change it a bit yourself. What you want is just a bit less wordiness, and a little more colorful vocabulary, a few less weasel words and explanatory clauses, and a bit simpler sentence structure. I hesitate to give examples, because I *don't* want you writing in my style instead of your own, but look at your very first sentence and compare:

The seizure of buildings by campus activists in April, 1968, in addition to changing for all time the relationship between students and administration on the American college campus, served to highlight the ambiguous position of the college athlete in 1970. A now-famous picture . . .	*When Columbia University fell apart in April, 1968, everybody knew that college life would never again be the same. But amid the riots and seizures and declarations of war, at least one thing seemed permanently unchanged: the role of the campus athlete. A now-famous picture . . .*

You can do better than both of these, I hope, but the passage on the right is, I think, somewhat more readable than the one on the left.

This passage is only about one-fourth of Sandman's critique, but it is enough to suggest both the flavor and substance. Critiques are never written in such detail unless the staff editor likes the article and expects his magazine to publish a revision, and they are rarely as long as this one. In this case, a revision was purchased.

It is important to point out why critiques are seldom written at such length. Many a writer has complained bitterly that, given detailed directions, he could bring his first draft up to the publishable level. This may be true in a few cases. More often, though, the editor decides quite accurately that, although the subject may be timely and provocative and all the information may be in hand, *this writer* is probably incapable of fashioning an acceptable piece. Without necessarily thinking in such terms, the staffer is actually making a distinction between writing as craft and writing as art. In effect, he is saying: "I could devote several hours to typing a critique that would suggest how this writer can use anecdote, example, illustration—all the techniques of appealing prose—and improve this article markedly. And the writer could probably follow my directions. But even though he'd get the *craft* right, something would be missing. He wouldn't have the flair and the style of the artist."

An editor of *Playboy* who has been through thousands of manuscripts that he considers "semiliterate" suggests another reason for rejecting manuscripts with a printed form, saying of many who submit to *Playboy*, "They couldn't write a letter to the gas company."

The Writer as Editor   On some publications, a staff writer *is* the editor—or vice versa. That is, many publications are produced by small staffs, some consisting of one person. Patricia Newport, who was for a time the editor of a fraternity magazine, wrote most of the first issues herself. She also wrote part of a special issue that was published the following spring, but she asked for contributions from fraternity members for the bulk of the issue. Her experience with amateur writers is instructive:

> This being the first time that I had done this, I was not explicit enough in my directions about what to write— people do want tight guidelines and need them or else you end up with an article having twenty different subjects, a lot of beginnings and no ends, i.e., the result is a lot of rambling thoughts. . . .
>
> All of the people were amateur writers, flattered beyond belief that they were asked to write an article. For this reason, I had to be careful with my editing, since most of them had worked for months on their articles and thought they were perfect. When they handed their pieces in, they did so with 101 excuses for why they were so poor, knowing full well that I had better think that they were masterpieces. For the most part, I ran them as they were, with minor construction and grammatical changes. I was careful

not to change the tone of each, since that was "the sign of
the author." Of course, after the magazine came out, they
all wanted to know the reactions to their articles.

The writer-editor can experience an exhilaration unknown to
most who perform only one role. Patricia Adams, who went straight
from the University of Miami to running a company magazine, has
expressed memorably her sense of excitement and pride.

My fifteenth issue has just come out. I've written every
blessed word in every magazine.

The magazine has progressed, although it's awfully
crammed. It's hard to cover 7,000 people, scattered all
over the country and working at different jobs, in just
sixteen pages. There's a terrific educational job to do with
it. The company grew so fast and the people were lost.

I've been reading, studying, and experimenting with the
magazine. Industrial journalism, if it's to be good, entails a
great deal more than the basic principles. It's a wonderful
challenge. The money's good—everything's good about it,
I think. It takes a lot of basic psychology—well, let's just
say common sense. You aren't just a reporter.

I'm trying to tell the story in terms of people. If top management wants to sell them on something, I don't talk in
terms of generalities; I try to find people who exemplify the
idea we're trying to put across. This brings everything
home and serves two purposes: informs and gives a few
deserved pats on the back.

I've tried to make the magazine very warm. I seem to have
succeeded. The International Council of Industrial Editors
gave me a high rating on content and writing. And the
people seem to put a lot of stock in the magazine—I suppose because it's their only real source of information
about the company.

CHAPTER TEN EXERCISES

1. Based on your interest in the subjects it covers, purchase a copy
of one of these magazines—*Sunset, Fortune, Newsweek, Time, Business
Week, Ski, Rudder,* or *Dallas*. Read the entire issue and write 500 words
to describe what was wrong with that issue. Were the articles too
long? Too short? Have the editors chosen the wrong articles?

2. Create the formula for a new magazine by listing ten subjects you
would include in the first issue.

3. You are the editor of a small specialty magazine published in New
York but distributed nationally. There are four other people on your

editorial staff. Choose a focus for your magazine (a sport, a hobby, an industry, and so on), then discuss how you will organize your staff to provide national coverage without leaving New York. How will you get information from other parts of the country?

CHAPTER 11
The Free-Lance Writer

Beginning free-lancers have one advantage over prospective staff writers—they do not need to persuade anyone to hire them full-time in order to start writing. In fact, many free-lance writers have eased into staff positions by becoming frequent and reliable contributors to a magazine. But a full-time position may not be your goal, especially after you have experienced the freedom and independence of free-lance writing. However, along with those attractive qualities are a number of constraints that make the free-lancer's lot less appealing.

HOW A FREE-LANCER OPERATES

Many aspiring journalists do not realize that free-lance writing is a business that in order to be successful, must be run efficiently and economically. The commodity for sale is magazine articles. In most cases, the free-lancer will be the business's writer, reporter, typist, accountant, advertising director, and salesperson. Beginners often expect to spend most of their time in the first two roles and are surprised when they discover that the last four can require as much or more effort. It is important to realize that being successful in these roles will enable a free-lancer to devote more time to writing and reporting.

Query Letters

A free-lance business is a lot like a mail-order company, without the benefit of a catalog. Instead the writer must rely on query letters that are written proposals to editors describing articles the free-lancer would like to write. (Chapter Fourteen discusses how to write effective query letters.) Once a query is in the mail, the free-lancer must be prepared to do a lot of waiting. Although some do reply sooner, it's not unusual for a national magazine to take six or eight weeks to respond to a query. Of course in the interim, an industrious free-lancer expects to be working on other articles and other queries, because there is no guarantee of when the response will arrive.

When the important letter finally comes, it will either make all the waiting worthwhile or make the free-lancer wonder whether another career might be in order. Many magazines rely on form-letter rejection slips which often provide little or no information about why a query was turned down. A proposal may be rejected for any number of reasons, including these:

1. the query letter was poorly written,

2. the idea was not suitable for the magazine,

3. the editor had already assigned a similar piece to another writer, or

4. the magazine had covered the subject in a recent issue.

Some editors do take the time to explain why they rejected queries; such responses can be very instructive to free-lancers who read them carefully. Consider the following rejection letters and how the free-lancer who received them might feel:

Thank you for giving us the opportunity to consider your article proposal. We appreciate your interest in contributing to *Ms.*, but unfortunately we cannot assign your proposed piece because it does not fit in with our current editorial plans.

Our editorial decisions are based on space allowance, material already covered or scheduled for future issues, as well as the projected interests of our readers.

Due to the number of articles, stories, and ideas coming into the magazine each week, it is impossible for us to send you a personal and detailed reply. We want to assure you, however, that the time saved on letter-writing has been spent on careful consideration of your idea by members of the *Ms.* staff.

Thank you very much for your inquiry about writing an article for HADASSAH MAGAZINE.

While we would like to answer every letter personally, the volume of our correspondence makes it impossible to give you a personal reply.

HADASSAH MAGAZINE, as a matter of policy, does not assign articles to authors who have not previously written for us. We do, however, give a careful and considered reading to all manuscripts submitted to us. Many articles which appear in HADASSAH were unsolicited.

The optimal length for our articles is 1,500 to 3,000 words. We pay 12¢ a word with a maximum of $300.00. Payable upon publication of the article. If you have pictures related to your story, include them. We pay $35.00 for each black and white photo we use.

We would welcome hearing from you.

Thank you for your article query on behavioral therapy. Although we cannot use this particular idea for the magazine, we do hope that you will send any other ideas that may be suitable for FAMILY HEALTH; we'd be happy to take a look at them.

P.S. Along with your next query, could you please include a few current writing samples? Standard procedure for freelance writers who are new to FAMILY HEALTH. Thanks.

I'm afraid the answer is No on your proposal for an article about————. That's one of the problems, I'm not sure what the article is about. The fact that women live longer? That's hardly news. Besides, the real point is that we almost never do articles *about*. We're doing a much more personal and anecdotal kind of journalism, as I explained to you when you came by. That's why we liked the birds. No articles about phobias—but a good piece on someone who overcame one. That's the path.

The first letter gives the writer little indication of why the query was turned down, whereas the last one contains a great deal of information. The writer who received this rejection knew three things right away:

1. She had not done an effective job of presenting her idea. The editor wasn't even sure what the story was about.

2. The magazine was not interested in that kind of story.

3. A previous article she had written for the magazine was more the sort of article the editor was looking for. Other suggestions for stories of a similar nature might be well received.

An Article Idea Is Accepted

If the response to a query is an acceptance, it generally comes in one of two forms. The editor may make the assignment entirely "on spec" (speculation), meaning that he or she indicates interest in seeing a manuscript usually of a specified length and by a specified date, and agrees to pay a certain amount for the article if it is accepted, zero if it is not. Or the editor may make the assignment on contract with a provision of a "kill fee" of 10 to 20 percent of the acceptance price if the article is rejected. In the first case, the writer takes all the financial risk in doing the article; in the second case, the magazine shares some of the risk by guaranteeing the writer a minimum payment. Editors also may indicate whether or not they will pay research expenses for an article, such as long distance calls, travel costs, or other related out-of-pocket expenses the writer may encounter. If the editor does not provide this information, you should inquire about it before starting work. If you have to pay expenses yourself, that may affect the kind of research you choose to undertake.

Getting Paid

Magazines pay either "on acceptance" or "on publication." Because a magazine may not publish an article for many months after accepting it, payment on publication can put quite a strain on the free-lancer's monthly budget. Unfortunately for beginning writers, most small magazines pay on publication because they operate on strict monthly editorial budgets and do not have the resources to pay now for articles they will publish later. Even worse, the mortality rate among small magazines is very high, which means that one may fold having accepted an article but without having published it. The writer may get back the article, but it isn't likely to be accompanied by a check.

Payment for articles varies widely. Most large national magazines pay more than small regional or local ones do. Some pay a flat rate per word of the published article. That means a writer whose 2500-word article is cut to 1500 words by an editor is losing more than space in the magazine. More often, however, magazines agree to pay a specified amount for an article and do not change that amount if the story is heavily edited or cut. Beginners may earn as little as $50 for a story in a small magazine or a short item in a large one. More experienced writers earn hundreds of dollars for their articles, and very well established free-lancers may earn thousands for a single piece. It's a long road from the hundreds-per-article to thousands-per-article stage, one that few writers travel very quickly.

Part-time Jobs Supplement Free-Lance Work

It doesn't take much calculating to see that free-lancing is not a lucrative occupation for beginners. Most have to rely on part-time jobs or other sources of income to supplement their earnings as writers. However, this necessity has the advantage of forcing the free-lancer to get out of the house and into the world, which is where most good ideas come from. Skillful free-lancers seek part-time jobs that either provide them with other kinds of writing or editing experience or which may produce material for articles. One of the authors of this book worked part-time as an editor and writer at a contract research organization concerned with issues in social science. These published articles came directly from subjects she encountered in her work there, and many of the research scientists she met have proven to be valuable sources of information for other articles.

THE ADVANTAGES OF FREE-LANCING

So far the disadvantages in a free-lance writing career seem enormous. Fortunately, there are a few facts about the magazine publishing world that provide the free-lancer some advantages.

Magazines Need Free-Lancers

Many magazines want national coverage but must operate with very limited staffs. They *need* free-lancers to give their publications the national focus they cannot achieve alone from their editorial offices. They do not have the bureaus of Time-Life, Inc., to gather information from different parts of the country, so they must rely on stringers or free-lancers to send them stories.

Next, look at the financial arrangement from the magazine's point of view. When an assignment is given on spec, the magazine gets an article on a subject that the editor has declared to be of interest to it for an initial outlay of the cost of a postage stamp. If the article is rejected, the magazine hasn't lost any money. Even if a kill fee is involved, the cost to the magazine is minimal. If the article is accepted, the magazine has acquired a publishable story, and that, after all, is what magazines need. From a financial standpoint, there is no reason an editor should not ask to see an article on spec, provided the free-lancer can convince him or her that there's a good chance the final product will be publishable. While these arrangements may be a hardship to the writer, he or she is still being given the chance to make it into print. One must consider the long view!

One Idea Leads to Another

Another factor working in the free-lancer's favor is that there are no restrictions on squeezing every last drop out of research on a particular subject. You can't sell the same article to more than one magazine, but you can sell different articles that use the same material. Usually this involves approaching the subject from a different angle, appealing to a different audience.

Sometimes one article simply leads to another if the writer is observant enough to notice the path. While covering a ski race for *Women's Sports* magazine, one writer met a contestant in the race who she felt would be a good subject for a *Women's Sports* profile. She sold the idea and traveled to a freestyle skiing training camp in order to interview the skier. She wrote the article and then decided that a piece on freestyle training camps would be suitable for another magazine, *Sportswoman.* The editor accepted the idea, and the writer went to one of the country's top freestyle training camps to do some interviews. While there, she met another skier, a young girl whose coach claimed that she could already do tricks that no other woman on the freestyle circuit was able to do. Not one to miss an opportunity, the writer interviewed the girl, took her picture, and sold both to *Women's Sports.*

Perhaps the ultimate example of how a writer can exploit a subject was described by Bruce Bliven, Jr. in an article titled "My Table Tennis Racket" that appeared in *The Atlantic*. As a beginning free-lancer, Bliven had managed to extract an assignment from *Life* to do a story about the national ping-pong champion. *Life* bought the article for $1000 but never published it. Bliven took the piece to *Look* after updating it and was rewarded by a check for $500. *Look* subsequently ran a one-page photo of the champion with a 200-word caption. Bliven then sold his story to *Esquire* for $400. This time the entire piece was printed. Several years later, he suggested another story on the ping-pong hero, who had managed to retain his title, to the new *Sports Illustrated*. They bought it for $750. At the time Bliven wrote *The Atlantic* story, the champion had finally retired, but the intrepid author still hoped for one more comeback.

Timeless and Seasonal Articles

Time can also function on the free-lancer's side—not the time it takes to get a query answered but the time it takes for a magazine to be published. Most monthly magazines have lead times of two to three months: that is, they are produced in the editorial offices two to three months before they are sold on the newsstands. This means that a magazine has to appear timely without actually being timely. Such magazines have to relinquish coverage of breaking news stories to weekly or daily publications, and instead concentrate on material that has enduring newsworthy characteristics. For example, a monthly magazine like *Women's Sports* cannot publish a story about who won a particular tournament in June because in June the editors are working on their September issue. By the time the magazine hit the stands, the story would be old news. Instead, the magazine might try to cover the same event from a different angle—such as what the future plans of the winner might be or whether there was some promising newcomer there to watch for in the future.

Because of the long lead times, editors have a great need for two kinds of articles. Seasonal stories are written long before the relevant season arrives. A free-lancer should think like a department store and advertise his Christmas specials in July! Editors also need stories that are not time-bound, stories which could be published at any time of year without losing their newsworthy qualities. Many magazines try to keep a supply of such articles on hand to use in emergencies when an assigned piece does not come in on time or arrives in unpublishable condition. Free-lancers should not hesitate to point out this aspect of articles they propose to editors in query letters.

THE FINANCES OF FREE-LANCING

An important part of running a free-lance writing business is keeping records for the Internal Revenue Service. This is no mere bureaucratic detail; it is the free-lancer's primary means of protecting his or her income from being eaten away by taxes. As in any business, the goal in free-lancing is to make a profit, but at tax time your primary objective will be to whittle it away as much as possible. This is done by deducting legitimate business expenditures from the total amount of payments received from magazines. The amount of income tax you owe is a percentage of that final figure; it's to your advantage to reduce that number as much as possible.

In general, any expense you incur that is *directly* related to your work as a free-lance writer is deductible. The list of legitimate deductions includes the costs of such items as postage for query letters, editorial correspondence, or mailing in articles; long distance phone calls to editors or sources of information; office supplies, such as typing paper, ribbons, and so on; magazines you buy for the purpose of your work; miscellaneous expenses such as photocopying charges for research materials, parking garage fees paid during reporting expeditions, or tapes for interviewing. One of the greatest boons to a mobile free-lancer is the mileage deduction allowed for use of your personal car for business purposes. The rate changes from year to year, but has been as high as 17 cents per mile.

Perhaps the largest deduction for many free-lancers is that allowed for home offices. Writers who qualify for this deduction can include expenses such as percentages of their mortgage payments or rent, property taxes, utility bills, and phone bills. However, there are very strict limitations on who qualifies for these deductions. The best way to find out if you do is to consult a knowledgable tax accountant.

The only way you'll know how much you've spent on your work at the end of the year is to keep accurate, ongoing records. A journal divided into categories in which you record the expense, its purpose, and the date it was incurred accomplishes this task quite well. It is also important to keep receipts whenever they are available. An envelope stapled into the journal is a convenient way to collect them until tax time. As an additional form of documentation for the IRS in case you are ever audited, you should keep copies of all your letters to editors and sources, as well as your manuscripts.

An experience of an author of this book illustrates how the finances of free-lancing operate. While working part-time as an editor at a research organization, she learned about the activities of groups whose purpose is to help women reenter the job market after many years as homemakers. She also found out that a national conference was scheduled that would bring together people working in these "displaced homemaker" programs from various parts of the country. The conference was in Baltimore, Maryland; the writer was in Seattle, Washington.

The free-lancer queried *Working Woman* magazine on an article about displaced homemaker programs, emphasizing the job-oriented thrust of most of them. In the query, she also mentioned the upcoming conference and suggested that attending it would help her write the article. The reply was favorable. *Working Woman* agreed to assign the story and to pay $500 for it on publication. The editor also specified that while the magazine would pay the conference registration fee of $30, it would not pay for the writer's airfare or other travel expenses.

The writer decided to combine attendance at the conference with a trip to New York to talk with editors at several magazines about future assignments. Most free-lance writers find that an occasional trip to New York for face-to-face exchanges with editors they correspond with regularly is well worth the expense. And she convinced the research organization to fund a third of the expenses of her trip to the conference in exchange for a fact-finding report upon her return.

While on the trip, the writer kept a daily record of her expenses. She arranged to stay with friends in both Baltimore and New York, so there were no hotel charges. Here are the items she recorded:

Airfare	$260.00 (discount rate)
Conference Fee	30.00
Taxi fares to and from conference	7.50
Meals	25.00 (Baltimore)
	40.00 (New York)
Train fare from Baltimore to New York	22.00
Taxi fares in New York	10.00
Mileage to airport in Seattle	8.50 (.17/mile, 50 miles)
Bus to airport in New York	4.50
TOTAL	$407.50

When the trip was over, the writer divided her expenses into three categories: (1) to be paid by *Working Woman*, (2) to be paid by the research organization, and (3) to be paid by the writer herself. As agreed, she sent the magazine a bill for $30 along with the completed manuscript. She then billed the research organization for one-third of the expenses incurred in relation to the conference, except for the registration. That came to $100. The remaining expenses, $277.50, were recorded in her accounts book as business expenses to be deducted from her total receipts at the end of the year.

Of course, one way to view the financial outcome of this situation is to say that the writer earned only $222.50 for writing the article ($500 fee minus $277.50 expenses). But that does not take into account the assignments she generated while in New York. At least one article for which the writer was paid $500 came as a direct result of meeting with an editor there, and others came indirectly, aided by the personal contacts she made during the trip. The adage "you've got to spend money to make money" applies as much to free-lancing as to any other business. The writer's task is to decide when and how to take that risk.

Compiling the information you need for income tax purposes will tell you how well your business is doing from a financial standpoint.

In addition, journal and letter copies can serve as reminders of when you sent queries or manuscripts, and how long it was between your submission and the response. And once you are a successful, prosperous free-lancer, you'll be able to look back on those lean early years and chuckle over the empty-looking "payments received" page. But for the present, concentrate instead on offsetting those few precious payments with all the deductions the government allows.

CHAPTER ELEVEN EXERCISES

1. If you decided to become a full-time free-lance writer, how many queries and articles would you expect to write each month? How would you organize your activities? How much time would you spend researching and writing a query?

2. Assume you are the editor of a national magazine that relies heavily on free-lance writers. How would you organize your exchange of ideas with them? Consider some of the problems you might face, such as two good writers who want to do similar stories, a usually reliable writer who turns in an unpublishable piece two days before deadline, or staff writers who resent your giving choice assignments to free-lancers. How would you handle these situations?

3. Examine the financial difficulties of free-lance writing by projecting how many articles you would need to write each year, and how much you would have to be paid for them, in order to make what you consider a reasonable living. Don't forget to deduct federal and state income taxes from the gross amount.

CHAPTER 12
Working with Photographers

It has taken less than a century for photography to overcome journalism's bias toward print. In the 1880s the halftone photoengraving process was perfected; in the 1890s a way was developed to run off photographs on a rotary press, making it possible to print photographs in newspapers and mass magazines. Thus, magazine writers have long had to compete for readers' attention with the color and allure of photographs beside their articles. As a result, magazines have been much more visually innovative than newspapers, and magazine writers have learned to coordinate their efforts with those of photographers.

For example, *People* is basically a picture magazine. Some have described it as television in print. It runs about 15,000 words an issue (*Time* runs three times that many), and its text and photographs offer a flashy, quick look and read into the lives of celebrities. Although most magazines cannot be described as "picture magazines," editors are more and more aware that photography is as powerful a tool as the words it accompanies.

THE WRITER-PHOTOGRAPHER RELATIONSHIP

Many free-lancers work with photographers on article assignments; most staff writers do. In fact, unless the staff writers are employed by magazines that do not publish pictures, the staff writers may spend a large fraction of their time on aspects of photography—anything from hiring free-lance photographers to making layouts of their own words along with the photographers' pictures.

Should a writer try to shortcut this process and *become* a photographer? The prospect may be especially attractive to a free-lance writer; perhaps his income would double if he could illustrate his own articles. A staff writer, too, might enhance his income by learning to take pictures. These are alluring prospects. Unfortunately, they are seldom realistic. The experiences of many who have tried to become true photojournalists by developing talents in writing and photography suggest that striking a balance is almost impossible. A journalist is likely to be so much more skilled as a writer than as a photographer—or so much more skilled as a photographer than as writer—that one talent far overshadows the other. A photographer whose pictures satisfy the exacting demands of the picture editor is not likely to write well enough to satisfy the text editors; but his pictures are almost certain to be light years ahead of those taken by anyone who writes regularly for the magazine.

There are related dangers. The talented writer who tries to develop his photographic ability may be stealing time from writing that is actually needed to develop his primary talent. It may be, too, that one who develops both talents to the point of publishing words and pictures regularly could have written (or taken pictures) for more demanding and prestigious publications if he had been content to develop one talent or the other. If this assessment is negative, it is nonetheless drawn from the experiences of many journalists. Most writers must learn to work *with* photographers rather than working *as* photographers and vice versa.

Photographers, like writers, are highly individual. Some expect the writer to suggest shots and even visualize pictures. This is especially true of photographers who are accustomed to working on public relations and advertising assignments. They are used to producing pictures on order—usually *exact* orders. Thus, Charlene Brown, who now teaches journalism at Indiana University, recalls from her experience in advertising:

> When I went out with a photographer, I had almost always designed the layout into which both his shots and my copy were going to fit. It was always useful—and good politics—to know what I wanted, quite specifically. It was to our mutual advantage if I could provide the photographer with a sketch of what I had in mind—without infringing on his artistic creativity, of course. If I knew I wanted a picture on the right-hand page, that information helped the photographer compose his picture so that the lines of force were not running off the edge of the page to the right, but into the layout to the left.
>
> My mother, an advertising supervisor who works a lot with photographers and artists, uses a system of tear sheets. She includes with her instructions samples she has culled from magazines or wherever which illustrate the mood, positioning, etc., she is after. This is quite effective for conveying the sense of her intentions. I also found this system quite useful since most photographers cannot be expected to come up with genius ideas every time they take an ad shot. . . . The fundamental advice from my experience is: know yourself what you want, be as specific as you can, and then let the photographer take as many pictures as he wants. Vague instructions waste everyone's time—the photographer's, the subject's, and your own. A

rough idea of the layout helps the photographer work within its scope. If the photographer has some great ideas of his own, he can always take his shots in addition to yours. And you can choose.

Many professional photographers are grateful for the sense of purpose in this approach. Ms. Brown also indicated, however, that some magazine photographers would probably be offended by this approach; as a matter of fact, they would be outraged. Camera journalists have developed a strong sense of identity.

In the following quotation, Mary Ord of *Sunset* presents another point of view on the relationship between magazine writer and photographer—and on how the two can work together effectively.

Unless a story has no prospects of photography, or the writer is taking his own pictures, the writer will be dealing with a photographer. The writer sets the scope of the story (though great photography may unexpectedly dictate a shift of emphasis), but since the photography is done before the layout, the photographer doesn't have to work within that sort of rigid framework.

The quality of the photographs makes the difference between a two-column and a two-page story, no matter how worthy the topic. So the writer chooses the photographer whom he thinks can do the job best. Some photographers are best at studio shots, some at wildlife shooting, some at house photography, and some at photographing children.

The writer tries to tell his photographer as much about his story as possible. If the story calls for going out of the studio to work, the writer tries to give the best idea he can what the situation will be, what lighting there is, what distance the photographer may be shooting from, how much legwork may be involved in getting the shots. The writer should say if he just doesn't know what they'll find, or if he has specific shots in mind.

If all this is communicated, usually the photography comes out all right. But my first experience working with a photographer was a disaster. The story was a Christmas crafts project and I signed up the only photographer who had any free time that week. The story required a how-to picture and one of the finished project, both to be done in the studio. For the how-to shot, nothing we tried seemed right after half a day's work. Standing there in the studio with the lights and all, I thought, "This glamorous world of magazine work sure isn't much fun." Finally I went and got my art director to set up the shot. It turned out that this photographer's forte was wildlife shooting and he was as new to studio work as I was.

Doing your own photography is encouraged. If you are competent at it, you are more useful. It is good if a writer can take at least adequate scouting photographs to help him sell his story to editors, to help determine if it is worthwhile to send a full-time photographer back, and also to show that photographer what kind of conditions he will find. Writers often do their own photography if the story is some distance away and is not of certain enough value to warrant the expense of a photographer's time.

In some cases, you, as a free-lancer or staff writer, may be assigned by a magazine's editors to accompany the photographer to produce an article. There must be a meeting of the minds as to whether words or pictures will determine the direction of the story. If the article is primarily a visual story, the photographer should have the right to chart the course. But if the words will dominate the published story, you should demand the right to shape it.

Even if you're not at all certain that you should be a photographer, taking a beginner's course in photography will help you understand its language, problems, and joys. As soon as you learn the fusion of words and pictures, you'll begin to understand the late Wilson Hicks, a picture editor, who was, in the view of some of the leading photographers, the most perceptive judge of pictures in the world. On retiring from *Life,* Hicks wrote brilliantly in *Words and Pictures:*

Man, in understanding what happens around him, depends primarily on his sight, secondarily on his hearing. In journalism, which makes use of words only, the words bear the entire burden of re-creating for the reader an experience undergone by someone else. Printed words being visual representations of spoken words, the sense of hearing is basically related to the act of reading. The eye, in conveying the sound symbols to the brain, appropriates the work of the ear, so to speak, and performs to a very limited degree its own peculiar function which, to put it quite simply, is to see. In journalism which makes use of words and pictures, to the stimuli of sound symbols there are added the stimuli of the forms of reality represented in the photograph. Together these stimuli call forth a collaboration of the two senses by which the quality of a re-created experience is enormously increased, and brought much closer to actual experience.

This particular coming together of the verbal and visual mediums of communication is, in a word, photojournalism. Its elements, used in combination, do not produce a third and new medium. Instead, they form a complex in which each of the components retains its fundamental character. . . .

The intent of photojournalism is to create, through combined use of the visual and verbal mediums, a oneness of communicative result. If a fusion of the mediums could come about on the printed page, the problem could be simplified to the extent that only one perceptive act on the reader's part would be required. As noted above, such a coalescence is impossible. A fusion does occur, but not on the printed page. It occurs in the reader's mind.

WRITING TO PICTURES

When writers have worked with photographers, their next task comes into sharp focus. Mary Ord suggests the best procedure for those who are writing to pictures. She speaks of the *headline,* which is the title of the article; the *display wording,* which refers to any type that is larger than the body print of an article; and the *captions,* which are the explanatory words accompanying a picture.

Writing to pictures is an important element of staff writing. We are told that when *Sunset* readers turn to an article, they look at the pictures first, read the headline and any other display wording second, read captions third, and then—if they are still interested—they'll read the lead (hopefully more). From these few elements the reader should get the gist of the article. *Sunset* articles have bold-face kick-ins in captions and leads to draw the reader's eye. So these words are especially key ones. They should say as much as possible; it's no time for leisurely writing. We try to avoid *a, an, the,* and prepositions as the first word so the reader gets to the key words quickly.

The headline, captions, and lead should be written out of the pictures. The headline should summarize the situation most directly; that is, the reader should be able to look at the pictures, then look at the head and have it sum up the point the pictures are making.

For example, in a story you see a map of a road running the length of Baja California and four pictures of different Mexican-looking scenes. The head says, "Should you try the Baja road this year? Now or soon is the best time. Here is *Sunset*'s report." The reader knows what he is getting. In another story, photographs show different baskets woven from flat strips which could be clay. They hold rolls and bread. Three other pictures show step by step the weaving of the strips which here look like some kind of dough. The head says, "The bread basket looks good enough to eat. (But don't nibble.) You roll, weave, and bake baker's clay."

If the pictures were at all puzzling, the reader now knows what the story is about.

After the headline, the next chance the writer has to attract the reader is in the captions. Caption writing requires that the writer really know what is going on in the picture, and more. The caption should *not* just restate what is obviously happening in the picture. Here's a simple example. With a picture of a hillside blooming with ice plant and daisies, the caption could have said jus⁺ "Ice plant and daisies cover a Southern California hillside." But instead it said, "Purple ice plant and daisy have been in bloom since midwinter." Now, besides knowing what is in the colorful picture, the reader gets a little more information to start him thinking. The caption writer should acknowledge what is going on that's clearly visible in the picture, then give more information or point out something less apparent in the photo to make the reader look more closely. The caption should draw the reader *in* to the photo.

The boldface words of the caption demand thought on the part of the writer; generally, here is the place for whatever clever writing you can muster, some alliteration or metaphor, for example, as long as it's used to amplify the photograph . . . and as long as it's done in the space allotted. Sometimes, when a series of pictures show the steps in a project, it is a good idea to start the caption for each picture with a boldface number to show the sequence clearly. This helps the reader know exactly what the pictures are telling him.

Of course, there are variations on this approach. On the *Field & Stream* annual, staff writers fashion captions for pictures that are generated outside the staff to go with commissioned manuscripts that the staff writer has no part in producing. In such cases, the staffer searches through the manuscript or does research on his own to find information to amplify the photographs. At *Business Week*, the copy desk writes the captions, using information from the copy to describe the photographs. If the photograph is of a prominent figure, they summarize his stand or accomplishment from the copy. At *National Geographic*, a special writing staff produces captions from the material in the article and from their own research.

Writing Captions

Many writers have discovered that they can write most successfully to a single picture by performing a simple trick: Imagining that the picture is the lead of a story and the caption is a continuation that explains and amplifies the lead. It is essential, however, that the writer first determine what is obvious in the picture and what must be explained.

Most captions can be written well following these rules:

Remember   that a caption is an explanatory paragraph that stands alone. Even if there is an accompanying story, the caption does not depend upon it.

Excessive explanation   is a mistake. The word *above* has no place in a caption running under a single picture. And if only a man and a woman are shown, a caption that explains that the man is "left, above" is ridiculous as well as superfluous. Similarly, when only two men are shown and one is identified at "left," pointing out that the other is "at right" or "right" is thoughtless.

The spirit   of the picture must dictate the spirit of the caption. Although captions are, as a general rule, lighter and more colloquial than stories, they also flow out of pictures and are geared to pictures.

The key   details that make pictures—among them names and things that need explanation—are the key words that must come near the beginning of a caption. It is usually a mistake to start a caption with a name, but if a person is the key to a picture, do not make the reader wait for the identification until he reaches the end of the caption.

The rule regarding tense   in captions unfortunately varies from publication to publication. Generally, captions for action pictures start with a sentence in the present tense. This is entirely in keeping with the idea of word-picture fusion: The photographer has captured a moment in time—the picture can be considered "frozen time"—and the words that enhance the moment are in the present tense, heightening the effect. However, sentences that are not so directly related to the picture—for example, references to the action of the subject at another time—are usually written in the past tense. A cardinal rule is that tense should never be changed within a sentence. In general, the writer should make a distinction between action pictures and posed pictures. Action is in the present; posed pictures are past.

WRITING PICTURE STORIES

Meaningful picture stories are essays. They must be planned. In fact, it is doubtful that a great picture story can be composed unless its producers have arrived at a theme or a central idea *before* the photographer starts work. Happy accidents have been known to grow out of haphazard shooting, but the weight of experience is on the side of the picture story that is developed rather than the one that is stumbled on while going through batches of photographs. The role of the writer in building a picture story is not merely accessory to that of the photographer as this step-by-step description of it should make clear:

1. Develop an idea.

2. Present the idea to an editor for discussion.

3. Plan the picture story on the basis of the discussion.

4. Research the story.

5. Brief the photographer on the general plan, then assist him during the making of pictures.

6. Select and organize the pictures.

7. Help an artist make a layout.

8. Write the cutlines and text that fuse word and picture into a graphic presentation.

A finished picture story is usually made up by:

1. Choosing a dominant picture.

2. Facing pictures toward the related text.

3. Avoiding the "rivers of gray" that are caused by captions meeting irregularly near the same level.

4. Arranging similar captions in the same width, type, and number of lines.

5. Focusing simultaneously on a subject or personality as well as a theme or mood.

Writing to a picture story differs markedly from writing to a single picture. The writer must at once focus on a single picture as he writes and remember that he must preserve continuity from photograph to photograph. This can be accomplished by

1. Providing a central copy block that relates to all the pictures and echoes the spirit of the pictures as a group.

2. Ruthlessly holding captions to a minimum. (The reader likes to leap rapidly from picture to picture.)

3. Avoiding superfluous words in direction as well as in description; captions can be related to pictures by proximity, keyed letters or numbers, or arrows.

A perceptive writer can observe a scene and describe it keenly, in rich or simple prose. But few written descriptions can compete for truth with pictures. As the philosopher Suzanne K. Langer has observed: "The correspondence between a word picture and a visible object can never be as close as that between the object and its photograph." The ancient Chinese had another way of expressing it: A picture is worth ten thousand words.

CHAPTER TWELVE EXERCISES

1. Using an issue of *Cosmopolitan* or *National Geographic*, read the captions for the pictures, then come to the next class prepared to discuss whether the writers have observed the rules for writing captions in this chapter.

2. After rereading "Writing Picture Stories" in this chapter, purchase an issue of *People*. Do the writers observe the rules for writing to pictures? Can you edit the captions by taking out unnecessary words?

CHAPTER 13
Generating and Developing Ideas for Magazine Articles

The ability to generate magazine article ideas is really the ability to see the world from a writer's point of view. When photographers walk down the street, they visualize the scenes before them as though they are looking through a camera lens. Mathematicians see the spatial relationships between the objects around them. Similarly, skillful magazine writers regard the everyday experiences of life as being full of story ideas just waiting to be discovered.

Beginning writers are often discouraged by their apparent inability to churn out ideas. What they do not realize is that this kind of thinking is an acquired skill, one that it is possible to develop. After three years of practice, one free-lancer remarked that she was never dismayed when she discovered that one of her ideas had already been published by someone else; she regarded such events as evidence that her skill in generating marketable ideas was improving.

Because of the sharp competition for the reader's time and attention, which causes fierce competition among magazines, nothing is quite so critically important in the magazine world as a good idea. Before he was elected to the United States Senate, the late Richard Neuberger of Oregon was one of the best-known free-lancers in the West. Editors welcomed his articles, but not because he was a richly talented writer. In fact, Neuberger was little more than a competent writer. More often than not, his phrases were somewhat matter-of-fact, and his sentences did not sing. Magazine staffers often had to rework long sections of his articles (and sometimes the articles themselves) to put them in shape for publication. But Neuberger had interesting ideas for articles and techniques for developing them, and he supported both with careful and wide-ranging research. Several of his pieces—notably "They Never Go Back to Pocatello," "The Decay of the State Legislature," and "My Wife Put Me in the Senate"—have been reprinted widely.

ANALYZING MAGAZINES

Before beginners can view the world from a writer's point of view, they must be able to see magazines that way. Detective Sherlock Holmes could deduce a person's occupation, character, and even recent activities simply by observation; likewise, astute magazine writers can glean a great deal of information about a magazine simply by looking at it. Holmes's expertise was in knowing what to look for and how to interpret the information once he had it. The same skills can help a writer both to generate ideas and to market them.

Covers   You can't judge a book by examining its cover, but you can learn a lot about a magazine that way. What kind of identity is the magazine trying to establish through its logo and cover art work? Imagine a newsstand and the magazines a person would be able to spot on it right away. Magazines like *The New Yorker, Life, Time,* and even *Cosmopolitan* are among the first that come to mind because each has established a clear, distinct identity that separates it from the dozens of other magazines on display. A buyer would never mistakenly pick up *The Atlantic* if he or she meant to buy *Sports Illustrated*. The former uses covers that illustrate ideas, while the latter generally relies on action shots that virtually scream "SPORTS!" at the reader.

Look at the cover lines. How does the magazine try to lure readers inside its pages? Are the cover lines informative or tantalizing? Are they characterized by "A Guide To . . ." or "25 Ways To . . ." or "How to . . ."? Some magazines that rely on formulas to fill their pages month after month seem to run the same headlines regularly. A parody of *Cosmopolitan* published by the *Harvard Lampoon* caught the spirit of that publication's cover with a photograph of a model posed in a revealing evening dress, Cosmo style. Only one detail of the picture was amiss—the model's eyes were crossed. A headline printed in the standard Cosmo typestyle read, "How To Tell If Your Man Is Dead."

Finally, note whether or not the article titles displayed on the cover are followed by the authors' names. If they are, there's a good chance that the magazine relies on well known writers and may not be very receptive to considering the work of a newcomer.

Mastheads   Take a look at the magazine's masthead. Study the organization of the editorial staff. Are there many layers of associate editors, department editors, assistant editors, writers, researchers or editorial assistants? If so, the magazine is probably written mostly by staff. But if the number of editors wouldn't even comprise a volleyball team, there's a good chance they have to go outside their own offices for articles. Check to see where the editorial offices are located. Although most national magazines are located in New York, there are some scattered throughout the country. A beginning sports writer living in Bellingham, Washington, was amazed to discover that the offices of one of her best potential markets, *Young Athlete*, were less than 50 miles away. The advantage, of course, was that the writer was able to visit the editor in person rather than rely strictly on letters to transmit ideas.

Tables of Contents   The most important information available on the Table of Contents page is how the articles in the magazine are organized. Often magazines arrange stories into regular departments that appear in each issue. Sometimes these are always written by the same person, but an examination of a few back issues should reveal whether or not the authorship of departments changes. If it does, and the names are not those that appear on the masthead, the magazine is probably using free-lancers.

Advertisements   Magazine advertisements can indicate who reads the magazine. If the ads are for Mercedes Benz, Chivas Regal, or Saks Fifth Avenue, the audience is likely to be an upper income group. It is safe to assume that these advertisers try to place their ads where people with money to spend on such goods will see them. Who uses the products advertised in the magazine? Are they old, young, male, female, athletic, middle class, or highly educated? Advertising salespeople sell ads not only on the basis of a magazine's circulation but on the demographic characteristics of its audience. They get this information through readership surveys and use it to show prospective clients that their readers are the people who buy the clients' products.

Are any of the articles related to the advertisements? Magazines do not allow advertisers to influence editorial content, but they do sometimes try to attract advertisers by publishing articles that are related to their products. Salespeople carry around lists of upcoming articles to show clients. At *Women's Sports* magazine, the advertising staff was sure to contact Bausch and Lomb, a leading manufacturer of optical supplies, any time there was an article on how to protect eyes from the sun. Advertising was sold by position in the magazine so a client like Bausch and Lomb could specify that its ad should appear next to the relevant article. The idea, of course, was that readers interested in the subject of eye protection would be exposed to the advertisement as they read the article.

Articles   Now have a look at the articles. Are they long or short or both? Count the words in a line and figure out how many words there are on a page. Translate that into a typewritten manuscript and see how many pages the writers are generating to produce each article. The trend in recent times has been toward stories that are "short and snappy," which means that an editor needs a greater number of articles to fill a single issue.

What types of articles are there? Do they tend to be serious, light, or both? Does the magazine rely on an eighth-grade vocabulary or are the articles written in a more sophisticated style? A clue to the overall tone can be found in the headlines. Are they informative, catchy, or both? It's unlikely that a headline published in *New West*, "A Wok on the Wild Side," would ever appear in *Good Housekeeping* even if the articles were on identical subjects. Do the articles cover subjects on a national, regional, or local basis?

Finally, who are the authors of the articles? Are their names on the masthead? Check the endings of stories for biographical information about the writers, such as "Jane Smith is a free-lance writer living in Oklahoma who specializes in topics related to health and medicine." Occasionally, magazines devote an entire page to descriptions and photographs of their writers. Read these for clues about the level of expertise the magazine expects from its free-lancers.

Graphics   Graphics can make a small magazine look big but can't make a poor magazine look rich. Color is the key component—how much is there and where does the art director put it? If there are lots of color photographs and illustrations with the articles (don't include color ads—the advertisers pay for them), the magazine is probably in good financial standing. Color is a very expensive part of art production, but because it enhances the visual appeal of the "book," as magazines are called in the publishing industry, everyone wants to have as much as possible. Articles regarded as the most important or most popular are the ones illustrated with color.

A seasoned writer can size up a magazine simply by glancing through it. For beginners, the process must be more deliberate and detailed. Information gathered in such analyses can be used to either match an idea to a particular magazine or to help the writer generate ideas for that magazine. Here are some additional tips to round out your analysis of magazines and to generate article ideas:

Think in headlines   Editors use headlines to help sell magazines; writers can use them to help sell articles.

Ask questions as the basis for a story   Is the private university a dying institution? Why can't Americans read? Who really controls our supply of gasoline?

Examine the other side of an issue   Why public universities are growing. Why Americans can't add. How to use less gas.

Don't limit ideas to subjects that have never been covered before   There aren't many left. Try to develop new angles for old subjects, or new markets for subjects that have been covered elsewhere. Of course, if a new subject comes along, approach it from as many different angles as possible.

Think in terms of magazine departments   That's what editors of magazines that are organized into departments do. Writers who can suggest ideas for particular segments of a magazine that appear regularly often find their work being published with comparable frequency.

Cherchez la femme   Or as one California free-lancer put it, "Look for the Lithuanian." In virtually every story there is another story, often one that appeals to a slightly different audience.

Think in terms of illustration   A dramatic photograph can often provide the basis for a good magazine article. Art directors have been known to suggest article ideas to editors after seeing the work of a photographer, and there is no reason why writers should not do the same.

SOURCES OF IDEAS

Article ideas are everywhere, but it helps to narrow the field somewhat. Here are seven fertile sources of ideas that beginners should consider.

Ideas from Campus   College students who hope to write for magazines may justifiably lament their regular class schedules and the tight financial conditions that prevent them from ranging widely on article research trips. But the campus itself can be an excellent source of ideas and information for articles. If the school maintains an alert news bureau, its staff can usually provide leads to dozens of article possibilities. However, the imaginative student writer seldom needs news bureau help. While he was a graduate student at the University of Iowa, Tom Fensch wrote for *Writer's Digest* a description of his campus writing career.

I read in the University of Iowa's student newspaper, *The Daily Iowan*, that some university students were involved in a national billiards tournament. It didn't sound like much, but because I liked billiards I talked to the director of the Union's bowling and billiards area, over coffee. He told me that one Iowa co-ed was headed toward a national championship in pocket billiards. I then checked my copy of *Writer's Market* and discovered that *National Bowlers Journal and Billiard Revue* magazine in Chicago bought free-lance billiard material. A stamp sent my query—would they be interested in an article about the co-ed champion? They would indeed and bought the article.

They then said that the billiards director—the man that I had talked to—was a nationally known tournament official. Could I do a second article for them about him? I could and did.

While writing his story, I wondered, could I sell the co-ed article again? The answer was yes, twice, at this writing. A college magazine called *Big Ten* bought it, as a short, and then because the girl is a Negro, *Sepia* magazine bought a third article about her.

Fensch then went on to prove that even writing about champions and celebrated tournament officials is not essential in getting published. Watching pinball players in a bar, he asked himself, "What is the attraction that makes students play pinball hour after hour?" He answered his own question with "Pinball: The Only Game That Plays You" for *Dude.* In the same bar, he listened to a recording of the Jefferson Airplane's "White Rabbit," which suggests that Alice in Lewis Carroll's *Alice in Wonderland* was on drugs. After rereading *Alice,* he wrote "Lewis Carroll—the First Acidhead" for *Big Ten.*

College experience also provided Diana Gleasner, a physical education major, with article ideas. She wrote and sold one article on physical education as a career and two on swimming. She was equally adept at turning experiences into article sales after her marriage. The pleasure of reading to her children gave her the inspiration for a story for *Jack and Jill.* Her involvement in PTA resulted in an article for *The Instructor.*

Ideas for Trade Journals   These are not the kinds of ideas or sales that make a writer rich, of course, but they enable the beginner to break into writing—to learn how to develop ideas and turn them into publishable articles. Some young writers go on from there to publish in the prestige magazines. Others make a career in what are known as secondary markets, which include trade journals. One writer for trade journals, Margaret M. Clayton, advised beginners, in an issue of *Writer's Digest:*

> The biggest advantage of writing for trade journals is that most are hungry for material and their editors are willing to help the promising beginner to shape his work. The competition is not as great as in some other fields because of the misconceptions and ill-informed prejudices held by so many writers concerning trade journal writing.
>
> The idea, in brief, is this, Keep your eyes open for new or recently remodeled stores, businesses with clever displays or promotions, firms with successful personnel, bookkeeping, etc. innovations. When you have spotted a good subject (for instance, a garden center that is doing a flourishing business by putting on educational clinics), write a query letter to the editor of the proper magazine (in this case a garden center magazine), asking if he would be interested in an article on this idea. If he answers yes, call the manager of the store for an appointment, telling him XYZ magazine is interested in an article about his successful operation and asking for an interview.

Deft trade journal specialists are among the most prolific idea men. Howard H. Fogel writes 300 to 400 articles a year, some for trade journals that pay as much as 10 cents a word. He is obviously a fast writer, but another reason he is able to produce so much is that he often generates several ideas from a single source. He visited a department store in Sioux City, Iowa, interviewed three employees, and walked out with notes for articles for four journals: *China Glass and Tableware, Photo Dealer, Photo Discount Buyer,* and *Sporting Goods Discount Buyer.*

Ideas from Reading   Nearly everyone who goes into free-lancing seriously becomes a careful reader, and clipper, of newspapers. Charles and Bonnie Remsberg, a husband-wife writing team in Evanston, Illinois, subscribe to the two major Chicago papers. When these seem to be yielding few items, the Remsbergs will subscribe to as many as six out-of-town papers, searching for local features and news items that were not carried by the wire services. They spotted in the *Chicago Sun-Times* a report that the Gallup Poll had discovered that six out of ten Americans favor establishing a system through which the innocent victims of violent crimes (such as when a mad killer shoots wildly at everyone he meets) would receive government compensation for physical, mental, and economic suffering. After doing extensive research in their own heavy files of clippings as well as in legal periodicals, libraries, and law enforcement offices, the Remsbergs produced "Should Crime Victims Be Paid?" which was published by *Family Weekly.*

This experience is an excellent example of what reading can do for writers—and what writers must do for themselves. That is, the Gallup Poll story was published so widely that thousands of professional writers must have seen it. It was simply a fact, not a magazine article sitting there for the plucking, until the Remsbergs thought imaginatively *about* the fact and how it might serve as the cue for an article. It is equally important to note that the writers thought of their article in relation to a particular magazine. They said that they were "aware from carefully studying the magazine that *Family Weekly* often runs stories anticipating burgeoning public issues." If they had not studied the magazine, they might have dismissed the Gallup Poll report as a profitless item. This underlines a vital aspect of generating ideas and one emphasized earlier: The writer must read and analyze magazines to get a feel of what the editors want. It follows that the writer should aim at magazines he enjoys reading. To attempt to write for a magazine one does not read is to send an engraved invitation to failure.

When reading newspapers for ideas, the writer must see more than the facts; he must see their implications. A story in the *Wall Street Journal* about the weather service led Frank Taylor, a leading free-lancer, to two *Reader's Digest* articles on jet streams. Another *Wall Street Journal* story on the business of building swimming pools for Hollywood stars led him to a search for the leading builder and eventually to write an article titled "Those High Jinks in Hollywood Pads." Still another mentioned the problems of finding homes for newly rich stars. This posed the question, "Is there someone who's tops in this field?" There was—a live-wire realtor on the Sunset Strip named Al Herd. From Herd's experiences came Taylor's "He Sells Houses to the Stars." Prosaic news stories about California's great irrigation projects resulted in a Taylor article for *Nation's Business* on how Californians were "moving the rain."

These experiences should clearly demonstrate that an article writer's imagination must always be at work. A newspaper item about a zoo's swapping kangaroos for a polar bear is just an amusing little story to the general reader. To the article writer, it is an invitation to look for a larger story. One did, and found that the San Diego Zoo had become one of the world's best zoos by astutely swapping seals (which could be caught nearby) for many kinds of animals other zoos considered surplus. The article that resulted was "Swapping Zoo Keepers."

Although metropolitan newspapers can be mined by imaginative free-lancers for scores of articles, professional writers often read much more widely. Some focus on publications that are not so likely to have been culled by their competitors. An article in a local farm publication led to "Lazy Man's Orchard." Another farm-paper story, this one on a young beekeeper who rented bees by the millions to orchardists to pollinate their blossoms, became "Hundred Million Bees for Hire" in *Reader's Digest*. Company magazines—especially the house organs of aerospace, oil, and electronics companies—are sometimes heavy with facts that can be used profitably by free-lancers who venture out on the growing edge of technology. Like university magazines that are a similarly rich source of material, these publications are usually available free to a writer who asks to be placed on the mailing list.

One eminently successful free-lancer began early in his career to subscribe to numerous obscure journals, looking for leads. An item in *Engineer's Digest* reported how many people are electrocuted every year because they think it is safe to handle a high-voltage wire with ordinary rubber gloves, when the fact is that rubber gloves will protect the wearer only from 110-volt wires around the house. He promptly wrote to the safety heads of such organizations as the American Red Cross, the National Board of Fire Underwriters, the National Safety Council, and the American Medical Association asking, "What are the most popular fallacies concerning safety which imperil the public's life?" From the 60 pounds of literature he received, the writer fashioned a manual for survival titled "Safety Rules That Can Kill You."

Ideas from Observing   The writer who is truly observant looks into his own experiences and surroundings with the clear eye of a newcomer. Working in a congressional office and reading many of the hundreds of letters from constituents that pour in every day—most of them on trivial but time-consuming matters—provided the basis for "Why Congressmen Can't Do Their Jobs." Living in Miami during a winter so cold that many of the luxury hotels went bankrupt suggested to one writer the idea for an article on the resort economy, "On the Shifting Sands of Miami Beach."

It is not necessary to live in an area that most magazine readers would consider colorful or exotic to generate article ideas from one's surroundings. Investigating the "Flowers by Telegraph" signs that appear in the windows of flower shops nearly everywhere led to "Their Business Is Blooming" in *Reader's Digest*.

Peg Bracken, a housewife whose husband became ill, needed to write more to help support her family, but she was kept close to home by a small daughter. She was a good cook, but she didn't enjoy it, and she began writing the tongue-in-cheek pieces that became the *I Hate to Cook Book*. This led to other whimsical books, many magazine assignments, a syndicate contract, and appearances on television and the lecture circuit.

Ideas from Experience   The young writer may think that only those who lead adventurous or important lives have experiences worth space in magazines. Braving danger certainly does provide the basis for an article, and serving as an assistant in the White House has led to many articles and often to books. But almost any kind of experience may yield an idea to a perceptive writer. A conversation is an experience, and some of the most casual conversations provide leads to articles. Mort Weisinger was led by a conversation to wonder whether all those who are tapped for Phi Beta Kappa become famous statesmen, jurists, or tycoons. He queried the Phi Beta Kappa Society and received a list of members and copies of its bulletin. (He learned that Franchot Tone, an actor, was a member and so was Nathan Leopold, a murderer.) Then he wrote to some of the members who had become national figures and asked how winning the Phi Beta Kappa key had affected their lives. The result was "America's Smartest Set," which appeared in *Cosmopolitan*. In one case, a vexing conversation was itself an article. Reflecting on his trouble trying to prove to a government official when and where he was born, a writer recounted his experience in "The Friendly Man from Medicare" for *Reader's Digest*.

Experiences need not be unusual. In fact, common experiences properly packaged by a deft writer often provide article ideas with which many readers can identify. Finding herself anchored to her home by a baby, Amelia Lobsenz sold many articles on pediatric problems to *Today's Woman* and *Parents' Magazine*. A college sophomore, Stephen Kelman, took advantage of the current interest in higher education to sell an article on the flaws in college board exams and the pressures the exams exert on high school students.

Experience articles that are cast in how-to form are often the most widely read pieces a popular magazine can publish. Paul Green paid off much of his mortgage on a new home by writing articles like

"How to Cut Down Fuel Costs." Caroline Bird's "How to Give a Cocktail Party" suggests that the subjects can be basic, even simple, provided the author treats them imaginatively. This form is used much more often than the number of "How to . . ." titles indicates. Green's "10 Ways to Save on Fuel Costs" and Caroline Bird's "If Your Child Cheats" and "Advice to Honeymooners" are all stories of this variety. Advice is a staple of many widely circulated magazines, some of it from experts, but much of it from diligent article writers.

Early in his career, one writer developed a special talent for generating successful articles from prosaic experiences. One of his best ideas came in the early days of television, when he bought the first television set in his neighborhood. It started a chain reaction among the neighbors that led to "Swooning in the Gloom" for *This Week*. The article began:

> I snuff out my cigarettes in a luminous ashtray. My wife washes the dinner dishes shortly before midnight. Our nextdoor neighbor takes art lessons in our parlor every Thursday night. Baby-sitters fight to sit in our home.

Similarly, a writer developed an article from listening to "Information Please" on radio. He collected scores of embarrassing moments when famous people were stumped, then wrote "How to Fool the Experts."

Correspondence is the kind of experience that might be considered in a separate category because of its importance. Many writers find that friends and well-wishers who are far away like to suggest ideas, many of which are valueless. Fairly often, though, a correspondent will point up first-rate ideas. Frank Taylor owes many good leads to letter writers. A persistent fan in Denver wrote several letters about a rainbow trout farm in Idaho operated by Robert Erkins. This led to "They Grow Trout by the Millions" for *Reader's Digest*. Several stories on Henry J. Kaiser, the great builder, were triggered by a single letter from a fan. "The World's Liveliest Art Show," the Laguna living art pageant, in which local citizens portray scenes from great paintings and sculptures, was suggested by a resident of the town.

Ideas from Publicists   Although it pains some writers to admit it, publicity and public relations workers are often the richest sources of ideas. The journalist's historic belief that the publicist must have an axe to grind is often well founded. "Sometimes, though," one free-lancer holds, "public relations people will suggest story topics that are not self-serving just because they are interested in being in on the start of a story. Most of them are high-caliber people who know a story when they see one."

For a journalist to ignore all publicists or treat their suggestions cynically because of some lofty "holier-than-thou" attitude is unfair. A worthy article is a worthy article, even though the person who suggests that it be undertaken may benefit from its publication. The writer need only guard against being used for unworthy purposes.

Publicists have certainly suggested or inspired some of the most solid and readable magazine articles. Among Hollywood publicists, the late Maggie Ettinger was a useful source. Her suggestions led to, among others, "Rubberneck Restaurant," a piece on the Brown Derby; and to two articles on Dr. Herbert Kalmus, the developer of color photography for the movies. Paul Snell, also a leading Hollywood publicist, has offered leads to stories for no other reason than they seemed interesting, as well as pushing those that benefit his clients. He suggested that the operations of the American Potash and Chemical Company, which extracted borax, potash, and other minerals from the brine drawn out of Searles Lake, would make a readable *Saturday Evening Post* story. It did, a piece titled "The World's Richest Mineral Stockpile."

Douglas Ann Newsom, an astute Fort Worth public relations counsel and a professor at Texas Christian University, points up the value of the publicist:

> This is such a specialized society we live in that trying to write about it is a problem for the man who is used to general assignment writing. He almost has to depend upon PR for ideas and materials—for ideas because he wouldn't even know about them if the PR man hadn't called them to his attention; for materials because he's not likely to have access to the information any other way.

Ideas from Editors   When a writer has begun to sell fairly regularly to a magazine, he can expect his editor to begin to suggest ideas. In time, half the writer's ideas may come from editors. This is the most important source to develop, since an editor who suggests an idea has a vested interest in it, since he wants it to become an article he can publish. A veteran writer explains his own procedures:

> I have always made it clear to editors that I am ready to check any leads that readers may send them, or that they may have from newspaper clippings or other sources. Sometimes these lead to stories, and sometimes they don't. I've made it a point, though, to tell the editors frankly how the story idea pans out. If after investigation it doesn't look as though it will make a good story, I tell them so and pass it up as a possibility, even though in some

cases I might have pushed a little and made it into a border-line story which they possibly would have accepted. But I think it has paid off to establish in the editor's mind the fact that I will make a cold, hard appraisal of any story lead I am checking, and he can be fairly sure that if he gives me a go-ahead after my report that it will turn out to *be* a story.

The task for the beginner is to reach the point at which he or she can deal with editors on this laudable basis.

DEVELOPING AN IDEA ONCE YOU HAVE IT

Articles often begin as little more than passing thoughts, images, or statements. Only in the process of developing an idea into one that is marketable does the writer decide upon the angle from which to approach the story, the form in which to write the story, and the possible sources of information for researching the story. It is not unusual for the final product to have little relation to the original concept, and writers must be flexible enough in their thinking to allow for that adjustment.

Beginners often have difficulty asking the questions that help to develop ideas. Here are two examples of story suggestions, and how they could be turned into publishable articles:

Art as an investment   The originator of this idea was not really certain who her audience would be. Serious art collectors or people interested in making large investments would probably not be interested in advice from anyone who is not an authority on the subject. But what about the average person? Is art a good investment for someone with $500 to $1,000 to spend? What kind of art could such a buyer invest in? Where could he or she go for help? How do relatively small investments in art compare to other types of investments available to people with the same amount of money, such as savings accounts or stocks? The answers to these questions could form the basis for an article that would be marketable to a wide range of magazines.

Controversy over the initiative to limit construction of high-rise buildings in San Francisco   The writer who thought of this idea knew that the story would be thoroughly covered by the local press. Her best chance for developing it was to examine the related issues from a national perspective. Have other cities passed similar initiatives? Have such initiatives been defeated elsewhere, and why? What are the long-range implications of such restrictions on the survival of urban areas? How do businessmen in different parts of the country view the issue? What do urban planners have to say on this subject? Is there a clear-cut division between various national groups that are for or against these initiatives? A well-researched article on this subject would have obvious appeal for many national magazines. (See Chapter Nine for an excerpt from this article as it was actually published.)

CHAPTER THIRTEEN EXERCISES

1. Choose three magazines of the same genre and analyze them according to the criteria outlined in this chapter. Then compare the three and discuss how each tries to establish a unique identity.

2. Choose two of the general subject headings listed below and suggest five topics related to each that could be the basis of magazine articles.

health	personalities
sports	art
money	politics
hobbies	minorities
environment	religion

3. Choose one of the topics listed below and discuss how it might be developed into an article. Include possible interview subjects and other sources of information.

alcoholism among teenagers	antique collecting
pottery making	declining enrollment in college humanities courses
health care cooperatives	

CHAPTER 14
Landing Magazine Assignments

A universal horoscope for all beginning free-lancers might read: "A stranger wearing a uniform will soon assume an important role in your life." That person is the postman.

Anyone who engages in the business of selling magazine articles long distance soon discovers that a well-written query letter is the most effective selling device. It offers advantages to both the editor and the writer. Editors prefer to receive queries rather than unsolicited manuscripts for two reasons. First, queries can be read more quickly, and editors generally have little time to spare. Second, a query enables the editor to participate in the process of developing the article. In reply, the editor can suggest an angle, specify a length, and discuss treatment of the subject. This has obvious advantages for the writer as well because it tells what kind of article the editor would like to receive, and it reduces the likelihood that the writer will spend a lot of time and effort to produce an article that no editor wants.

WRITING A QUERY LETTER

In writing a query, try to accomplish three things:

Give the basics of the story. Do this by explaining not only what the story will be about but what your sources of information will be and who you plan to interview. It is not necessary to have already done the research and interviews; it is necessary to have decided what topics you will cover and how you will do it.

Show why this is a good story for this magazine. Use your skills as a magazine analyst to point out the relevance of the subject to the magazine's audience or how the article fits in with the magazine's editorial policy. If you have a particular department in mind for the article, say so.

Convince the editor that you are the person to write this story. Think of the query as a short article, written by you in your best style. It is a sample of your writing that you know the editor will read. Including additional clips from previously published articles is also a good idea, but beginners often have none so the letter itself must do the job. More experienced writers simply mention the names of publications in which their work has appeared.

Show the editor that you are in an especially good position to do the story, either because you have access to some key information, are well informed about the subject, or know someone who is an expert.

Although it is unethical, editors have been known to assign articles to staff members based on a free-lancer's suggestions simply because they do not have confidence in the free-lancer's ability to produce publishable manuscripts. Unless the free-lancer can prove that this has happened, he or she has little recourse. When the editorial offices are in New York and the free-lancer is in Omaha, the chances of his or her knowing the full story behind the "Sorry, but we've already assigned a piece on this subject . . ." replies are slim. The best way to avoid such disappointments is to write a good query.

A query letter should never exceed two typewritten single-spaced pages. If it does, that is evidence that the writer really does not have a clear idea of what the story will be about. It's a good idea to include your phone number in the return address; magazine editors, especially those with access to WATTS lines, often like to telephone writers to discuss articles. Make sure the editor doesn't have to search for your number.

The elements discussed above are the Yin and Yang of query writing because they must be in balance for harmony to exist in the letter. A good idea that is poorly presented, either by sloppy writing or insufficient reporting, won't stand a chance. Likewise, a well-written query about a good idea could be rejected if the editor lacks confidence in the writer's ability to cover the subject. The three elements must work together for the query to be successful.

In a few special cases, querying an editor to suggest an idea may be difficult. For example, some articles cannot be outlined, among them very short features. Most humor pieces depend too much on the *way* they are written—the charm of the writing—to be outlined successfully. Some heavily editorial articles—the kind in which the writer is getting something weighty off his chest—may be similarly impossible to outline. Still, the query letter to an editor is one of the writer's most valuable tools. Why this is true is illustrated by the following letter:

> I have run across a character who would provide material, I believe, for a lively story. He is a voluble and energetic little Italian fellow with an Irish first name, Patrick Lizza. His enthusiasm is fireworks, and he is the largest fireworks manufacturer in the country. Lizza puts on fireworks shows at state and county fairs, American Legion gatherings, the Hollywood Bowl, and any other place that will be an excuse for lighting up the heavens.
>
> Lizza lives down at Redondo, a seaside town in Southern California, and has two fireworks plants, one at Saugus

and another at Redondo Beach. Never satisfied with just putting on a display of colorful illumination, Lizza's specialty is telling stories with fireworks. Last summer, for example, I saw one of his unusual shows, an engine and a train that moved, done in fireworks. He also put on portraits of famous people. One of his prides is his Niagara Falls. He has flying saucers, the flag raising at Iwo Jima, the aurora borealis, the fountain of youth, to mention only a few of his spectacular ideas.

A good deal of Lizza's success has been due to his ability to go before the Board of Directors of a fair or some other pageant and talk them out of a few extra thousands of dollars to try out one of his new ideas. He gets them all laughing over his excitable Italian-English, and usually comes away with the money.

The big payoff in Lizza's business is his assignments from the Army and Navy to load rockets which are used to turn wartime no-man's-land and any enemy territory into artificial daylight. His two plants are going full blast on this, and while he is up to his ears in war work, Lizza has not let up on his fireworks displays and has a series of shows lined up for this summer that will be bigger and better than anything he has ever done before.

If you wanted to make a try at it, I think we could get set and line up some color of some of these displays. If successful in kodachrome, it ought to make a most spectacular layout.

In view of the fact that Lizza is such an effervescent and entertaining character, I think there would be ample material for an amusing human interest story about him and his unusual game. How does it look to you?

Note especially that although this is the query letter—the first correspondence on this subject—the writer has already done some of the research for this article. Much more fact gathering lies ahead, but the query is fairly detailed. The writer does not say merely that he wants to fashion an article on an interesting man who manufactures fireworks. Instead, the editor learns *why* the subject may interest millions of readers. And, although the writer and the editor are friends, the writer does not presume on the friendship nor even on the fact that he has already written many articles for the magazine. In short, he *works* at writing an attractive, informally phrased query— exactly as he might if he had never met and never written for the editor. The result was this go-ahead:

Patrick Lizza seems a good bet for a piece. We'll be glad to have you go ahead on this one whenever you can get to it.

One minor word of warning: Please make it quite clear that this fellow's business is selling fireworks for community displays and not to kids. As you know, there is high feeling in many parts of the country against the indiscriminate sale of fireworks to young fry, and many towns and cities have laws against it.

Such direction from an editor can be very helpful to a writer, particularly when it comes in detailed form as illustrated in the following excerpt from a query and reply. Note that in this case the writer and editor had already discussed the article in person, but that the editor had still requested a written proposal before giving the "okay."

One of the subjects we spoke about was a first-person account of how I overcame my phobia of birds. By coincidence, just two days after we met, I faced the most severe test imaginable of my freedom from fear. I was walking down 37th Street toward Madison Avenue when suddenly I noticed something falling from above, slightly in front of me and to the right. It landed with a thud on the sidewalk, followed by the scraping sound of wings against pavement. Imagine a claustrophobic caught in an elevator and you'll know how I felt.

The odds of a wounded bird falling from the sky onto one's head are quite slim; the odds of one falling inches away from a bird phobic are even slimmer. An estimated one in ten people suffer from phobias of some kind. Each could describe a terrifying scene in which all their worst fears come true. Depending on the degree to which a phobic believes what he or she most dreads will happen, the problem can rule the individual's life. A person with fear of heights cannot go into tall buildings or ride in airplanes; an agoraphobic cannot leave the house; a car phobic must walk to go anywhere.

A year ago the episode that took place in New York would have sent me screaming and crying hysterically into the nearest bird-free place. Shaking and panic stricken, I would have imagined it happening again and again. I'm happy to say that because of therapy, my reaction was far less dramatic. I just kept walking. Moreover, I was able to remain calm and did not conclude that the sky was about to rain dead birds down upon me.

My other accomplishments as a former phobic may sound less exciting, but they represent real progress. I can walk down the street without crossing to the other side if I see a bird on the sidewalk ahead of me. I can sit in a restaurant where there are birds in cages and enjoy my meal. I can walk around in my backyard without searching the grass for dead birds. Sometimes I can even enjoy the graceful picture of birds in flight, or laugh at ducks sliding on a frozen pond.

The treatment that helped me overcome my fear was a brief, relatively simple process. It lasted less than three months, involved only half a dozen sessions, and cost about $300. My therapist was Dr. Gerald Rosen, chief psychologist at Providence Medical Center in Seattle and author of *Don't Be Afraid*. The behavior modification techniques Dr. Rosen used to help me can be applied to any severe, irrational fear, whether it is of snakes or of public speaking. Unfortunately, most people who suffer from phobias are either too ashamed to seek help, are unaware that such help exists, or believe that it would be too expensive. In fact, visits to a clinical psychologist are covered by many health insurance plans.

I would like to write an article about my experience for *Good Housekeeping*. The story is one I'm certain would strike a common chord among your readers, for almost everyone is truly afraid of something that the rest of us find only mildly unpleasant or downright nice. The article would also represent an unusual treatment of the subject— though I have seen stories about phobias, I have never seen one written by a phobic who had been cured. As a service to your audience, the story might provide some phobics with the information they need to get help. Naturally I would obtain the advice and approval of Dr. Rosen before submitting the article.

Thank you for your consideration. I look forward to hearing from you.

The following response was received just one week later, breaking all previous records for response-time to this free-lancer's queries.

I remember your visit and your mention of the bird phobia piece. I do think it would make an interesting article— especially if you can do it in a light, conversational style. Since you have never written for us, we would have to request that you do the piece on speculation. That means that if it proves satisfactory for use in *GH*, we pay you $1,000. If it doesn't work out, you get it back. The piece should not run more than 1,200 words. I suggest you save the episode of the falling bird for the end—a kind of clincher to prove that your cure really worked. You might start the article by saying how glad you are to be cured of your phobia, then describe the phobia and how your fears interfered with your life, how you found out about the treatment, what the therapy was like and how it worked out for you. When you're talking about the behavior modification techniques, please be very specific and don't burden the piece with a lot of theories. We look forward to receiving the manuscript from you by the middle of February.

COMMON PROBLEMS IN QUERY WRITING

Because a query letter is a bit like a short article, it presents similar problems to the writer. There is no room for words or paragraphs that are not essential to either presenting or selling the story. Here is an excerpt from a query written by a beginner that illustrates some common difficulties.

Clay Felker, Editor
Esquire
488 Madison Avenue
New York, New York 10022

Dear Mr. Felker:

Recently, I had occasion to reflect upon the past brilliance of the late great American motor car industry. To clarify, a motor car carries the distinguished marque of a Duesenberg, Stutz, Cord, Mercedes, Rolls, or Bentley, to name a few quality machines from the golden era of classic machines. An automobile is the throughway vehicle built by Detroit, subsequent to World War II.

Last month as I shopped for a new car, immersed in cloudy thoughts about the fuel shortages and even gloomier thoughts about the uneven craftsmanship so evident in post-war American automobiles, I really tried to buy American. It was no use, after driving ten new cars, I ended up doing the inevitable: I bought a foreign car. What a shame! The United States dominates the aircraft industry, because our airframes and engines are the very best available, yet we can't build a competitive quality motor car.

Our motor cars, at one time, were among the very best. Stutz and Duesenberg racing machines gave many a European race team heartburn during the early decades of the century because of their speed and stamina. As a youngster, growing up in New England—the mecca of classic cars, with the net assets of one canary yellow straight-8 Stutz roadster, I developed an early appreciation for fine machinery. Today, I begrudgingly drive my father-in-law's Seville. It doesn't have 20-inch red wire wheels, it doesn't have a one-shot lube system, and worst of all, it doesn't even have a menacing set of exhaust cut-outs protruding from the hood—at the exact height of the average Radcliffe girl's bicycle seat. Essentially, our best has neither elan nor character; it's a eunuch in the company of fine motor cars.

Aside from the obvious need for editing in these opening paragraphs, there is another problem that detracts from the writer's presentation of his idea. After reading these three paragraphs, the editor still will not know what the subject of the article is. Does the writer intend to produce a story about why American cars aren't what they used to be, or does he want to do a nostalgic piece about the classic automobiles of the past?

A Query Letter Should Have a Good Lead

Like magazine articles, query letters should have leads that grab the reader's attention. Like newspaper articles, they should present the most important information in the opening paragraphs. Many beginners tend to take a long warm-up before the pitch; in writing a query it is essential to get the point across quickly. Here are some that do:

> Who decides which trees are cut? Right now an apparent deadlock exists between the lumber industry and environmentalists. Housing shortages and an expanding economy are demanding an increase in production of timber. But people all over the U.S. are reacting with horror and disbelief to the possibility of a treeless future. Is there an answer to the dilemma?

> Most people are familiar with the McDonald's Restaurant chain, but few realize that the company has concerns that extend beyond the realm of the Big Mac. Owners of McDonald's Restaurants in Northern California and Northern Nevada together with the Children's Hospital at Stanford Parents Group have recently completed construction of Ronald McDonald House, a home away from home for families of catastrophically ill children at the hospital.

> At a time when Disco Fever is sweeping the country, I fear we may be overlooking a much older but no less serious disease which afflicts thousands of college students yearly: Potomac Fever.

> The symptoms are many and varied: a burning interest in public affairs and governmental policy, an itch to see Ted Kennedy in person, a phobia of that contradiction in terms—"summer school," and an uncontrollable urge to find out what people really do in a cloakroom besides hang up coats.

Over 3,000 young people descend upon Washington, D.C., every summer to visit the healing waters of the Potomac. Everyone is treated differently, and some are cured—permanently. Many others find that the condition is chronic, but controllable.

The Next Task: More Correspondence

For many writers, correspondence with editors begins with one mailing and ends with another: first, a query letter suggesting a subject; then, if the editor has answered affirmatively, an envelope carrying the article.

But there is reason to believe that a free-lancer should undertake much more correspondence. A writer who once gave relatively little attention to correspondence, contenting himself with a query letter and an article mailing in each case, found that nearly half his manuscripts were coming back with rejection slips saying, "Sorry, we can't use this." Deciding that a full dialogue with editors might help, he began to work more industriously at correspondence. He not only wrote an original query letter outlining an idea but also followed up, after doing much of the article research, with another letter—sometimes two or three—sketching his progress and asking for the editor's reaction to the shape the article was beginning to take (which was sometimes quite different from the shape suggested by the initial query). The result was that fewer manuscripts came back, and the writer was almost always able to modify those that did to the editor's specifications. Sometimes two or three rounds of correspondence—after as well as before the first submission of the article—were necessary before an idea would jell at both ends of the correspondence line.

The value of this process should be apparent. Correspondence helped the writer involve the editor in the project. After two or three letters, the editor had a stake in the writer's success. Sometimes the idea became more the editor's than the writer's; the idea the writer originally proposed to the editor evolved into an even better idea—at least from the editor's point of view.

One value that is less apparent is that editors are part of an editorial team on most magazines. Few of them can or will decide independently whether an article should be published. Editorial conferences are often a process of argument and compromise. When an editor has become deeply involved in an article, he or she is much more likely to argue strongly for it and is much better able to present it winningly. Of course, not all editors have the time or inclination to engage in a dialogue by mail, but those who do can be a great help to writers.

Here is an example of a follow-up letter—not a query—that was written to an associate editor after the writer had received a go-ahead on an article and had completed much of the research. The article that eventually grew out of this correspondence was titled "His Millions for the Big Outdoors."

By way of a report on the story line for the Rockefeller story, the theme seems to be that it calls for more sweat and tears to give the public a hundred million dollars worth of outdoor and historical treasure than it did to make the hundred million to pay for it. The Rockefellers have carried out what is probably the most magnificent one-family conservation program in history, and they are still going strong in the face of attacks on their motives that would have deterred a less single-minded family.

Laurance Rockefeller is the brother who picked up the play started by John D., Jr., four decades back. The five brothers are more scientific givers than their father was. They have a partnership, Rockefeller Brothers, Inc., to make the millions, and another, Rockefeller Brothers Fund, to give them away. However, to keep themselves out of the spotlight, they work largely through other organizations such as Jackson Hole Preserve, Inc., and American Conservation Association. However, Laurance R. frequently plunges on his own, if he thinks an outdoor treasure is in danger, just as John D., Jr., did.

The total of gifts for conservation is well over the $100,000,000 mark, but the canny Rockefellers have doubled this ante by matching federal, state, or other private funds wherever possible. Laurance says they are not "wilderness boys" and they don't propose to invest in virgin areas to "put them in deep freeze for future generations." They think the people should be using the natural recreational areas now. In fact, the Rockefellers talk as much about human resources as about natural resources, when they are on the subject of conservation.

The natural and historical gems they have saved, in many instances in the nick of time, pretty well blanket the country. They range from Williamsburg to Grand Teton Park to Corkscrew Cypress stands in Florida; from the Calaveras Grove of Sequoia gigantea and the Bull Creek Grove of Sequoia sempervirens on the Redwood Highway, to the Great Smokies, Acadia National Park, stands of sugar pines along the roads to Yosemite, museums at Mesa Verde and other parks, roadside clean-up in Yellowstone, "seed money" for a survey in Mt. Rainier to find a way to provide facilities for the public, one of the Virgin Islands now a national park, and numerous others. There is a story behind nearly every one of these projects.

My plan is to put the story together in the rough and have it checked by Horace M. Albright, who acted as front man for the family in lining up many of these purchases. Robert

L. Hoke, Room 5425, 30 Rockefeller Plaza, has gathered together many photographs, both color and black and white, and these are available if you want to use any of them. If you can let me know when you would like to have copy, I'll shoot at that deadline.

If you're still not convinced of the value of correspondence, this report from a prominent free-lancer should win you over:

Early in my article-writing career, I hit on the idea of keeping a box score on a large sheet of paper of my article suggestions submitted to editors. The best average I could achieve that first year and the next was one acceptance out of ten ideas submitted. Of course, I could rewrite the letter about a rejected idea and try it on another editor or another magazine. The first year of the box score I submitted ninety ideas and got nine go-aheads. These were not exactly assignments; they were merely the editor's word that he was interested in seeing the manuscript and that nobody else was doing that story for him. He had staked out the idea for me and would give me a reasonable amount of time, usually up to six months, to send him the manuscript. If he wanted it in a hurry, he would tell me and I could put on a night shift (myself) and rush it.

Gradually, as I learned what the different editors did not want and quit submitting sure-fire duds to them, I worked the average down to one acceptance in five ideas submitted, and eventually down to one in three—which is about the best I've been able to achieve. But just because one editor turned down an idea didn't mean that another wouldn't go for it. Editors' choices are as variable as the winds. All this time, as the go-ahead rate improved, the article acceptance rate was zooming until I was batting around .900—selling nine of every ten articles I wrote, and at top rates. All this proves that it pays to write good letters—good sales letters.

TALKING IDEAS OVER WITH EDITORS

Part of the cost of free-lancing is financing trips to the magazine publishing centers, especially New York, to discuss ideas with editors. A writer who lives far from his editors must rely primarily on correspondence, but he cannot rule out travel simply because it is expensive. He learns too much on these "apple-peddling expeditions," as one editor calls them, to forego them. He acquires insights into what the magazine may want for months ahead. During a lunch with two or three editors, an idea may strike a spark with one even though it may not interest the others. Often, an idea a writer suggests is developed in conversation, enabling the writer to refine his understanding of an approach to a subject in a way that could not have been accomplished in ten exchanges of letters.

Talking to editors, however, is not automatically valuable. Like the other aspects of free-lancing, discussions must be planned. Several general principles are involved in the planning. First, the writer must make appointments well in advance—a month or more, if possible—because many editors travel and because other writers are also making appointments. Writing short notes and making phone calls can enable a writer to set up a schedule that will allow him to talk with editors at several magazines during one trip. The beginner must write letters that will persuade editors that a face-to-face discussion is worth their time. (Practices vary from magazine to magazine. On some magazines, a beginner is not likely to be able to meet even the most junior editors. In any case, it is usually wise to ask for an appointment only after your query letters or articles have brought a stronger response than a printed rejection slip.)

The second, and most important, principle is to be prepared to talk specifically about article subjects. A writer's asking vaguely whether there is anything in an area he might cover for the magazine is almost certain to waste everybody's time. Be prepared to discuss your ideas as carefully as you would prepare an extensive query letter. In other words, some of the research must have been accomplished before you visit magazine offices.

One veteran writer began early in his career to prepare for talks with editors as though he were on a campaign:

> Before taking off on an expedition, I always sifted through my ideas and jotted down enough facts in a pocket notebook to talk about each story intelligently. If I didn't have enough facts to talk up the story, I got on the phone or did some in-person interviewing to case the story idea. I also checked *Readers' Guide to Periodical Literature* to make certain that the magazine had not recently run an article that I was proposing. It's most embarrassing to have an editor advise you to look at an issue two months back and read the story you're proposing—written by another man. No matter how carefully a writer tried to keep up, he'll probably miss a few articles in his magazines. And these are the ones that trip him up. Checking *Readers' Guide* is his protection.
>
> The pocket notebook invariably intrigued my editors. Before we had downed the first cocktail, one of them would say, "Get out your little notebook, and let's see what's in it." Some topics would win a go-ahead right away. The editor might want more information on others. That was my cue to say, "How would you like to have me case the

idea and send you a report?" The answer usually was, "Okay, we'll protect you on the story until you can give us an outline." Often, editors offered to pay my expenses while I was casing a story, and sometimes they would pay for my work even if they eventually decided against giving me a go-ahead.

As soon as I return from one of these expeditions, I write to the editors to thank them for their time and to outline the story ideas they want me to turn into manuscripts and those that I am to case. This firms up the assignments and guards against misunderstandings.

HOW ABOUT AN AGENT?

Perhaps the worst malady that can afflict the beginning writer is "agentitis." All the vexing details, he may think, would be taken care of if he could only hook up with a sharp literary agent, especially one who would take over the "business" aspects while the free-lancer devotes his genius to the serious work of writing. This is a dream.

There are a few agents—very few—who can and will shoulder much of the business load for *established* writers. For 10 or 15 percent of the earnings of a writer who has proved that he can turn out profitable prose, agents will try to do the selling. Some agents have developed such close relationships with their writers that they occasionally serve as confidante, idea generator, and, when their writers are in slack periods, money lender. Some writers consider their agents as essential to success as vigorous verbs.

The pivotal point, however, is that topflight agents will almost never take beginners on as clients. A good agent can afford to give little time (if any) to a writer who is just learning his trade. The agents who specialize in helping beginners charge reading fees (their ads can be found in writers' magazines). They may be able to help a writer get started, but few of them are held in high esteem by editors. In short, the neophyte should cultivate his own relationships with editors.

Further, it is questionable whether one who specializes in article writing for magazines should ever hook up with an agent. Some successful article writers have developed mutually profitable relationships with agents. But agents are far more useful to writers who concentrate on fiction and books. The article writer is primarily a reporter; his work with magazine editors resembles the relationship between the newspaper reporter and his editor. In addition, neither a writer nor an editor wants to convey messages through a third party.

A highly successful article writer summed up his experience with agents as follows:

Over the years, I have worked with three literary agents, two of them of high caliber and one not so good. None was of any great help in selling article ideas, although it was reassuring on occasion to talk over ideas with them before talking with the editors. Agents are sometimes able to line up new markets for a writer, but when it comes down to the hard business of selling ideas, the writer must do it himself. In all three cases, after working with these agents for from one to eight years, we have terminated the relationship by mutual agreement, and with good feelings.

Where the agents were able to do good, and justify their 10 percent commissions, was in persuading editors to raise my rate of pay. They may have pushed some editors a little too hard. Most editors are alert to the need of raising rates after eight or ten articles. If they forget, I'm not squeamish about calling it to their attention in a letter. That usually does it.

In principle, agents are supposed to check manuscripts before they go to an editor and suggest revisions. But I've found that agents' guesses as to what editors want are not much better than my own, and sometimes not so good. Also, I've found that agents hesitate to go to bat for a writer if there is a misunderstanding with an editor, for fear of jeopardizing their other clients.

Obviously, if you plan to work through an agent, you must choose one carefully. Perhaps the best approach is to ask magazine editors to recommend an agent they respect. But if you think that working with an agent will solve all your business problems, you are certain to be disappointed.

CHAPTER FOURTEEN EXERCISES

1. Write two queries based on one of your story ideas to two different magazines. Explain how you tailored your subject for each one.

2. Exchange your two queries with one of your classmates. Tell him or her which of the queries you would prefer if you were an editor.

3. Assume that you are a full-time free-lance writer who earns an average of $500 per article and has a total income of $12,000 per year from free-lancing. How many queries will you need to write each month to maintain your income if 30 percent are accepted? Calculate this figure for other acceptance rates.

CHAPTER 15
Writing the Long Magazine Article

Many beginning writers have the mistaken impression that it is easier to write a short article than a long one. Experienced free-lancers often claim that it's really just the opposite. Of course, the rigors of precise language, tightly knit structure, and well-chosen quotes and anecdotes apply in both cases. However, in a short article, a writer cannot afford to include a single line or paragraph that is not essential to the story, and if the subject is broad or complex, the need to extract the most important points without omitting any crucial ideas can be quite demanding.

And even in a long article the writer is rarely free to loosen the reins and trot along at a leisurely pace. In order to keep the reader's attention from beginning to end, the writer may even want to quicken the pace somewhat. Smooth transitions are essential to keep readers moving from one paragraph to the next without losing their attention. Paragraphs are usually short, no more than four or five sentences; otherwise, the printed page begins to look like a mass of gray that is not only difficult to read but is unappealing to the eye. To maintain visual appeal, magazines often break up long articles into sections and add subheadings or sidebars that are either interesting quotes from the article or summations of the main ideas.

Long articles are especially good barometers of whether or not the writer has done a thorough research job. It's not hard to tell when the author has used every last quote and every drop of information squeezed from other sources. Regardless of the length of the story, it is always better to have far more research material than you actually use. The surplus allows you to be selective, to choose the best quote, not just the only quote you happen to have on the subject. In addition, extensive knowledge about the subject gives the author feelings of confidence and authority and that translates into sure, thoughtful prose.

Having a desk piled high with research material can itself be a problem for beginners. The difficulty lies in how to organize the material before you start, and in how to use it as you go along. Writers' solutions to these problems are as individual as their styles; the best way is simply the way that works best for you. In this chapter, you'll read how some experienced writers tackle the task. Try the methods that seem most appropriate for you.

Steve Ames, who writes often for sports magazines, has proposed some general guidelines on how to write long articles. Here are his suggestions:

1. Type notes double-spaced, reorganize them, number them, then cut and paste to insert new ideas.

2. Draw an outline from your reorganized notes.
Suggested order:
    Anecdote or general statement of fact
    Main thought development
    Quote as example
    Underlying, or secondary, thought briefly stated
    Example

3. Write a lead built around the ideas as you have organized them and decide whether an anecdote would be fitting to precede the lead.

4. Try writing at least a 1,000- to 2,000-word story nonstop. Writing is an artistic method of stringing words together. However, what it is not is an elongated newspaper story. It must have depth, background, color; write to one point of view. The author must completely submerge himself in the topic. Step away a bit, then write like an observer.

5. Come back to the writing after a brief time. Reread the story. Look over your notes and finish writing. Be selective. You owe nothing to anyone you have interviewed. Just because you have spent fifteen minutes or even two hours with someone who has produced nothing that will make an important contribution to your article doesn't mean that you have to include his name or anything he has said.

6. Come back a day or two later. Look at your story cold. Read it aloud or have someone else read it to you. Ask yourself, is it conversational?

7. After you have done some thinking about it—make that *critical* thinking—retype it.

8. Read it into a tape recorder.

9. Play back the tape. Check for transitions as the tape plays back. How do the words sound that you have strung together?

10. Rewrite for the final draft. And now, reresearch your article. Are quotes transcribed correctly?

Let's look in depth at how to apply some of Ames's suggestions for writing the long article.

FIRST PRINCIPLES OF GOOD WRITING

Organizing the Material   It is far better (if extraordinarily difficult for some writers) to organize the material first. Impatient writers can force themselves to do this by telling themselves that they must work efficiently rather than temperamentally. They may have to submerge their artistic egos, but this will enable them to use all their time, energy, and talent more effectively.

Patient writers will stay away from the typewriter for as long as is necessary to organize facts and thoughts. Although individual writers work at different speeds, and no system will transform a plodding writer into a fast one, anyone will benefit from organizing the attack on research material. Consider four levels of organizing, each of which lends itself to variations.

Level 1 is almost ridiculously simple. It involves nothing more than reading the research material. Yet some writers *never* reach this level. Itching to write, they simply try to remember the clippings they have read and the releases and passages from books they have scanned, referring to their notes and to a clipping or a passage only when they want a direct quotation. The occasional need for one item or another leads them on a time-wasting, frustrating search through the stack.

In general, writers should be so familiar with their material that they can put their hands on the right source for a particular item in a matter of seconds. This means that not only should you read your material once, you should reread it two or even three times.

At least a few writers reach the first level and stop there, too impatient to go on to Level 2. This level requires arranging notes, clippings, releases, pamphlets, and books by placing similar materials together—descriptive passages here, anecdotes there, and so on —and by marking the items that are likely to figure heavily in the article. Writers who work at this level often surround themselves with research, using not just desk space but spreading notes and clippings in an arc around their chairs. The more careful the writer, the greater the probability that he or she will organize the material rather than merely open it to view.

Level 3 of organization, after reading and arranging the material for easy access, involves outlining the article. Among professional writers, this is seldom the academic outline made up of roman and arabic numerals and capital and lowercase letters. It is more often a simple, general-subject outline that starts with a thematic sentence and indicates how and when the various elements—anecdotes, statistics, incidents, descriptions—will be used to point up the theme and flesh out the characters.

Level 4 is a quantum jump. It calls for organizing research material in a way that many might consider extravagant. One variation has the writer jotting sequences of his projected article on index cards, then putting the cards in order to firm up the pattern of the article. Another has the writer putting sequences on sheets of paper that are then fastened to the wall above the typewriter. Perhaps the most elaborate method is used by an extremely successful free-lancer. He describes it as ''the perspirational system of writing.''

This is purely mechanical, and it's a fine warm-up exercise for writing. First, I cut up the small pocket notebooks that I use in note taking and paste the pages on sheets of typewriter paper, four pages to a sheet. Then I add to that stack of sheets whatever notes I've made on tablet paper and organize the releases, tear sheets, bulletins, and books, which also go on the stack. My live field notes—most of my best stuff from interviews and on-the-scene reporting—go on top of the stack. Then I go through all this and number each sheet and item.

By this time, I'm warming up to the task ahead of me and am eager to get to the writing. But I don't start beating any typewriter. Instead, I take a large sheet of paper, about the size of a newspaper page laid sidewise, which is divided into four columns, and which has a space at the top about three inches deep for random notations like lead sentences or titles that might occur to me. I use so many of these special pages in my work that I have them printed.

Then, reading through my notes and the other material, I jot down sequences in my prospective story in the columns on that big page. I number each sequence to correspond to the page number in the stack of notes. This is for quick reference when I'm writing, so I won't have to thumb through a wilderness of notes for a fact, a figure, an anecdote, or a quotation. After I've outlined all the material, I scan the whole sheet for what seems to be a lead, then mark that sequence with a red pencil, "1." Then I look for the next sequence and mark it "2," then "3," and so on. Soon, my story is organized on that big sheet of paper right down to the last paragraph.

At this point, I back off and look at the sheet of sequences and say to myself, "Do I have a story or don't I?" If I decide that I do, I'm almost ready to start writing. If I decide that I don't, I know that I'll have to do some more research. It's much better to learn this before I start writing rather than after I've spent hours or days pounding the typewriter only to discover that my piece is too thin to send to an editor.

Even when I have everything I need, I hold off on the writing until I answer this question: "Exactly what am I trying to say in this piece?" I try to answer in one sentence, which I then condense into a few words or a phrase. This serves as my working title, my guide as I write. I jot them down in the space at the top of my page of sequences, and sometimes I have twenty titles before I'm through. I pick the one that looks best, knowing that the editor may decide on another. After all, he may think he's a better title-writer than I am—and he probably is. Why don't I just forget all about titles? Because a title, even one that's rejected, gives me a mental picture of my story. And I must have one or I can't write.

This is a complex system, and it is doubtful that many writers have the patience for it. More writers use a simpler approach that pivots on subtopics. This requires making a list of important subtopics that the article must cover (the length of the list varying with the length and complexity of the article). The writer numbers each research item (notes, clippings, and the like), reads each item to decide which topic it concerns, then places the appropriate number next to the relevant topic on the list. Next, the writer organizes the list into an outline. When he is ready to write a subtopic, he can prepare a small pile of relevant materials by referring to the outline.

How carefully each writer organizes his material will vary with temperament, will power, habit—indeed, with all the qualities that make a writer one kind of worker or another. It would be absurd to suggest that every writer attempt to adapt himself to any one pattern of work. But a writer must read and organize his material in some way before beginning to write.

Determining the Theme   One should write to a title or at least to a thematic sentence. This practice is desirable because a writer must know where he is going; and a thematic statement, whether it is expressed in a title of a few words or in a complete sentence, will guide him. The absence of a thematic idea (many writers call it "the angle" or "the slant") is nearly always damaging. A writer may wander through sentences that add little to the thrust of the article or, worse, through sentences that are peripherally relevant; they seem central because they are fairly close, but they are the most voracious time wasters imaginable.

Consider the danger of working without a theme: Thousands of words *can* be written about almost anything. A simple room, a simple object, a simple man—an imaginative researcher-writer can explore any of these in paralyzing detail. Without a theme that states the salient features of a subject, the writer has no guide to tell him what to point up, what to ignore. Of course, a thoughtful writer has some vague notion even without a theme because he has read extensively and because his own interest in certain aspects of the subject will guide him toward a proper emphasis.

But it can be little more than a vague notion unless the writer makes a conscious effort to state a theme specifically. Thus, it is not enough for a free-lancer to begin to write about the UCLA basketball team or the president of the United States *in general*. He must decide, for example, that he will write about the ruthless efficiency of UCLA, including the seriousness and the rigor of the training that produced the team. Entire books could be written about the team, but the article writer needs a focus that will enable him to contain his piece in 3,000 to 4,000 words. The fact that he places his focus on UCLA's efficiency does not require that he ignore evidence of locker-room horseplay or practical jokes during travels to out-of-town games. If these sidelights exist, the writer would be dishonest to ignore them. Instead, he subordinates them, recounting an example or two to indicate that the players are not always serious.

What the focus on theme really means is that the writer has an instrument that will enable him to *select*. For example, the sequences in the UCLA article may seem, superficially, to be quite diverse—everything from the coach's religious training to the All-American guard's family life. The writer deals with the coach's background, however, because it is central to understanding why he runs the team as he does. The writer deals with the guard's home life not merely to make the point that the player is pleasant during the off-season and barely civil during the winter, but to show how one player reacts to the rigors of efficiency athletics.

Similarly, a story on the president (or almost any other subject) must be thematic. One can write volumes about the presidency in general, or even about the current president in particular. *What* about the president? Is this an article predicting that he will run for reelection? Is it about his sense of humor?

Asking and answering such questions is a commanding necessity in beginning an article. Most careful writers determine the theme at the beginning—while writing the query to the editor about writing the article or early in the research process. Themes that have been developed early sometimes change. Editors may suggest different themes, often in responding to queries from the author, sometimes when responding to a writer's progress report on research, and occasionally—alas!—when they have read the article in the form that the writer fondly supposes to be final. Ideally, though, the writer shapes a captivating theme quite early, when the idea begins to emerge, and only if research yields new facts and thoughts that thrust forward a compelling new theme will the writer change his initial idea.

Even when the theme is in mind, many writers postpone putting words on paper and indulge in rituals that help them absorb the feel of a story. One writer becomes so wound up that he paces up and down the corridor outside his office. Another leaves his desk to walk around and sometimes digs out and reads similar articles he has written for the magazine at which he is aiming. A third broods about the form of his article while absently working in his garden. Eccentric though these may seem, all are designed to search out the feel of the article. No one can quite define it, but when one has captured the feel, the writing flows.

Basic Writing Considerations   For the beginner, there are other considerations before starting to write. We might group them under the headings: (1) mechanics, (2) forms, (3) style, and (4) market.

Mechanics   Some beginners worry endlessly over whether they should use longhand, type, or dictate. Each method has been used successfully, often by the same writer at different times. A writer should adopt the method that suits him. Writing in longhand has one striking advantage: It cuts down verbosity. Most free-lancers find that their handwritten articles are seldom flabby with words. But longhand can be slow and tiring. Typing goes faster for almost everyone, especially those who have learned to "think on a typewriter." Ernest Hemingway, who was a newspaper reporter for years, eventually turned to longhand for much of his writing, but he usually typed dialogue because it came to his mind so rapidly that he felt the need to get it on paper as fast as possible. But some writers avoid the typewriter because they believe typing requires too much time and energy feeding pages in and yanking them out. They suspect that the speed of typing encourages them to write too many sentences that find their way into the wastebasket. For those who work from detailed outlines, dictating is undoubtedly the fastest method, but one who does not outline carefully can become lost in his own sentences. Dictation can turn out a smooth article that flows well from point to point. But few writers are really capable of dictating well, and even those who develop a talent for it often find that the result is startlingly verbose. One writer who turned to dictating said, "I've always had dictated manuscript transcribed with a wide margin, usually a third of the page, so that I can condense and refine the story—sometimes through as many as six or eight revisions."

Forms   Another question that troubles most beginners is the form of the magazine article. Those who have been told that there is a structure for the news story and a structure for the formal essay and various structures for various kinds of poetry worry about "the proper form of the article." There is none. One can analyze *categories* of articles. Profiles, descriptives, narratives, personal experiences, informatives, how-to-do-its, analyses, and essay-reviews are the categories identified and illustrated in the chapters of this book. But the structure of each article varies with the material. That is, even within a single category, the articles begin differently, develop their themes differently, and end differently; the possible variations are limitless. This is suggested by one of the best articles written by *Life*'s Robert Coughlan.* A profile of a controversial assistant secretary of defense named Roger Kyes, the article was in the form of a trial, with those Coughlan interviewed speaking for and against Kyes, much as they might have had they been on a witness stand. Was Coughlan wrong to cast his article in this eccentric form? No. There are no wrong forms. There are only ineffective forms—and they, too, are countless. Ultimately, the material and the writer's ideas about it determine the form the article should take.

Style   The fact that the mechanics of writing and the forms of articles are numerous may seem to suggest that anything goes in

---

*"Ugliest Man since Abe Lincoln," *Life* (August 10, 1953), pp. 86–94.

article writing, that it is idle to try to establish general rules. But when we consider style and content, the focus sharpens. Although there are certainly exceptions to almost any rule one might propose, one may generalize confidently about the style and content of most magazine articles.

Rather than devote page after page to questions of style (in the traditional and stale manner), this book is arranged so that the reader learns primarily by covering the high points of style in this chapter and by analyzing the articles reproduced in later chapters. Study the sentences. Note that the writing is hardly ever the choppy style common to many news stories (most of which are designed to do little more than impart information). Nor is it the leisurely prose of most essays or the specialized jargon of articles in scholarly journals. Magazine prose does vary from article to article and from magazine to magazine because subjects and audiences differ. Without being formularized, however, magazine writing is a distinct body of prose, usually made up of words the reader can understand without a dictionary and information he can absorb without being gravely purposeful about improving himself. Vivid writing is prized, but the writer must use the restraint dictated by taste and common sense.

The general style favored by most magazines consists of crisp, original phrases made up of familiar words. It seeks to avoid the trite. Where possible, the words and phrases are concrete and visual rather than intangible and abstract. Where numbers will help, they are not piled on one another in a statistical morass; they are used infrequently for maximum effect. Pointed quotations are sprinkled through most articles to change the pace, to enliven the reading, and to present facts and ideas distinctively. Although long articles may be broken into sections (much as a book is broken into chapters), the general rule is that the writing flows from beginning to end through smooth transitions. Because the reader is not automatically interested in hard fact and analysis, he is *led* to them. For example, a profile never begins with the vital statistics of the subject's birth and parentage. These are worked in only after the reader has been given so many interesting facts, incidents, and insights that he wants to know about the man's beginnings.

Market   The writer must study each magazine he or she is considering articles for and that means much more than reading a few issues. Whether he is a beginner or a professional, the free-lancer must devote hours, even days, to analyzing a particular market. One highly successful writer says that he aims at a magazine for the first time by reading all the issues of the preceding year. He analyzes the style and he tries to understand the essence. "The feel of the articles," he says, "is just as important as the mechanical analysis."

Use the techniques described in Chapter Thirteen of this book to help you analyze the magazines you are aiming toward; then use that information to help shape the content of your articles.

WRITE AND REVISE

The following case study illustrates some of the important points in shaping and reshaping readable articles.

Changing Yosemite

Critique of Article	Article	Revision
The first paragraph doesn't build to its point; the point is made in the middle of the paragraph. In the revision—right column—the paragraph builds to the point. It's difficult to picture a *word* like "commercialism" infiltrating anything. ("Infiltrate" is a visual term.) Yet one can visualize commercialism (a kind of blight) enveloping—right column—a place like Yosemite.	Yosemite National Park has been widely publicized since its early history. In fact, just six years after the valley was discovered, the first tourist party was brought in by English adventurer James Hutchings in 1855. The terrible word "Commercialism" that has infiltrated so much of America during the last decade has regretfully not forgotten about Yosemite. Tucked away in the high Sierras, Yosemite National Park is now just five to seven hours driving time from both San Francisco and Los Angeles.	Perhaps the future of Yosemite National Park was forecast at the beginning. Just six years after the Yosemite Valley was discovered in 1849, English adventurer James Hutchings brought in the first tourist party. Now, although Yosemite is tucked away in the High Sierras, it is just five to seven hours from both Los Angeles and San Francisco—and the commercialism that has tainted so much of America is slowly enveloping it.
One speaks of "amounts" of sugar, sand, etc.; of "numbers" of people, bricks, trees, and the like. Are there visitors who are *not* transient?	Yosemite Valley, although still abounding in natural beauty, is evolving to keep up with the whims of modern America. Every summer, the amount of tourist inhabitants increases to a record number. Due to this alarming number of transient visitors, last year over one million, the valley has had to make some corresponding changes.	The valley is still rich in natural beauty, but Yosemite is evolving with the whims of modern America. Every summer, the number of tourists sets a record; last year, Yosemite lured more than one million. And every summer the valley changes.
Test each use of "for example." If your next statement is quite obviously an example of a generalization you have just written, "for example" wastes words.	For example, no longer do the park rangers think it wise to let the entertaining bears conduct their nightly raids. This season, for the first time, nearly all of the bears were carted to the uplands	No longer will the park rangers allow the resident bears to conduct their nightly raids. For the first time last summer, the bears were carted away to the uplands. Only two of the thirty escaped

If you must identify Yogi Bear with Jellystone, the point is lost. Instant recognition of his name is essential. "Pic-in-ic," on the other hand, asks too much of the reader.

of the park. Only two of the usual thirty were sly enough to avoid capture so that they could continue on their usual summer capers of robbing "pic-in-ic baskets" as Yogi Bear of Jellystone National Park fame would say.

the exodus and continued their amiable robbery of picnic baskets, Yogi-Bear style.

This probably isn't contrary to what the reader would think. The friendly park bears are widely known. "Contrary" makes a "rather than pleased" superfluous.

The point about the limitation *by park officials* to ten days comes much later. The reader won't understand.

Contrary to what the reader might think, this move disappointed rather than pleased the loyal Yosemite visitors who have been returning faithfully to the park for their allotted ten days of vacation every summer. The bears used to put on a nightly show at the valley garbage dump which drew an intrigued crowd of regular spectators every night. This event began the evening's entertainment program which was culminated by watching the Firefall.

The disappearance of so many of the bears was a stark disappointment to regular Yosemite visitors. They can remember the years when everyone crowded around the valley garbage dump to watch the bears put on a nightly show.

Few readers know what is meant by "Firefall." Don't use it until you define it (as you do in the next paragraph).

In addition, late in the season, usually in September, every night after the Firefall precisely at 9:45, garbage can lids were heard to bang in every campsite as the bears began their nightly raiding parties. Some campers left a jar of food out by their campsites waiting for the bears to appear so they could get a close-up look.

And late in the season, precisely at 9:45, garbage can lids banged in every campsite, the signal of the bears' nightly raiding parties. Some campers left jars of food out beside their tents to bring the bears near enough for a close-up look.

Note that through this paragraph and the beginning of the next there's a slight drift away from the theme, almost as though the writer of the article had forgotten the point he was making and was beginning to offer general information. It's important for a writer to keep his theme in mind throughout. He may

But there are more than the bears to worry about feeding during the summer tourist season in Yosemite. Many campers forgot to bring the necessary food and supplies with them, and ultimately just two years ago another significant change occurred in the valley. A supermarket was built as the nucleus of a new shopping center right in the middle of

Now, instead of wandering wildlife, Yosemite features all the comforts of suburbia. Since many campers forgot to go to the store before heading for the valley, the store has come to the campers. Two years ago, a supermarket went up—the nucleus of a shopping center. Yosemite, ex-wilderness, now has everything from a bakery to a barber shop.

certainly bring in matters that may seem extraneous—bears, campsites—but only insofar as he can fit them into the framework of theme.

American ex-wilderness. The new Yosemite Village also contains a bakery, barber shop, garage, filling station.

Now the left column is getting back to the theme. But recognize that the use of "so-called" precludes the use of quotes around *backwoodsman.* And note that the column at right makes clear the relevance of the theme to the change in campers.

Another change in Yosemite is in its tourists and campers. It seems that the so-called "backwoodsman" type of camper gets more scarce every year. Now camping in Yosemite is like moving into your backyard. If it is too much effort for the tourist to set up his own tent, then all he has to do is move his family into one of Yosemite Valley's "pre-fab" tent towns already set up for the increasing number of visitors, who prefer, as the brochures say, "Less rugged living."

And, of course, the character of the typical Yosemite camper is changing. The "backwoodsman" has apparently gone way back in the woods, leaving Yosemite Village to the backyardsman. If the new tourists are too fagged to set up camp, they can move into the "pre-fab" tent towns available to those who prefer, as the brochures say, "less rugged living."

This paragraph gets a bit heavy with sarcasm. Better a touch of subtlety.

If this is still not enough of a homey touch to suit our friend "Joe Tourist," then he can rent a housekeeping cabin at Camp Curry. Of course, there are hot showers, a cafeteria, post office, gift shop and heated swimming pool nearby, lest the hardy traveller need to indulge in "wilderness activities" missing at home.

The tourist who dies a little at the thought of any kind of tent can settle at Camp Curry where hot showers, a cafeteria, a post office, a gift shop, and a conveniently located heated swimming pool are guaranteed to whisk away any vestige of wilderness fever.

First Draft, Second Draft, Third Draft   Should one write the first draft hurriedly or painstakingly? A writer may choose to blast ahead, giving little attention to phrases or sentence structure, trying to get the basic framework on paper in the first draft, saving deftness and polish for revisions. Or he can shape and polish as he goes, phrasing as vividly as his talent allows the first time through, smoothing one sentence before he moves on to the next. There can be no rule about such matters, of course, but most writers advise beginners to try to develop the habit of writing the first draft rapidly. Because the theme is likely to be nebulous and the process of worrying each sentence can lead the writer down dead-end paragraphs, it is far better to build a basic structure, however unwieldy, and polish everything in sub-sequent drafts. This may be impossible for some writers. In fact, one of the authors of this book sometimes finds that he cannot bear to leave a page without polishing and revising. But he recognizes that the ability to run through a first draft rapidly is a valuable quality.

When the writer has rapidly written a first draft, what does he have? Usually a crude framework for an article. Converting this into publishable prose requires restraint, for the impulse to move directly to a final draft is strong. A better course is suggested by a veteran free-lancer:

> I've found that it pays to have each rewriting, each draft, serve a specific purpose. My article is barely hatched with the first draft. I compare it to my notes and other material and insert anything I've overlooked that will make the story stronger. I don't try to do too much refining in the second draft, which is longer than the first—and much too long for the editor. The third draft is the one in which I do the refining, cutting unnecessary paragraphs or sentences or even words, and often changing the position of se-quences. This gets the manuscript down to length, and this is usually the semifinal copy. Now I begin sandpapering and polishing. You might call this a fourth draft, but it's probably just an upgrading of the third. It's overwhelm-ingly important, though. With *Roget's Thesaurus* and Rodale's *Word-Finder* at hand, I go through the entire man-uscript looking for words I can upgrade to make the story more vivid or lively or moving. I try to replace static words with those that have action. It's amazing what refining a dozen to a score of words will do for a manuscript.
>
> It's especially important to rework the lead. If I rewrite a manuscript three to six times, or more—and I often do—I usually refine the first two or three paragraphs ten or a dozen times. And that's no exaggeration. I have about one minute flat to catch my editor and my reader with that first paragraph or two. So I try every combination of words and phrases that seem challenging. Often, I've tried a few of these combinations before I start to write the first draft. If I can hit the right one, it's a guideline when I'm doing the first draft. The probability is that I'll distill out a better one when I finish the first draft.
>
> The target in distilling out a lead is to make every word say exactly what you want it to say. If a word or a phrase doesn't say enough in the right way, then you have to find a better one. This process of making words say exactly what you mean goes for the rest of the story as well as the lead. It's the difference between sharp writing and fuzzy writing.

THE VALUE OF ANECDOTES

Reading the articles reproduced in Chapters 5 to 9 in conjunction with the letters and memos from editors (which follow) will point up central matters of content. Note how many anecdotes and incidents are used in almost every article. Sometimes a writer must tell about a subject, at least in part, but how much better it is to *show!* Frank Taylor's article "He Sets the Sky on Fire!" begins with a revealing anecdote—because it is one thing to say that Patrick Lizza is a colorful, eccentric figure who sells his fireworks with his own enthusiastic presentations. It is quite another, and more vivid, thing to present him as Taylor does here:

In Sacramento the directors of the California State Fair were deep in parley over how to stay within the budget, when a chunky little human bombshell in baggy clothes pushed his beaming face into the room and loosed a burst of verbal pyrotechnics. He could, he said, produce a more magnificent fireworks display than anyone had ever seen this side of Mount Vesuvius, near whose slope our hero, Patrick Lizza, was born.

"I got a great idea, gentlemen, the greatest idea that ever comes to me before. All we need is a little more money, just a few thousand dollars more, and we put on the greatest fireworks show in any state fair. You gentlemen go along with me for a little more money and we really light up the sky."

As usual, after half an hour of Mr. Lizza's salesmanship and kidding, the directors were in great good humor and ready to go along—and the budget be damned.

No other element of an article is more important than the anecdote. It need not be funny, it need only reveal. Quite often, anecdotes are used to support generalizations. Thus, in an article titled "New Winds in the South, New Splash in the North," the author suggests that the sleazy reputation of the *San Francisco Chronicle* springs in part from the maladroit banner headlines on its street sale editions. Then:

There is daily evidence. . . . For example, one morning the *Chronicle* published an amusing story about a man who called in his friends to show them home movies of his vacation. The movies had just been processed, and he hadn't seen them himself. He darkened the living room, turned on the projector, and out came one of those stag-party dirty movies. In its home delivery edition, the *Chronicle* played the story adroitly—in a small, double-column box on the left side of Page 1, sitting there as welcome relief from the major news of the day. But in the street sale edition, the innocuous little story was plastered under a huge banner which proclaimed across the top of Page 1: PORNOGRAPHIC MOVIE SHOCKER. The story was transformed from an amusing sidebar to a silly piece of empty sensationalism.

Because an anecdote *confronts* the reader with a subject while other kinds of writing merely tell about it, a well-chosen anecdote is memorable as well as readable. In "Why Congressmen Can't Do Their Jobs," a general point is made with, "There are some correspondents who write letters so they can say they know a senator on a first-name basis." That establishes a fact, but it hardly drives the point home to the reader. This, however, does: "The first letter is formal: 'Dear Senator.' The second runs: 'Dear Senator Sparkman.' The third is 'Dear John.' A fourth received in Senator Sparkman's office started: 'Sparky.' "

Anecdotes come in hundreds of forms and lengths—all of them precious to a writer. No matter how serious the article, anecdotes will give it a lift. Too many beginners assume that no more than an opening anecdote or two—and perhaps one at the end for a punch conclusion—are needed to sugarcoat the important things they have to say that will make up the bulk of the article. They should remember that Boswell's *Life of Johnson,* generally considered the greatest biography ever written, is made up largely of what Samuel Johnson said and did. Boswell knew the value of anecdotes. The point is that many of the important things a writer has to say can be presented graphically, but finding and developing graphic anecdotes is sometimes hard work. It is much easier to sit back and reel out abstract sentences and impressions—easier, but deadening.

MEMOS FROM EDITORS

When a free-lancer or staff writer has completed an article and submitted it to an editor, the learning process may be just beginning. For this much is certain: Perceptive editors have much to teach writers who will listen. Contrary to the beliefs of some disgruntled writers, an editor is not hired to make the life of a staff writer miserable and the life of a free-lancer impossible. The chief responsibility of most magazine editors is to produce successful magazines, and this requires that they discover and cultivate writers who can provide the articles that make a magazine successful. The point is that it is to an editor's advantage to help writers. The excerpts in this chapter from editors' letters and memos show how they try to help with sharp, but friendly, criticism. These excerpts should also demonstrate some of the important techniques in writing magazine articles.

Study Your Magazine before You Write for It

Thank you for letting me see "The Anatomy of the Shark Scare," which I return herewith. Like all your work, this is extremely well-written, with considerable flavor. It is not, however, the kind of article we would use. It is subjective and literary, whereas our pieces are more apt to be objective and factual.

To write successfully for the national magazines, the writer must aim each article at a specific magazine. He must familiarize himself with the kind of article used by that magazine by long reading and study of its pages. No longer—perhaps unfortunately—can the writer simply write an article and then send it out to be published.

You will see that preparing such an article entails a great deal of work—preliminary as well as final. It is altogether different from writing a newspaper story: long and careful research is necessary, and then great attention to content, construction and writing. Our successful contributors sometimes spend much more time on preparing an outline than the average writer spends in writing a finished article for other magazines.

Stick to Your Theme

There should be only one main theme in your article— i.e., the fact that the police are unpopular and why. This would include both the themes mentioned in your letter, that hooligans have been making violent attacks on police, and that the police are unpopular with the general public. Naturally, the piece would go on to tell what is being done constructively about the problem in various cities. But if you go too much into techniques of handling crowds, for instance, you get away from the main theme. Remember that the article came out of our conversation which was devoted to the two closely connected points: *Why* do we have this wave of attacks on the police? and *What* can be done to stop it? Naturally, you are going to describe such attacks, using your most dramatic case histories. I feel sure you can put the piece together solidly, so that it will have the coherence and unity to make it convincing.

Tell Only One Story at a Time

The Boss asked me to write you about "Lazybones Gardening Is for Me," which we have concluded is a darned good subject, but not "as is." The problem, we think, is that you have tried to tell two stories in one: (a) how gardening has become a lazy man's job for you and (b) how others developed various gadgets and chemicals that help the gardener become lazy.

Honestly, we think the first story is the best one, the most widely appealing one—and while the other relates to it, you have let it more or less take over, which, in addition to the effect it has on the story organization, also throws too much emphasis on particular products.

What we would like to have is a fairly straight story about lazy man's gardening from your own experience and that of your gardening friends. It should be told with a light touch, of course, but shouldn't strain to be humorous; we think there is an extensive interest in gardening that will welcome a fairly serious, informative article. There are a lot of puzzled gardeners, caught between the traditional back-breaking systems, and the plethora of new plant foods, fungicides, insecticides, soil conditioners, and the array of gadgets. We can't, of course, do a how-to-do-it guide, but certainly you can tell how you and some other gardeners have licked this dilemma. Keep the focus on the lazy gardener—the kind we all hope to be.

Personalities Make Your Story Come Alive

The chief trouble with this piece is that it comes out a rather dull piece of copy. Somehow it becomes largely a catalogue of philanthropies in the field of conservation and seems to be done at arm's length. It just doesn't have the breath of life in it. And of course this is the most difficult of all rewriting problems to solve, but it will have to be solved somehow if we are to have an acceptable article.

I think one element, now missing, that would help would be to give us some personality stuff on your character— how he works, what kind of guy he is, maybe a few more quotes from him about people and problems he deals with in this work. In the present manuscript, he seems to be only a shadowy figure in the background. Is he really a self-effacing character, or does he just come out this way in your article?

One thing I think you should *not* do in trying to get more life into the article is to make it more breezy and slangy. You have a bit too much of that kind of writing in the manuscript now. This technique is all right for a lighter vein piece, but it doesn't seem to belong in a serious article like this one.

Enliven with Examples

Your Indian girl story arrived this morning—and you are going to be just as disappointed in my report on it as I was in reading it. To put it bluntly, the story misses the mark entirely. I am extremely puzzled by this, because there is wonderful material here for a striking and memorable piece. I find myself wondering whether you have really read our magazine carefully, studying the articles to familiarize yourself with the kind of things we use.

I still believe, however, that you *can* write for us successfully, and that you will do so in the future. Anything I can do to help, I shall gladly do. But I think it would be wise for you not to attempt any more articles until we have had a chance to sit down and discuss matters of technique again. Why don't you wind up your story investigations when convenient and come back to New York? Then we can go over everything carefully, and you can write the other pieces you have in hand when you get home. Working together more closely, I have every hope that they will end up in the magazine. I hope you don't mind me writing thus frankly to you, pulling no punches. That is the only way I know how to talk to someone I like and whom I want to help.

As to detailed criticism of the Indian girl piece, I shall list some of its failings. In the first place, it lacks anecdotes. There are really only two good ones in the whole article —the lead story of finding the little girl, and the story of Marie-Yvonne picking a thief to guard the Red Cross goods. As I have pointed out before, a successful article must be constructed almost entirely of anecdotes, a series of short narratives vividly representing particular events and places. In your article, you *tell* the reader about Marie-Yvonne's life in general terms; what you must do is show the reader the most interesting events of that career in anecdotes and narrative.

You tell the reader that Marie-Yvonne is accustomed to do this and that when she visits the Indians. How much more effective this section would be if it were the narrative of one specific trip, one specific scene around the campfire, with actual quotes of her conversation. You write: "When her father was with her on similar expeditions, he made it a point to tell them his history, and how he had adopted and raised her. It always made them like him better." This is an indirect and passive presentation of what could be a most interesting point—you are asking the reader to take your word for an opinion. But write that scene as an actual occurrence—the half-naked savages around the campfire, the white man standing before them, the Indian girl trying to make the two understand each other, the shadows, the jungle, etc.—and you will have the kind of effective anecdote that makes a moving piece.

Perhaps you are writing too much for yourself, and not enough with the reader in mind. This is never a successful approach for us, except by accident. Our articles are written for a calculated effect on specific readers—the successful magazine writer never loses sight of that. He must say to himself continually, "Is my reader still with me? Am I losing him? Would this interest him more than that? Now I shall make him laugh, now I shall make him choke up," and so on. And the way to do this is to give the reader a continuing narrative, formed of a series of memorable anecdotes. General exposition and leisurely description do not make a good magazine piece.

Part of this calculated effort to interest the reader is of course the presentation of pictures, sharp images. In the lead of your article, for instance, the only description you give of your heroine is that she was a "two- or three-year-old girl, showed marks of severe mistreatment, and she was terrified." Well, what did she look like? Was she fat or thin? Was she clothed or naked? If clothed, with what? Black hair? Color of eyes? As a matter of fact, nowhere in the whole article do you tell us what Marie-Yvonne looks like, either then or later. Of course there should be two descriptions—of the tiny savage found in the jungle, and of the civilized young woman twenty years later. But you do not even tell the reader the color of her skin, whether she is short or tall, how she dresses, what her figure is like, or the sound of her voice.

Dr. Vellard's first glimpse of the child, in the jungle, should be one of the highlights of the story. You hardly mention it, merely quoting from the doctor's diary. Compare the lead of your article—which is written in general terms—with the detailed, vivid picture of the same scene which could be written. You say that Dr. Vellard and his Indian guides were walking through the jungle under constant attack by unseen Guayaki Indians with bows and arrows, that two of the guides fled, and that on September 23, "a strange thing happened." In transcribing from his notes later, Dr. Vellard made this simple entry in his journal: "Our fugitive Indian guides returned. On the way they found a small Guayaki camp, two women and a child." But nowhere do you *show* us the "constant attack with bows and arrows"—you merely tell us that it occurred. There is no description of the guides, or even of the "small Guayaki camp, the two women or the child." Yet think how effective and memorable could be a vividly painted scene of savages in the jungle, arrows quivering in trees, and Dr. Vellard stepping out into the small clearing, here and there a hut or two, the naked women lamenting and crying, the tiny child, and so on. This could be an extraordinary scene;

it must not be thrown away with a noncommittal quotation from a diary. This is such a dramatic story that it is begging to be written. I know that I am going to be writing you my hearty congratulations one of these days. I look forward to that day.

Omit Slang, Please

I am sorry to say that your piece needs more work. Your material is good, and I am sure you will be able to produce an acceptable article, but, to state the matter candidly, we think the writing is pretty darned bad in the present version. In revising the manuscript, the following matters will require your attention.

We don't like your excessive use of slang in this article. Slangy writing may be all right with some subjects, such as sports or perhaps Hollywood characters, but it seems out of place when you are writing about a great university and its president. Even in this sort of article, we don't object to an occasional slang expression, but you have loaded the whole piece so heavily with this type of writing that it gives the effect of being overly cute and kittenish. I haven't gone through the manuscript and marked these too-slangy spots, because there are some on virtually every page.

There are also a number of fuzzy, unclear spots in the manuscript. I have marked most of these marginally. These places need careful recasting and clarification and in some cases additional information. A particularly bad example is the section telling what Stanford is doing to develop its large land-holdings into profitable property through residential and industrial developments. It is simply impossible to tell what is going on from reading the present manuscript.

In rewriting the piece, I think you need to bring the biographical material about Sterling's earlier career up much closer to the front of the article. As it stands now, you merely hint at some of his previous experiences, then launch right into the job he has done at Stanford. I think his work at Stanford will be much more meaningful to the reader if you first give us a good glimpse of the man himself. Your present lead, the piano-playing incident, makes a good beginning. After that, you should state briefly, in a paragraph or two, that Sterling has done a remarkable job of reviving Stanford. Then, it seems to me, you should tell the story of his earlier life and give us a good picture of the man. After that could come your detailed story of his accomplishments at Stanford. And, finally, your present ending, giving some nice personality glimpses of the man is okay.

Make Your Piece Move

I have messed up your manuscript, in an attempt to make it more dramatic. If this piece is to be successful for us, it must really be the exciting and breathless account of an extraordinary occurrence. Everything leisurely or inconsequential must be pared away from it, so that the piece moves with the utmost speed from beginning to end. Short, staccato sentences will help, and short paragraphs, too.

I have cut out a number of the more leisurely descriptions in an attempt to speed things up. What I have not succeeded in doing is to add to the piece the idea that Rummel, having been shot point-blank twice, should have been mortally wounded or at least thought he was. Perhaps you can get this in at several places. Did Rummel fall down when he was shot? Or was he still standing up, one wonders why he didn't stagger over to the car and empty the gun into Clark. Perhaps he was unable to walk? Have you any information as to how many bullet holes were found in Clark's car afterward? Was Clark himself hit?

I think the lead is pretty good as edited—at least as far as construction is concerned. You get right into the story quickly, and it moves. Indeed, I think the construction of the whole piece is sound—the framework. But I do feel that it will need some "sheer writing" and that, of course, is up to you. You can throw aside all restraint on this one, and really let yourself go. You might get the idea of your title into the piece at several places—the fact that Rummel had three lives. When he finally gets out of the car after its turning over, you might say that for the third time that night he had brushed by death.

Why You Can't "Dash Off an Article"

Your article, "Ten Ways to Cut Your Medical Bills in Half," which I return herewith, is a beginning—but it is far from being the finished article we would require. Writing a magazine piece is considerably different from knocking out a newspaper story—as I can assure you from my own experience. The articles we buy are most thoroughly and carefully researched, sometimes for months; then are checked and re-checked; and are written and re-written. When finished, you and I both should be able to say that the article is just as comprehensive, just as perfect, as it can be made. It is because we demand such a high standard that we pay generously for the articles we accept.

You have an excellent idea for your article, and some of it reads well as it stands. But the piece gives the impression of being hastily put together, and it is by no means complete and comprehensive enough. As the piece now stands, there is a tendency to jump around from subject to subject; whereas we prefer to have everything on one subject brought together logically. Each section of the text needs careful thinking out before it is written.

Incidentally, we do not use the newspaper style of one-sentence paragraphs which you have used in this piece. It might be a good idea for you to read ten or twelve of our medical articles published over the last year or so, to give you an idea of the way in which we handle articles of this kind.

I hope you will spend at least an additional month on revising the article. Every section should be checked carefully with authorities to be sure that it is as complete as it can possibly be made. Would it not be a good idea to ask the directors of a number of hospitals what ways they can suggest in which people can cut their medical bills? And a number of other doctors as well? After all available material has been assembled, the article should be carefully constructed from start to finish. Finally, the writing itself should be done with great care.

You have an original and promising idea here, and it should make a fine article. I know you can make it just that if you will devote plenty of effort to it.

Detail Makes the Story Vivid

I wish you would have another go at this piece. The main trouble is lack of detail, clear pictures of what went on, and ease of understanding. It is better to write in detail, clearly and completely, about a certain number of events than it is to skim over many more. We like the easily understandable narrative style, which consists of a series of sharp pictures. Your opening paragraphs are excellent examples of this. It is also advisable to remember that the average American has little knowledge of foreign words and phrases and even less of remote geography; therefore, when using any such references, they must be explained; it is better to avoid them when possible.

Perhaps a good example of what I mean by the detailed narrative approach is afforded by your account of the capture of Riyadh. Rarely, in this account, does the reader get a clear picture of what went on. The town itself is not described, except to say that it has 50,000 inhabitants and has a wall and a moat around it. Yet, to make this important incident memorable to the reader, it will be necessary to give him a vivid picture of the town, the scene of the struggle, the fighters on either side—nowhere is there a word as to how they are dressed or armed—and so on.

Perhaps you have been trying to condense the article as you wrote it. But this is a handicap—you should forget all about condensation, leaving that to us, and simply write your story as vividly and as interestingly from the reader's point of view as you can. The more detail, the more color, the more pictures there are, the easier it is for us to make a lively condensation. I suggest you read a number of the biographies and adventure stories in recent issues and note the unusual amount of colorful detail you will find in each. All these pieces, it should be remembered, were three or four times as long when originally written.

Make Your Writing Clear

There is some mighty fine writing in this piece, and it is a fresh subject that seems sure to interest many of our readers. I feel, however, that a certain amount of revision and addition would make the piece even better than it is, and I am hoping you will be willing to make the changes.

As it stands, the piece takes for granted too much ready comprehension on the part of the reader. For a large audience, it is necessary to spell things out somewhat more than you have done. We try, first of all, to make each of our articles crystal-clear to every reader. Just keep in mind the reader who doesn't know the West, or anything accurate about Indians, or ranching, or the country you describe. If you can make the story easily comprehensible to him, you will have achieved what I have in mind.

I feel that the piece reads too much like fiction. I think you can help this by introducing some facts and figures. This information is needed to complete the story. How many students has the Indian school graduated or placed in jobs? How long has it been in existence and how many students does it normally accommodate? What are the buildings like, the teachers, etc.? Is there some outstanding personality connected with the school who is responsible for its success? If so, can't we have a short profile of him? In brief, the normal data of a nonfiction article, inserted here and there throughout your present script, would make the piece more realistic, with less of the sound of fiction.

The Eager Market for Humor

Thank you for letting us have a look at the piece on the perils of remodeling an old house, which I return herewith. I read it with personal, as well as professional, interest—for I am similarly entrapped. I wish I could give you encouragement on this article, but I fear I cannot. In the first place, the subject is not a fresh one, it having been treated many times in different ways. And then I think you have set down approximately what actually happened in your own case, whereas a successful humorous article of this nature should be *based* not only on actual experience, but also built up of the purely imaginary. The whole thought of the writer should be entertaining the reader, and not of reporting what has happened in real life to the writer. This requires a great deal of creative effort. You certainly have the gift of humor in your writing, and if you would give your imagination free play—forgetting the facts—I should think you could bring off some very amusing pieces. As usable humor is the hardest thing for a magazine editor to find, there is always an eager market for it. But it has to be very good, quite fresh and original.

A CHECKLIST ON WRITING

In summary, these are some of the techniques involved in successfully writing the long magazine article.

Grammar, Spelling, Punctuation   The literary genius need not bother with such mundane matters. If one is not certain that he is a genius, however, he must focus on these "mechanical" matters. Editors certainly will. In fact, editors are likely to wonder whether a writer who spells shoddily and writes drunken sentences is similarly careless with facts.

The Audience   One must write for an audience, not for himself at one extreme or for the entire universe at the other. In the magazine world, the audience one writes for is fairly easy to discern: It is made up of the readers of the particular magazine. This seems simple, and yet failing to write for a magazine's audience is probably the most common fault among beginners.

Words and Phrases   Writers should shun the trite. They must try endlessly to fashion evocative and memorable phrases. Instead of using clichés, they must strive to make phrases so captivating that they will *become* clichés—phrases that are so attractive that other writers will steal them and use them over and over to the point of exhaustion (which is exactly how the current clichés became trite). Not every sentence can, or should, be so captivatingly fashioned that it calls attention to itself. But a sentence that is not fresh and lively should at least be written in straightforward English rather than in clichés.

Anecdotes, Examples, Concrete vs. Abstract   Anecdotes (*little* stories, not necessarily *funny* stories) are among the most compelling devices in writing. Properly used, they point up, they illustrate. Their value is suggested by the difference between merely *saying* that an attorney is "like a tiger in the courtroom" and relating an anecdote that proves the point.

Anecdotes are actually examples of behavior. There are other kinds of examples, of course. One can write that some United States senators have been demagogues and yet not be especially convincing. But citing Senator Joseph McCarthy of Wisconsin offers a persuasive example of demagoguery. It is useful for anyone who writes a generalization to pause and ask himself, "Can I give two examples of this?" If he can, he should.

Few techniques in magazine writing are as pivotal as *showing* the reader a point rather than merely telling him about it. (Anecdotes show.) It is one thing to tell the reader that the subject of an article is a great humorist. It is another, and much better, thing to show his humor by recounting some of his jokes.

It is nearly always true that the specific is more readable and interesting than the general ("He has two billion dollars" is better than "He is rich"), and the concrete is more readable and interesting than the abstract (writing about a wealthy man is better than writing about the idea of wealth).

Description   Following many of the preceding suggestions will help the writer describe people, places, and things more vividly. It should also be emphasized that describing routinely ("He weighs 210 pounds, has blue eyes, and smiles often") invites yawns. It is far better to color in a person as a distinct personality. How does he walk? How does he talk? What are his distinctive mannerisms and gestures? Similarly, describing a place or thing requires that the writer focus on its distinctive qualities. What is it about Boston (or the Florida Keys or a Kansas wildflower) that makes it interesting and worth reading about?

Theme and Tone   Speaking of the "angle" or the "slant" of an article refers to its theme. Whatever term is used, the requirement is the same: The writer must decide what he is going to say *about* his subject—what aspect he will emphasize and develop fully—and write a title or a thematic sentence that will guide him.

The theme and the audience together will help the writer determine the tone—sinister, serious, straightforward, light, flippant, or whatever. It is fairly common for beginners to change the tone of an article inadvertently. Although light elements can appear in articles that are essentially serious, the article that seems never to be able to make up its mind about tone leaves readers puzzled. The problem of varied tones does not usually arise for the writer who selects a magazine to write for and a theme to write about at the beginning.

Rewriting   A first draft is never as good as a second. A second draft is never as good as a third. Perhaps there is a point in rewriting at which improvement ceases. It may even be true that an article begins to deteriorate with too much rewriting, but it is easy to suspect that if this occurs it is during the thirty-seventh rewriting, or the fifty-fifth, and is thus not much of a threat to many writers.

It is important, of course, to know what to *do* in rewriting. Going at it aimlessly merely because one has been persuaded that a revision is necessary seldom improves an article. It may be necessary to put the writing aside for a time and return to it with a fresh eye and attitude. It should be possible to improve a piece by analyzing it against the items in this checklist and against the many other suggestions about writing in this book.

CHAPTER FIFTEEN EXERCISES

1. Choose two long magazine articles from any current publication, one of which is interesting and the other of which is not. Then analyze the structure, style, and content of the articles, and decide how these elements contribute to each article's overall impact on the reader.

2. Select a subject you think would be suitable for a long article. Then make a list of topics and subtopics you would expect to cover in the article and organize them into an outline. Finally, develop an alternative structure for the article by rearranging the outline. Discuss the differences that would result and the reasons you might choose one outline over the other.

3. Find a long magazine article that you think needs improvement. Assume the role of editor, and write a detailed critique of the article for the writer, suggesting ways the article could be revised. Remember to be as specific as possible.

CHAPTER 16
Descriptives and Profiles

Like the color stories found in newspapers, magazine descriptives and profiles rely on visual writing to make the readers see subjects in their minds. There was a time when such articles comprised at least half the content of popular magazines, but competition from television has reduced that percentage significantly. It has also changed the way magazines handle these stories. Some depend heavily on full-cover photographs to supplement the text while others use illustrations, but nearly all insist that descriptives and profiles be tailored specifically to the interests of their audiences.

One of the staples of descriptive writing in both magazines and newspapers is the travel story. This kind of article takes readers somewhere through descriptions of the sights, sounds, tastes, smells, and other sensations they would experience there. Yet despite the popularity of travel articles, magazine editors still demand that such stories appeal to the particular preferences, interests, and income of their readers. You won't find an article on New York budget hotels in a magazine like *Carte Blanche*. Its readers are upper middle class and affluent; they're more likely to be interested in four-star hotels and restaurants. Likewise, a magazine like *Working Woman* that has an even narrower audience wouldn't run an article on travel in San Francisco simply because it's an interesting place to visit. The story would need to have an angle of interest to women with careers, such as how a woman can combine a business trip to the Bay Area with a special vacation deal at one of the city's best hotels.

The same selection process applies to profiles. A person who is merely interesting in general probably won't make a good magazine profile; a person who is interesting because of some particular accomplishment or characteristic will, provided there is an audience with an appetite for the story. Few magazines today publish profiles that fit the mold of the *Reader's Digest*'s "Most Unforgettable Character" series. Instead, editors seek profile subjects that will interest their particular audiences.

Both descriptives and profiles benefit from a "news peg"—a newsworthy justification for running a particular story at a particular time. A profile of an actress might be published before her opening in a local theatrical production. A travel story on a city might run the month before a convention or some other event is scheduled to take place there. A news peg isn't necessary, but it's a handy tool for selling a story idea.

DESCRIPTIVES

The following two excerpts are descriptive passages—the first from "New 'Old' Homes," the second from "Freestyle Camps," both by Shelley Smolkin. As you read the two, try to determine how they help readers "see" their subjects. Is one passage more effective than the other? Why?

In beautiful old New Orleans homes, the complaint that "they don't build 'em like they used to" no longer applies. Not only has a local real estate lawyer found a way to build houses like the ones built here a century ago, she's done it by replicating the best aspects of the old in combination with the convenience and practicality of the new. The result is a row of charming Creole Porte-Cochère townhouse reproductions located on the street whose name best characterizes these new "old" homes—Harmony.

At first glance, the coral and beige colored buildings could easily be mistaken for well-restored uptown homes. That is the effect lawyer Jacqueline McPherson wanted to achieve when she first hit upon the notion to build reproductions two years ago. A preservationist with 10 years experience, she was working on her 19th Century home on Exposition Boulevard near Audubon Park, when a stream of admiring and envious friends and neighbors convinced her that many New Orleanians were looking for a combination of classic design and modern comfort that was nearly impossible to find uptown. The answer, decided Ms. McPherson, was to build new houses from old designs, using modern building materials.

Arnold Palmer wouldn't recognize his old golf course in Stratton, Vermont. People in wet suits with dripping hair and sunscreened noses slosh from the pond at one end to the trampoline at the other toting skis and poles instead of irons and drivers. Formerly the peril of the fairway, the pond is presently the most popular place on the course, only now it's bodies instead of balls that land in the drink. Across the green, skiers dig their edges into artificial turf as they maneuver down a wooden ramp.

These grass-bound skiers may appear somewhat confused, but as participants at a summer freestyle skiing training camp, they're well aware that snow is four months away. Skier Mike Shea's Stratton camp is one of half a dozen sites run by professional freestylers, ski equipment manufacturers and ski resorts around the country. For fees of about $300 for a ten-day session, campers learn how to perform the aerial, ballet and mogul routines that have given freestyle skiing the reputation as a good sport for the incurably insane.

The broken bones and bruised limbs of early freestylers are past history to today's hotdoggers, who are coached not only by their predecessors but by experts in tumbling and gymnastics as well. Unlike freestyle's pioneers, they don't just trudge out to the snow and hope for the best. Instead, they go to summer training camps where trampolines, carpeted ski decks and water jumps cushion the blows so frequent to beginners. Fellow campers may include professional freestylers, many of whom travel the training site circuit during the summer in preparation for winter competition.

The most obvious difference in the language of these two excerpts is that the first relies heavily on adjectives while the second depends more on verbs and nouns in helping the reader "see." A comparison of phrases from the two shows this clearly:

New "Old" Homes

beautiful old New Orleans homes

the best aspects of the old in combination with the convenience and practicality of the new

a row of charming Creole Porte-Cochère townhouse reproductions

the coral and beige colored buildings

a stream of admiring and envious friends

a combination of classic design and modern comfort

Freestyle Camps

people . . . slosh from the pond at one end to the trampoline at the other toting skis and poles instead of irons and drivers

bodies instead of balls that land in the drink

skiers dig their edges into artificial turf as they maneuver down a wooden ramp

they don't just trudge out to the snow and hope for the best

While no editor would advise a writer to discard adjectives altogether, most would agree that it is best to use them sparingly, even in a descriptive story. Vivid verbs often do the job more effectively as the above example illustrates.

The Essentials of the Descriptive

A focus on distinctive characteristics.   By carefully selecting minutiae, a writer can sketch a picture that sets forth the unique quality of a place.

Careful phrasing.   Descriptives depend largely on the way words are put together to achieve their effect. The substance of the descriptive may, of course, be important also.

A reading and viewing experience.   The success of a descriptive is not determined by whether readers *learn,* in the sense that they learn facts or ideas from other kinds of articles. Success pivots almost entirely on whether readers finish a descriptive with the feeling that they have been through a satisfying reading experience. The most evocative descriptives—those fashioned by writers who have developed and refined a talent for using visual words—are also a *viewing* experience.

PROFILES

The axiom that "people are interested in people" holds doubly true when applied to magazine articles. It is a safe estimate that nearly half the articles now appearing in popular magazines are woven around interesting characters, their hopes, their problems, foibles, and adversities, and how they finally got around or over the hurdles in their paths.

In editorial parlance, these articles are "profiles." The first profiles were definitive character sketches written for *The New Yorker* in the early 1930s. Gradually, the term was tacked onto almost any personality piece. Many were articles about crusades, institutions, companies, sports events, political episodes, and the like, told in terms of a lead character involved in a struggle. This method gained popularity because editors and writers discovered that the surest and easiest way to make an otherwise heavy topic come alive was to cover it from the viewpoint of a person involved. Readers could easily put themselves in his or her shoes, whereas they had a hard time pulling on the boots of a corporation or an institution.

Profiles have since become even broader. It is now fairly customary in many magazine offices to speak of "profiles" of places and events. In such cases, the profile is often much like the descriptive.

Consider the short profile of actor Peter Falk, which appeared in *Newsweek* of 13 November 1972.*

The Real Columbo

<table>
<tr>
<td>

Comment

Note that the writer begins immediately to describe the character, Columbo. The writer has been allotted only two columns, one of which will carry a small picture of Columbo. As a result, he hasn't the space for leisurely writing which he would have had if, for example, the *Newsweek* executives had decided that Falk would be the cover story.

The writer works consciously for descriptive phrases: "the wardrobe of a flood victim," "would seem hopelessly out of place in a Rolls-Royce or a pair of Gucci shoes," "like an off-duty janitor." No doubt the writer worked for hours—perhaps days—through many rewrites to get just the right tone.

The readers are induced to read on by the careful structure and phrasing of the profile.

Notice the link between this paragraph and the

</td>
<td>

Profile

He has the face of a broken-down pug, the diction of a poolroom hustler and the wardrobe of a flood victim. He never flashes a gun, throws a punch or nestles against a voluptuous bosom. When tracking down a killer, his manner is so apologetic and stumbling that his quarry invariably regards him with bemusement rather than fear. In short, "Columbo" is the absolute antithesis of the typical television detective, a misbegotten dropout from the Rock Hudson-Gene Barry School of Sophisticated Sleuthmanship. Top marks from Nielsen, however, have made the "Columbo" segment of "The NBC Sunday Mystery Movie" series one of the five highest-rated shows on TV this season. The reason, of course, is Peter Falk.

Like the detective lieutenant he portrays, Falk comes across as a lovable, low-keyed Everyman who would seem hopelessly out of place in a Rolls-Royce or a pair of Gucci shoes. Clad in a graying white shirt and crumpled trousers, he shambled into Universal Picture's executive dining room last week, looking more like an off-duty janitor than an affluent actor who has won two Academy Award nominations and two Emmies. When the waitress informed him that the booth he had taken was reserved for a Universal VIP, Falk obligingly picked up his gnawed, 10-cent cigar and slouched to another table. But when he began analyzing his TV role for *Newsweek*'s Malcolm MacPherson, it quickly became evident that Falk's unpretentious pose—like that of Columbo—disguises a shrewd, sensitive intelligence.

"Columbo says things that children say and adults only think," rasped Falk, twisting his head upward in order to see through his one good eye (the right eye is glass, the legacy of a childhood tumor). "He asks naïve questions not because he wants to look like a farmer, but because he is genuinely inquisitive. He knows they're going to write him off as a rube, but he's not offended by it. It works to his advantage if he's taken for a farmer."

Fool: You don't have to be a buffoon to enjoy identifying with Columbo. He is the eternal doormat who always trips up high-and-mighty villains. The show's very predictability is part of the fun. Columbo may make a fool of himself, but the audience knows full well that in the end, his simple, unaffected virtue will triumph over such polished murderers as the smug symphony conductor (John Cassavetes) or the super-sophisticated private eye (Robert Culp).

Peter Falk has been living the life of Columbo for most of his forty-five years. Not long after graduating from high school in Ossining, N.Y.,

</td>
</tr>
</table>

preceding one, which began: "You don't have to be a buffoon to enjoy identifying with Columbo." Then, to go all the way back to describe his childhood, the writer makes the transition with, "Peter Falk has been living the life of Columbo for most of his forty-five years." He adroitly writes himself up to the present by the time he reaches the end of the story.

Give close attention to the way the writer saved possibly his best story for the end. This gives the reader the pleasure of finishing the story on a high note.

he signed on with the merchant marine, then embarked on a carousing tour of Yugoslavia with a girl friend. Returning to the U.S., he graduated from Syracuse University and served an unlikely tour of duty as an efficiency expert in the Connecticut Revenue Department before drifting into the theater. ("You mean," asked his father, the owner of a dry-goods store, "that you're going to paint your face and make an ass of yourself all your life?") In 1956, Falk had his first success in an off-Broadway production of *The Iceman Cometh*. Four years later, his portrayal of a hoodlum in the movie *Murder, Inc.* won him his first Oscar nomination. More recently, he has been acclaimed for his performances in Cassavetes's film *Husbands* and Neil Simon's play *The Prisoner of Second Avenue*.

Incredibly enough, NBC originally wanted Bing Crosby for the part of Columbo—but Crosby was too much of a golf freak to spare the time. Falk liked the role immediately, and within a short time made the character almost indistinguishable from himself. Columbo's ratty raincoat, brown suit and 1950s tie, for example, came out of the actor's own closet. Nor do the similarities between the two end off-camera. Recently, Falk's battered, 1959 Jaguar lost its forward gears as he was driving along Beverly Hills's Wilshire Boulevard. Undaunted, Falk found the one operable gear and happily drove along in reverse for several blocks. "Right now," he says with a one-eyed twinkle, "there isn't a car anywhere that goes better backward. I go backward everywhere." Columbo would understand that perfectly.

The piece on Falk is a skillful profile. The writer had only about 700 words in little more than a column and a half. He wrote the essential factors tightly. Obviously, he hadn't the leisure that permitted another writer to spell out one particular aspect of another profile, as demonstrated in this anecdote:

One day before the Big Game several years ago, Professor Gurley ambled up onto the stage in an Economics I class as he had done for several years in a row: slowly, meditatively. As the students filed in, he charted several graphs on the four blackboards. When the boards were strangled with odd lines, letters, and jottings, he turned around and rapidly began to go through an incredible explanation far above the level of Economics I. As he wandered through several highly abstract concepts, he added new lines to his blackboard maze.

The amazed students scribbled everything down as fast as they could, understanding nothing. "Now, are there any questions?" he asked, suddenly turning. Four hundred hands blossomed. He stood silently, scrutinizing the faces with his sincere look, not moving an inch.

Within a second the auditorium blew up in a mixture of hissing, clapping, whistling, and screams. The graphs on the boards spelled quite clearly: "BEAT CAL."

For contrast, here is another description of the same teacher by another writer, who tries to portray the professor's humor using only a simple sentence:

His dry wit is scattered throughout the lecture to keep everyone watching.

The least important error here is the use of the phrase, "to keep everyone watching," which, because it is not *precisely* the phrase you want, is irritating. The most important error is to make a point, then just let it sit there. If you want to say he has dry wit, prove it. Cite some of his witticisms.

The Essentials of the Profile

What the subject says.   In direct quotations and in paraphrase.

What the subject does.   His actions, including anecdotes that illuminate him.

Description of the subject.   Including not only such routine facts as height, weight, and color of eyes and hair, but especially how the subject walks, talks, gestures, and makes small movements.

History of the subject.   Although what the subject is like *now* is the important aspect, failing to color the person's background in at least a few paragraphs may suggest that the subject was always this way—that he or she was never in the process of *becoming.* Ideally, historical tracing helps to show how the subject became what he or she is. (But it is usually a mistake to begin an article with history. At least a few paragraphs should be devoted first to the subject at present, so that the reader will *want* to go back into history.)

What others — friends and detractors — think and say about the subject.

Like descriptives, good profiles make the readers see their subjects. Consider the following excerpt from a story about a black general, written by William Greider of the *Washington Post:*

> The general is a man of heavy presence, tall and broadshouldered, with a deep and serious voice, a natural "command voice" that subtly extracts deference from those around him.
>
> So it was a rare moment, listening to this man after hours over drinks, in the standard red-brick general's house assigned to the base's vice commander. His voice turned soft and rheumy as he stretched out in the lounge chair and sketched word pictures from his past.
>
> "When I was going to school with my mother, we always did shows," he said. "We'd have an Easter operetta, a Fourth of July patriotic blast and I'd have the largest speaking parts."
>
> Lt. Gen. Daniel James, Jr., 55, talked about a small boy nicknamed "Chappie" standing on a stage, dressed in a pink tuxedo with white lapels while his cousin Mabel sang to him a song written by his older sister.
>
> The general's voice shifted to a falsetto imitation of his cousin Mabel and he began to sing:
>
> "Handsome is as handsome does, so the wise man say. Feathers fine may make fine birds, but folks are not that way.
>
> "It's what is in your heart that counts, deny it if you can. I'm not impressed with how you dress, cause clothes don't make the man."
>
> The general laughed at his own singing. Why, he wondered, do those words stick in his memory after all these years? He was growing up poor in Pensacola, Fla., only he didn't know it. His mother never told him. . . .

In this profile, Greider creates both General James and the South in which he lived as a black officer. We see.

Long before Greider's article was published, the novelist Joseph Conrad wrote: "My task is to make you hear, to make you feel—it is, before all, to make you *see*." Magazine writers should make Conrad's goal their own.

CHAPTER SIXTEEN EXERCISES

1. Read again "The Essentials of the Descriptive" from this chapter, then write a descriptive article of about 1,000 words on any place you

have observed. Analyze the devices you have used in your article to make readers see the subject. Do you rely on verbs or adjectives, words or phrases? What other senses besides sight have you used?

2. Choose an interesting person who would make a good subject for a profile, then discuss how you would tailor the article to suit three or four different magazines. Which aspects of the person's career or personality would you emphasize for each and why?

3. Find a magazine profile and a newspaper personality sketch that were written about the same person. (Use the *Readers' Guide, New York Times Index,* and other reference books to help you.) Compare the two stories and discuss how they are alike and how they are different. Does the fact that one is in a magazine and one in a newspaper affect the content or style of the articles?

CHAPTER 17
Personal Experiences and Narratives

I could a tale unfold whose lightest word
Would harrow up thy soul, freeze thy young blood
Make thy two eyes, like stars, start from their spheres,
Thy knotted and combined locks to part,
And each particular hair to stand on end,
Like quills upon the fretful porpentine.
Hamlet, Act I, William Shakespeare

Not all stories promise as much as this one, but that does not diminish the pleasure of telling them. Personal experiences and narratives bring out the storyteller in most writers. The role is one they relish because it offers considerable freedom. The only absolute requirement is that the story be a good one.

PERSONAL EXPERIENCES

The temptation to write articles in the first person is strong, particularly now that the New Journalism has given its blessing to participation by the writer in his or her story. Yet most subjects are not suited to the first-person approach. When the subject is more important than the writer's reaction to it, his or her presence often becomes obtrusive.

How can you decide whether or not you have a first-person story? Did you actually experience what you are writing about, or were you there only as an observer? If you were a participant in the events you describe, that is an argument in favor of using the pronoun "I."

Answer these questions: Would the readers of my article want to have been in my place? Would they have wanted to meet the person I met, to see the place I visited, to do what I did? If the answers are yes, you can probably share your first-hand experiences most effectively by using the first-person approach. If you interviewed Jackie Kennedy Onassis, your readers might want to know how you felt and what you thought upon meeting her, but if you interviewed Jackie Doe from the local theater group, you'll need to concentrate instead on interesting your audience in your subject.

Publishable articles on personal experiences are rare. While they are prized by some editors, selling a personal experience to even the most receptive editor is difficult. The reason is probably obvious. Before the writer can do a readable personal experience story, he must have a thrilling adventure or an experience that is highly amusing or one that strikes home intimately with a million readers. The thrillers happen once in a lifetime—if then. Amusing incidents that can be woven into a tale that will draw chuckles are more frequent. But the writer must see the funny side of the experience and be able to tell it entertainingly—usually with himself as the fall guy.

The light approach can even be used when the subject is a serious one, as in this excerpt from an article on how the writer overcame a phobia (see Chapter Fourteen for further discussion of this article):

> Some people cross the street to avoid a black cat. I used to cross at the sight of a bird. It wasn't superstition that sent me zigzagging from one sidewalk to the other, it was fear. The mere mention of birds made me cringe. Their presence terrified me. I had a bird phobia—and a bad one.
>
> Phobias are severe, irrational fears that compel people to avoid the things that make them afraid. Phobias actually interfere with people's lives. An aquaphobe will not go swimming; a person with fear of heights will not travel by plane. For me, a pet store was a chamber of horrors. Parakeets, even fluffy little chicks, filled me with terror.
>
> The robins who visited my yard in the spring were as welcome as a flock of vultures. I once served leftover spaghetti to dinner guests rather than go through the ordeal of taking a chicken out of the refrigerator.

The rest of the story describes the writer's treatment by a clinical psychologist and how it helped her overcome the fear. Note how in describing her problem, she also provides the reader with information about phobias, such as what they are and how they affect people. This is obviously a first-person story, but it isn't one the writer will be able to repeat unless she develops other phobias. Even for a hungry free-lancer, that is asking too much.

Personal experiences needn't always be dramatic or humorous to be effective pieces of writing. This is particularly true when the writer has some expertise in the subject. Consider this excerpt from a nostalgic article about classic American cars:

> Howard Carter could have had no greater sense of discovery entering Tutankhamun's tomb than Bobby Paine and I had, stumbling out of the warehouse lift into a fairy-

land of cars, caissons, machine guns and artillery pieces. The sight was so unexpected that we were momentarily dumbstruck. Once the shock was over, we raced past the merely fine cars toward the five great ones, parked together in a separate enclosure. The closest was a Duesenberg SJ Towncar. In back, almost obscured by the massive Duesenberg, were two Auburn sedans and a Packard phaeton. All the way over by the wall was an equally massive canvas-covered shape with huge red wire wheels.

We climbed into the Duesenberg. Her sleek black hood was a block long, or seemed so. Despite signs of superficial neglect, she looked like she was doing 80 miles an hour standing still. Lifting the hood with reverence, we found the biggest eight-cylinder engine we'd ever seen. It had dual overhead camshafts, four valves per cylinder, dual ignition, and of course, a supercharger.

Even in these two short paragraphs the writer communicates his love of old cars and knowledge about them. He is entitled to write in the first-person because his point of view is essential to the article.

The Essentials of the Personal Experience Article

In writing about personal experiences, remember to do two things:

Share your experience. You must work to enable the reader to participate in your story. This can be accomplished only by graphically describing actions and emotions. It is very difficult to write about experiences that occurred in the distant past because you probably won't be able to recall significant details. Inventing them often results in strained and artificial-sounding sentences.

Maintain an unrelenting focus. Avoid digressions that are unrelated to the experiences you are describing. Occasionally an article succeeds even though the writer rambles through a long introductory passage that attempts to explain entertainingly who he is and how he was equipped for the experience, but it doesn't happen often. Keep the experience the center of attention, but be sure to give enough information about yourself and others in the story to create human characters. Do this without letting people overwhelm events. This balance is a delicate one to achieve.

NARRATIVES

Narrative-style articles are essentially factual short stories. Like fiction, they rely on the unfolding of episodes for their compelling interest (this episodic structure makes many personal experience articles narratives also). The narrative is so easily the simplest form that a beginner may ask himself, "Why don't I write all my articles this way?" There are good reasons. The most important is that many manuscripts just don't get airborne when told chronologically from start to finish. Many articles require a carefully contrived lead to capture the reader's interest and hold him until he is absorbed in the story. Furthermore, editors consider pure narration an old-fashioned style of writing. Years ago, almost all articles were narratives. Today, to capture readers, a writer often has to jump into the middle of his tale for an exciting or significant sequence for his lead, and he may not get around to the narrative part until the middle or near the end. However, when the events that made up an article lend themselves to the narrative treatment, no other form provides such satisfying reading.

The Essentials of the Narrative

The essential elements of the narrative are largely those of the personal experience. The difference is that the writer is not a factor in the narrative. Rather than relating an experience *he* had, he is reporting someone else's experience. The narrative is less a sharing of experience than is found in personal experience writing. It is nonetheless possible to present a story so graphically that the reader becomes involved in it. One must focus ceaselessly on the crux of the story in writing a narrative to hold the reader's attention.

In preparing to write the narrative that appears below, Rusty Todd of Austin, Texas, took copious notes on the campaign trail of Lieutenant Governor Ben Barnes. From these notes, he fashioned a revealing series of episodes. When he had finished this story, he called one source to verify a quotation. He used two books—*Texas Under a Cloud* by Sam Kinch and Ben Proctor, and *Money, Marbles & Chalk* by Jimmy Banks—to crosscheck factual information. This report comes almost entirely from his notes. Pay particular attention to the comments on the narrative; they should give you some ideas on how to fashion your own narratives.

Comment

This begins boldly— "which has no middle"—as though the piece has no identifiable middle (although it does, of course).

The article *could* begin with the second paragraph. Should it?

Narrative

This story, which has no middle, begins in Amarillo, where Lt. Gov. Ben Barnes started his campaign for governor by boarding a rented train and storming across Texas in the grandest Woodrow Wilson style. It ends in the Capitol on election night.

Amarillo has been called less than a dream city. It lies smack in the middle of the flat, treeless Texas Panhandle, and its most glorious aspects include an old zinc smelter that gives the city the state's

(Probably.) One could ask whether the atmosphere is basic to this story.

highest respiratory disease rate and the Helium Monument, a stainless steel atrocity whose plaque modestly informs one that Amarillo is the "Helium Capitol of the World."

On Feb. 22, 1972, a bitter northwest wind was smashing through Amarillo from across the prairie, and thick rain clouds obscured the approaching dawn. At this hour the Barnes campaign staff, the press corps, and more than 400 local residents were awake and getting ready for the 7:30 A.M. departure celebration.

It is important to help readers see Barnes. Give him a sentence or even a paragraph that will enable readers to see him in the flesh.

A "rung"? He "waltzes" in "to the tune"? Move the readers swiftly to the next point with precisely the image you want them to see. "With this rung, though, there were problems" gives the readers nothing precise or visual. In addition, the images are confused.

None of them wanted to miss the beginning of another campaign for the biggest political *prima donna* Texas had ever seen, the man who in 1960 got tired of selling vacuum cleaners and in less than a year became a twenty-one-old state representative. Four years later he acquired the House speakership and the political support of Lyndon Johnson and John Connally. In 1968 he waltzed into the lieutenant governor's office to the tune of the largest majority in recent Texas history, and now it was time for Ben Barnes to tick off the next rung of the political ladder.

With this rung, though, there were problems, substantial problems. First, the Capitol was being racked by a scandal of enormous proportion. The present governor, the speaker of the House, and various legislators had been implicated by the Securities and Exchange Commission in a stock fraud attempt. No evidence pointed to Barnes, but his three opponents were trying hard to associate him with the outrage.

This section uses transitions well. Each paragraph is tied to its predecessor, even though the writer covers a great deal of Barnes's history: from the reference to a stock fraud attempt, divorce and sexual escapades, a new marriage, and finally a reception, which enables the writer to return to the reporters.

Second, Barnes had in 1970 committed what can be a fatal error in Texas politics: divorce. Grandiose rumors of his sexual escapades (all unsubstantiated) had surrounded the split, and the odious image of "Bedroom Ben" had slowly crept across Texas. A popular bumper sticker read: "It's 10:30. Do you know where Ben Barnes is?"

A year later he married a deceased lobbyist's widow, who was eleven years his elder; writers wondered in print if the marriage had been arranged as a political expedient. At last night's press reception, Barnes acted like Nancy had been his wife for as long as he could remember.

The reception, incidentally, had been a wet one, and most of the reporters in the motel coffee shop this morning were nursing hangovers. The headaches were doubly intense since yesterday's Barnes-furnished aircraft from Austin had been amply stocked with liquor.

Two men who were not reporters (though they both had been) and who were not hung over (they had been that, too) also sat in the shop, talking about the train ride and their plans for it.

This is a skillful touch that gives good visual imagery of Read. That's just enough, since he isn't the central figure.

The one who looked like a king-sized Kennedy in a dated blue suit and narrow tie was Julian Read, who plotted the strategy of every one of John Connally's campaigns. He and George Christian, the same Christian who had been LBJ's White House press secretary, were running this campaign. Read was ravenously consuming a steaming plate of fried eggs and country sausage.

Across the table sat Terry Young, a heavier man than Read, of early rather than late middle-age, the number two man in Read's public relations organization. Young is normally unflutterable but tends to grow hypertense and lose weight during a campaign. His breakfast this morning consisted of black coffee and black coffee.

"By God," Read said to him. "This sausage hits the spot. We ought to have some Jimmy Dean sausage put aboard the train when it stops in Plainview."

"A fellow from the factory is bringing boxes of cooked sausage and bread to the depot there," said Young, who had thought of it himself.

A reporter and a Barnes cameraman joined the two publicists. The reporter had worked for Read and Young until last November and had known about the train even then. He had not seen Read since Christmas, but then Read was seldom seen outside an office. He and Young were good friends, though, and met often.

Here, the writer begins a nice passage that runs several paragraphs, providing the readers with information swiftly and also a highly readable short sketch of the scene. The natural question is, What does this contribute? Its primary purpose is to show readers the kind of reporter who is covering the story and the casual informality of such meetings. Such words as "Faaantastic" add to the informal tone.

"Good morning, Mister Read. Hi, Terry," the reporter said. He always called Read "mister" and always noticed the unconscious tendency to do so.

"Good morning. I'm glad you're getting to make the trip with us," Read said.

A waitress came for the orders, coffees for the newcomers and another coffee for Young. The reporter asked how the trip was looking.

"Faaantastic," said Young, characteristically stretching his favorite word. "You won't believe the train."

"Yeah," Read said. "But it's too bad that damned Nixon had to go to Peking this week and steal part of our thunder."

"Do you expect much of a crowd in this weather?"

Read was busy chewing eggs, and Young tried to look nondescript as he shrugged.

"We'll see. I think it'll be alright," he said.

The cameraman, Pickle, had not been saying much because of his headache, but Read roused him with a question about filming plans.

"It's gonna be tough to stay within the budget Wayne has us on," Pickle said.

By Wayne he meant Ralph Wayne, state representative, Barnes's best friend and nominal head of the campaign.

"Shoot what you need and we'll work out the budget," Read said. "The depot will be good this morning. It's cold and the crowd will be trying to jam inside."

"Yes, sir," Pickle said.

Everybody at the table but Read had another coffee before boarding the big Greyhound out front. During the drive Young talked with other reporters, trading wisecracks and helping out where he could.

Here, the writer describes the station in a quick sentence. It's far better to do the description in a single sentence because he can continue the reporter's action without interruption.

Santa Fe Station's old depot looked like a decrepit red brick castle in the dim light of a muted dawn. The reporter was startled when he saw the size of the crowd trying to squeeze its way inside.

The writer in the seat beside him said, "They really did some advance work on this one. You'd have to pay me to come out on a morning like this."

They threw sidelong glances at each other and laughed as the bus emptied. The fifty-two member press corps trudged around to the back of the building to stash their typewriters and get a look at the train.

With "Its six silver cars," the writer abandons his attention to the reporter

Its six silver cars had been rented through Amtrac for a flat $16,000. Besides the engine and generator car, there was a dome car where

and concentrates on description.

These are excellent paragraphs, drawing in the atmosphere swiftly. Note especially that he does not make every sentence carry adjective after adjective. It's often a temptation for a writer to add heavily to his description. Yet you cannot find a sentence in which he has used adjectives and adverbs too strongly.

reporters and dignitaries could view the passing country, a big lounge car to serve as the press room, a pullman where the candidate could rest, and a caboose with a special speaking platform.

Cocktail bars had been installed in the dome and press cars, and big signs on the doors said "Refreshments Must Be Left on Board." Horn speakers on the rear platform were blaring "Wabash Cannonball" by the Nashville Brass, the same background music used on the University of Texas Longhorn football show, which Read produces.

Around the platform milled a riding club on horseback. A couple of the steeds had the audacity to defile the yard with piles of pungent, steaming excrement.

A belly-to-back crush inside the depot was thwarting the police efforts of thirty or so Jaycees in matching gold vests, and the local television crew was having a time keeping its equipment intact for this morning's live broadcast. The nasal, amplified wail of two high schoolers, one of them playing organ, subjugated any conversation attempts. They were performing a ditty called "Ben Barnes for Texas."

Here, the reporter introduces himself into the story with, "the reporter." Nowhere does he use "I," even though he is on the train throughout this campaign tour.

Many in the crowd were no older than the singers, and the reporter wondered if perhaps they had come to see the professional football players making the trip instead of the candidate.

He now heard the rumor spreading: They are here, they will be on stage any minute now. Ralph Wayne leaped onto the makeshift platform and commandeered a microphone.

"Okay! Okay now!" he screamed. "They're coming! They're at the back door! Everybody help us sing for the television! Come on now, real loud!"

He had the nasal singers burst back into "Ben Barnes for Texas," and half the audience sang lustily along, familiar with a song that had been "premiered" last night at the press reception.

Suddenly the celebrities stepped into sight: Dallas Cowboys Dan Reeves, Bob Lilly, and Walt Garrison; Baltimore Colt Bubba Smith; Cleveland Brown Bob McKay; and gubernatorial contender Ben Barnes. They were all from small Texas towns.

Ralph Wayne thrust his arms into the air, a tumultuous cheer erupted, and the television commentator began speaking quietly into his own microphone. Pickle, resembling a six-foot-four-inch mustachioed cyclops with a protruding metal eye, plowed through the crush, getting close-action footage.

Julian Read had climbed onto a sort of scaffold back in a corner to view the execution of his plans. Below him, Young zipped about, taking care of correspondents, speaking to supporters, happily tending whatever needed attention. That is the way Young works: Tell him to take care of one or two things, but he ends up taking care of everything.

> **Although the writer of this article *is* "the reporter" in the next paragraph, notice that the reporter never stresses himself. He is suitably not at center stage; he is never "I."**

He stopped by the reporter, his face flushed red, his eyes flashing exuberance.

"Don't worry about taking notes if you like," he said. "We've got secretaries taking down quotes and a mimeograph machine in the press car."

He vanished swiftly into the herd of people.

On stage, Reeves had taken over the microphone to get the program underway. His first remarks drew girlish screams from the audience.

> **Reeves's quotation is revealing; it shows for the first time that Barnes is a fighter.**

"I'm for Ben Barnes because he's got guts," Reeves growled. "He'll fight for you all the way."

Nancy Barnes now joined the group on stage, and Reeves decided to extemporize: "Nancy is a gracious and charming lady, a real pro in a professional role."

> **The "verbal fumble" is in keeping with the football players, who are speaking.**
>
> **Here, the writer gives a quick flash of description—"freckled face and sandy red hair"—but at no point does he *show* Barnes. That seems a mistake. Barnes is the primary actor in this drama. He should be given a full description.**

The press wrote that one down, knowing very well it would not make the mimeo sheet. That was the only verbal fumble the players made in three days of touring, but then it was the only time any of them attempted an extemporaneous remark.

As the football stars descended into the autograph hunters, Barnes began his address. His freckled face and sandy red hair made him look younger than his thirty-four years. He thanked the crowd for "a warm welcome on such a cold morning," something he did at every stop until the weather warmed up.

"I want to tell you that Amarillo's future is important to me," he was saying. "And I'll not let the state arbitrarily close an important industry like your smelter. . . ."

High on his perch, Julian Read intently watched his candidate, now and then allowing his gaze to sweep across the crowd. Young had left the press to its business and was talking with a Barnes worker.

"If I am elected governor," Barnes was saying, "we are going to have a state water plan to supply West Texas the water it needs. . . ."

In West Texas it was the water plan; in Central Texas it would be revitalizing agriculture; along the Gulf it would be hurricane insurance revision. The stock speech called for tougher welfare qualifications, better education, and so forth, but one well-researched segment of every address was keyed to the locality. The campaign strategists had decided to avoid the morals issue completely and would mention the stock scandal only in Houston and Galveston, where Barnes already held great support.

" . . . and I think more and more people realize the man to beat in the governor's race is the peanut farmer from DeLeon."

With that Barnes, who had indeed come from a peanut farm in De-Leon, Texas, plunged into the crowd while the ubiquitous theme song clattered about the room. The audience was ecstatic. The commentator busily spoke into his microphone, telling his viewers what they had just heard Ben Barnes say.

Young was again circulating some information.

"The governor will speak from the caboose platform in a few minutes," he said. "When the trail whistle blows, you have two minutes to get aboard."

The back door of the depot swung open, and Barnes led the throng to the train. Several of the horses started and reared, their nostrils spouting streams of steam into the frigid air. Somebody suddenly released several hundred helium balloons.

As the "Wabash Cannonball" faded, Barnes climbed onto the caboose to thank the crowd and predict "a victory for everyone." The big engine whistle blew its warning only to be nearly overwhelmed by a sudden barrage of sharp explosions.

A moment of confusion seized the celebration, but the salvo turned out to be only fireworks, a large display of fireworks flashing those three American colors against the dead gray sky. When a rocket

---

Note especially how the writer goes into a transition that will enable him to move smoothly into the next paragraph: "where Barnes already held great support" merges into the next quotation.

Note that the writer manages to sustain his theme. He is switching from one episode to another, but he nearly always controls his theme by giving close attention to transitions. Note that the beginning of each paragraph is tied to the

preceding paragraph: "sudden barrage of sharp explosions" is tied to "a moment of confusion"; "a tiny parachute was ejected" is tied to the end of the first sentence in the next paragraph "attached to each chute," and so on.

exploded, a tiny parachute was ejected to carry some cargo earth-ward.

The reporter trotted across the yard to discover a small American flag attached to each chute. Smaller children in the court began fighting over the momentoes.

Once again the whistle sounded, and the reporter jumped on board. A few of the crowd jogged along behind the train but were left behind as it gathered speed. Young and the reporter met in the press car.

"Terry, those flags. That was too much."

"Yeah, bad scene. I didn't know about that," Young said. He was grinning and bouncing from one foot to the other, barely jogging in place. "But wasn't that a fantastic beginning?"

Drinks were already being served at the back of the car, and the reporter took a Bloody Mary from the elderly black bartender. He walked up into the dome to consider a thought he had not been able to shake. . . .

(After the reporter explores his thoughts, he closes with this note that sums up his story:)

More and more articles are using this kind of ending, which does not attempt to sum up what has been said in the article. Instead, the writer decides that Pickle's comment is the apt quotation: "Maybe to them it did." (They lost.)

Pickle and the reporter walked back through the granite halls and left their empty glasses in the rotunda. They dashed through the mist to the car.

"It's too bad," the reporter said as they drove away. "I don't feel too bad about Barnes, but Julian and Terry did what they could, and it didn't matter."

"Maybe to them it did," Pickle said.

CHAPTER SEVENTEEN EXERCISES

1. Find a personal experience article that has recently been published in a magazine. After reading it, answer the following questions:

Why do you think the editor of the magazine accepted this article?

What formula did the writer use to tell the story? (Example: statement of problem,

Could this article have been published in other magazines? Which ones?

development of problem, change, solution)

2. Write a 1,000-word article about a personal experience you have had. Explain why you think the subject is a publishable one, and which magazines might use the story.

3. To practice presenting a good narrative, choose a familiar story (such as a fable, or a fairy tale), then think of three different ways to tell the story by changing such things as the order of presentation, the style of writing, the point of view, etc.

CHAPTER 18
Informatives and
How-to-Do-Its

A magazine publisher once told an editor, "Any issue with a how-to on its cover sells better than an issue without one." As a result, the editor struggled to write at least one how-to coverline each month, regardless of whether the article inside warranted cover treatment.

The popularity of how-to articles, guides, and informatives is most evident in the rise of city magazines like *New York* that feature page after page of material telling readers how to shop, eat, decorate, and even sleep. There was a time when such articles were the exclusive territory of women's magazines (also called service magazines in the publishing industry), but now these stories are the standard fare of even such "literary" magazines as *Esquire*.

Consequently, informatives and how-to-do-its have acquired a new respectability among magazine writers. Beginning staff writers will almost certainly be asked to write many of each, and free-lancers can count on a steady market for both.

INFORMATIVES

All magazine articles should be informative, but those that take the readers behind the scenes of a process or service are given this particular name. Usually the subject is one of general interest, such as how the Internal Revenue Service uses computers to keep track of your income. But if the magazine has a particular focus, such as sports, the subject might be as specialized as how athletes train for the decathlon.

The cardinal rule in preparing an informative is that the writer cannot stint on research. Moreover, he must be selective with his information, remembering that his aim is to capture the reader's interest. For example, before he began writing an article on superports, Tim Ord noted that he had first done the following research:

1. Read all or parts of the reports mentioned in the article.

2. Got information on petroleum refineries, demand, and imports from such as *Petroleum Encyclopedia*, Bureau of Mines, California Department of Conservation's recent energy report, etc.

3. Interviewed: Col. Wm. E. Vandenberg, who's running the study for the Corps [U.S. Army Corps of Engineers]; Richard Eng, who's the coordinator of the study for the Corps.

4. Went to two public workshops given by the Corps to get public input.

5. Read three books on tankers and tanker terms, as well as much background information on the oil industry.

Then Ord wrote this fine piece:

Comment	Article
Although the writer's subject is serious, he realizes that he must attract the reader. Note that he addresses the reader *directly*. This is an effective beginning.	Do you remember the two Standard Oil Company of California tankers which crashed in San Francisco Bay in January 1971, spilling 800,000 gallons of bunker fuel? Those were 16,000-ton tankers.
	Do you remember the *Torrey Canyon* which went aground in the English Channel, fouling miles of beaches in Britain? That was a 119,000-ton tanker.
At this point, the writer recognizes that continuing "you-you-you" becomes monotonous. Although he has now dropped the direct address, he has established that he is still speaking directly to "you," even though he doesn't use the word.	If you were among those cleaning fouled beaches or trying to save scum-covered birds, you might have thought those were pretty big tankers. After all, if the *Torrey Canyon* were afloat today it could dock fully loaded into only two ports on the whole west coast of the United States: Puget Sound and Long Beach. It could squeeze into San Francisco Bay if it were partially unloaded and came in at high tide.
	But as far as the oil companies are concerned, such tankers are just not big enough, because the bigger the tanker, the lower the cost of transporting oil. In fact, the U.S. Corps of Engineers estimates that quadrupling the size of a tanker cuts the per-ton transport cost in half.
	So now the oil companies are in a race to see who can build the biggest tankers the fastest. By 1975, Standard Oil of California (SOCAL) will have thirty-two "supertankers" of 250,000 tons or more. Each of these tankers will be over fifteen times the size of the SOCAL tankers which crashed in the Bay, and double the size of the *Torrey Canyon*.
	Not to be outdone, Shell Oil Company recently ordered two tankers of 533,000 tons each. If one of these tankers were stood on its end, it would be taller than the Empire State Building. These quarter-mile-

Consider how difficult it is to maintain the direct tone when the writer finds it necessary to report so many numbers. Yet, Ord manages this marvelously—making the numbers interesting by comparing the length of the ships to things the reader can visualize.

long ships will have a draft of 92 feet—two and one-half times that of the biggest aircraft carrier. If a tanker this size emptied its cargo at the rate of one SOCAL Bay oil spill per week, it would be four years before she were dry.

The Federal government seems to be going along with the oil companies' switch-over to larger ships: The Commerce Department is subsidizing the construction of at least eighteen supertankers in this country at a government cost of $286 million.

Safety Factor

The oil companies claim that carrying oil in big tankers will actually be safer than carrying it in small ones because there will be fewer tankers to get in each other's way.

The writer often leans on the words of higher authorities rather than declaring his own bias against the supertankers. This technique is worth keeping in mind.

However, this overlooks the fact that the bigger the tanker, the harder it is to control. A 1972 Maritime Administration report stated:

> Because of their somewhat limited maneuverability and the distance required for them to stop, the use of large tankers in existing port channels would be extremely unsafe. The most important factor in connection with collisions and groundings is the "crash-stop" ability. Unfortunately, the ability of the mammoth tankers to come to a "crash-stop" as compared with smaller tankers has decreased as their size increased . . . For example, a T-2 tanker of 16,000 tons can come to "crash-stop" within a half mile in five minutes while the straight-line stopping distance for a 200,000-ton tanker is about 2½ miles requiring about 21 minutes.

The *Wall Street Journal* recently reported that the propeller shaft on a 250,000-ton tanker "cannot even be stopped, much less reversed, inside of seven minutes."

And oil tanker collisions are by no means rare occurrences. The Maritime Administration reports that, "Within the last 10 years, there have been over 500 tanker collisions worldwide with 80 percent occurring while these vessels were entering or leaving ports. . . . Oil spills from tanker collisions average at least a million tons annually causing some $40 million in damage."

It is possible that supertankers have other inherent dangers not shared by smaller ones. . . .

(The article goes on for several pages. It ends:)

Even though Ord's article is opposed to the

To hear some people tell it, superports are about the greatest things around. In the words of the Nathan study, "The United States has an supertankers, consider how carefully he writes this strong ending. It is thought-provoking—not the kind of ending that seems to bludgeon the supertankers.

historic opportunity to achieve a bulk commodity port delivery system which *optimizes* economic benefit and benefit distribution and which provides *acceptable levels* of protection of environmental and ecological values." But if one of those behemoth tankers goes down in either our Bay or in Monterey Bay, San Franciscans may well have reason to wish that statement had been made the other way around.

The Essentials of the Informative

When she visited Stanford's Overseas Campus in England, Mary Sharp Liebersbach was as intrigued as her companions with the country pubs. She saw in them an unusual quality that led to the following article that we can use to point up the essential elements of informatives.

Unearthing Facts Most informatives cover subjects that could be explored by anyone. That is, few are so esoteric that only the specialist can investigate and understand. The writer of an informative customarily unearths the facts that undergird ordinary phenomena.

Dressing Up the Facts It is important that facts be interesting, which means that the writer must select them carefully and present them pleasingly. This is true of all magazine writing, of course, but it is especially important in writing an informative because the unadorned presentation of facts about everyday phenomena and institutions is likely to bore readers. One way to dress them up is to be aware that readers are usually more interested in people than in things. When facts about things can be presented in relation to people—the people who use the things, the people who produce them, and so on—interest heightens.

Pub-Hopping in Britain

Comment

It's important, especially in a light piece, to make points as deftly as possible. Thus, specifying the subject (pub-crawling) in the first part of the sentence and repeating it again in the last part labors the point.

Article

Tours of England ~~would~~ *are* never ~~be~~ complete without at least a night or two of local pub-crawling; but caution—*it is not like,* ~~bar~~-hopping in the United States ~~cannot be thought of as parallel to pub-hopping in Great Britain.~~ One can *bypass* ~~miss~~ Joe's Local Bar without missing a vital part of American culture, but *to bypass the Blue Man is to miss* ~~this is not so with~~ the British. The pub is an *ranking with teatime*

institution ~~as is tea.~~ No town, whether 25,000 or 25, is complete without a church and the local pub. ⚥

Social life in many small towns and villages consists of nightly excursions to the Arms, the George, or the Pig to play darts, have a pint of bitters, and chat with fellow cohorts. *One who frequents* ~~Frequenting~~ the same pub nightly usually ~~results in one~~ acquir~~ing~~ *-es* his own stool, yet the British countryman seems only too pleased to share his corner with a foreigner who wishes to engage in some of the local chat or join in a friendly game of darts.

A note to the woman traveler—for the most part, men make up the clientele of these country pubs, though women are welcome if escorted. The British wife usually stays home while the men go for their nightly dart game and pint of beer.

The higher-class pubs, though without the consistent clientele and the ~~quite so~~ *in-*formal surroundings, can prove to be quite jolly and entertaining (and women frequent *them* ~~these~~ pubs more often). *On the main road to Nottingham,* You can visit a popular local pub such as the Wheatshed Mouston Gap—"The Gap" to regular customers—~~on the main road to Nottingham~~ and meet any class of people from the tweed-jacket-wearing, pipe-smoking country gentleman to the rough-hewn shopkeeper. After a performance many of the Nottingham theatre crowd race ten miles along twisting roadway (partially "dual carriageway," i.e., four-lane road) to The Gap to enjoy a quick pint of bitters and hash over the latest plays in the warm, friendly atmosphere. There is always a fire going, and many interesting conversations brewing in each of the three quaintly furnished rooms. If you go there more than three times the bartender may even remember your drink.

The repetition of "miss" is awkward; "bypass" is a bit more precise.

"Not so with the British" is not parallel structure.

"As is" is less direct and forceful than "ranking with."

"Results in one acquiring" seems a bit awkward. In fact, "frequenting" and "frequents" are probably stilted in *this* article. (Whether a word choice is right depends largely on the tone of the article.)

This could be made more flavorful with a sentence or so of the local chat. The skill of the dart throwers, many of whom are excellent, might also be covered in a couple of sentences.

There's no real objection to using "quite" twice, but the repetition doesn't add anything.

Here, "pubs" has been used so often as to become monotonous.

"On the main road to Nottingham" has been moved up to the beginning of the sentence to bring the two verbs ("visit" and "meet") closer together. A small matter, but read both versions of this sentence aloud before judging.

Again, something specific would help. That is, two or three sentences from one of the "interesting conversations" would allow the reader to *confront*, rather than merely be *told* about, what goes on in a pub.

Be convincing; name another such attraction. (Don't list *all* the oddities you know—certainly not if you know eight or nine. Be selective—but be convincing first.)

The different placement seems to make the sentence more graceful.

This is just the right number of names to cite. It gives the flavor without being boring.

Such odd attractions as a duck that drinks a couple of pints of beer per day are always popping up in some of these out-of-the-way pubs. To experience British culture one need merely leave ~~to get out of~~ the big cities and spend a week or so touring the countryside and stopping by the endless variety of pubs that seem to pop out of every hedgerow. Within the limits of one English town *of about 20,000* called Grantham, ~~consisting of about 20,000 people,~~ there are *sixty-six* different pubs bearing such titles as The Blue Man, the Angel and Royal, The Blue Pig, Sir Isaac Newton, Knipton, Gregory Arms, The Fox and Hounds, etc. Local people *consider one their* ~~usually find one pub they prefer as their~~ second home, but they frequently drop by others as well. . . .

HOW-TO-DO-ITS

One can consider how-to-do-it articles as informatives or classify them separately. Because how-to articles seldom depend on the conventional techniques used to excite reader interest, we will treat them as a separate type. How-tos are durable—one of the oldest types—and they continue to be popular among the readers of a great many magazines. *Sunset*, for example, is packed with information on how to garden, build additions to homes, cook more appetizing meals, or plan a trip. The "shelter" magazines (those that deal with the home)—among them *The American Home* and *Better Homes and Gardens*—offer similar fare. *Popular Mechanics* is fat with information for hobby shop buffs.

One distinctive kind of how-to article is the list—"Ten Ways to Save Your Marriage," "Seven Steps to Better Grades," and so on. Not all "lists" are identifiable as how-to articles, but many contain the basic elements of the how-to.

The Essentials of the How-to-Do-It

Information and Advice   The how-to is usually loaded with information, but its major reason for being is to offer advice.

Clarity Foremost   More than any other type of article, the how-to depends on clarity for its effect. Indeed, most of these articles sacrifice other qualities of readability, the writer reasoning that attempting to inject reader interest through metaphor, alliteration, anecdote, and other literary devices is likely to affect clarity.

Depending on the amount of space allotted to the how-to article, the writer may proceed directly to the instructive information or may be able to provide a great deal of background on the subject. Consider these two excerpts from articles that appeal to the treasure hunter in all of us.

Comment

In this paragraph, the writer realizes that she has a limited time to capture the reader. She opens with a serious sentence, then begins to show the joy of spending an afternoon panning for gold. The sentence beginning "Or it can be" is important because it tells the readers that finding gold isn't easy.

As soon as the writer begins the paragraph, she realizes that it's all business to the end of the story. Everything is written as plainly as possible, which is the best kind of how-to-do-it.

It's important for you to realize that in writing a how-to-do-it story you must physically carry out all the operations necessary. If you fail to carry them out yourself, almost certainly you will leave something out. One critic of how-to-do-its, Holly Arpan, has said: "It *seems* to be so easy that its users forget the overriding necessity for extreme clarity of expression. Even professionals have a deplorable habit of leaving out one step in a process, or one detail, and somehow that omission always is the vital one without which

How-to-Do-It

Gold mining can be hard, back-breaking work that requires long hours of concentrated effort, cold wet feet and a lot of luck. Or it can be a marvelous way to spend a spring afternoon by the side of a streambed, soaking in the sun and the wildflowers in bloom. The difference is how hard you want to work for your find, whether it be a small glass vial filled with minute gold flakes or that fabulous 100-pound nugget. Old-timers contend that looking for gold is like any other gamble—there are those who strike it rich by placing the first bet and those who acquire wealth by building up their winnings slowly. The choice is yours.

Gold is one of the heaviest metals and, with proper care, will settle to the bottom of the pan with heavier black sand in your mixture. To do this, submerge the pan in the riverbed by keeping the rim level with the top of the water, being careful not to lose any of the contents. Pick out the largest pieces of gravel with your fingers, stirring to break apart any clumps of clay or roots so that everything is soaked and moving freely about.

Then, hold the pan with your hands on either side, tipped slightly away from you but still under the water, and shake it with a quick clockwise and then counterclockwise motion, swirling the water to remove the lighter sand and coarse gravel over the rim of the pan. Repeat this several times, tapping the pan often to keep the gold from washing over the rim. Now hold the pan outside the river and give it the same clockwise-counterclockwise motion again.

Alternate dipping the pan and rotating it out of the water, each time settling the heavier black sand and gold at the bottom. Carefully tip the pan occasionally to let the pebbles and lighter sand wash over the side until only the fine black sand seems to remain.

Keep washing the mixture gently until most or all of the blonder sand is removed and the blacker sand is settled on the bottom of the pan. Use a magnet to remove the last of the black sand and expose the gold. . . .

the whole process falls apart!"

Because this writer went through the process before she wrote about it, she has carried through everything in her description.

How to Find Florida's Lost Treasure

Comment

Article

Unlike most how-to articles, this one uses anecdotes and history. That is because this article is not a step-by-step explanation of how to carry out a process but a guide to lost treasure.

An ambitious young map maker once set out to do his bit for mankind by listing the best sites for treasure hunters along the coasts of the United States. He started counterclockwise at Oregon, ran down the Pacific Coast, jumped across Lower California and Mexico, marked the X's on the coastal waters of Texas, Louisiana, Mississippi and Alabama—and quit work entirely when he hit Florida. There he went hunting for treasure himself.

This cartographer was a victim of the lure that eventually attracts every get-rich-quick schemer in the Sunshine State who doesn't go into the motel business. For Florida is to treasure hunting what Fort Knox is to gold.

Not only did Gasparilla, Lafitte, Blackbeard, John Rackham, and the other bloody-handed pirates who sailed the Florida mains cache gold and silver on the little islands that dot the sweeping Florida coast, but the storms that assault South Florida during the bad-weather seasons sent many a gold-laden galleon to the bottom. Now, thanks to modern underwater gear, the treasure is being brought to the surface.

It is important to mention the Smithsonian quite early to establish authenticity. So many articles about buried and lost treasure are contrived that a respected institution like the Smithsonian is a valuable ally. Note, too, that the next paragraphs cover a buried treasure museum.

Only a few months ago, the Division of Naval History of the Smithsonian Institution sent divers five fathoms deep off the Southern Coast to hit the richest historical jackpot in the annals of coastal treasure hunting. The treasure in this case was precious mainly to the Smithsonian: rare artifacts with a few coral-encrusted gold and silver coins. Far more important commercial finds have been made. But the 200-year-old shipwreck the Smithsonian located is important, too, because it shows that the stories are far from false and that tales of Florida gold are based on fact.

Unlike the long-dead pirates, who can be

The Smithsonian find also demonstrated once again that Arthur McKee, who operates McKee's Museum of Sunken Treasure on

**mentioned only to appeal
to a sense of adventure,
the museum provides
concrete evidence.**

**Citing specifics about the
weight of the ingots, the
cost of the building, and
the valuable memorabilia
McKee has collected is
more persuasive than
merely saying that a
museum exists.**

**These paragraphs
are not obviously**

Plantation Key in South Florida, should be the man to hold the floor
when the discussion swings to underwater searches for gold and
silver.

McKee, who was one of the four divers who went down to the wreck
wearing only a helmet, has long been considered the foremost Flo-
ridian in the treasure hunting division. Formerly a recreation director
and underwater moviemaker, McKee was down in the waters of
Florida's fabulous keys in 1949 shooting pictures when he found a
sunken galleon and brought up three silver bars weighing 65, 70, and
75 pounds. He sold the 70-pound ingot to the Smithsonian for $1,000.
Dr. Alexander Wetmore of the Institution offered to buy a second
ingot on the same terms after learning the bars assayed at 99.36 percent pure silver, but McKee put them on exhibition in his museum
instead.

A black flag emblazoned with the skull and crossbones flies over
McKee's museum. Inside the $65,000 building are pieces of eight,
doubloons, a 3,000-pound coral-laden cannon, bar shot, grapeshot—
and ivory elephant tusks recovered from the wreck of a slave trader.
Collecting such valuable memorabilia has been so profitable that the
museum is incorporated.

The home for ship relics began on a much less lavish scale, but it is
now far from the roadside stand type of vacation attraction. It has an
observation tower 65 feet high that affords a view not only of the
Atlantic Ocean and the Gulf of Mexico, but also of the Gulf Stream
itself, the route followed by Spanish galleons returning to Madrid
from the New World with treasure.

McKee, who is not a man to overlook the obvious, has taken a lease
on the treasure hunting rights in the area off the key. The tower not
only serves as a tourist-catching throwback to the days of the great
sailing ships when crows' nests were in fashion, but also is a lookout
to preserve the claim. The organization headed by McKee, thanks to
the lease, is working a wreck in the staked-off area, and recently
recovered two silver platters, pieces of eight, a silver cup and other
objects.

The State of Florida issues treasure leases and these leases do double
duty, for a hunter in shoal waters usually needs both kinds the state
offers—exclusive and nonexclusive.

The nonexclusive permit, which retails at $100, gives a bullion seeker
a chance to search in waters that may cover four or five counties.

how-to—they do not tell the prospective treasure hunter exactly how to apply for a permit—but anyone interested could derive the essential information from this passage.

After looking around the large territory until he has pinpointed his treasure, the leaseholder is then ready to return to the Land Agent in Tallahassee and swap his nonexclusive permit for an exclusive right which also costs $100.

The exclusive permit limits the search to one acre but it's valuable because no one else can jump the claim during the year the permit is in effect.

By the terms of the permits, the applicant agrees to return 12¼ percent of the value of all treasure he finds to the state, if the find is within the territorial jurisdiction of Florida.

That's the official necessity, but, of course the Land Agent is aware that many treasure hunters never bother to comply with the special statute. And of those who do follow the letter of the law and pay for permits, few admit their discoveries.

Again, no explicit how-to information is offered, but the next few paragraphs suggest avenues for prospective treasure hunters.

However, one method of determining which of the hundreds of sites would be best for an expedition is to check on the areas that have proved most popular with permit-buyers.

There is, of course, no single best site but one of the most popular has always been the mouth of the Suwannee River on the Gulf Coast. One expedition or another is busy in this area at least every 10 years looking for an estimated $5,000,000 in gold coins. The money was part of the indemnity paid to Spanish subjects who were forced to move when the United States negotiated a large-scale real estate deal with Spain in 1820.

The $5,000,000 was carried first to Pensacola, far up the Northwest Florida Coast, then loaded aboard a Spanish schooner for the long trip around the tip of Florida to Havana. However, a storm separated the gold-filled vessel from its escort, the ship sprung a leak and the captain ordered a run for the beach. Instead, the craft landed on a sandbar and was pounded to pieces while the crewmen escaped to the mainland.

Is the fortune in gold still there? Professional treasure hunters insist that it is—and prove that they really believe it by fitting out elaborate expeditions.

At least $7,000,000 in silver bullion is awaiting the discoverer of the Spanish galleon *Santa Margarita*, which lies in only 15 or 20 feet of water. The problem: where is it exactly? All anyone is now certain of is that the ship went down near Sebastian inlet, north of Vero Beach, which is on the Atlantic Ocean side of the Peninsula State. . . .

___

In the first article, writer Rita Stollman wastes no space on the history or attractions of gold mining. By the second paragraph, she begins the how-to part of her article. In contrast, the writer of the second story devotes the first ten paragraphs to developing the readers' interest and to showing them through examples that sunken treasure can be found.

Aside from space allotments, another factor influences how much background information should be included in a how-to. How much knowledge will the average reader have about the subject? If you are writing an article for a sports magazine on how to improve your tennis serve, you can assume your readers are well acquainted with tennis. Likewise, if you are writing an article for a business magazine on how to play the stock market, you can expect your readers to know in general how the market operates. But suppose you are writing an article on the same subject for a general interest magazine. Then you would need to explain how the stock market works and what it is before you give any advice about how to invest money in it.

The magazine market for how-to articles is large and reliable. It is worth the effort for a writer to master this form and to regard any piece as a prospective how-to.

CHAPTER EIGHTEEN EXERCISES

1. Write an informative article of approximately 1500 words on a subject of your choice. Explain why you think the subject is a good one and which magazines might publish the article.

2. Write a short article on how to drive a car. Be sure to include every action a person would need to perform.

3. Choose one magazine and examine six back issues to determine whether it publishes how-to articles and informatives. Then list five topics you think might be published in this magazine in either category, and explain why. In addition, describe how you think the magazine would handle each article in terms of format, angle, and visual display.

CHAPTER 19
Analyses and Essay-Reviews

More than any other kinds of magazine articles, analyses and essay-reviews offer an opportunity for the writer to leave behind the garb of detached objectivity and don a cloak of subjective opinion. Many regard this as an intellectual challenge, a chance to exercise their analytical and interpretive skills. It offers them the role of thinker as well as journalist, and many can hardly wait to set their great thoughts down on paper.

The danger is that beginners often become so preoccupied with the magnitude of their thoughts that they neglect their presentation. The writing in analyses and essay-reviews should be forceful and concise. Important points should be carefully developed and illustrated by well-chosen examples. The writer must exert tight control over any tendencies to use flowery language or to present opinions without supporting illustrations. As in other magazine articles and features, it is essential to show rather than to describe. In short, all the discipline of good writing should be applied.

ANALYSES

Most analyses are background articles aimed at answering the question "What's it all about?" when a war, a social explosion, a political upheaval, or any other momentous event splashes the headlines. They are built primarily on prosaic fact, only secondarily on incidents, anecdotes, and personalities. Now that more newspapers are turning toward interpretive reporting and analytic writing, magazines are being pushed into developing analyses more carefully and thoughtfully.

Since most magazines run many analyses, the beginner naturally assumes that there is a ready market for his talent. There is—but with built-in obstacles. Analyses call for generous use of facts and figures. Most analyses require firsthand reporting and intimate knowledge of the subject. Before he realizes it, the writer is bogged down in numbers and in quotations borrowed from books, which make dull reading. The veteran writer surmounts this hurdle by larding his analysis with episode and anecdote.

The Essentials of the Analysis

Dissection   The central purpose of an analysis is to *examine*. In a profile of a scientist, for example, a writer might cover the scientist's chief theory fairly superficially and focus on other aspects of his life and work. But writing an analysis calls for shining a fierce light on the central matter—the scientist's theory—and dissecting it with words that reveal its components, values, and implications.

Anticipating Arguments and Questions   A thoughtful editorial writer anticipates the arguments that will be used to counter his viewpoint and hence counters *them* in advance. The writer of an analysis tries to present a balanced examination rather than an editorial, but he, too, must anticipate arguments and questions.

Clarity and Unity Foremost   Like the how-to writer, the writer of an analysis must work for extreme clarity. Almost any analysis will be considered by some readers to be argumentative, which makes it essential that the writer be understood. To be persuasive, an analysis must be unified, sentences marching along decisively, major point following major point in a way that seems inevitable. These are the essential stylistic qualities, and the writer of an analysis will leaven his work with devices that lend color and flavor only if they do not impair clarity and unity.

Consider how the following excerpt (by William Rivers) has incorporated these essential elements into an analysis of a highly charged political and academic situation.

Associate Professor of Maoism

Comment   **Article**

Although the San Francisco Bay area is almost universally pictured as the storm center of academic activism, Stanford University has contributed relatively little to that image. This is not because Palo Alto has been a sea of tranquility but because the loud confrontations there have often been drowned out by real explosions at nearby Berkeley and San Francisco State College. If close observers of the troubles of academia are right, however, in holding that the emphasis nearly everywhere is slowly shifting from student discipline to faculty discipline, Stanford can now be considered the leader of the vanguard. Recent events at Stanford place a powerful focus on central questions about faculty and institutions, including whether the actions outside the classroom of a self-professed revolutionary should be considered relevant to his regular duties—and thus subject to the kinds of questions that may be asked about his classroom performance and scholarship.

Stanford has seldom asked any questions at all about its tenured professors. Like most universities, its policies are marked by what the President's Commission on Campus Unrest termed "reluctance to enforce codes of behavior other than those governing scholarship" and by the assumption that "a minimum of regulation would lead to a maximum of freedom." That puts a sharp point on President Richard Lyman's suspension of an associate professor of English, H. Bruce Franklin, for his part in a campus confrontation. Lyman has informed Franklin that he faces possible dismissal and has obtained a preliminary injunction barring him and some of his supporters from the Stanford campus. In the academic world, such actions seem breathtakingly decisive, but summarizing them that way obscures the lessons they may teach as well as the tortuous path by which they were reached.

Note how the writer uses information about Franklin's background to make the reader see that he is clearly not a "troublemaker" who simply got what he deserved.

Franklin, 36 years old, is a fairly recent convert to revolution. The son of a poor family in Brooklyn, he went to work at 14 to help support his family. He attended Amherst on a scholarship and was graduated magna cum laude in 1955. After working briefly as a tugboat mate in New York harbor, Franklin served as a navigation and intelligence officer in the Strategic Air Command. Then he went to Stanford for graduate work, earned his Ph.D. in 1961, and immediately became an assistant professor of English. He went to Johns Hopkins in 1964, but the Stanford Department of English thought so highly of him that Franklin was lured back with a promise of promotion. He was a Melville scholar, and the documents supporting the promotion cite his "unusual intellectual drive" and say that his many publications "show evidence of his originality and ingenuity." He was made an associate professor with tenure.

The writer begins to bring the story up to date, and to introduce controversy by citing other examples of Franklin's behavior.

Until that time, Franklin had been a fairly conventional academician. He has described himself as a "Stevenson liberal" during his term as a SAC officer. His year at Johns Hopkins coincided with the 1964 Presidential election, and Franklin was a precinct captain in Baltimore for Lyndon Johnson. But not long after his return to Stanford, Franklin made it clear that his beliefs—or at least his way of expressing them —were changing rapidly. In March 1966, he and about 70 others opposed to the Vietnam War were on hand to protest when the port commission of Redwood City, near Stanford, began consideration of leasing 2.1 acres to the United Technology Center for a napalm plant. When Franklin spoke vehemently and at length in opposition, he was gaveled down and eventually removed by force from the meeting. During the ensuing confusion, the port commissioners voted quickly to grant the lease. Hearing of the decision, Franklin raced back and shouted into the microphone: "This is what America has come to! This is our democracy!"

But Franklin did not become a genuine revolutionary until he went abroad several months later to teach at the Stanford campus in France. Reading Marxist literature and talking to Vietnamese Communists visiting in France, he has said, helped persuade him of the rightness and inevitability of the people's revolution. He and his wife, Jane, established a Marxist-Leninist study group in a "free university" in Paris. They returned to Stanford in 1967 as fervent Maoists. Franklin has led many confrontations and demonstrations since then, has been arrested several times, and in 1969 was barred from the campus of the nearby College of San Mateo.

Having used Franklin's background to relate other incidents, the writer easily moves into a discussion of the events leading to the current controversy.

The climactic events at Stanford began on Jan. 11 when former Ambassador Henry Cabot Lodge was scheduled as the keynote speaker at a campus conference marking the 25th anniversary of the United Nations. The shouting and chanting of a group of about 50 people, including Franklin, in the audience of 800 prevented Lodge from speaking.

By quoting directly from the central characters, the writer shows their positions more forcefully than he could through description.

President Lyman said the next evening in one of his regular broadcasts over the campus radio station:

> A university can't afford to have potential audiences for all sorts of speakers one by one deprived of their opportunities because a limited but very vehement minority wishes to deprive them. . . . Freedom for people you agree with is no freedom at all. Freedom for people you feel mildly about is not very hard to achieve. It's freedom to listen to the full expression of points of view which you regard as sinful or disastrous or catastrophic in their outcome—that's when freedom really means something.

Lyman then wrote to Franklin that he was proposing suspension without pay for one academic quarter because Franklin had "deliberately contributed" to the disturbance. Responding with a letter whose salutation read, "The Chief Designated Agent of the Board of Trustees of Leland Stanford Junior University, Heirs of the Family Who Stole This Land and the Labor of Those Who Built Their Railroad, War Profiteers and Rulers of the U.S. Empire," Franklin wrote:

> I do not deny demanding that Lodge answer to the massacre of the men, women and children of My Lai, the fire bomb and herbicide raids on the countryside of Vietnam, Laos, and Cambodia. . . . I would agree that whatever I and others did on Jan. 11 constitutes an inappropriate response. The appropriate response to war criminals is not heckling, but what was done to them at Nuremberg; they should be locked up or executed.

This chronological account of the story allows the reader to interpret the actions of people and groups for himself.

In accord with tenure policy, the Advisory Board, seven professors elected by the faculty, was to consider Lyman's proposal that Franklin be suspended. Franklin protested that he should appear instead before the Stanford Judicial Council, a student-faculty group which was to hear the cases of the students involved in the Lodge incident. (Subsequently, it recommended that seven students be expelled.) Lyman held that the Advisory Board was the appropriate body because it acts in cases involving faculty discipline.

But a hearing on Lyman's original proposal quickly became obsolete. Soon after Franklin addressed a rally on Feb. 10, radicals took over the Stanford Computation Center. Many occupied the building; Franklin himself was on the lawn outside. The building was emptied shortly before the arrival of 80 sheriff's deputies. Shortly thereafter, following a dispersal order, several persons were arrested during a police sweep of the area. Franklin and other radicals addressed another rally that evening. Moments later, three members of the conservative Free Campus Movement were beaten by a roving band of radicals; within an hour, an unidentified gunman fired several shots near the headquarters of the conservative group and wounded two bystanders.

Two days later, Lyman suspended Franklin with pay and sought a preliminary injunction to bar him and several others from the campus, explaining in a letter to Franklin, "I regard your continuance in your regular duties to constitute a threat of immediate harm to others." Fifty-five faculty members, including Nobel Laureate Linus Pauling, filed a petition of intervention with Santa Clara County Superior Court, seeking to block the injunction. But more than 400 faculty members signed an open letter backing the University's court move. After a week-long hearing, the injunction was granted barring Franklin, six students, and seven outsiders from the campus. Under its provisions, Lyman gave Franklin permission to come on the campus for five hours a day to gather evidence for his hearing before the Advisory Board. That hearing will now turn on Lyman's proposal that Franklin be dismissed.

Having completed his discussion of events, the writer now begins to analyze the situation.

None of the charges bear directly on Franklin's performance in the classroom, where he teaches highly popular courses like "Melville and Marx" (a change from "Melville and Hawthorne" that Franklin grounded on his belief that Melville was a proletarian writer). The charges center on Franklin's participation in the Lodge incident, which he does not deny but characterizes as "heckling," and on a presumed cause-and-effect relationship between Franklin's exhortations and violent actions that followed them. Several who attended the rally prior to the occupation of the computation center say that

Franklin called for a shutdown of "that most obvious machine of war." Others say that prior to the beatings and shootings that evening Franklin urged listeners to "break into small groups, and do whatever you feel you ought to do, as late at night as possible." Franklin has denied that he advocated the particular acts of violence that occurred.

Early in April, 13 professors drew up a petition asking that Franklin's petition be lifted and protesting that they had found it difficult at the beginning "to understand how Professor Franklin's continuance in his regular duties—which we interpreted to mean teaching classes, holding office hours, and fulfilling departmental obligations—endangered anyone." When the injunction was granted, they argued, it eliminated the reason for the suspension. They wrote that the suspension "may constitute a violation of academic freedom since a professor is being unnecessarily prevented from teaching prior to a hearing by the Advisory Board and because of activity outside the classroom."

Although the petition was circulated widely, only about 50 other faculty members signed it. Perhaps a few did not sign despite their sympathy for the petition. It is certain that many did not sign because they agree with the Stanford attorney who argued in seeking the injunction that, after years of turmoil, it is time to say, "Enough is enough." But it is also probable that some have begun to question whether "teaching classes, holding office hours and fulfilling departmental obligations" actually defines teaching duties today. The structure of higher learning has changed to the point that the central role of the classroom has been eroded almost everywhere.

In this case, the author is able to interpret the motives of students and faculty members because he is a professor at the university. He does not need to attribute the analysis to anyone else because he is an "insider" and therefore a credible source of information.

As for the students, few are committed to Franklin's cause, perhaps no more than the 100 to 125 hard-core radicals. The many protest rallies and demonstrations that have been held at various milestones in his case draw few more than that and some of those who do appear are merely curious.

It is certain that the feeble support for Franklin among students can be traced in many cases to the extremity of his political stance. Many more students would surely have supported an outspoken liberal professor, or even one professing a less extreme radical doctrine. They hesitate to work for a Maoist. But the chief reason Franklin is receiving little support from students is no doubt that many of them are simply tired of protests, protestors, and protesting.

Ironically, Franklin himself has inadvertently argued against those who petitioned for him. When Ian Watt, the chairman of the Department of English, wrote to Franklin to ask about his failure to meet several recent classes Franklin released Watt's letter and a biting response of his own. He pointed out that on one occasion he could not meet the class because he was serving as defense counsel for a group of students. At another time, he invited his class to meet him in a Redwood City courtroom because he was being arraigned. The third and last time he missed class, Franklin wrote to Watt, was the afternoon of the occupation of the computation center. "On that day, I went to the classroom at 1:15, the appropriate time, and discovered that there were no more than ten (at the most) of the 150 registered students in the room. Most of the rest had gone on the march to the computation center. In order to meet the class, I put a note on the blackboard stating that the class would meet outside the computation center. . . ."

Note that this is *not* an editorial. In summing up, the writer does not conclude that Franklin should or should not be suspended. He analyzes the situation, but does not judge it.

For some, the key question in the Franklin case involves free speech and incitement to possible violence; for others, the broader question of a professor's fitness for his job is central. Although the Franklin case may be exceptional, faculty committees at universities across the country which are now trying to define professional duties and faculty disciplinary procedures may have to take account of teaching beyond the walls of the conventional classroom.

Franklin's own opinion on the meaning of his case is self-evident in his comment: "What this means is that no one with my views will be allowed to teach in a university. This proves that tenure doesn't mean a Goddamned thing. As long as speech is ineffective, it's free—but not when it begins to threaten the rulers of the empire."

ESSAY-REVIEWS

The chief difference between an analysis and an essay-review is that a book (or movie or play or other work of art) is the center of the latter. In fact, the work of art is the reason the essay-review exists. But it is much more than a conventional review, which often consists merely of the reviewer's reaction. The essay-review of a book, for example, is usually approximately half-article, half-review, with the part that is article focusing on the general subject of the book but not on the book's particular treatment of that subject. The review, of course, does focus on the book's treatment of the subject, but the effect of reading a perceptive essay-review is much more like reading an analysis than it is like reading the conventional book review. In other words, the essay-review provides a larger context in which to consider the book.

The Essentials of the Essay-Review

The essential elements of the essay-review are much the same as those of the analysis: dissection, anticipating arguments and questions, and clarity and unity. An important additional element, of course, is *opinion*—the writer's opinion of the work he is reviewing. And to present his opinion persuasively, the writer must provide examples and evidence. Although analyses and essay-reviews differ in tone along with the subjects they cover, it is likely that the writer of an essay-review can often do more than can the writer of an analysis to enliven his article with color and flavor.

Magazine editors usually assign essay-reviews to free-lancers or staff writers who are specialists in the field covered by the book. In such cases, the writer is likely to have a mind so well-stocked with relevant facts, ideas, and insights that he need do little more than read the book he is assigned to review, then write. But many writers choose to research an essay-review in much the same way they would prepare to write a more conventional article. That was the approach of an author of this book when he was asked by the editor of *Columbia Journalism Review* to write an essay on three books about the underground press.* The following is an excerpt from that article.

Notes from the Underground

Comment

Although this is an essay-review of three books, it need not begin by mentioning them. The books *could* have been dealt with in the first paragraph. The author chose instead to use the first paragraph to set forth his attitude toward the underground press—which also served to inform those readers who knew little about the undergrounders.

Article

The Open Conspiracy. By Ethel Romm. Stackpole. $6.95.

Famous Long Ago. By Ray Mungo. Beacon Press. $5.95.

The Underground Press in America. By Robert Glessing. Indiana University Press. $6.50.

Anyone who is guilty of being forty-five years old, as I am, is probably so afflicted with the tunnel vision of his generation that he can judge other generations only by his standards rather than theirs. Thus, for a long time I dismissed the underground press because it seemed to have all the stability of a floating crap game. My opinion began to change because of these events:

• The Los Angeles *Free Press* installed a time clock. I didn't like time clocks when I had to punch one twenty years ago, and I wouldn't like to punch one now. But an underground paper that begins to check on

---

*Reprinted from *Columbia Journalism Review* (May/June 1971) © 1971. By permission.

the comings and goings of its staff members takes on a businesslike aura that might lure a smile from William Randolph Hearst.

• The owner of the Berkeley *Barb*, Max Scherr, and his staff began to fight over money. The staff wanted to buy out Scherr and cited evidence that he had been making $5,000 a week from the paper. Although reading the *Barb* fairly regularly persuades me that I do not share many values of Scherr and his staff members, this financial wrangle suggests that they share one of mine.

Note that the reference to DeWitt Wallace is not explained. Because the article was written for *Columbia Journalism Review*, whose readership is made up largely of journalists and others who are knowledgeable about journalism, it was assumed that almost all readers would know that Wallace founded *Reader's Digest*. To spell out this fact would have insulted most readers of *Columbia Journalism Review*.

• Citizen Zenger Company, publishers, of Fairfax, Calif., has issued a prospectus for a kind of *Reader's Digest* of the underground press. In keeping with the casual underground spirit, some of the pages are numbered and some are not. But the prospectus is thick, it seems to cover all the factors that might bear on the success of the venture, and it reflects a serious effort to raise $100,000 to start the *Underground Digest*. Reading these plans sets me to wondering whether, like these entrepreneurs, DeWitt Wallace was foresighted enough to copyright *his* prospectus.

If these examples are almost embarrassingly commercial, that is because the instability of the underground has caused me so much trouble that I welcome any sign of order and purpose. A recent book of mine titled *The Adversaries* carried a long analysis of an underground paper that folded while the book was being bound. In another recent book, *A Region's Press*, David Rubin and I attempt to assess the newspapers of the San Francisco Bay area. Because this area's climate seems to spawn publications and then smother them with a fine impartial hand, I often found myself agonizing over analysis of an underground paper that had died the day before. All this leads to pondering a dictum of the late Ed Lahey that I had once dismissed as impossibly cynical: "All I ask of a publisher is that he stay solvent."

The points in this paragraph and the next are significant. They represent the anticipation of counterargument (and they present important information). If they did not appear, readers who know of the attitudes represented by the young men quoted here would surely read this essay-review with growing antagonism.

There are, of course, undergrounders who retain the original purity. One, John Sinclair, has written of copyright:

> *Who says the words belong to us? How did we get to own them? Copyright is just another bullshit Western ego trip and a capitalist greed-scheme.*

In an underground office, a visitor who called a staff member's attention to uncashed checks strewn on the floor was told: "Oh, forget 'em; God provides money when we need it." Perhaps most undergrounders are like this, but enough of the acquisitive kind exist to show that materialism is not quite dead.

There are other reasons to regard the underground press as something more than a fad—among them the fact that the field is beginning to generate an impressive library. It began to build early this year with Ethel Romm's *The Open Conspiracy*, which imparts the spirit and the flavor of the underground unforgettably. Filled with pungent quotations, *The Open Conspiracy* offers wide-ranging samples of underground literature without either leering or moralizing. Mrs. Romm quotes classified ads:

> Athletes Beware: *New girl in town bored with old methods seeks new ways to play same old game with bigger and better toys. Send photo and suggestion to P.O. Box 650, San Leandro Cal.*

She also quotes one of the most famous underground articles, Gerald Farber's "The Student as Nigger," which has been widely reprinted since it was first published in the Los Angeles *Free Press*:

> Students are niggers. When you get that straight, our schools begin to make sense. It's more important, though, to understand why they're niggers. If we follow that question seriously enough, it will lead us past the zone of academic bullshit, where dedicated teachers pass their knowledge on to a new generation, and into the nitty-gritty of human needs and hangups. . . .

Although Mrs. Romm is sympathetic, she is by no means a blind partisan. She even questions whether the young journalists deserve the honor of the name "underground," pointing out that it was a term for the anti-Fascist resistance press of Europe and that *those* undergrounders risked their lives if they were caught, for example, with a copy of *L'Italia Libera*. To use the term "underground" for papers that can be purchased on newsstands seems absurdly romantic to Mrs. Romm. (Introducing the editor of the *Peninsula Observer* to one of my classes last year, I tried to make the same point by saying that the *real* underground was symbolized by Albert Camus writing for *Combat* in Nazi-occupied France during World War II. The editor, a bright young man named David Ransom, reproved me gently by saying that the modern American "underground" refers to what the papers are reporting *on* and speaking *for*—the causes and protests of youth, for example—rather than to the resistance efforts of an outlaw press.)

Famous Long Ago is similarly flavorful, and it offers the perspective of a participant who writes well. It is a sort of autobiography of Ray Mungo, one of the founders of Liberation News Service, which was a sort of syndicate for the underground press. Mungo devotes four pages to his early life and what Holden Caulfield termed "all that David Copperfield kind of crap." The rest of the book is an intensely

---

Here, well into the article, is the first reference to one of the three books. Note that the writer does not *leap* from the introductory statement to the book; an effort is made to move smoothly into reviewing. Quoting briefly gives readers a notion of both the flavor and substance of a book.

Note that the transition is achieved by referring to the other book: "is similarly flavorful."

Although there is seldom space enough for a reviewer to document *every* point he makes, some must be documented. The reviewer has said that the book is candid, then quotes an example of candor to prove the point.

personal view of the underground world. Much of it is refreshingly candid, as when Mungo confesses:

> *Lots of radicals will give you a very precise line about why their little newspaper or organization was formed and what needs it fulfills and most of that stuff is bullshit, you see — the point is they've got nothing to do, and the prospect of holding a straight job is so dreary that they join "the movement" (as it was then called) and start hitting up people for money to live, on the premise that they're involved in critical social change blah blah blah. And it's really better that way, at least for some people, than finishing college and working at dumb jobs for constipated corporations; at least it's not always boring. . . . That's why we decided to start a news service—not because the proliferating underground and radical college press really needed a central information-gathering agency staffed by people they could trust (that was our hope), but because we had nothing else to do.*

It is important to realize that although essay-reviews are based largely on the opinion of the writer, he does not allow his presence in the article to overwhelm the subject he is discussing. Thus, in the article above, the author first reveals his biases about the underground press, but then moves rapidly into a discussion of the books without continually using "I."

The same applies to the next excerpt from an article by Dena Dawson. Although her opinions color the entire article, she does not intrude on the subject by writing in first person.

Police Women: TV's Newest Heroes*

Comment

Article

Note how the tone of the first two paragraphs informs readers that this is a review, not a straight news story.

The new TV season's creators seem finally to have grasped the plain fact that among the many million evening or prime-time viewers are several million non-WASP males, which they cleverly term "ethnics," and even a few dozen women.

Since the purpose of television is to SELL! SELL! as well as, of course, to provide Quality Entertainment, it's surprising that those feverish players of the Ratings game haven't turned their attention to the women in the audience until now. On the other hand, if the Hero

---

*Reprinted by permission of the author.

represents the ideals of a culture, would Americans, whatever their genealogy or sex, accept a hero or Top Person belonging to the non-dominant group? It seems they do. If the producers think they do—they do.

By the third paragraph, the writer has already begun to discuss the shows in the larger context of society. She does not digress for long, and returns quickly to the topic of her story in the next paragraph.

Not only is every ethnic group from Aborigine to Zulu represented in the new shows, *two* of the new weekly police programs star women. This can only mean one thing—that our culture symbols *are* changing—and that the long arm of the women's movement is reaching even here, into nine out of ten U.S. homes.

Refusing to abandon the stock-in-trade of police and adventure stories—i.e., murder, rape, kidnapping, larceny, etc.—the "creators" of TV police shows give you a hard-hitting, sexy Hero-cop who brings all the bad guys to justice. Lately, this mythic figure has become more vulnerable and sensitive, at times even poetic.

This unusual development of the police-hero figure seems to be, at least partly, a result of a significant attitude change in the public towards the police of the 60's—remember Berkeley and Chicago. Throughout the world, it is common to fear and/or despise the police, but only here, I suspect, has the Word come down to make them lovable, or at least human.

At any rate, the trend toward humanization continues with the emergence of the police woman. If the steely automaton is no longer tolerated in males, it would be unthinkable in females.

Having set the stage for her discussion, the writer then begins to review the two shows.

The opening episode of "Police Woman" is characteristic of the new mode in which Hard-hitting is replaced by Tough-tender. As Sergeant Pepper Anderson ("Beauty, Brains and a Badge") and her partner arrive at the scene, a young policeman has been shot and is dying in the street. She kneels by him, reassuring him about the ambulance on its way. He looks youthfully and sadly into her face and says, "Will you hold me, please?" She cradles his head in her arms and lowers her cheek to his. He dies.

Well-chosen examples and quotes from the show are used effectively here to make a point. The writer believes her readers will get the message without being told directly.

The next scene shows her going into the office and sobbing against the file cabinet. The boss, sympathetic and resigned, says, "It's part of the business Hon . . . but no way you get used to it."

This particular episode exists only to set up the character and has no connection with the main story of a team of bank robbers, two white males, a black female and a white female. Later, in the climactic scene, Sgt. Anderson, disguised as a bank teller, shoots and kills the black woman, to save an innocent person's life. But even this realistic note of violence does nothing to reduce identification with her.

Note the smooth transition here from the discussion of one show to another through a comparison of the main characters.

In "Get Christie Love" the character of Christie is more geared to the entertainment value of the star, Teresa Graves. Based on the widely read mystery novels of N.Y. policewoman, Dorothy Uhnak, the character has changed from Irish to Black and from serious to comic.

Christie calls everyone "sugah" and is so smart 'n' pert 'n' sassy, you wonder why she didn't go into show biz instead of joining the force. Nevertheless, unlike her NBC counterpart, she makes small, human mistakes which lead to danger.

In "Police Woman," the danger to Sgt. Anderson is usually a breakdown in the transmitter wired into her bra. At this point, in a '74 variant of the Maiden-in-Distress-Rescue, her one black and one white (and shaggy) partner rush in, save her life, and help "apprehend the suspect."

CHAPTER NINETEEN EXERCISES

1. One of the key elements of writing analyses and essay-reviews is concise language. To increase your awareness of wordiness in commonly used phrases, edit the unnecessary words from the phrases below:

his other alternative	his advance predictions
found strangled to death	will start off soon
its future prospects	a bald-headed man
was of an oblong shape	

Choose a single word to replace these phrases:

in the neighborhood of	at this point in time
owing to the fact that	lent a hand to the efforts of
have openly voiced complaints	in the majority of instances
managed to overcome	

2. Write a review of a movie, play, concert or other performance. Explain who the readers of your review would be and why they

would be interested in the items you have criticized. What publication might use the article and why?

3. Bring to class an article by a reviewer whose writing you like and explain why his or her reviews are effective. Comment on the person's writing style, general approach to reviewing, knowledge about the general subject, tone, etc.

CHAPTER 20
Humorous Articles

Several years ago a student handed in an article that was so good that the instructor suggested that he send it to *The Atlantic*. Unfortunately, a rejection letter came, and he was so despondent that to cheer himself up he went to a printer and made up a letterhead for a fictitious magazine, *Fish and Game*. He listed the instructor as the publisher, himself as editor-in-chief, the instructor as managing editor, himself as associate publisher, and two staff writers: himself and the instructor.

The instructor began to use the letterheads for notes to friends, rejecting articles that they had supposedly submitted for publication. One such bogus rejection notice went to Wilbur Schramm, a highly respected teacher and colleague:

> Dear Dr. Schramm:
>
> It has always been the policy of *Fish and Game* that every article be read by the Publisher, the Editor-in-Chief, the Managing Editor, the Associate Publisher, and both Staff Writers. Halfway through reading *your* manuscript, half the staff gagged and quit. We have decided that your manuscript is much too fishy and gamey for us. Please visit our spacious offices and pick up your manuscript. In its present rank state, it could not pass through the federal mails.
>
> Sincerely,
> Chief Sniffer

The instructor congratulated himself then forgot it—until he received a letter from Schramm:

> It seems that something untoward, not to say fishy, has happened. My wife, while talking on the telephone, apparently fried one of my manuscripts, and mailed the fish to you. The manuscript, with horseradish, tasted better than many of the things we have had to eat at our house, but, until we heard from you, we were somewhat puzzled as to what had become of the fish.

Knowing something of your *Fish and Game,* and your editorial ability, I am not surprised that you and your staff read halfway through my fish without realizing it was not a manuscript for your journal.

I must now insist that you return the fish to me promptly. May I remind you that your refusal to return the fish is fishnapping, and your calling it a manuscript is fishlander.

Thus, the anecdote began as a rejection, which was topped by the writer, who was topped by the instructor, then he was topped by Schramm. Is that humorous? Of course—provided you, or someone, laughed. Still, that doesn't get you any closer to understanding humor. The question should be: What is humor? If you'll explore a dictionary, you'll probably find the word defined something like this:

Humor is the quality that makes something funny or fanciful. It includes satire, a work in which vices, stupidities, and follies are held up to ridicule. It also includes wit, which is the ability to make clever or ironic remarks, usually by expressing it in a surprising or epigrammatic manner.

All humor starts with incongruity. That is, anything that deviates from the usual is potentially humorous. Humor begins with incongruity and ends when imagination dries up. Any subject may be approached humorously.

LEARNING TO WRITE HUMOR

A more accurate title for this chapter could be "Can You Teach Yourself to be a Humorist?" Although an instructor can teach you about writing in general—assigning papers, criticizing them, having you rewrite, and so on—the instructor cannot cajole humor out of you. Imagine the instructor beginning the class by saying: "All right, be *funny.*" Even if you are a budding humorist, it is almost impossible to respond with something funny.

When you're casting about for a topic that's humorous, don't try to think about something bizarre. Consider what Chic Young, the creator of "Blondie," has accomplished. He has been writing and drawing that comic strip for 40 years and reaches 60 million readers throughout the world in 17 languages. What is the secret of his success? Young says: "It's durable because it's simple. It's built on four things that everybody does: sleeping, eating, raising a family, and making money." Even though you may not yet be charged with raising a family, that leaves you with the other three. Extend them a bit. In the rest of this chapter you'll find articles on a health center,

Shakespeare, and suicide: three topics that most of your fellow students will think about at some time during their academic careers. Note the devices the writers use to create humor.

Pairing Unlike Elements

The following article, written by a student, Carolyn Manning, depends upon the effect of her matching two unlike elements:

There comes a time in almost everyone's college career when they feel compelled for one reason or another to go to the student health center. . . . The visit is an entertaining break from calculus and a chance to pinch the nurses. For others, sickness overtakes them so that their enfeebled minds are foolish enough to think that the health center may even be able to help them. Unfortunately, my number came up last week. I'm not saying that it is bad, but just the other day my roommate went in with a sore throat, and walked out with a cast on her arm.

I went in suffering from a severe headache that had gone on for nearly a week. They had originally diagnosed my problem as a severe case of split ends and recommended a change in shampoos. But, in spite of my dedication to Earth Born the problem persisted and I was forced to visit once again.

The jammed waiting room displayed a pitiful cast of characters; they looked like the cast of extras from "Airport 77." The man sitting next to me looked like he was the lone survivor of a Macy's bargain basement sale—and had tried to carry the basement home. He sat clutching a limp handkerchief to his face, and managed to read excerpts of his Spiderman comic between sneezing fits.

"What're you in for?" I asked, trying to take my mind off the heart attack victim to my right.

"Seven to life. Yuk, yuk. That's a joke, get it? Seven to life, jail, get it?"

"Ha, ha. Yeah," I said. Holy hypodermics! Who'd I get stuck talking with? Maybe I could find some pepper and set him off on another sneezing fit. But where was I going to find pepper in a health center? And why do they call this place a "health center" when everyone here is sick? . . .

Exaggeration

A primary form of humor in America is exaggeration. To put history in contemporary terms should be funny—especially if you've read Shakespeare. In the following article you'll find a student exaggerating Shakespeare to humorous effect.

There have been so many present-day authorities ready, willing, and running-at-the-mouth with explanations on flying saucers that today we reach way back to check with one of our favorite commentators, a fellow named Shakespeare, who attained at least local fame during the late sixteenth and early seventeenth centuries.

The bard never mentioned flying saucers as such in any of his works, but he too was somewhat intrigued with the many and various sights in the heavens. He was clever, however, and didn't commit himself one way or the other. In view of the controversy today, it could be that the "experts" might take a leaf from his book.

Not only is Shakespeare not committing himself through his characters in the following dialogue, which is in Act Three of *Hamlet*, he leaves Hamlet and Polonius with possible retreats in every direction.

> Hamlet: *Do you see that cloud that's almost in the shape of a camel?*
>
> Polonius: *By the mass, and it's like a camel, indeed.*
>
> Hamlet: *Methinks it is like a weasel.*
>
> Polonius: *It is back'd like a weasel.*
>
> Hamlet: *Or like a whale.*
>
> Polonius: *Very like a whale.*

As you may see, Polonius is an adaptable fellow. He doesn't exactly have a mind of his own, which may be for the best; it prevents controversy and leads to a general agreement all around that doesn't entangle one and all in quasi-scientific discussions of refracted light and discs whirling through space.

However, we would have preferred that Shakespeare imbue Polonius with a bit more spirit. For example, he might have ended this conversation with the following lines and settled the saucer question for all time:

> Hamlet: *And riding on the tail of that whale, methinks I see a greenish-appearing specimen with large eyes and a dour look.*
>
> Polonius: *Methinks you're drunk.*

Parody

Because the primary form of humor is exaggerating, we must end this chapter with an exaggerated, parody article written by a student, Eric Peterson, entitled "Writing Your Own Suicide Note":

A suicide note may be the most important thing you'll ever write in your lifetime, particularly if you're a failure. Unfortunately, most people put off writing their suicide note until the last desperate minute, and what might have been an eloquent and touching account is obscured in a muddle of hackneyed rambling phrases, bad punctuation, and inexcusable spelling errors.

Ideally, what you say and how you say it can mean an eternity of guilt and suffering for your family and friends, according to Gibby Mandrell, a young free-lancer who has found a niche for himself ghostwriting suicide notes.

"In my work," Mandrell says, "I'm dealing with your run-of-the-mill slob who's had it with the world. All of a sudden he decides he wants to be a Hemingway or a Faulkner on his farewell message. Well, he might as well be Toulouse Lautrec trying to dunk a basketball. If he doesn't know what he's doing and he doesn't seek some sort of help from a professional note writer, his whole suicide's going to be pointless."

But suicide notes don't have to be written by "experts." More and more people are writing their own notes, and doing it just as effectively.

Although there are no rules that must be strictly adhered to, experts agree that all "good" suicide notes have certain characteristics in common:

—They are always written on plain white paper.

—They usually start and end with good anecdotes.

—They contain a minimum number of suicide clichés. (Find your own way to say "I can't go on any longer" and "Don't blame yourself, Harry.").

—They are written in ink and tend to be slightly smudged.

—They are never sealed in an envelope and mailed. (Singing telegrams are in bad taste.)

Vern Muntjac, a popular suicide note ghostwriter working out of New York who claims a great number of show-business celebrities as former clients, emphasizes the importance of maintaining a singular theme throughout the suicide note.

"You don't want to minimize the meaning of your death by leaving a note that says 'Don't forget to pick up the cleaning Friday' or 'See if you can get something done about the rattle in the car.' When you've got your theme, whatever it is, for pete's sake, stick with it."

For many people the biggest obstacle in writing a suicide note is where to begin. A colorful anecdote is a good way to get your note off the ground, but keep it short and to the point. You might want to reminisce about an especially bad time in your life, or a relative who was mean to you.

No writer should ever use the first draft of his or her suicide note as the actual note. *Plan* on rewriting it at least once—or until the pills take effect.

Don't waste time searching for that ever-elusive "perfect" word. Remember what successful magazine editors say: "Don't get it right, get it written!"

Try to tailor your suicide notes to your personality. Make it sound like *you*. Find your natural voice. That's the voice that your friends and relatives will recognize, and that's the voice that will cause them months, even years, of agony. If you're a schizoid, don't be afraid to use *we* instead of *I*. And if you're catatonic, you might just want to leave a blank piece of paper as your suicide note. The most common public misconception about suicide notes is that they are mandatory. In fact, they are optional. Because of their inherent straightforwardness and practicality, suicide notes have become the convention in our society but not necessarily the rule.

"The truth is," says Columbia suicide psychologist Psol Abrahams, "other means of post-mortem communication have been just as effectively left. Suicide paintings, often depicting the vast amounts of inner-turbulence within the suicidee, have been left, as have a great number of suicide poems. We even have one case on record of a suicide sailboat being left behind."

If you're intent on leaving a suicide note, though, and aren't satisfied with your own writing efforts, you might want to consider hiring a professional writer. Even if he doesn't end up ghostwriting your note, most offer consultations and sound advice at reasonable prices. Many, like Gibby Mandrell, guarantee their work.

"I consider myself a specialist," says Mandrell from his plush San Diego office with a sweeping view of the ocean. "My work's guaranteed. Hey, that means when you're gone, baby, if Gibby Mandrell wrote your suicide note, people are going to miss you. They're gonna' be sick about it. And you *know* they're at least gonna' cry."

If you do enlist the services of a professional suicide note writer, be prepared to pay cash. "I have to work on a strict cash-in-advance basis," says Muntjac. "I got burned a coupla' times on bounced checks and people leaving me their dogs and cats in their wills. I don't need that," he says emphatically.

According to research conducted by Professor Abrahams, most suicide note writers are already at a psychological disadvantage when they attempt the note. "Most are down on their luck. They lack confidence. They're trying to succeed at writing the note when they've already failed miserably at most everything else."

Abrahams has worked extensively with potential suicide victims to restore their confidence in their note-writing ability. "Often the new-found confidence at having written a successful suicide note carries over to the actual suicide attempt, which as a result succeeds on the first try," Abrahams says proudly. "It's good to see the results."

"The main thing is for people to realize that they *can* write their own suicide note. It doesn't take a lawyer or a scholar or a published writer. One of the best notes I've ever seen was written by a high school counselor. My god, if he can do it, anyone can."

The ironic thing about a suicide note, Abrahams observes, is that it can be the first—and the last—thing that a miserable failure of a human being does right.

Why don't we explain why we think each of the articles in this chapter is funny? Because William Frye wrote a book on humor entitled *Sweet Madness* so unhumorously that he ended it with this: "When you put a butterfly on a pin, he soon is dead."

Humor, too.

CHAPTER TWENTY EXERCISES

1. If you're writing humor for the first time, you should think of a personal experience that you remember as funny. After writing the first draft, read it carefully. Does the experience no longer seem funny? If so, you can fictionalize the experience by exaggerating—provided it's clear to the reader that you're writing humor. Write a humorous article of at least 500 words.

2. Emulate Carolyn Manning's article on the health center by putting together unlike elements. Read her article again before attempting to write that kind of humor. Write a humorous article of approximately 750 words.

PART FOUR

The Professionals and How to Become One

CHAPTER 21
Laws, Ethics, and Etiquette

Journalists' work involves hundreds of decisions each day. In the course of their normal activities, they must decide what to write about, whom to interview, which information to use in the story, what order to present the information in, what kind of story to write, what words to use, and so on. Many of these choices affect only the final product, so writers are free to act on their judgments about what will produce the best story. But many decisions affect things other than the story itself, such as writers' relationships with their sources or editors, their relationships with other writers, or their professional standing in the publishing world. Such decisions often involve issues of law, ethics, and etiquette.

No writer can expect to practice the craft without having to confront situations that demand such choices be made. It is therefore reasonable for writers to acquire a practical knowledge of the laws that not only protect their work but that limit their use of other people's work. In addition, they should be familiar with the legal incentives society provides for writers to publish accurate and truthful statements about their subjects. They should also be aware that their ability to protect the confidentiality of their sources is not absolute.

Beyond the areas of journalism that are regulated by law are territories governed solely by ethics. Decisions involving ethical choices are often more difficult to make than those involving legal choices because of the absence of absolute guidelines. Should you allow a source to read an article before it is published? Suppose that person asks for changes? Are you obligated to make them? Is it all right to submit articles to several magazines simultaneously? Suppose two magazines want the story. Should you sell to the highest bidder? What if you stumble across a story that someone doesn't want made public? How can you decide whether or not to go ahead with the article? These kinds of decisions can be made only on the basis of an individual's standards of professional conduct. As such, they can greatly influence your standing among your peers.

Finally, the unwritten code of publishing etiquette should guide a writer's activities. Who pays for what in a relationship between writer and source, or writer and magazine? How much revision should an editor expect a writer to do on an article without a guaranteed payment? How much revision of an article by a magazine's editorial staff should a writer accept before claiming that his or her work has been substantively altered? And when that does happen, how should the writer handle the situation?

Recognizing that many practices are not covered by statute—and that legal action is often so cumbersome and expensive that it is all but useless in many cases—the American Society of Journalists and Authors (ASJA) has developed a code of ethics and fair practices. The code, reprinted in Appendix C, is excellent for spelling out pivotal matters affecting the relationships between writers and editors. This code is not entirely satisfactory for the purposes of this book because it is largely limited to writer-editor relations and is designed for professionals, who take for granted many points that are perplexing to beginners.

The code is limited in another respect. Although the ASJA is a healthy organization having nearly 500 members, many other writers make agreements with editors that do not conform to the code, and members of the society are sometimes unable to persuade editors to conform.

Whether editors observe the code is their decision. If many of their best writers insist that their assignments be governed by the provisions of the code, they are likely to acquiesce. So many editors have backgrounds as free-lancers that sympathy for the code is apparent, even in magazine offices where editors find it difficult or impossible to live up to its provisions.

Thus, the code is both a set of practical guidelines and an ideal to be attained. In this chapter, we cite some of the provisions of the Code of Ethics and Fair Practices—in the context of discussing questions that are important to beginners as well as to professionals.

LAW AND THE WRITER

No matter what its constitution states, nearly every society restricts free expression. The basic restrictions take the form of laws to protect individuals or groups against defamation, copyright laws to protect authors and publishers, statutes to protect the community standard of decency, and statutes to protect the state against treasonable and seditious expression. Volumes have been written about these laws. A short work that writers find valuable is Paul Ashley's *Say It Safely*. Much larger and more complete books are *Mass Communication Law* by Donald M. Gillmor and Jerome A. Barron and *Law of Mass Communications* by Harold L. Nelson and Dwight L. Teeter, Jr. Writers interested in the laws governing communication are referred to such books for full discussions. In this chapter, we will consider some of the highlights of the laws governing a writer's career.

Libel

Any false statement, written or broadcast, is libelous if it causes anyone to suffer public hatred, contempt, or ridicule; or if it causes one to be shunned or avoided; or if it injures one in his business or occupation.

In 1964, the United States Supreme Court decided in *New York Times Co.* v. *Sullivan* that even false statements that tend to injure public officials must be protected by law unless facts were deliberately misstated or unless there were reckless disregard of the question of truth or falsity. In 1971, the Court decided in *Rosenbloom* v. *Metromedia* that private individuals who are involved in matters of public or general concern also should be severely limited in their ability to recover damages in libel actions. Like public officials, they must prove that they are the victims of actual malice or "calculated falsehood" to sue successfully no matter how great the damage. It is obvious from this that the Court continues to uphold a broad umbrella to protect writers who attempt to present facts about public issues—even if the writers are mistaken and the "facts" turn out to be false.

In presenting opinion, writers have long enjoyed the privilege of "fair comment and criticism." This means that people, measures, and social institutions that seek public approval are fair game for the writer's judgments. The judgments may be cruel—as when a drama critic wrote in a scathing review, "I have knocked everything but the chorus girls' knees, and God anticipated me there"—but they are fully protected.

There is much more to the law of defamation, and every writer should study it. In public affairs journalism, the writer who takes due care to present facts rather than distortions and does not write maliciously avoids the principal dangers. In most states, if a defamatory publication is true, the injured person cannot recover damages except in highly unusual circumstances. But the writer must prove the statements are true if a suit is filed. Studying the laws of libel should be an important part of the education of every public affairs journalist.

Privacy

Here, too, the writer's freedom has been growing; the courts support the public's right to learn about their fellow citizens. This does not mean that a writer is free to invade privacy at will. It means that the courts weigh the public interest against the interest of the person who believes that his privacy has been invaded. Where it can be shown that issues or matters of general concern are involved, the courts tend to rule in favor of publication. Courts sometimes go much further. In a famous case, a one-time child prodigy named William Sidis was the subject of a profile in *The New Yorker*. Repelled by the publicity that had enveloped him when he was a child, Sidis, who had lost his passion for mathematics and was leading an obscure life as a bookkeeper, sued on the grounds that *The New Yorker* had invaded his privacy. But the court ruled that he had been a public figure and still was.

Since the majority of magazine articles are written with the cooperation of those who are prominently featured, few writers have been threatened with suits based on the right of privacy. Writers who become defendants in such suits usually recognize while researching an article that danger looms, and this gives them time to seek legal help. There are enough exceptions to these rules of thumb, however, to suggest that writers should study the passages covering privacy in one of the books on communications law cited above, or in *Rights and Writers* by Harriet F. Pilpel and Theodora S. Zavin.

Copyright

How can I protect my work from being stolen? This is a question that worries beginning writers much more than it should. Since January 1, 1978, when the Copyright Revision Act of 1976 went into effect, a writer's article has been protected by federal copyright laws from the moment it is written. Even if the article is never published, or for that matter, never leaves the author's desk, it is subject to copyright restrictions for the author's lifetime and for 50 years afterward. Two criteria must be met for a work to be copyrighted: (1) it must be original, and (2) it must be "fixed in a tangible form." Magazine articles that are the unique work of an author clearly meet these specifications.

Another source of comfort to beginners should be that the cost of the text material represents a small fraction of the total cost of *any* magazine. *Playboy* pays $3,000 for some articles, but producing and distributing a single issue costs hundreds of thousands of dollars. The publisher of a down-at-the-heels journal who can afford to pay no more than 3 cents a word may begrudge the $90 he lays out for a 3,000-word article, but he is certain to grieve more over the thousands of dollars that must go for other expenses. The outright theft of a manuscript makes so little sense that the editor who risks a lawsuit by stealing one should have his sanity questioned.

The "Theft" of Ideas   This does not mean that there are no dangers. There are many fewer than the fearful beginner imagines and most of them lurk in evils subtler than thievery. If 100 free-lancers submit an article each to a magazine tomorrow, one can bet confidently that no article will be stolen outright. It will be almost as unlikely—but not a certain bet—that a magazine staffer will steal a passage or a paragraph from any of the articles. But just as it is not safe to assume that college students will neither cheat on exams nor plagiarize in writing term papers, fresh thoughts are so important in the magazine world that assuming that nothing will be taken is risky. Perhaps a young staffer eager to impress his superiors will appropriate a title or a phrase—or perhaps the article he is evaluating carries an anecdote that would sparkle in the article he is writing. The culprit need not be a beginner. A seasoned editor may be captivated by an article idea but may think that the article itself is not up to his standards and that the writer is not likely to revise successfully. He may then reject the article and assign the subject to one of his regular writers. These kinds of thievery need not be conscious. Such is human frailty that one can easily rationalize guilt to the point that it disappears. It is especially easy for a staffer to persuade himself after some time has passed, that the title, the phrase, or the idea was original with him.

Unfortunately, ideas are not subject to copyright laws. Only their expression in a certain form is protected. Thus, there is no legal recourse for a writer who feels that a magazine has stolen his article idea. Because the magazine world places such a premium on new ideas, or good ideas, this situation sometimes causes problems for writers and editors. The American Society of Journalists and Authors has proposed some guidelines on this subject in its "Code of Ethics and Fair Practices":

> An idea shall be defined not as a subject alone, but as a subject with an approach to the handling thereof. A writer shall be considered to have a property right in such an idea. Under ordinary circumstances he shall have priority in the development of it. When an editor likes an idea, he normally is bound to permit the writer who presents it first to proceed with it.

These guidelines reflect the spirit of the federal law, which distinguishes between ideas and their form of expression.

Magazines and Copyright Law   Published magazines are protected by copyright laws, as are the individual articles they contain. This does not prevent a writer from asserting his right to separate copyright because he is regarded by law as the first owner. Although individual registration with the copyright office is not mandatory, a writer cannot sue for infringement without having registered, nor can he collect damages or attorney's fees for any infringement that occurred before the article was registered.

In general, when a magazine buys an article, it purchases specific rights to publish the article or to authorize others to publish or reprint the article. Some magazines give reprint royalties to writers, but others do not. It is important for free-lance writers to understand exactly what they are selling when they sign contracts and receive payments for articles.

A writer who produces an article working under contract to a magazine is considered to have written a "work made for hire." In such cases, the magazine is considered the "author" for copyright purposes and is thus entitled to initial ownership of the copyright. Staff writers also work under this condition.

Since most publishers are fair-minded and since so few articles have a life beyond first publication, it seldom pays an author to copyright his own work or to worry about which rights he is giving up. Once most articles have been published, rights to them are no more valuable than used theater tickets. But enough authors have had cause to rue the cost of their once-careless habits to suggest that knowing the law and reading contracts carefully can be important. Consider this excerpt from a magazine contract:

> In consideration of the sum of $ —— (in payment of which we herewith enclose our check), the author grants to —————— Publishing Company, its licenses and assigns forever, all rights in and to the material and all rights of copyright and renewal of copyrights therein, including, but without limitation, the exclusive right to publish the material in magazine, newspaper and book form, and to use it in dramatic, motion picture, radio and television productions anywhere. The rights herein granted include the right: to edit, revise, abridge, condense and translate the material; to publish the same in one or more install-ments; to change the title thereof; to use the author's name, biography and likeness in connection with the pub-lication, advertising and promotion of the material; and to make such other promotional use of the material as —————— Publishing Company may determine.

Copyright Law and the Doctrine of Fair Use   Most magazine writers find that protecting themselves is less significant than how they use the copyrighted work of others, sometimes quotations from other articles, more often quotations from books. How much can I quote? This question centers on the doctrine known as "fair use," and as one panel of distinguished judges pointed out, "The issue of fair use . . . is the most troublesome in the whole law of copyright."

The Copyright Act says nothing about fair use, and as the courts have developed the doctrine it is imprecise at best. No fixed rules have emerged to tell a writer how much he may quote. In some des-peration, most book publishers tell their authors that they must seek permission to quote any substantial amount of copyrighted ma-terial, and that in any case the author must obtain permission to quote a passage as long as 300 words—or 400, or 500, varying with the publisher. Seldom does anyone fear that quoting a sentence or a paragraph will infringe on copyright. But if mere length were the criterion, one might freely quote four lines from an eight-line poem. The pivotal question is whether the quotation represents substantial use—and especially whether quoting, whatever the length, may prejudice the sale or diminish the need for the original work.

Some magazines and books carry notices that not a word may be reproduced. The *Reader's Digest* masthead states, "Reproduction in any manner in whole or in part in English or other languages prohibited." This is nonsense. Publications cannot pass their own laws. Those that issue such warnings are as subject as others to the rules of fair use.

Writers should also know that general facts cannot be copyrighted, and a writer can paraphrase almost at will. Copyright is not a prison for ideas or reports of events; it protects the sequence of ideas, words, phrases, and the phrasings themselves. Conceivably, copyright can be infringed by paraphrase—if the writer paraphrases at length and so deftly that a court might rule unfair use—but that danger is remote.

Copyright Infringement   Infringement of copyright is illustrated by the case brought by writer Gene Miller of the *Miami Herald* against Universal City Studios, Inc., American Broadcasting Companies, and Post-Newsweek Stations Florida, Inc. In 1971, Miller covered the story of the kidnapping of Barbara Mackle, who was abducted from an Atlanta hotel and buried alive in a coffin for five days before she was rescued. Miller and Mackle agreed to write a book together about her experience called *83 Hours Till Dawn*. A producer for Universal Studios subsequently saw the book, decided it would make a good movie for television, and gave a copy of it to a screenwriter. The producer offered to purchase the rights to the book from Miller, but Miller wanted more money than the producer was willing to pay.

Universal went ahead with the movie, called *The Longest Night*. Miller then sued on the basis of infringement of copyright, and in 1978 the case was decided in his favor. The decision was based largely on the fact that the movie script contained a number of similarities to material in the book that was not available in other accounts of the kidnapping, including some factual errors. The decision was that Miller's research, that is, those facts he discovered through his own effort during 2500 hours of interviews and digging, was subject to copyright restrictions. It was evidence of the originality of his work and its form of expression. In its opinion, the court stated the following:

> To this court it doesn't square with reason or common sense to believe that Gene Miller would have undertaken the research involved in writing *83 Hours Till Dawn* (or to cite another more famous example, that Truman Capote would have undertaken the research required to write *In Cold Blood*) if the author thought that upon completion of the book a movie producer or television network could simply come along and take the profits of the books and his

research from him. In the age of television "docudrama" to hold other than research is copyrightable is to violate the spirit of the copyright law and to provide to those persons and corporations lacking in requisite diligence and ingenuity a license to steal.

Magazines and Copyright Infringement   Magazines often seek to protect their own legal interests by inserting provisions in their contracts in which the writer guarantees various aspects of his work. The following paragraph is an example of this kind of protection:

You represent and warrant originality, authorship and ownership of said contribution, that it has not heretofore been published, that its publication will not infringe upon any copyright, proprietary or other right and that it contains no matter which is libelous, obscene, or otherwise contrary to law.

Copyright Law and U.S. Government Publications   Few writers are aware that the law holds that "No copyright shall subsist . . . in any publication of the United States Government. . . ." Like all other works that are not protected by common law or statutory copyright, government documents are in the public domain and may be quoted freely. There can be questions about particular works because the Copyright Act does not define "government publication," but the only practical danger is that a government publication may reprint copyrighted material. This does not transform the reprinted work into a government publication. A copyrighted magazine article reprinted in the *Congressional Record* is still protected under copyright law.

Access to Government Information   While Federal law permits one to quote freely from government documents, writers sometimes have trouble getting at them. Government secrecy is an old story.

As we are all now well aware, secret dealings have been common in every presidential administration. For example, some members of Congress were as disturbed by governmental secrecy during the Eisenhower administration as were spokesmen for the mass media. They began in 1955 to work for an amendment to the Administrative Procedure Act. It was a laborious process. Representative John E. Moss's Subcommittee on Government Information held 173 public hearings and investigations and issued seventeen volumes of hearing transcripts and fourteen volumes of reports, all of which documented widespread secrecy. By 1966, both houses of Congress had passed an amendment to the public information section of the Administrative Procedure Act. But by the time the amendment became the law known as the Freedom of Information Act, *nine* categories of information had been exempted:

1. Information specifically required by executive order to be kept secret in the interest of national defense or foreign policy.

2. Information related solely to internal personnel rules and practices of any agency.

3. Information specifically exempted from disclosure by statute.

4. Trade secrets and commercial or financial information obtained from any person and privileged or confidential.

5. Interagency or intraagency memorandums or letters that would not be available by law to a private party in litigation with the agency.

6. Personnel and medical files and similar files the disclosure of which would constitute a clearly unwarranted invasion of personal privacy.

7. Investigatory files compiled for law enforcement purposes except to the extent available by law to a private party.

8. Information contained in or related to examination, operating, or condition reports prepared by, on behalf of, or for the use of any agency responsible for the regulation or supervision of financial institutions.

9. Geological and geophysical information and data (including maps) concerning wells.

Understandably eager to promote and protect their own policies and programs, officials often hide and manipulate information. As the American public learned during the revelations of the Watergate scandal during the second half of the Nixon administration, sometimes their purpose is shady. In one relatively innocuous example, the commander of the Military District of Washington, D.C., once attempted to withhold a letter that pressured liquor lobbyists and wholesalers to provide free drinks for 1,200 guests at an army party. He tried to justify his action by citing the first exemption to the Freedom of Information Act, which protects national security information.

Despite its flaws, the Freedom of Information Act has enhanced access at the federal level. More than half of the states have passed laws that provide access to state, county, and municipal records and require open meetings of public bodies. These laws, too, are flawed by exemptions. But it seems clear that the writer's freedom to find facts in the labyrinths of government is improving.

ETHICS AND THE WRITER

Plagiarism and Fair Use

The writer should understand the distinction between plagiarism and the unfair use that is copyright infringement. Plagiarism is not necessarily illegal (although it is certainly unethical). That is, one may steal a few sentences or a few paragraphs by passing them off as one's own. This act is one of failing to give credit, but it does not necessarily infringe copyright.

A writer may satisfy the courts that he has not infringed copyright and thus settle the legal question. Whether he can satisfy his conscience—or in the absence of a conscience, whether he might be able to satisfy a jury of other writers—poses the ethical question. Although it is easy to rationalize and explain away plagiarism, anyone who has the intelligence to write for publication *can* tell when he is failing to give appropriate credit. It is unnecessary, of course, for the writer to try to trace down the origin of every captivating phrase. The man who coined "credibility gap" to describe one of the problems and failings of the president of the United States would probably like to be credited every time the phrase is used, but that would be absurd.

It is not at all absurd, however, to give credit for a sentence. One worth using should be clothed in quotation marks and attributed to its author. (Not, for most magazines, with the footnoting that is common in scholarly journals—but in a smooth note in the text: "As James Thurber pointed out in . . ." or "Gunnar Myrdal's *An American Dilemma* cites . . .") If the phrasing of a sentence a writer wants to use is limp but the idea is attractive, the writer should paraphrase and give credit.

These guidelines are not rigid for the writer who uses them sensibly. For example, an article on the crushing troubles that afflict New York City must deal with financial problems and air pollution. The writer might take facts and figures from an article or book and accurately feel that he owed no credit because dozens of articles and books carry the same information. He must ask himself in each case: Did the person who wrote this have to work for it—dig—or are these facts widely known and readily available? This criterion can apply in almost any situation. Facing it squarely and answering it honestly will suggest whether giving credit is necessary.

When honest answers to such questions result in paragraph after paragraph of attribution to others, a writer should not assume that he is spreading credit too liberally. Rather, like the bad scholar who leans so heavily on other scholars that he does little more than move bones from one graveyard to another, the writer is merely rehashing.

Playing Fair with Sources and Readers

The newspaper reporter learns quite early that he must play fair with those he interviews. If he misconstrues ideas, garbles quotations, or identifies an interviewee who expected anonymity, his source may decide to be a source no longer. This problem is seldom so acute in magazine writing because so few free-lancers or staff writers must return to a source again and again. Writers often obtain information from a different set of sources for each article.

No ethical writer will take unfair advantage of his sources. The unethical writer soon develops a reputation for casual attitudes toward the truth; outraged sources complain to editors. Young writers, however, may get into trouble or fail to get information because they do not know that the conventions of interviewing enable them to protect a source who fears being quoted directly or being identified with the information he provides. The conventions include:

Indirect Quotation   These are remarks which may be quoted only in substance (not verbatim). Usually, however, they are attributed to an identified source. A little-used convention, this is sometimes valuable for someone like the president, whose words will be studied for shades of meaning if he is quoted directly.

Off the Record   Information that is to be held in complete confidence, off-the-record facts are not to be printed under any circumstances or in any form. For the most part, these are facts needed to grasp the significance of complicated events. Off-the-record information is usually given to writers to orient them to future events that will require special handling by those who are thoroughly informed.

Not for Attribution   This is information that should not be attributed to a named source but to one who is identified generally: "a reliable source," "a longtime friend of the entertainer," "an authority on international law," or the like. In many instances, the source is not named because the fact that he disclosed the information might embarrass or injure him.

Background   Information that may be used by a writer entirely on his own responsibility, background may not be attributed even to "a reliable source." The writer presents the information as though it had been developed from original research. Ordinarily, the reason background may not be attributed in any way is that even a reference to a general source might lead to identification and cause embarrassment or injury.

These conventions are useful primarily because the writer can offer them as cloaks to one who is reluctant to be quoted directly. On the other hand, they can be dangerous for two reasons. First, a writer may offer anonymity of one sort or another too freely and thus hide sources who should be identified. The writer may even discover that he has granted anonymity to so many sources that his article reads as though he had made it all up. Second, the conventions that allow anonymity tempt the source to grind his axe as he likes, unobserved. At bottom, anonymous interviews circulate information for which no one takes public responsibility. The writer may wake up to discover that he held a cloak behind which a source was manipulating facts and fashioning his own version of truth.

The worst of it is that these interview conventions may serve or destroy the ultimate aim, which is to play fair with the reader. This is a dilemma. Presenting the facts provided by only those who will be identified is not likely to add up to the truth. For example, the president of the United States will talk on the record to present his version of the truth about foreign policy. A civil servant in the State Department who has a firmer grasp of the facts is not likely to contradict the president publicly. Granting anonymity to the civil servant will best serve the reader. But the writer may inadvertently grant anonymity to a source who hopes to mislead. In the end, the writer must protect everyone by granting anonymity when it seems desirable or necessary, then checking carefully to try to make certain that he is not being used to mislead the public.

Direct Quotations   Playing fair with sources and readers is also at the center of problems with direct quotations. The most common question about quoting—How exact must quotations be?—can be answered simply: Never use quotation marks unless you are certain that the words are precisely what was said. If it ever made sense to quote *approximately* what was said and to improve the grammar of public figures—once fairly common, but dubious practices in journalism—it makes no sense today.

Writers seem to agree almost unanimously that only in unusual cases—highly technical articles, for example—should sources be allowed to read before publication the articles in which their quotations appear. A source makes a contribution to an article but the writer is responsible for the whole of it. A source views a completed article from a point of view distorted by his own self-interest. Most writers will agree to call a source (or write to him) when an article is complete and give him a chance to check his own words. These are practices that raise a question of ethics only when the writer has promised that a source may read all or part of an article before publication and fails to follow through. Professional writers rarely make such promises.

Quoting Out of Context   There is a real danger that a source who is allowed to read an article before publication will try to influence a revision selfishly; but another danger may arise if the source is not allowed to read it. For one of the most acute problems in journalism is quoting out of context. This is never so blatant in article writing as it is in theatrical advertising, where a reviewer's "The play is a terrific bore" is quoted highly selectively in ads that attribute to the review this judgment: "Terrific!" The problem is much subtler in magazine writing. Quite often well-intentioned writers are so intent upon the point they want to make that they fix upon (and write down) sentences that support a theme and ignore another that counters it. Or the writer quotes a part of an interview that fails to reflect the meaning of the whole of it.

Perhaps the best way for writers to avoid injuring a source and misleading readers is to remind themselves over and over that quoting out of context is a persistent danger. Seasoned magazine writers avoid it by a method no more complex than putting themselves on guard.

An Article's Publishability   Everyone who is approached for an interview deserves an honest judgment of the likelihood that an article will be published. Interviewees give time, energy, and information, and a writer should repay them with honesty. Beginners should make it clear that they are speculating about the possibility of publication—if they are—even though many sources will probably give them less time and attention than they would give a well-known free-lancer or a staff writer on assignment. Honesty offers several compensations. If the writers have admitted that their articles may not be published, the source is not as likely to call periodically to ask when the article will appear. Also, some public officials who are inclined to guard information are more relaxed with beginning journalists (especially students) and tell them more than they would tell established writers. Finally, some sources will try to help beginning writers by giving them much time and attention. All this does not negate the fact that, in many cases, the established writer has a distinct advantage. But the beginners who try to pass themselves as writers who are virtually certain of publication are virtually certain to fail.

Expense Account Journalism   In one dark area, many writers and sources (not to mention editors) seem to be united against readers. This may be a harsh judgment of the practice of sources who try to promote favorable articles by arranging free travel and other expensive assistance for writers. But seldom are readers informed that the writer of the glowing article on Oahu was able to explore the island because someone with an interest in promoting tourism there paid the bill. In some cases, the editors are not told of the arrangement. Normally, however, editors know or can guess, if only because they are paying a $400 fee to a writer whose expenses were $750.

The fact that an interested party paid the bill is not the essential point. The ethical question springs from the fact that the reader is not fully informed that the article may have been biased.

Simultaneous Submissions

Should a free-lancer submit an article to more than one publication at a time? If the world of magazines observed the rules of the retail marketplace, the answer would be "Of course." But editors make a vociferous case for single submission. They point out that an editor may devote hours, even days, to reading and evaluating a manuscript. A staff conference involving a dozen editors may be given over to discussing an article. If an editor of *Cosmopolitan* sends a four-page letter suggesting revisions, many hours and hundreds of dollars are wasted if the writer responds that *McCall's* bought the article the day before.

This does not mean that there are no reasonable exceptions. When a writer has an idea or an article so timely that waiting for an editorial decision may jeopardize it, some editors consider simultaneous submission appropriate. The cardinal rule in such cases is that all editors must be informed.

Beginners sometimes reason that their articles have so little chance of acceptance at major markets that they can safely submit to four or five simultaneously on the off chance that one will buy. This is usually a safe assumption because few beginners *can* publish in a major magazine without serving the apprenticeship of writing first for minor magazines. But even a beginner jeopardizes his future by submitting simultaneously without informing each magazine.

Double-Duty Articles

Imaginative writers can make one research project go a long way—perhaps far enough for three or four articles. Should they? It is easy to pose an example that clearly suggests an affirmative answer. Certainly, a slow journey down the Mississippi can yield the material for a profile of the river, a profile of a port city, an article on a riverboat, and another on a riverboat captain. In fact, given the time, energy, and ingenuity, a capable writer might fashion a hundred articles for a hundred different magazines from a single trip. If passages in the articles do not duplicate one another, and the information in each article is substantially different, the ethical question disappears.

But there are questions in this area that must be answered closely. For example, what of writing on one entertainment personality for different magazines? Two factors are now pivotal: the similarity of the articles and the similarity of the magazines. If the articles are similar, the magazines must be different. If the magazines are similar, the articles must be different. Thus, one might write an article for a magazine circulated in the Southwest and a similar article for a magazine circulated in New York. One might also write a profile of an entertainment personality for one magazine and barely mention that he loves to cook and, for a similar magazine, base an article on the same man's prowess as a gourmet cook.

The requirement that either the articles or the magazines be quite different is easy to understand. If readers of *Harper's* and *The Atlantic* were to find one month that an author had written similar articles on Edward Kennedy for both magazines, many would feel cheated because they subscribe to both. If the articles were quite different, though, the readers of both magazines would probably feel only that that was a bit too much Kennedy. If similar articles by one writer are published in magazines that have quite different sets of readers, clearly no harm is done.

Whatever the writer believes about the similarities and differences in magazines and audiences, he should inform the editors. Their judgments may not square with his. An author of this text once agreed to write for a magazine a 3,500-word essay-review of three books. A short time later, he agreed to write a 900-word review of one of the books for another magazine. The reviews were so strikingly different in substance and tone as well as length that he did not trouble to inform the editors. When the 900-word review was published, the other editor called long-distance to say that its appearance had ruined his day.

Informing everyone who is centrally involved is also essential when a writer wants to sell once again an article purchased by a magazine that died without publishing it. The writer should get a letter of permission from the publisher of the defunct magazine and show it to any editor interested in the article.

ETIQUETTE AND THE WRITER

Points of etiquette have been treated generally in earlier pages of this book, but several that are important to the free-lancer and the staff writer are discussed specifically here.

Writer and Source

One of the most important points of etiquette arises from the fact that many articles are built on massive research. If the writer interviews widely and gathers much more information than he can use—and he should—how does he explain to his sources why he ignored their contributions? Explaining should begin not after an article is published but during interviews. A writer should tell his sources that he is interviewing not only for quotations but also for background information. This is, of course, quite true, and very few interviews yield *nothing* of value. It is true also that many interviews do not show up in articles because space in that issue of the magazine was limited. Most interviewees are mollified by one explanation or the other, even though they may not be happy. Sources who are quoted as well as those who are not are often gratified by thank-you notes from writers, just as most are pleased when a writer calls for an appointment and arrives punctually.

With few exceptions, writers should take sources to lunch, not the other way around. It is easy to overemphasize the point that in many cases, the source is likely to benefit at least as much as the writer (introducing a note of sticky piety where it does not belong), but the writer should not yield to that easy rationalization. A writer who establishes businesslike relationships is not likely to find some day that his sources will expect too much of him.

Writer and Revision

The knottiest problem of etiquette in the writer-editor relationship is revision. It poses questions like these:

1. How much rewriting should an editor be able to ask a writer to do without guaranteeing that the article will be bought and published?

2. To what degree should an editor himself be allowed to rewrite an article?

3. What recourse has the writer when he thinks editing has ruined his article?

The code of the ASJA states:

> No writer's work shall be rewritten without his or her advance consent. If an editor requests a writer to rewrite his manuscript, the writer shall be obliged to do so. Alternatively, he shall also be entitled to withdraw the manuscript and offer it elsewhere.

Although this provision falls far short of covering all questions, it offers useful guidelines. Like the rest of the code, however, it is designed for the established writer. It assumes that writer and editor settled on an article fee beforehand. This is unlikely for the young writer. What should a writer do if an editor asks for an extensive revision but does not promise to pay for the result?

As always, circumstances alter each case. If the writer thinks the revision will improve the article (and make it more salable elsewhere), he or she might simply revise as suggested. But if the revision requires extensive research and rewriting, the writer might ask for a guarantee. The rankest beginner is justified in asking for a guarantee when a revision is requested in a way that suggests that the editor is strongly interested in the article and is optimistic about publishing it.

The Manuscript

If it seems too elementary to advise that manuscripts should be neat and easy to read, the many that arrive in magazine offices looking as though they had endured a bad trip suggest that it is not. Editors face stacks of manuscripts every day. Are they likely to enjoy those that writers have edited heavily in pencil, those that are typed in purple on yellow paper, those that are creased and dog-eared? Genius or great talent is welcome in whatever form it arrives. No editor will reject an article he wants because the writer is a slovenly typist. But writers who are not geniuses or great talents—those who must compete with thousands of others—must submit manuscripts that eye-weary editors can read without groans. (See the example of standard form for a manuscript on p. 278.)

The most considerate writers mail their manuscripts flat and put them in folders before inserting them in manila envelopes. (Folders are essential when pictures accompany an article. Pictures should be protected between two pieces of corrugated cardboard held together by rubber bands.) Because most editors like to work with loose pages, manuscripts should be paper-clipped, never stapled.

A stamped, self-addressed envelope should accompany query letters and manuscripts until the writer is established as a professional *or* until a relationship with a particular magazine is established. A beginner who has received a highly favorable response to a query need not enclose an envelope when submitting an article. A writer who has come close to selling ideas or articles to a magazine and receives encouraging letters also need not.

Whether a covering letter should accompany an article depends on the reason for the letter. *Never* should a letter be written to explain the article. If the rows of words that make up the manuscript fail to do their own explaining, a letter will do no more than mark the writer an inept amateur. Covering letters are always in order when writer and editor have corresponded extensively about an article. An editor will usually want a letter explaining that the writer did not pursue one aspect as planned for this reason, or could not interview a recognized authority for that reason.

IN SUMMARY

Laws regarding communications vary somewhat from state to state. Precepts of ethics and points of etiquette are likely to vary at least slightly from magazine to magazine—and on some publications from editor to editor. Such variations make it impossible to describe exactly how writers and editors should behave in all cases. The principles set forth in this chapter, however, sketch the central bodies of law, ethics, and etiquette. The wise writer will give them as careful attention as he gives to fashioning evocative sentences.

CHAPTER TWENTY-ONE EXERCISES

1. You have discovered that a young woman enrolled at your school is a former star of a popular television series. According to your source, she has had a nervous breakdown because of the pressures of Hollywood and has come to escape being a celebrity. Her activities are closely monitored by the dorm supervisor, and he refuses to help you arrange an interview, stating that she wishes to be left alone. You know an article about her would be a good one for a magazine, but you have not figured out how to get an interview. What should you do?

2. A national magazine has responded favorably to one of your queries. The articles editor who writes back to you says that the magazine will give you the assignment on spec, and will pay you $1,000 for the article if it is published, zero if it is not. You write the article, then wait anxiously for a month to hear from the magazine.

Finally you get a phone call from the articles editor. Your article has been accepted, but the editor-in-chief feels that the magazine should pay only $500 for it because you are a new writer. The articles editor apologizes profusely, and reminds you that you can refuse the offer and try to sell the piece elsewhere. If you demand $1,000 as agreed, the magazine will simply reject the story. What should you do?

3. You have written a profile for a national magazine published in New York and it has been accepted. One day you get a phone call from an editorial assistant at the magazine saying that she has spoken to the person you wrote the article about, and has been told that your story is riddled with factual errors. Your research for the piece included conducting a two-hour recorded interview with the person, reading a book written by her, and reading numerous articles in which she is mentioned. You did the interview when you happened to be passing through the city where the person lives, and have not spoken to her since then. What should you do?

```
Your Name

Your Address
                              Title of Article

                           Your By-line


     The title is typed about one-fifth down the page to leave

room at the top for the editor's instructions to the printer.

The manuscript should be double-spaced to facilitate easy reading

and to leave room for editing marks between lines.

     The second and all succeeding pages should carry the writer's

name in the upper left corner; the page numbers should be at the

center or right corner.  All pages after the first should start

in the conventional place, a few spaces down from the top, and a

margin of about one inch should be left on all sides.

     A pica or elite typewriter should be used (never script or

other unconventional type).  Black type on white paper is preferred,

and only one side of the paper should be used.

     Where possible, a page should end at the end of a paragraph.

This has several advantages, among them the fact that in writing

memos to other editors or to the writer, an editor can refer to

"the last paragraph on 5" rather than to "the paragraph that begins

on 5 and ends on 6."
```

APPENDIX A
An Article's Passage

A typical magazine article undergoes extensive changes from its inception to publication. At every step in the process, from query to acceptance to first draft to edited final version, it is subject to revision by the author and often by several editors. This appendix provides an example of how that process works, using an article that was written by an author of this book and published in the July 1979 issue of *Working Woman* magazine. At the time Shelley Smolkin proposed the story, she was listed on the magazine's masthead as its Seattle correspondent and had already published one 2,500-word article in *Working Woman*.

It was during the research phase of the first article that she first heard the term "displaced homemakers." It refers to women who have spent most of their adult lives as homemakers but who suddenly must find jobs outside the home because of divorce, death of a spouse, illness, and so on. Several women's magazines and newspapers had published articles about displaced homemakers, and a few stories about programs to help them had also appeared. Most of the stories focused on the personal problems faced by women in this position.

Smolkin felt this might be a good subject for *Working Woman*, but she knew that the angle would have to be particularly suited to its audience, which is primarily composed of career women. She decided to focus on the jobs aspect of the displaced homemaker movement, and to emphasize the work being done by women who were displaced homemakers to insure that others would not have to face the same problems. Here is the query she sent to the articles editor:

> This year for the first time, the Comprehensive Employment and Training Act (CETA) being considered by Congress cites "displaced homemakers" among the list of economically disadvantaged groups eligible for a wide range of government assistance programs. As defined in the national legislation, a displaced homemaker is one who "has not worked in the labor force for a substantial number of years but has, during those years, worked in the home

providing unpaid services for family members . . . , " who has been dependent upon a source of income that is no longer available (such as a deceased or ex-husband) and who is either unemployed or underemployed.

The inclusion of displaced homemakers in the list is no accident—it is the direct result of the efforts of many women, most of whom could have been described by the above definition at some point in their lives. Three years ago the term "displaced homemaker" did not exist. It was coined by Tish Sommers, a California divorcee who decided to do something about the plight of the millions of women who, for whatever reason, suddenly are compelled to seek employment outside the home after many years as homemakers. Implicit in Congress's definition of a displaced homemaker is the recognition that a woman who has spent most of her adult life caring for others is extremely disadvantaged when she tries to reenter the job market. The skills she may have acquired years ago are outdated; her paid working experience is not considered recent enough to qualify her for many jobs. Displaced homemakers are of every age, but many are older women who are ineligible for government-sponsored apprenticeship or training programs.

Together with Laurie Shields, a widow, Tish Sommers set out to do something about this appalling situation. The two enlisted the help of Barbara Dudley, a young attorney, and drafted legislation that was passed by the California state legislature in 1975, authorizing funds for the establishment of the first Displaced Homemaker Center in the country to be located in Oakland, California. They formed the Alliance for Displaced Homemakers, organized a national letter-writing campaign, and took their message cross-country to legislators, women's groups, and anyone else who would listen. Within two years, 16 states had enacted displaced homemaker legislation. From an idea in the mind of one woman, the displaced homemaker movement had gained national momentum, culminating in the CETA legislation. In a recent speech before Congress, Assistant Secretary for Employment and Training Ernie Green promised to allocate $5 million in the coming year to programs to help displaced homemakers. In October, the first national conference on displaced homemakers will take place in Baltimore, Maryland.

I would like to propose an article on the displaced homemaker movement for *Working Woman*. In addition to describing how it began, the article could provide information on the many displaced homemaker centers already operating in the country. Programs like the one here at Bellevue Community College offer a variety of services, including vocational guidance, counseling, and job referral. Once the CETA legislation passes, many other government-sponsored programs will also be open to displaced homemakers. Of particular interest in the story would be an interview with Evelyn Farber, a labor economist in the Women's Bureau of the Department of Labor, who is an expert on the subject of displaced homemakers and who is instrumental in authorizing funds for the establishment of programs throughout the country.

Over a month later, Smolkin received the following reply:

We are indeed interested in your proposal for an article on displaced homemakers, CETA, the countrywide programs, the women who started it all and the October meeting.

Your approach, as outlined in your query, seems very sound and thorough to us, and we'd like to add just one other ingredient to be included in the article: namely, Why should the younger, employed woman be much concerned about it all. The answer, as we see it, is twofold: 1. She can learn something from any woman or women who successfully initiate and run a program of this scope and 2. (without being too dour about it) the possibility that any of us at some time in our lives could find ourselves in a similar situation.

Giving emphasis to these points, we think, will involve the *Working Woman* reader in an issue that, in the main, she herself doesn't now face.

Unfortunately, we can't pay travel expenses, so the October meeting part of the piece will have to depend on whether you are planning to come east on your own.

I'm enclosing a contract herewith. If there's anything further you'd like to discuss, please phone me collect.

Note that the editor took this opportunity to offer some advice to the writer on the angle she thought the story should take. She also specifies what financial arrangements the magazine is willing to make: first, that it will not pay travel expenses to the conference, and second, that it will assign the story on contract. For a detailed discussion of the financial arrangements for the article from the writer's point of view, refer to Chapter Eleven.

Smolkin signed the following contract and returned it to the magazine:

This is to confirm that we will pay on acceptance $500.00 for your grant to HAL Publications, Inc. of certain rights to the contribution entitled "DISPLACED HOMEMAKERS".

You hereby grant to HAL Publications, Inc. (a) exclusive North American serial rights; (b) the right to reprint said contribution from WORKING WOMAN magazine or to authorize third parties to make such reprints; (c) the right to use said contribution in publicizing, promoting or advertising WORKING WOMAN; and (d) the right to include said contribution in any volume of WORKING WOMAN material published or authorized by HAL Publications, Inc.

You represent and warrant originality, authorship and ownership of said contribution, that it has not heretofore been published, that its publication will not infringe upon any copyright, proprietary or other right and that it contains no matter which is libelous, obscene, or otherwise contrary to law.

If the foregoing terms are acceptable, kindly sign and return the enclosed copy of this letter.

Virtually all the research for the article was done at the two-day conference, which was attended by over 300 women from around the country. Smolkin wrote the article and submitted it to *Working Woman* in the following form:

Carol was 35 years old when she lost her job. Suddenly, there was no money in the bank and no prospect of employment. Everywhere she went Carol heard the same story. Her current skills were not saleable in today's market; her early working experience was not recent enough to qualify her for jobs now. In despair, she sought help from the government. As she made the rounds from one agency to the next, Carol discovered that her situation did not fit the guidelines of any assistance programs. Too old for job training, ineligible for Social Security, she felt helpless and betrayed.

Though she didn't know it at the time, Carol was a displaced homemaker. After 15 years of running her household, caring for her children, and working as a volunteer in community organizations, Carol was suddenly forced to find another job. The divorce had in fact been her idea, confident as she was that her abilities would enable her to earn a living. A few months of rejections finally convinced her that she was wrong.

Carol's situation is not unusual—on the contrary, about seven million women in this country face similar problems. They may be divorced, separated, widowed, or married to men who are unable to work, but regardless of the details, the outcome is the same. Their contracts to provide homemaking services in exchange for financial support have been canceled. In an employment market that places a premium on youth and has yet to open the same doors for women that it does for men, they face the double barriers of age and sex discrimination. They are displaced homemakers.

But thanks to the work now being done by hundreds of these very women, future generations will not have to fight the same battles. Through persistence, hard work, and sheer guts, these women have moved the U.S. Congress and changed the law of the land. They have forced the rock of bureaucracy to budge and have commanded the country's attention. Who would have thought that a bunch of unemployed older women could do that?

Tish Sommers, a 64-year-old divorcee from California, not only thought so, she was certain. A veteran of the civil rights movement and the anti-war campaign of the 1960s, Sommers had been an agent of social change for some time. Through her work with the NOW Task Force on Older Women and the Oakland, California Jobs for Older Women Action Project, she became aware that the problems she had faced after her divorce at 57 were all too common. "These women were falling through all the cracks," she said. "My gut told me the time for older women's issues had come."

A collective name was the first thing the women needed to identify themselves as a group and to call the attention of others to their plight. Sommers first coined the term "displaced homemakers," intentionally choosing harsh words that would convey the notion of forced exile. No indication of age was included, for displaced homemakers range from 18 to 80, though most are over 35. The response from women who recognized themselves in the name surprised even her. After an appearance on the "Phil Donahue Show" in which Sommers talked about the problems of displaced homemakers, she received over 2,000 letters.

In 1975, with the aid of attorney Barbara Dudley, the California group filed a bill in their state legislature to allocate funds to establish a program to aid displaced homemakers. Soon a national bill was filed, and the Alliance for Displaced Homemakers was formed to work for its passage. At the group's first meeting, Sommers encountered a woman whose willingness to work and determination to succeed matched her own. The woman was Laurie Shields, a widow with a knack for political maneuvering. Shields's ability to store information about politicians and their constituencies quickly became an invaluable asset to the Alliance.

The women embarked on a cross-country campaign to garner support for the national bill and to encourage state bills similar to that passed in California. Model programs were established in Oakland and in Baltimore, Maryland. By 1977, legislation to help displaced homemakers had been introduced in 28 states. From an idea in the mind of a California divorcee, the displaced homemaker concept had grown into a national movement. Hundreds of requests for information on how to start assistance programs poured into the offices of the Alliance and the Oakland and Baltimore centers, as older women throughout the country realized that they were not alone in their struggles to start careers. A national training conference was planned for October 1978 as momentum for passage of the bill in Congress increased.

On October 13, 1978, the conference convened, and on that very day Congress passed the Comprehensive Employment and Training Act (CETA) reauthorization bill, the first national legislation to cite displaced homemakers as an economically disadvantaged group eligible for federal assistance programs. As a first step toward solving the problem, the CETA bill is significant, but as an indication of the political clout of exiled women, it is a legislative milestone. It is also irrefutable evidence that displaced homemakers are a skilled group and a resource whose talents have previously been wasted by our society. That situation is changing because, as Tish Sommers put it, "We are learning to use the system, and well we should, for it has certainly used us."

The CETA bill is by no means a comprehensive solution, but it does provide the essential mandate for federal support that displaced homemaker programs need. In a speech before Congress, a Department of Labor official promised to allocate $5 million for this purpose. In addition, other federal agencies such as the Department of Health, Education, and Welfare, have begun to include displaced homemakers in their programs.

But it's a long way from enactment of a law to change in society, and the 300 women at the Baltimore conference realized that their work had just begun. To ensure its continuation, they formed the Displaced Homemakers Network, a national organization headquartered in Washington, D.C. with representatives in each of ten regions around the country. Among the Network's many objectives are to share information, to lobby for passage of legislation favorable to displaced homemakers, and to serve as a clearinghouse.

Underlying this political and organizational structure however, is the understanding that the difficulties shared by displaced homemakers are intensely personal. Sommers distinguishes between internal and external problems. The first are primarily subjective judgments that the woman makes about herself. Having lost the role she held for most of her adult life, she has little sense of self-worth, sees nothing of value that she is capable of doing, and often has no self-confidence. Circumstances compel her to seek employment just when she may be least ready to do so effectively. External problems are those found in society itself. Employers are not anxious to hire older workers; training programs are often closed to people beyond a certain age. Those jobs that are available are dead-end opportunities with little room for growth or advancement.

The notion that older women deserve not just jobs but careers is perhaps the most revolutionary concept of the displaced homemaker movement. Marita Heller, program coordinator for the Metropolitan Center for Displaced Homemakers in St. Paul, Minnesota explained, "Many women have never thought in those terms before. The concept of long-range planning is completely foreign to them." Planning for the future while learning to cope with the realities of the present is a major emphasis of the 60 displaced homemaker programs now operating throughout the country. The feelings of women involved in these groups are best summarized by one who said, "The general attitude is, 'Why don't you sit back and let us give you services?' Well we don't want social services. We want jobs!"

The task of converting an anxious, often frightened, displaced homemaker into a career woman is not an easy one. Often the most pressing immediate problems are financial. Though some programs have emergency funds to help in extreme cases of need, most aid participants through preparing them to seek employment. Strategies for accomplishing this goal are varied, but all come under the general heading of "job readiness."

"One of our first objectives is to teach them how to translate their homemaking skills into business skills by using a business vocabulary," said Marita Heller. "This also gives the women confidence that they do have marketable abilities." Workshops in resume writing and job interviewing are often part of the programs. Everything from videotaped mock interviews to trial-run information-seeking appointments at real businesses are used to reintroduce displaced homemakers to the techniques for marketing their skills.

One of the most inventive methods is used by a Buffalo, New York program. Called "On-the-Job Shadowing" (OJS), it is a four-week part-time program in which a woman actually goes to a firm to try out the kind of job she is considering. The OJS takes place midway through a skills course, so it enables a participant to see if the day-to-day reality of the career she is planning matches her expectations. Betsy Hopkins, executive director of the

Everywoman's Opportunity Center, Inc., said, "At first it was hard to talk employers into doing this, but eventually they began to see the advantages. Because the program pays the woman a stipend, the employer gets free labor and a chance to see a prospective employee at work." The results for participants are often job offers. Any reluctance by the women to participate in such an unusual arrangement is countered at the center by one very effective statement: "Do this, and you'll never be in this position again."

The training programs offered by the Everywoman Center are for non-traditional jobs. Through sub-contracts with local technical schools, participants can learn everything from welding to automotive repair to carpentry. Many displaced homemaker programs have turned to non-traditional jobs as an alternative to the dead-end prospects of some sales or clerical positions. Armed with the knowledge that equal opportunity employment laws will necessitate the hiring of women in various fields, they are ensuring that displaced homemakers will be among those qualified to fill the jobs. For example, by May 8, 1979, at least 3.1 percent of any construction crew working on a federally funded project over $10,000 must be women. The contractors have no choice, but the women must be prepared.

Occasionally that preparation requires more than skills training. Non-traditional jobs often demand more physical stamina than displaced homemakers have when they begin. A CETA representative in Pittsburgh cited a case in which U.S. Steel contacted her office to complain that the women they were hiring were unable to stand the physical strain of the work. As a solution, the company donated heavy shoes, hard hats, and samples of the heavy equipment the women would have to use to a training program that would condition the prospective employees before they actually began work. A similar program was developed through the University of Oregon when contractors trying to meet affirmative action quotas reported to the regional CETA office that after two days on the job, their female employees were too sore to work.

Another strategy used to find employment for displaced homemakers is job creation, that is, utilizing the skills a woman already has to develop a business or career. Often those skills are not formalized by a degree, but as one woman at the Baltimore conference put it, "We're a room full of life experience here. That's our education." An underlying philosophy of the movement is that displaced homemakers should fill staff positions in its programs whenever possible. This approach has been used throughout the country because it not only creates jobs, it provides counselors who are certain to understand the problems of the people they seek to help. Grace Webb, a career counselor at the New Directions for Women program in Baltimore, said, "We have shown that you don't really need a degree in counseling to be successful. Empathy is the most important requirement."

June Crowe, activities and volunteer coordinator at the Displaced Homemakers/Widowed Services Program at the University of Oregon, is proof that the idea works. The day after her husband died in 1975, Crowe saw an article about the program in a local newspaper. A month later, she finally summoned the courage to go, certain that her situation was beyond hope. "I walked up the steps wishing the place would be closed," she recalled. "It was open." Looking back on her experience, Crowe added, "The help I received there is the reason that I did not choose to join my husband, and believe me, I considered it."

Though jobs are the focus of displaced homemaker programs like the one in Oregon, staffers are quick to point out that having a job does not solve all the problems. Counseling to help the women cope with the emotional difficulties created by their situations plays a large role in every group. "We recognize that a woman in the trauma of divorce will not be able to hold a job," explained Barbara Turner, director of group services at the Baltimore Center. The program there includes workshops conducted by a lawyer who teaches participants how to deal with their own lawyers. The "know your rights" theme of the workshop attracts 20 to 30 people each month. Courses on credit are also offered.

Sometimes a displaced homemaker who needs to work to support herself simply does not want to do it. "Many women resist going to work," said Barbara Turner. "They don't want to work and they can give you 50 reasons why they can't work. Usually the problem is fear." Such feelings may be related to low self-confidence, but they are often based on beliefs that work has to be dull and unsatisfying. One 35-year-old displaced homemaker who needed to work for financial reasons fought adamantly against the idea because she did not want to give up her daily round of golf. Her idea of work was sitting behind a desk for eight hours. With the help of a counselor, she eventually learned that there were alternatives. Now a successful L'eggs pantyhose salesperson, she drives a van instead of a golf ball.

Other problems faced by displaced homemakers are common to most working women. One of the movement's goals is to encourage the creation of alternative work patterns, such as flex-time and job-sharing, to meet the needs of women with children. Meaningful part-time employment that is accorded the same professional regard as full-time employment and offers opportunities for growth and advancement is also sought. In addition, the movement is working toward developing career paths in jobs that are now dead-ends. U.S. Department of Labor statistics show that 62 percent of the country's service workers and retail sales workers are women, as are 79 percent of the clerical workers.

In the employment market itself, the displaced homemaker movement hopes to educate employers about the value of skills acquired in unpaid positions such as homemaking and volunteer work. Part of this effort will be to promote the use of job application forms that do not limit descriptions of previous experience to previous salaried experience. Displaced homemaker programs encourage participants to work as volunteers when it is financially possible to do so as a means of acquiring expertise and training. Ultimately, the movement seeks to have homemaking recognized as "work" for Social Security so that displaced homemakers will at least be provided with some financial support.

Long-range goals such as these are a long way off, but recognition of the problems of displaced homemakers is here now. Laws are being changed, stereotypes are being revised, but as President Carter's special assistant on women's issues said in Baltimore, "What has changed more than anything else is our concept of ourselves. We are our biggest strength."

The article was reviewed and edited by several people on *Working Woman*'s staff. A complementary story was planned for the same issue, so any duplication of material was eliminated. Here is how the article appeared in final form:

GOOD NEWS   by Shelley Smolkin

When a Homemaker
Loses Her Job

Nationwide network is set up to help displaced homemakers fight for their rights and prepare to reenter the job market

Seven million women in this country have had their jobs canceled and find themselves without financial support. They may be divorced, separated, widowed or married to men who are unable to work; regardless of the details, the outcome is the same. Their contracts to provide homemaking services in exchange for financial support have been terminated. They are displaced homemakers, and in an employment market that places a premium on youth and has yet

Each year, thousands of suddenly single homemakers are joining the millions of women already in the job market. Many of the problems faced by these displaced homemakers are shared by all working women. Some of their problems are unique ones that call for unique solutions. To answer their needs, displaced homemakers are helping themselves—with support, with counseling, and with political action.

to open the same doors to women that it does to men, these women face the double barriers of age and sex discrimination.

Now, thanks to the work being done by hundreds of these very women, future generations of displaced homemakers will not have to fight the battles that are being waged on their behalf today. Through persistence, hard work and sheer guts, the displaced-homemakers movement has even convinced the US Congress to recognize the situation and change the law of the land. Who would have thought that a bunch of unemployed older women could do all that?

Tish Sommers, a 64-year-old divorcee from California, didn't just think so—she was certain. A veteran of the civil-rights movement and the antiwar campaign of the 1960s, Sommers has been an agent of social change for some time. Through her work with the NOW Task Force on Older Women and the Oakland, California, Jobs for Older Women Action Project, she became aware that the problems she'd had after her divorce at 57 were all too common. "My gut told me the time had come for older-women's issues," she said.

A collective name was the first thing the women needed to identify themselves as a group and to call the attention of others to their plight. Sommers coined the term "displaced homemaker," intentionally choosing a harsh term that would convey the notion of forced exile. Although most are over 35, displaced homemakers range in age from 18 to 80. The response from women who recognized themselves in the name surprised even Sommers.

In 1975, Sommers and attorney Barbara Dudley drafted legislation to allocate funds to set up centers for displaced homemakers. They took the draft to Washington with the intention of having California Congresswoman Yvonne Burke file a national bill for federal funds. On further consideration, they decided a national bill would have a better chance if a similar bill were filed first at the state level. Back they went to California, and in April 1975 a state bill was filed to set up a pilot project for displaced homemakers. With that as a precedent, Burke filed the national bill in May of the same year. To speed the bill's passage, it was later amended and tacked onto an existing vehicle— the Comprehensive Employment and Training Act (CETA) which was up for refunding. Sommers and her fellow activists formed the Alliance for Displaced Homemakers to lobby for the passage of the displaced-homemakers legislation on both the national and state levels. When the Alliance was founded, Sommers met a woman whose willingness to work and determination to succeed matched her own. The woman was Laurie Shields, a widow with a knack for political maneuvering. Shields's ability to store information about politicians and their constituencies became an invaluable asset to the Alliance.

Workshops for displaced homemakers teach them how to utilize their homemaking skills to develop a business or career. Everything from résumé writing sessions to videotaped mock interviews are used to reintroduce displaced homemakers to the techniques for marketing their skills.

There's still no unemployment insurance, no pension plan, no social security benefits for the homemaker who has lost her job after years of working in the home. But thanks to the persistence of the displaced-homemakers movement, the federal government is beginning to recognize its responsibility to this disenfranchised group.

FOR MORE INFORMATION, WRITE:

Displaced Homemakers Network
c/o Business and Professional Women's Foundation
2012 Massachusetts Avenue, NW
Washington, DC 20036
202-293-1200 ext. 34

In September 1975, the state bill was passed and the push was on for passage of national legislation. Shields, then national coordinator of the Alliance, embarked on a cross-country campaign in early 1976 to garner support for the national bill and to encourage state bills similar to the one passed in California. Model programs for displaced homemakers were established in Oakland, California, and in Baltimore, Maryland. By 1977, legislation to help displaced homemakers had been introduced in 28 states. Hundreds of requests for information on how to start assistance programs poured in to the Oakland and Baltimore DH centers as older women throughout the country realized that they were not alone in their struggles to start careers.

The First Big Breakthrough

On October 13, 1978, a national training conference for displaced homemakers convened in Baltimore, sponsored by the Older Women's League Educational Fund. On that very day Congress passed the CETA reauthorization bill, the first national legislation to cite displaced homemakers as an economically disadvantaged group eligible for federal assistance programs. As a first step toward recognizing the problems of displaced homemakers, the CETA bill is significant. Sommers summed it up this way: "We are learning to use the system, and well we should, for it has certainly used us."

The CETA bill is by no means a total solution. What it does provide is the essential mandate for federal support that displaced-homemaker programs need. In testimony before a Congressional committee, Ernest Green, assistant secretary of labor, confirmed the Department of Labor's intent to allocate $5 million for displaced homemakers. In addition, federal agencies such as the Department of Health, Education and Welfare have begun to include displaced homemakers in their programs.

Still, it's a long way from the enactment of a law to any real change in the society. The 300 women at the 1978 Baltimore conference realized that their work had just begun. To ensure its continuation, they formed the Displaced Homemakers Network, a national organization headquartered in Washington, DC, with representatives in each of ten regions around the country. Among the network's many objectives are to share information, to lobby for passage of legislation favorable to displaced homemakers and to serve as a clearinghouse.

From Dead-End Jobs to Careers

That older women deserve not just jobs but careers is perhaps the most revolutionary concept of the displaced-homemaker movement. Marita Heller, program coordinator for the Metropolitan Center for

Tish Sommers
Laurie Shields
Older Women's League
Educational Fund
3800 Harrison Street
Oakland, CA 94611
415-658-8700

Betsy Hopkins
Everywoman's
Opportunity Center, Inc.
190 Franklin Street
Buffalo, NY 14202
716-847-1120

Displaced Homemakers in St. Paul, Minnesota, explained: "Many women have never thought in career terms before. The concept of long-range planning is completely foreign to them." Planning for the future while learning to cope with the realities of the present is a major emphasis of the 60 displaced-homemaker programs now operating throughout the country.

One of the most inventive methods is used by Everywoman's Opportunity Center in Buffalo, New York. Called "On-the-Job Shadowing" (OJS), it is a four-week, part-time program in which a woman actually goes to a firm to try out the kind of job she is considering. The OJS takes place midway through a skills course, so it enables a participant to see if the day-to-day reality of the career she is planning to enter matches her expectations. Betsy Hopkins, executive director of the center, said, "At first it was hard to talk employers into doing this, but eventually they began to see the advantages. Because the program pays the woman a stipend, the employer gets free labor and a chance to see a prospective employee at work." The results for participants often are job offers. Any reluctance by the women to participate in such an unusual arrangement is countered at the center by one statement: "Do this, and you'll never be in this position again."

Opportunities for
Nontraditional Fields

The training programs offered by the Everywoman Center are for nontraditional jobs. Through subcontracts with local technical schools, participants can learn everything from welding to automotive repair to carpentry. Many displaced-homemaker programs have turned to nontraditional jobs as an alternative to the dead-end prospects of some sales or clerical positions. Armed with the knowledge that equal-opportunity/employment laws will necessitate the hiring of women in various fields, they are ensuring that displaced homemakers will be among those qualified to fill the jobs. For example, as of May 8, 1979, at least 3.1 percent of any construction crew working on a federally funded project costing over $10,000 had to be women. The contractors have no choice, but the women must be prepared.

Occasionally, that preparation requires more than skills training. Nontraditional jobs often demand more physical stamina than displaced homemakers have when they begin. A CETA representative in Pittsburg cited a case in which US Steel contacted her office to complain that the women they were hiring were unable to stand the physical strain of the work. As a solution, the company donated to a training program the heavy shoes, hard hats and samples of equipment the women would have to use on the job in an effort to condition prospective employees before they actually began to work. A similar program was developed through the University of Oregon when contractors reported to the regional CETA office that after two days on the job, female employees were too sore to work.

Helping Others While You Help Yourself

An underlying philosophy of the movement is that displaced homemakers should fill staff positions in its programs whenever possible. This approach has been used throughout the country, because it not only creates jobs but also provides counselors who will understand the problems of the people they seek to help. Grace Webb, a career counselor at the New Directions for Women program in Baltimore, said, "We have shown that you don't really need a degree in counseling to be successful. Empathy is the most important requirement."

June Crowe, activities and volunteer coordinator at the Displaced Homemakers/Widowed Services Program at the University of Oregon, is proof that the idea works. The day after her husband died in 1975, Crowe saw an article about the program in a local newspaper. A month later, she finally summoned up the courage to go, certain that her situation was beyond hope. "I walked up the steps wishing the place would be closed," she recalled. "It was open." Looking back on her experience, Crowe added, "The help I received there is the reason that I did not choose to join my husband and, believe me, I considered it."

Though jobs are the focus of displaced-homemaker programs like the one in Oregon, staffers are quick to point out that having a job does not solve all the problems. Counseling to help the women cope with the emotional difficulties created by their situations plays a large role in every group.

Sometimes a displaced homemaker who needs to work to support herself simply does not want to do it. "Many women resist going to work," said Barbara Turner, director of Group Services at the Baltimore center. "They don't want to work, so they can give you 50 reasons why they can't work. Usually the problem is fear." Such feelings may be related to low self-confidence, but they are often based on beliefs that work has to be dull and unsatisfying. One 35-year-old displaced homemaker who needed to work for financial reasons fought adamantly against the idea because she did not want to give up her daily round of golf. Her idea of work was sitting behind a desk for eight hours. With the help of a counselor, she eventually learned that there were alternatives. Now a successful L'eggs pantyhose saleswoman, she drives a van instead of a golf ball.

Toward a Better Deal
for All

Some problems of displaced homemakers are common to most working women. The movement's goals include efforts to encourage the creation of alternative work patterns, such as flexitime and job sharing, to meet the needs of women with children. [See "Hotline," page 20.] Another goal is to make available more part-time employment that is accorded the same professional regard as full-time employment and offers opportunities for growth and advancement. In addition, the movement is working toward developing career paths in jobs that are now dead ends. US Department of Labor statistics show that 62 percent of the country's service workers and retail-sales workers are women, as are 79 percent of the clerical workers.

In the employment market itself, the displaced-homemaker movement hopes to educate employers about the value of skills acquired in unpaid positions. Part of this effort will be to promote the use of job-application forms that do not limit descriptions of previous experience to salaried jobs only. Ultimately, the movement seeks to have homemaking recognized as "work" for Social Security, so that displaced homemakers will at least be provided with some financial support. Long-range goals such as these are far off, but recognition of the problems is here now. Laws are being changed, stereotypes are being revised, but as Sarah Weddington, a special assistant to President Carter, said at the Baltimore convention, "What has changed more than anything else is our concept of ourselves. We are our biggest strength."

---

*Reprinted courtesy of HAL Publications, Inc., from *Working Woman* Magazine, © 1979.

APPENDIX B
The Journalist's Rule: Conventions and Principles

Writers who know most of the grammatical and stylistic conventions cited in this appendix have become comfortable with them through daily use. Practicing writers learn to employ these principles almost instinctively. But even long-established conventions do change, if ever so slowly. Inventive writers establish new styles that eventually take on the force of "law."

The usage entries in the following pages try to avoid the bookish, the stilted, and the stuffy on one side, and the colloquial, the slang, and the cliché on the other. The purpose of this appendix is to promote conventions and principles that make writing similar to speech but to avoid the looseness of spoken language.

Abbreviations. Most publishers have a style guide that tells writers which words should be abbreviated. Newspapers, which try to present a great deal of information in a small amount of space, tend to abbreviate more words than do most other publications. The following abbreviations are used by most publications:

1. B.A. (A.B.), B.S., M.A., M.S., Ph.D., M.D., Ed.D., D.D.S., and other academic degrees and professional degrees.

2. Mr., Mrs., Ms., Dr., Jr., and Sr.

3. Political and military titles when they precede the full name, as in Gov. John Jones, Sen. Margaret Atkin, Col. Reuben Johnson, and Lt. Henry Douglas. When such a title is used with the last name only, it is not abbreviated: Senator Atkin, Colonel Johnson.

4. Mph, rpm, P.M., A.M., A.D., B.C., and No. when they are used with figures: 90 mph, 1,500 rpm's, 8:00 P.M., 4:00 A.M., A.D. 104, 450 B.C., and No. 1 choice.

5. U.N., U.S., C.O.D., TV, hi-fi, and stereo.

Above. Avoid using "The figures above" whenever possible, and always avoid using "above" as a noun ("The above will make clear . . ."). "These" or "These figures" is preferable. When it is necessary to use "above," make it "The figures above" rather than "The above figures."

Acronyms. An *acronym* is an abbreviation pronounced as a word, which is made up of the first letters of the major words in the title: CREEP for Committee for the Re-Election of the President, SAC for

Strategic Air Command. When a writer is not certain that all his readers know what an acronym stands for, he usually writes the full name and puts the acronym in parentheses—Southeast Asia Treaty Organization (SEATO)—then uses only the acronym in later references and removes the parentheses: "The SEATO nations decided. . . ." This is common practice in writing all initials, but many readers consider it odd to see widely known organizations so identified, as in Federal Bureau of Investigation (FBI).

Active voice. See *Verbs.*

Actual, Actually. See *Modifiers.*

Adjectives. See *Modifiers.*

Advance planning, Future planning. Planning is laying out a future course. *Advance* and *future* are redundant.

Adverbs. See *Modifiers.*

Affect, Effect. These words are often confused. The verb *affect* means "to influence, concern, or assume," as in these examples:

> Hemingway's writing *affected* (influenced) the writing of John O'Hara.

> Brando *affected* (assumed) the manner of Hamlet.

The verb *effect* means "to cause or to bring about," as in this example:

> The manager *effected* (caused) a change by substituting Pete Rose.

Affect is used as a noun only as a technical term in the social sciences. The noun *effect* means "the result," as in this example:

> The *effect* (result) was that Oakland won the game.

Aggravate. This is not a synonym for irritate or exasperate. *Aggravate* means "to increase or make worse."

Agreement. This is the formal correspondence of one word with another, usually referring to the subject and verb in a sentence. Most of the common errors in agreement result from carelessness, as in:

> If a writer has any ability, the teacher will help *them* develop it.

Verbs and pronouns must agree in number with a preceding noun or pronoun—a verb with its subject, a pronoun with its antecedent. Most problems of agreement can be solved easily by keeping pronouns close to their antecedents and verbs close to their subjects. But even professional writers are sometimes troubled by a few problems, as in the following cases:

1. Collective nouns take either singulars or plurals, depending on the writer's intent and the context of the sentence. If the writer is thinking of a group as a unit, he must use singular verbs and pronouns:

> The group *has* been ready to act on *its* major assignment since November.

The team *prays* before every game.

The committee *is* to meet at 8:00 P.M.

If the writer thinks of members of a group as individuals taking individual actions, he should use plural verbs and pronouns:

By the time the committee had been in session for an hour, *they* were shouting.

When the team took the field, *they* ran from the dugout.

2. A compound joined by *and* takes a plural verb and pronoun, as in:

Hubert Humphrey and Jerry Brown were at *their* best in political debate.

3. After a compound joined by *or* or *nor,* the number of the verb and pronoun is determined by the nearer subject or antecedent, as in,

We don't know whether the quarterback *or* the linebackers *are* to appear on the television program.

The senators *or* the president *is* certain to be here soon.

4. Most good writers seem to decide that indefinite expressions such as *another, anybody, each, either, everybody, everyone, neither, nobody, no one,* and *none* take singular verbs and pronouns, as in:

No one *is* likely to want to go if *he* must buy a ticket.

But some writers and grammarians hold that *no one* and *none* can be singular or plural depending on the sense. In this example, *none are* seems preferable: "The children's home has received no contributions, and *none are* expected."

All ready, Already. *All ready* means that "everything is ready"; *already* means "by this time" or "beforehand in time": "She was *already* at the bus stop."

All right, Alright. *Alright* is all wrong.

Allude, Allusion, Refer, Reference. To *allude,* or to make an *allusion,* is "to mention indirectly," leaving it to the reader to use the allusion to make the identification. A *reference* is direct, as in, "I *refer* to the first sentence, not to the entire paragraph."

Although, Though. *Although* is preferable.

Ambiguous, Ambivalent. Writing that is *ambiguous* has more than one meaning or interpretation and is thus uncertain or obscure. *Ambivalent* refers to simultaneous attraction and repulsion.

Among, Between. Use *between* for two elements ("*between* you and me"), *among* for more than two ("*among* the three of us").

Amount, Number. *Amount* is used to refer to many things of the same kind or to many similar things considered as a whole, as in, "The *amount* he paid was not enough." *Number* is used to refer to separate units, as in, "The *number* of coins was different when she counted."

Anachronism. This is an error involving misplacement of words or actions in time. For example, "George Washington was a bit stern even when he was a teen-ager" uses *teen-ager* to discuss a time when the word was unknown.

And/or. This legalism is seldom useful in nonlegal writing and always sounds legalistic. *Or* will usually do the work of *and/or*. When it will not, use "——— or ——— or both."

Angry, Mad. Use *angry* to refer to the emotion. Use *mad* to refer to the mental condition. Using *mad* for *angry* sometimes leaves readers wondering, at least momentarily, whether the writer is referring to the emotion or to the mental condition.

Another. See *Agreement.*

Antecedents. See *Agreement.*

Anybody, Anyone. *Anybody* should not be written *any body* unless the meaning intended is "any corpse" or other inanimate object such as a body of water. *Anyone* should not be written *any one* unless the intended meaning is "any one thing." See also *Agreement.*

Any more, Any way. *Any more* is always written as two words. *Any way* should be written as two words unless the intended meaning is "in any case": "He didn't care *anyway*."

Anyplace, Someplace. These should be *anywhere* and *somewhere.*

Apostrophes. Among the many uses of the apostrophe are to:

1. Mark the possessive of nouns:

   John's book

   the boys' books

(Except for *one*—"*one's* best book"—the apostrophe is not used to mark the possessive of pronouns: *hers, yours, his, its, ours, theirs.*)

2. Mark the omission of one or more letters in contractions:

   doesn't

   it's (Note that *it's* means "it is"; *its* is the possessive.)

   I'll

   we've

   she'll

   who's (Note that *who's* means "who is": *whose* is the possessive.)

3. Mark the omission of one or more numbers:

   a '75 Cadillac

4. Form the plurals of symbols:

   He rolled three 7's.

She earned two A's.

I use too many *the's* in writing.

Article. *A* should be used before *h* when the first syllable is accented: "a *hus*band," "a *half*back." *An* should be used before a silent *h*: "*h*erb." Using *an* before *historian* and *historical* is an affectation.

A and *an* are indefinite articles. They refer to members of a class: "*a* book," "*a* football," "*a* man," "*an* ostrich." *The* is the definite article. It refers to individual persons or objects: "the woman," "the table." A fairly common fault is for a writer to forget that his readers know nothing about his topic and to write, for example, "Henry was pushing *the* wheelbarrow when he stumbled." In most instances, an object should be introduced indefinitely—"Henry was pushing *a* wheelbarrow when he stumbled"—so that readers will not wonder: *The* wheelbarrow? What wheelbarrow? When it is mentioned again, the writer should shift to the definite article: "A dozen bottles of gin spilled from *the* wheelbarrow and broke on the sidewalk."

As, Like. Use *as*, not *like*, as a conjunction: "The cigarette tastes good *as* a cigarette should."

Avoid using *as* for *because*. If a writer uses *as* and *because* interchangeably, readers have no way of knowing what is meant by expressions such as this: "As I was swimming, I began to think." Did he begin to think *because* he was swimming or merely *while* he was swimming?

At. Avoid using *at* after *where*. "Where is it *at*?" says no more than "Where is it?"

At present, At the present time, Presently. Instead of using *at present* and *at the present time*, use "now," which says the same thing crisply. Some writers misuse *presently*, thinking that it means "now." It means "soon," and when that is the intended meaning, use "soon."

Because. Avoid using ambiguous substitutes such as "since" and "as."

Behalf. "In his behalf" means "in his interest." "On his behalf" means "representing him."

Between. See *Among*.

Bimonthly, Biweekly. *Bimonthly* means "every two months"; *biweekly* means "every two weeks." These are so often confused with "semimonthly" and "semiweekly," which mean "twice a month" and "twice a week," that it is better to write "every two months," "every two weeks," "twice a month," and "twice a week."

Blond, Blonde. *Blond* refers to a man, *blonde* to a woman.

Boat, Ship. A *boat* is usually a small open craft. Larger vessels are *ships*.

Brackets. These [ ] a writer uses to insert his own words in a direct quotation. Parentheses should not be used for this purpose because one who is quoted may say something parenthetical that will require parentheses. Most newspapers use parentheses for brackets because their type fonts have no brackets.

Burglary, Robbery. These are not the same. *Burglary* is "breaking and entering with intent to commit a felony." *Robbery* is simply "stealing from."

Can, May, Could, Might. *Can* and *could* usually express ability or physical possibility:

> He *can* play on Saturday.

> He *could* win if he tried.

May and *might* usually express permission or possibility:

> You *may* attend the game.

> She *might* want to go.

Cannot, Can not. Either may be used. *Cannot* is used more often, perhaps because *can not* seems more emphatic.

Can't hardly, Couldn't hardly. Both expressions have the force of double negatives and are illiterate.

Capital letters. The style guides (or style books) adopted by publications spell out rules for capitalizing that may differ somewhat from one publication to another, but all are based on one principle: The name of anything unique begins with a capital letter. The term "proper noun" is derived from names that are the property of something unique: Susan Sanders, Sears and Roebuck, Continental Can Company, November, Texas, New Year's Day, Germany, William Shakespeare, Tuesday, the Mississippi River. Adjectives that grow out of such nouns are also capitalized: Texan, Shakespearean. In addition, titles that are used in place of names are capitalized:

> I'm writing, *Mother,* to ask whether you can send me an advance on my allowance.

> Please, *Mayor,* listen to the voice of the people.

The principle of uniqueness in capitalizing is a fair guide, but there are several exceptions. A writer should refer to "John's *mother*," not to "John's *Mother*," and to "a call from the *mayor*," not to "a call from the *Mayor*." In these instances, the writer is not using a title in place of a name but is using descriptive words.

Seasons ("spring," "fall") are not capitalized in constructions such as "next *spring*" or "last *fall*." Sections of the country are capitalized when referring to a region or culture—"the *West*," "the *South*"—but not in referring to them as directions: "I expect to go *north* in September."

Titles of books, plays, films, and the like are capitalized, but not conjunctions, articles *(a, an, the)* and prepositions, unless one of these is the first or last word:

The Man Who Was Not with It

One Flew over the Cuckoo's Nest

The World We Live In

Once upon a Mattress

Pride and Prejudice

Capitalize the initial letter in an independent clause after a colon ("It was a wild collection: *She* had everything from campaign buttons to camp tents"), but do not capitalize the initial letter of a dependent clause after a colon ("It was a wild collection: everything from campaign buttons to camp tents").

Centers around. This is often used. It is wrong. *Center* refers to a point. Use "centers *on*" or "revolves *around.*"

Chord. Do not use with "vocal," as in "vocal *chord.*" It is "vocal *cord.*"

Cite, Site. To *cite* is "to refer to or to quote." *Site* means "a location."

Classic, Classical. *Classic* connotes importance, as in "The Battle of Gettysburg was a *classic.*" *Classical* refers to Greek and Roman culture, serious music that has lasted, and basic bodies of knowledge (*"classical Hebrew," "classical philosophy"*).

Colon. The colon usually tells readers that a pointed explanation of the preceding part of the sentence comes next, as in:

He had only three choices: flight, surrender, or suicide.

The colon is also used to introduce a quotation:

Hemingway wrote of Gertrude Stein: "It seemed to me at first that she was always right."

Commas. An old printer said he used this rule for punctuating: "I set type as long as I can hold my breath, and then I put in a comma. When I yawn I put in a semicolon. And when I want a chew of tobacco I make a paragraph." Some beginning writers are likely to sympathize. The conventions of punctuation, especially those governing the use of the comma—the most common and the most commonly misused mark—may seem unbearably complicated. The many conventions will not seem complicated to one who remembers that punctuation is an attempt to reflect the pauses, intonations, and pitch of the spoken language. Thus, the writer who reads his work aloud can often guide himself to the appropriate marks.

Commas are used to impart meaning and prevent confusion. Their primary functions are to separate main clauses (usually with the help of conjunctions), to separate items in a series, to set off introductory words and phrases, to set off parenthetical groups of words, and to avoid ambiguity. Following are the main conventions of comma use:

1. Commas should be used to separate clauses, but not to splice groups of words that should be independent sentences. Here the comma is used appropriately:

> The team won, but every player was exhausted.

Here the comma splices two sentences:

> The president spoke at length, later he said that he regretted speaking so long.

Reading the first sentence aloud shows the slight pause and makes it clear that the words before the comma and those after it are naturally connected. Reading the second sentence aloud shows the much stronger pause at the comma, which suggests that the comma should be a period. When an independent clause is short, no comma is needed:

> If I win I'll be happy.

But a pair of commas is always needed to set off a nonrestrictive clause—the kind that does not define or limit as restrictive clauses do, but could be made a separate sentence, as in:

> The player, who was injured throughout the 1975 season, decided that his baseball career was over.

That could have been written:

> The player decided that his baseball career was over. He was injured throughout the 1975 season.

2. Commas separate items in a series, like this:

> The tree was alive with lizards, bugs, and birds.

> She went to the kitchen, to the bedroom, and to the porch.

Some publications prescribe that no comma should be used before the "and" that signals the last item in a series: "The tree was alive with lizards, bugs and birds." That system works in most instances, but in some it causes ambiguity: "The relationship of industrial recruitment, airport expansion and public transit and the problems of pollution and land use will soon be known." Readers cannot be certain whether "airport expansion and public transit" together represent one item or whether "public transit" is the last item in the series.

3. Commas set off introductory words and phrases like this:

> Well, you know I wouldn't do anything like that.

> When the quarterback tried to pass, he was overwhelmed.

As reading each sentence aloud will show, the comma reflects a break. The words "know I wouldn't" in the first sentence, for example, run smoothly together, not at all like "Well, you." In most instances, failing to use commas to set off such introductory words causes confusion for at least a few readers.

4. Commas are used to avoid ambiguity:

Below, the senator was speaking to his colleagues.

Had the sentence been written, "Below the senator was speaking to his colleagues," many readers might expect the words after the first three to tell what was below the senator.

5. Some conventions of comma usage have been established because commas are needed to show pauses, or to reflect a drop in the voice of a speaker, or both. Commas are used:

a. To separate cities from their states: "Kansas City, Missouri, is growing."

b. To separate the parts of dates: "It happened on November 12, 1958, in Boston."
(When only the month and year are used, a comma is omitted: "November 1958.")

c. To indicate direct address: "You told me, John, that Harry would go."

d. To set off mild interjections: "Oh, why should I care?"

e. To separate modifiers: "She wore a pair of old, tie-dyed jeans."

f. To set off appositives: "Amy, the valedictorian, has the highest scholastic average."

g. To introduce quotations: "He said, 'Let the music begin.' "

Compare to, Compare with. In likening one thing and another, use *compare to*. In examining two things to show differences and likenesses, use *compare with*.

Complected. Use *complexioned*.

Complement, Compliment. *Complement* means "making something whole or complete": "The dancers *complement* each other neatly." *Compliment* means "praise": "Applause is the *compliment* actors seek."

Compose, Comprise. To *compose* is "to constitute or to make up." Thus, "The parts *compose* the whole." To *comprise* is "to consist of or to be made up of." Thus, "The whole *comprises* the parts."

Consensus. Because a *consensus* is a general opinion or belief, both "general consensus" and "consensus of opinion" are redundant. This is enough: "The *consensus* was that. . . ."

Consider, Consider as. In a sentence meaning "believed to be," *as* should not be used:

Jim Plunkett is considered the greatest quarterback.

In a sentence meaning "speak about" or "think about," *as* should be used:

> In judging him fit for the job, they considered him *as* a worker as well as a leader."

Contact. Avoid *contact* as a verb by stating the action specifically:

> The workers should call [or write, or visit] the precinct leader.

Contemporary. Use *contemporary* to mean "at the same time," but make certain that the time meant is clear to readers. "Babe Ruth's *contemporaries*" is clear, but perhaps not "The *contemporary* view of Babe Ruth's batting records . . . ." The "contemporary view" could mean "that of Ruth's time" or "that of the present." In such cases, it is usually better to use "Babe Ruth's *contemporaries*" or "In his time, the view of Ruth's batting records. . . ."

Continual, Continuous. One can practice the piano *continually*—in frequently repeated practice sessions—but not *continuously; continuous* means "without interruption." (One could, of course, practice *continuously* for several hours). *Continual* and *continually* are meant much more often than *continuous* and *continuously*. It is wise to mark the difference by thinking of the *o-u-s* at the end of *continuous* as standing for "*o*ne *u*ninterrupted *s*equence."

Contractions. See *Apostrophe.*

Could have, Could of. Use *could have,* never *could of.*

Council, Counsel. A *council* is a group with legislative or administrative functions. *Counsel* is advice, and *a counsel* is one, such as a lawyer, who gives advice.

Couple, Couple of. A *couple,* like a "pair," is singular. Using either term sometimes leads to awkward expressions. The phrase "a couple of" is too breezy for any writing except the most relaxed.

Criterion. See *Greek and Latin words.*

Curriculum. See *Greek and Latin words.*

Dash. The dash is one of the most useful—and one of the most overused—marks of punctuation. Dashes are used to set off a strongly parenthetical expression within a sentence, as in the preceding sentence. The dash is also used in informal writing to indicate a break in a sentence, as in this:

> It was horrible, terrifying—oh, I can't tell you how bad it was.

The dash is often misused near the end of a sentence:

> The club should also be a place where all members of the community can relax and be comfortable—adults as well as children.

The dash is misused in that example—a comma would have been better—because the dash is strong punctuation that demands strength of the words it isolates. A dash used near the end of a sentence asks readers to pause, then rush into the remaining words. Readers should not be made to rush into weak words.

In typing, the dash is made with two hyphen marks to distinguish it from the hyphen.

Data. See *Greek and Latin Words.*

Different from, Different than. *Different from* is preferable because things differ *from* each other. In a few instances, *different than* is acceptable, as in:

> The constitutions of all the nations are different, but those of the democracies are more *different than* the others.

Dilemma. *A dilemma* is a choice between two distasteful alternatives. The word is often mistakenly used to refer to a choice that one wants to make and a choice that one should make.

Discreet, Discrete. *Discreet* means "prudent." *Discrete* means "distinct or separate."

Disinterested, Uninterested. To be *disinterested* is "to be impartial, to have no selfish, private, or emotional interest." The word suggests neutrality. *Uninterested* means "lack of concern or enthusiasm, even boredom."

Double negative, more than one negative. The need to avoid double negatives is widely known. "He did *not* do *nothing*" means that he *did* do *something*. Not so widely known is the need to avoid using more than one negative in a sentence, even though the negatives may not cancel each other. When readers come upon "The city council decided *not to* consider the *failure* of the city manager to *void* the contract," they must stop and puzzle out the meaning of three negatives: *not to, failure,* and *void*.

Due to. The broadcast networks often apologize with *"Due to* circumstances beyond our control," thus further popularizing the use of *due to,* which has long been wrongly used. *Due* is an adjective. In nearly all cases, "because of" is preferable.

E.g., I.e. *E.g. (exempli gratia)* means "for example." *I.e. (id est)* means "that is." Thus, in giving one or more examples, *e.g.* is appropriate. In naming all the members of a class, *i.e.* is appropriate. But both expressions are better used in footnotes or in scholarly texts than they are in other writing.

Each, Every. *Each* is singular. So is *every*. *Each and every* is merely an emphatic way of saying *each* and should take a singular verb:

> *Each and every* man was ready to join the posse.

Each other, One another. Use *each other* for two, *one another* for more than two.

Effect. See *Affect.*

Either, Neither. "Or" is used with *either,* "nor" with *neither.* When *either* means "one or the other," it takes a singular verb: *"Either* John or Bill *is* to play third base."

Ellipsis. The ellipsis (plural, *ellipses*) is made up of three periods and indicates that part of a sentence or a quotation has been omitted. A fourth period is used if the omitted material occurs at the end of the sentence. Here is an example of both kinds of omission.

> The man who would be greater than he has been . . . will make a greater effort. . . .

That sentence reads in its entirety:

> The man who would be greater than he has been, greater than his friends think he can be, will make a greater effort than he has made.

Some who have discovered ellipses use them too often. Journalists seldom find ellipses necessary because in most instances, readers understand that quotations are not complete.

Emigrant, Immigrant. An *emigrant* leaves a country. An *immigrant* enters a country.

Enormity, Enormousness. *Enormity* means "atrociousness, wickedness." An *enormity* is an "outrage." The word for "great size" is *enormousness.*

Enthuse. A back formation from *enthusiasm, enthuse* is a gushing word that should be avoided.

Equally as. *Equally* does not need *as:* "The books were *equally* readable."

Etc. Using *etc.* seems lazy and makes a sentence trail off. It is better to name specific items, but when naming them would become tedious for readers or unnecessary, substitute "such as" or "including" at the beginning of a list to indicate that there are others. When *etc.* or a substitute for it seems unavoidable, use "and so on" or "and the like."

Euphemism. Some *euphemisms*—substitutes for plain words—are useful in avoiding vulgarity or grossness. Some are damaging because they substitute fanciness or abstractions for words that are weighty. To write "pass away" for "die" and "casket" for "coffin" is too fastidious. The task of the writer is to decide when he is avoiding vulgarity and when he is using words as veils to hide something better displayed in its plain form.

Everybody, Everyone. See *Agreement.*

Exclamation point. Like the dash, the exclamation point is strong and calls so much attention to itself that it should be used infrequently. It should be used, of course, with all exclamations:

Oh!

Damn!

How sweet it was!

Then I understood. It was Dave wearing the mask!

A writer should not merely be wary of using many exclamation points. He should guard against using many exclamations. The tendency to use many exclamatory sentences is usually a sign of overstatement in general.

Farther, Further. The first is used to express physical distance, as in, "It is *farther* from Los Angeles to Chicago than it is from New York to Chicago." *Further* is used to express figurative distance: "I have much *further* to go on this term paper than I thought I had." Many good writers sometimes use the terms interchangeably, but *further* is indispensable in expressing "more," as in, "The committee will consider the matter no *further*."

Fewer, Less. *Fewer* refers to "how many" and is used with countable units: "San Francisco has *fewer* people now than it had in 1970." *Less* refers to "how much" and is used with abstract and inseparable quantities: "There is *less* bourbon in the bottle today." In general, *fewer* is used for numbers, *less* for amounts, but some units that could be counted, such as money, are often considered single quantities, as in: "I have *less* than a hundred dollars in the bank."

Figuratively, Literally. These words are responsible for two bad writing habits. One is using *literally* for *figuratively*, probably because it seems stronger. The other is using *literally* with an old metaphor to intensify it or to try to make it seem fresh, as in, "He *literally* ate them out of house and home." Neither *figuratively* nor *literally* is often useful. If a writer who uses *figuratively* correctly will examine his use of it, he is likely to find that the expression, "The banker was *figuratively* at the edge of disaster," is obviously figurative; the meaning is the same without the word. *Literally* is of no use as an intensifier. It should be used to make a point, as in:

> Justices Black and Douglas believed that the Constitution means *literally* what it says: that there should be no restriction on free expression. They held that anyone may call another a liar, or a murderer, whatever the truth of the charge, without fear of successful court action.

Here *literally* is useful to make it clear that the other justices did not interpret *literally*.

Firstly. This and its companions such as "secondly" and "thirdly" are old-fashioned. Cut *ly*.

Flaunt, Flout. To *flaunt* is "to wave, to make a boastful display, to parade," as in: "The candidate *flaunted* his military record." To *flout* is "to ignore, to reject, to treat with contempt," as in: "The candidate *flouted* the law of slander."

Folks. Except in letters home, use the specific terms: "parents," "mother," "father." To write of people as *folk* or *folks* is usually both arch and archaic.

Foreign words and phrases. Some foreign words and phrases, such as *matinee* and *negligee,* are now part of the American version of English and should be used. The task of the writer is to decide whether he is using a foreign word or phrase because it best expresses his meaning and will be understood by readers or whether he is using such a word or phrase merely to show off his knowledge. See also *Greek and Latin words.*

Former, Latter. Avoid using these when they made readers look back. Repetition is usually better. In using *former* and *latter,* make certain that there are only two antecedents. It is wrong to write, "Senators Long, Church, and Mansfield spoke yesterday, but only the *latter* spoke at length."

Formula. See *Greek and Latin words.*

Fortuitous, Fortunate. *Fortuitous* means "accidental" or "happening by chance." *Fortunate* means "lucky."

Fulsome. This does not mean "full." It means "overfull, offensive, insincere."

Future planning. See *Advance planning.*

Gender. This refers to the sex of words, not people. Unlike many other languages, English has many neuters. The gender is usually indicated by the context of the sentence.

Gerund. See *Verbal.*

Greek and Latin words. The plural forms of some Greek and Latin words that are commonly used in English are widely known and used: *criterion* is the singular, *criteria* the plural; *curriculum* is the singular, *curricula* the plural; *phenomenon* is the singular, *phenomena* the plural. But the plural forms are not entirely consistent, and we have further complicated the use of some Greek and Latin singulars and plurals: *formula* becomes either *formulae* or *formulas; index* becomes either *indexes* or *indices; datum* is the singular, but some good writers use *data* as both singular and plural; the plural of *stigma* is neither *stigmas* nor *stigmae* but *stigmata; agendum,* the singular of *agenda,* has all but disappeared; the plural form of *spectrum, spectra,* is rarely used except in technical exposition. The only way to steer through such confusion, especially with change occurring relatively rapidly, is to consult a recently published dictionary.

Hanged, Hung. *Hanged* is the past tense for "the execution of a person." *Hung* is used to refer to "the suspension of objects."

Hopefully. This does not mean "I hope," "We hope," or "It is to be hoped." It means "full of hope." "*Hopefully,* the motel will have a vacancy," means that the motel is hopeful, which is ridiculous. The correct usage is: "She looked at him hopefully."

However. Many sentences in which *however* is used as a conjunction meaning "but" are smoother if *however* is tucked into the sentence rather than used at the beginning. If it is used at the beginning (*but* or *nevertheless* is sometimes preferable there), it must be set off with a comma so readers will not confuse it with *however* as an adverb, as in, "*However* haltingly he speaks, he is certain to win the election."

Hyperbole, Litotes. *Hyperbole* is heavy exaggeration, as in, "He worked like a demon." Like all strong techniques, hyperbole loses force and may seem extravagant or even odd if it is used often. *Hyperbole* sometimes misleads readers who do not realize the writer is purposely overstating. The same dangers are apparent in using *litotes,* which is understatement. "Henry is able to restrain his enthusiasm for politics" may be an admirably dry way of saying that "he dislikes politics," but some readers may take it to mean that "Henry must work to restrain his enthusiasm." The effects of *hyperbole* and *litotes* depend on the context in which they are used and especially on the writer's control of tone.

Hyphen. The hyphen has many uses:

1. To indicate compound nouns: "father-in-law."

2. To indicate compound adjectives: "jet-black hair." The effect of the hyphen in compound adjectives (and in compound nouns) is to make two or more words read as one. In contrast, "father in law" and "jet black hair" seem halting and possibly ambiguous. Phrases that are customarily read as one word, as when "high school" becomes a compound adjective in "*high school* student," are not hyphenated because readers are accustomed to the combination. Compound adjectives are hyphenated only when they appear before the noun. Write "nine-year-old boy," but "The boy was nine years old." Compound adjectives should not be confused with combinations of adverbs and adjectives. No hyphen should be used in "overly praised performance" because "overly" is an adverb; readers are accustomed to reading "ly" words into the next word so that they seem to be one, which produces the same effect as the hyphen in the compound adjective.

3. To prevent confusion: "He *re-covered* the furniture" makes it clear that he put on a new covering. The hyphen marks the difference between that action and the action suggested by *recover.* Other words, such as *re-creation* and *re-form* are hyphenated to indicate their difference from *recreation* and *reform.* Many publications favor using the hyphen to avoid the awkwardness that results from doubling vowels at syllable breaks: *re-elect, pre-eminent, re-entry.*

4. To join prefixes and suffixes: "anti-Semitic," "senator-elect," "self-evident," "ex-wife," "arch-conservative."

The hyphen is also used, of course, to break a word at the end of a line when there is not room to type the entire word. Such breaks should be made between syllables: *drug* at the end of the line, *store* on the next line, not *drugs* at the end and *tore* on the next. Some editors, however, tell writers not to break a word at the end of a line even at a syllable break, but to type the entire word into the margin or type it on the next line. These editors fear that typesetters will not know in some instances whether the hyphen was used because the word is always hyphenated *(drug-store)* or merely to break it at the end of the line.

I.e. See *E.g.*

Idiom, Idiomatic. Foreigners can more easily learn the proprieties of another language than they can learn its idiom, which is a form of speech that is peculiar to itself within the usage. They find it difficult, for example, to understand why Americans "go *to the stadium* to watch a game" but "go *to town* to buy some clothes." Why not "go *to* stadium"? Why not "go to *the* town"? There is no reasonable answer. Over centuries, we have come to develop the idiom. In some instances, of course, native Americans use unidiomatic constructions, as when some say, "I graduated high school." To write idiomatically is to write sentences as they are used by most educated Americans: "I graduated from high school," and "I am able to do that work," not "I am capable to do that work."

If and when. *When* usually has no value in this tired phrase. *If* it happens, it will happen at a particular time.

Immigrant. See *Emigrant.*

Implement. Use it as a noun, not as a verb.

Importantly. Like *hopefully,* this is often misused. *"Importantly,* he then made the decision," means that he made the decision "with a sense of his own or its importance." The writer meant that "it was important that the decision was made at that time," but the sentence does not say that.

Imply, Infer. One who speaks or writes *implies;* one who hears or reads *infers.*

Include, Including. To write either word immediately before a list indicates that not all items are listed.

Incredible, Unbelievable. Both words are often misused to express amazement at actions that are actually credible or believable. It is far better to reserve their use for occasions when one wants to say that something cannot be considered credible or believable.

Index. See *Greek and Latin words.*

Individual. This is often used when *person* would serve better. The *Oxford English Dictionary* (the traditional arbiter of the English language) says that substituting *individual* for *person* is a "colloquial vulgarism."

Infer. See *Imply*.

Infinitives. Like the rule that a writer must not use a preposition at the end of a sentence, the rule that a writer must not split an infinitive is now weak. Good writers point out that in some instances, splitting an infinitive produces a more readable sentence, as in, "The news caused the soldiers *to simply shout* in happiness." Placing *simply* before *to shout* or after would not be as smooth as splitting *to shout* to make room for *simply*. But splits should be infrequent, limited to natural sounds. Most readers have been taught that an infinitive should not be split, and many are likely to pause when they see one split. Moreover, a writer who feels free to split infinitives may insert adverbs as weak intensifiers: "to *really* understand," "to *better* see the picture." In general, do not split infinitives. In particular, judge whether a split reads better than a solid infinitive.

Interesting. In most instances, referring to something as *interesting* says nothing worthwhile. A writer should substitute specifics for this generality. To begin a sentence or a paragraph with, "It is *interesting* to note" or "It is *interesting* to consider" is usually no more than a lazy way to begin. Is the point that is about to be made important, significant, pivotal? If so, say so. If not, do not salute the point. To say that what follows is "interesting" does not persuade readers that it is, and if they are not taken with what follows, it is made doubly insignificant by the salute.

Irregardless. This is a nonword that tries to say what *regardless* says.

Italics. Italics are made in typing by underlining and are used:

1. To emphasize words or parts of words: "He said that he would *not* run for office" and "No, I told you I *dis*like apricots." Although such emphasis is occasionally necessary, writers who underline often to emphasize should remember that all strong techniques become weak when they are overused. Emphasis can usually be expressed by selecting words carefully and constructing sentences carefully.

2. To show the titles of periodicals, books, films, plays, works of art, and vehicles:

Newsweek

An Inquiry into Chaucer's Use of Imagery

The Heart Is a Lonely Hunter

Bonnie and Clyde

The Thinker

Merrimac

Spirit of St. Louis

3. To mark foreign words and phrases that have not become part of our language (as, for example, *matinee* has): *dossier, Realpolitik*.

Its, It's. See *Apostrophe.*

-ize. Americans are turning nouns and adjectives into verbs by adding *ize* so freely that writers who care for the language are beginning to complain. Perhaps there was no outcry when, long ago, *civilize, familiarize, patronize,* and the like grew out of *civil, familiar,* and *patron.* Good writers are not happy, however, with the pace of change that has brought us words such as *utilize, personalize,* and *familiarize.* The "ize" words that are trying to make their way into the language are better avoided.

Joined together. The first word says it all. Delete *together.*

Kind of, Sort of. Although "kind of a" and "sort of a" should never be used, *kind of* and *sort of* are useful to indicate an item in a species: "Winesap is a *kind of* apple." *Kind of* and *sort of* cannot be properly used to mean "somewhat" or "rather" or "in some way," as in, "He is *kind of* angry" and "She is *sort of* pretty." In the first instance, the writer should specify how angry. In the second, the writer should describe the features that make her pretty or say in what way she is pretty.

Latter. See *Former.*

Lay, Lie. These words are often confused because of one confusing element: *Lay,* which means "to put" and is used to refer to an object, is also the past tense of *lie,* which means "to recline." Thus, one should write:

> I *lay* my books on the desk.

> I *lie* down every night at 11:30 to try to go to sleep.

> I *lay* down last night at 11:30, but sleep wouldn't come.

The best way to distinguish these is to remember that *lay* as an independent verb always needs a direct object, *lie* never needs an object, and *lay* is the past tense of *lie* in addition to its independent status.

Leave, Let. The first means "to go away"; the second means "to allow." Either can be used with "alone," but the meanings are different. To "*leave* someone alone" is to "leave him in solitude." To "*let* someone alone" is to "allow him to be undisturbed."

Lend, Loan. The first is the verb; the second is the noun. To write, "The bank *loaned* him $500" is wrong.

Less. See *Few.*

Lie. See *Lay.*

Like. See *As.*

Literally. See *Figuratively.*

Litotes. See *Hyperbole.*

Loan. See *Lend.*

Mad. See *Angry.*

Manner, Nature. Both words are often superfluous: "He worked in a skillful *manner*," "The work was simple in *nature*." Such sentences say no more than "He worked skillfully," and "The work was simple."

Masterful, Masterly. *Masterful,* which means "domineering" or "imperious," is often misused for *masterly,* which means "expert" or "skillful."

May. See *Can.*

Media, Medium. *Media* is the plural. *Medium* is the singular.

Militate, Mitigate. *Militate* is nearly always used with "against" (sometimes with "for") and means "to have influence or effect," as in:

> The evidence gathered by the House Judiciary Committee *militated against* the president.

Mitigate means "to soften, to make milder or less severe," as in:

> The jury's sympathy for the prisoner's wife *mitigated* his punishment.

Modifiers. Adverbs, adjectives, and participles (verbal adjectives) are the main modifiers. Nouns also modify, sometimes too much, as in an example the grammarian Bergen Evans found in a newspaper: "The River Street fire house Christmas Eve party funds." And, of course, phrases and clauses modify. Remembering that modifiers are not independent but do their work on other parts of speech—they are qualities, and have neither the substance of things nor the vigor of actions—should help a writer limit their use. But modifiers are strong enough to be dangerous. They sometimes wander around sentences, pillaging and plundering. In these examples, where the writer places *only* determines meaning:

Only he scored a first-quarter touchdown.

He *only* scored a first-quarter touchdown.

He scored *only* a first-quarter touchdown.

Dangling modifiers sometimes seem to modify nothing, but more often they seem to modify the wrong thing, as in these examples:

> Opening the door, the room seemed huge. (Did the room open the door?)

> Attractive from a distance but gaudy on closer examination, he decided not to buy the picture. (Was he attractive but gaudy?)

> While driving the car, her eye was caught by an odd scene. (Was her eye driving?)

Modifiers such as *actual* and *actually* are useful only when they contrast the truth with error, as in, "He thought the paper would have to be long. *Actually,* he was assigned to write only three pages." Never use *actual, actually, real, really,* and *true* as intensifiers (as in "*true* facts").

Momentary, Momentous. Anything *momentary* lasts only a moment. Anything *momentous* is extremely important.

Myself. This word is misused by some writers who fear *me* (probably because they are uncertain about *I* and *me*). "The book was written by Bill and *myself*" should be "Bill and *me*"; "Bill and *myself* wrote the book" should be "Bill and *I*." *Myself* can be used for emphasis; as in, "He was punished for that? Why, *I myself* have done the same often." Or, *myself* can be used reflexively: "*I* injured *myself*."

Nature. See *Manner*.

Nausea, Nauseous. *Nausea* is a sick feeling in the stomach. But one who is *nauseated* is not necessarily *nauseous*. To be *nauseous* is "to cause others to be nauseated." An object as well as a person can be *nauseous*, can turn the stomach.

Negative. See *Double negative*.

Neither. See *Either*.

No One, None. See *Agreement*.

Not too, Not un-. *Not too*, as in "He is *not too* handsome" and "The play was *not too* good," is an increasingly popular form of understatement that may be acceptable in speaking but is much too imprecise in writing. *Not un-*, as in "The film is *not unlike* a Hitchcock production," is precise in that it expresses a distinction finer than "The film is like a Hitchcock production." But writers are sometimes so seized with *not un-* that they use it merely for the sake of using it. George Orwell suggested that they memorize this sentence: "A not unblack dog was chasing a not unsmall rabbit across a not ungreen field."

Numbers. In trying to conserve space, most newspapers use Arabic numerals for all numbers above nine. Other publications have established different rules, with many requiring numerals for numbers over ninety-nine, many others requiring numerals for numbers over twenty. Nearly all publications use numerals in these cases:

1. All numbers that have decimal points or involve fractions or other technical figures: 18.5 percent, $9.95, 7½

2. Dates: March 17, 1925; June 1975

3. Addresses: 7803 Cayman Road

4. Numbered items in a series: 7 Catholics, 14 Protestants, 11 Hindus

5. Page numbers: page 50, pages 104–111.

Off of. Delete *of*. Write "The plan was already *off* the ground" and "He jumped *off* the ledge." In some cases, *from* is more natural: "She came down *from* the ladder." *Of* is seldom useful with *outside* and *inside*. Make it "*outside* the classroom" and "*inside* the building."

One. Using *one* for *you* or for impersonal expressions sometimes sounds stilted, as in, "*One* must do what *one* can to make *one's* own way in this life." In an earlier time, grammarians tried to change idiom by ruling that *one* must be followed by *one, one's,* and *oneself,* never with *he, his,* and *himself.* There are signs of change; some good writers and some grammarians hold that this construction is now permissible: "*One* should do it in the traditional way, but *he* can change if the tradition seems outdated." It is probably safer to observe the old rule, avoiding stilted expressions by using "A person," "A man," "A woman," and the like. To speak of *oneself* as *one* to avoid using *I* is pretentious: "*One* saw *The Sting* and recommends it to all who enjoy comedy."

One another. See *Each other.*

One of the . . . (those). A common error is to use the singular verb in these constructions: "One of the best actors who *was* ever on stage" and "One of those women who *is* smooth on a tennis court." The intention in these examples is to place one person among many. The ability of the many is the pivot and determines the form of the verb: "One of the best *actors* who *were* ever on a stage" and "One of those *women* who *are* smooth on a tennis court."

Only. See *Modifiers.*

Parallelism. This is a technique writers use to match two or more concepts or two or more grammatical elements, usually placing the same word forms in phrases or clauses. "I came, I saw, I conquered" is a sentence made up of parallels. Caesar would have jarred the ear had he written, "I came, I saw, and victory was the result." In its simplest form, parallelism is contained in sentences that begin, "First . . . , Second . . . , Third . . . ," or sentences that contain balancing words such as "either . . . or," "neither . . . nor," and "both . . . and." The more imaginative parallels satisfy the reader's sense of rhythm and balance, but using many calls attention to the technique. Had Caesar written many sentences on the order of "I came, I saw, I conquered," readers would have begun to pay more attention to the sound than to the sense. Most conventional parallelism, however, merely repeats tense, person, voice, and grammatical structure to make sentences smooth. These are the constructions to avoid:

1. Shifting tense: "He *visited* his home town and *sees* his old friends." (*saw*)

2. Shifting person: "First hit the ball, and then *you* run." ("*First you*" or "*and then run*")

3. Shifting voice: "The speech *was made* by the senator, and then *he shook* hands." ("The senator *spoke,* then *shook* hands.")

4. Shifting grammatical structures: "The president was subdued and his voice was low, and he seemed to be apologizing with every word." ("Subdued, the president spoke in a low voice and seemed to apologize with every word.")

To make appropriate parallels, a writer should use articles and prepositions consistently. *A, an,* and *the* can be used once for all items in a series ("The sun, sea, and sand are inviting in Hawaii") or they can be used with each item ("The sun, the sea, and the sand"), but they cannot be used irregularly ("The sun, sand, and the sea"). Similarly: "In speaking, writing, and studying we should do our best," or: "In speaking, in writing, and in studying we should do our best." Not, however, "In speaking, writing, and in studying we should do our best."

Parentheses. Use parentheses:

1. To show the initials of organizations that will be mentioned later: Committee for the Re-Election of the President (CREEP).

2. To enclose numbers or letters that separate the items in a series: "The points are: (1) . . . ."

3. To direct the reader's attention to similar or more detailed references "(see *Who's Who in America*)," or, in some instances, to indicate a source: "(*Harper's*, July 1974)." In most instances, sources are shown in footnotes or are written as part of the text: "In Larry King's article in the July 1974 *Harper's.* . . ."

4. To enclose material that digresses and is not important enough to be enclosed in commas or in dashes: "To make the point clear (or as clear as it is now), we must. . . ."

Commas always appear after, never before, parentheses, as is demonstrated in items 3 and 4 above. Periods go inside parentheses if the parenthetical expression is a complete sentence and is not contained in another sentence; outside if the parenthetical expression is not a complete sentence.

Participles. See *Verbals*.

Passive Voice. See *Verbs*.

Passed, Past. *Passed* is a form of the verb *pass*. *Past* is a noun or an adjective:

Time *passed* slowly.

The *past* is prologue.

Past time should not dictate present action.

Past is often used redundantly, as in:

His *past* experiences taught him much.

All that is *past* history.

Past serves no purpose in either example because *experiences* and *history* are in the past.

People. Use *people* for large numbers, as in, "Many *people* enjoyed the game." Use *persons* for small, exact numbers, as in, "Ten *persons* attended the performance." Both *people* and *persons* are used too often. More specific terms are usually better: "fans" and "playgoers." Instead of referring to students as "people," as many student writers do, refer to them as "students." If the context calls for more specificity, write "art students" or the like.

Per. Use *per* in technical writing, *a* and *each* in all other writing:

90 miles an hour

$50,000 a year

$100 payment for each (rather than *per person*)

Person. See *People*.

Personal, Personally. As intensifiers—"It is my *personal* opinion," "*Personally*, I think"—these words have no value. "I think" serves well in both cases, although writing that is dotted with such phrases is usually unconvincing. "*Personal* friend" has no value because we have no impersonal or nonpersonal friends. "*Personal* acquaintance" says no more than "acquaintance." *Personal* and *personally* can, of course, be used to distinguish from the impersonal:

Professionally, he rejects such actions, but *personally*, he enjoys them.

Restrict *personal* and *personally* to such uses.

Phase. This refers to a stage in a cycle and should not be confused with *faze*, which means "to daunt."

Phenomenon. See *Greek and Latin words*.

Plagiarism. This means "using the work of others without giving credit." Extensive plagiarism is "piracy."

Possess. This is often misused to mean nothing more than "have," as in, "I *possess* a strong mind." Writers who know the weakness of *has* and *have* tend to use *possess*, hoping that it will add strength. Choose another verb.

Practical, Practically. Do not use these as substitutes for "almost," "almost always," and "almost never." *Practical* is derived from *practice* and refers to the terms of "practice and practical purposes," as opposed to the terms of "theory or theoretical purposes."

Prepositions. Prepositions, which relate nouns to other words, should ordinarily be used within sentences instead of at the end. But many good writers think it nonsense to torture sentences merely to follow the no-preposition-at-the-end rule, as in, "He doesn't know from where his next meal is coming." In such instances, write, "He doesn't know where his next meal is coming from." Observe the old rule when it makes sense.

Presently. See *At present*.

Principal, Principle. The adjective *principal* means "leading, chief, foremost." The noun *principal* is closely related, meaning "chief official," or, used as a financial term, the sum on which interest is calculated. *Principle* is always a noun and means "rule, truth, or assumption." One could speak of the "*principal principle* of Roman law."

Proof, Proved, Proven. Be careful in writing of *proof*. Anything *proved* (*proven* is archaic) must be demonstrated beyond doubt. In most instances, instead of "This is proof that . . . ," one should write, "The evidence seems to show that. . . ."

Prophecy, Prophesy. *Prophecy* is a noun meaning "a prediction," as in, "The *prophecy* was defeat." *Prophesy* is a verb meaning "to predict," as in, "To *prophesy* defeat is to give up before the battle has begun."

Protagonist. The *protagonist* is the leading or main character in a literary work. "The main *protagonist*" is redundant. It says "The main main character."

Proved. See *Proof*.

Proven. See *Proof*.

Provided, Providing. Except when *provided* is used as the past of *provide*, it sets a condition, as in, "He will get the loan *provided* he has collateral." *Providing* should not be used as a substitute.

Punctuation. See *Brackets, Commas, Colon, Dash, Exclamation point, Parentheses, Quotations,* and *Semicolons.*

Pupil, Student.   One who attends an elementary school is a *pupil*. One who attends an institution of learning higher than an elementary school is a *student*.

Quotations. Indirect quotations are remarks a writer attributes to others without using the exact words. No quotation marks should be used when quoting indirectly:

> It is not true, the mayor said, that the city will sell bonds for the project.

Note that *the mayor said* is set off between commas just as such words of attribution would be set off in attributing a direct quotation. The British base their practices in quoting on single quotation marks. The American practice is to use double quotation marks, except that a quotation within a quotation takes single marks. (Quotations in American newspaper headlines, but not in news stories, are placed within single quotation marks.)

The primary use of quotation marks is to show which words are quoted directly, or verbatim. A secondary use is to mark words that are used in an unusual sense or in an unfamiliar way, as in:

> A politician can seldom indulge in the "luxury" of integrity.

This secondary use should be infrequent. Placing quotation marks around slang or clichés:

> The candidate has always won with a real "blast" of a campaign because he never hesitates to "tell it like it is,"

is like apologizing for using such expressions.

Most of the conventions in using quotation marks are strictly observed:

1. Commas and periods are placed within quotation marks whether the quotation is one word or many:

"Let us make merry while we can," said the king.

The king said, "Let us make merry while we can."

According to Franklin Roosevelt, we have nothing to fear except "fear itself."

2. Colons and semicolons are always placed outside quotation marks.

3. Exclamation points and question marks go inside or outside quotation marks depending on the sense:

Who was it who said, "Eat, drink and be merry, for tomorrow we die"?

He asked, "Why won't you vote for me?"

He had the nerve to say "Vote for Kennedy"!

Patrick Henry said, "Give me liberty or give me death!"

4. Titles of literary works such as articles, short stories, poems, and parts of a book are placed within quotation marks (most newspapers place book titles within quotation marks):

The article is entitled "The Public Agony of Political Journalists."

T. S. Eliot wrote the poem "Ash Wednesday."

The winning short story is "The Egg Is All."

5. Nicknames are customarily placed within quotation marks the first time they are used, then are used without quotation marks.

6. When one paragraph ends with a quotation that continues without interruption at the beginning of the next paragraph, no closing quotation marks are used at the end of the first paragraph, but quotation marks are used at the beginning of the next paragraph.

In scholarly writing and in many books, quotations longer than eighty words are introduced by a colon, begin on the next line, and are indented at both margins. Because the indentions indicate quotations, no quotation marks are used, but if an indented quotation itself contains a quotation, the writer sets off the interior quotation with double quotation marks.

Re-. See *Hyphens.*

Real, Really. See *Modifiers.*

Refer. See *Allude.*

Reference. See *Allude.*

Reason . . . because, Reason . . . why. "The *reason* is *because*" and similar constructions weaken sentences by adding needless words. "The *reason* the Forty-Niners can't win is *because* they have no quarterback" can be said more crisply: "The Forty-Niners can't win because they have no quarterback." "The *reason why*" is more acceptable than "The *reason* is *because*," but it can usually be eliminated as easily. "The *reason why* they won is that they followed the game plan for a change" can be revised to say, "They won because they followed the game plan for a change."

Rebut, Refute. To *rebut* is "to argue against." To *refute* is "to disprove." Be careful in saying that an argument was *refuted*.

Redundant. This means "excessive or superfluous."

Replica. A *replica* is not a model or a miniature. It is "a facsimile or close copy."

Respectively. This word is often used redundantly. Its purpose is to relate the members of one group to the members of another in order. "John, Bill, and Joe became professional athletes in baseball, football, and basketball, respectively," means that John plays baseball, Bill plays football, and Joe plays basketball. In most instances, readers automatically make the appropriate connections without *respectively*.

Robbery. See *Burglary*.

Semicolons. The semicolon is sometimes called "the intellectual's punctuation mark" because using it well seems to demand study and because it sometimes connects the parts of long sentences. But no one should fear it, and the mere length of a sentence is not decisive. The semicolon is used:

1. As a substitute for the comma when the comma has already been used:

> Study is difficult because one must find a quiet place, perhaps a corner of the library; because one's mind wanders, especially in the evening; and because friends are eager to have fun.

2. To separate the independent clauses of a compound sentence that are not joined by a coordinating conjunction:

> He worked hard; he was paid well; he enjoyed life.

3. To show more separation and a stronger pause between the independent clauses of a compound sentence that has a coordinating conjunction:

> The Senator decided not to run for reelection; and his wife was happy.

As these examples show, the semicolon marks the midway point between the comma and the period, or both.

Shall, Will; Should, Would. Nice distinctions were once made, but they have largely given way to idiom that does not observe the old rules. In an earlier time, *shall* and *should* were to be used with *I* and *we; will* was to be used with *I* to express determination ("I *will* go to the concert"). *Should* was to be used with *I* instead of *would* in conditional statements: "I *should* not have won the office without your help." *Will* is now more idiomatic than is *shall* in most instances, and using *should* conditionally sounds stilted. Idiom now dictates that *will* shows determination, as before; *should* shows obligation ("You *should* give him a hand"); and *shall* is used only interrogatively ("Shall I pay him?" and "Shall we go to the movie?").

Ship. See *Boat.*

Should. See *Shall.*

Sic. This Latin word should be placed in brackets immediately after an error in a quotation to show that the error was made by the source, not by the writer:

> *Editor & Publisher* magazine carried an editorial saying that "The media is [sic] certain to be blamed for the government's troubles."

Sort of. See *Kind of.*

Spelling. See the list below.

Split infinitives. See *Infinitives.*

Stet. A Latin word for "let it stand" used by an editor to show that an editing mark he made was mistaken. *Stet* means the word or words indicated should stand as they were written, not be changed to conform to the editing.

Stigma. See *Greek and Latin words.*

Structure. Use it as a noun, not as a verb. *Structured* can be used as an adjective, especially in the social sciences. A "*structured* interview," for example, is different from a "free-flowing interview."

Student. See *Pupil.*

Such as. Like *including, such as* used before one or more examples means that not all members of the class are listed. It is pointless and redundant to use "and so on," "and others," or "and the like" after a list preceded by *such as.*

Frequently Misspelled Words

absence	dependent	its/it's
accept	describe	khaki
accommodate	desert/dessert	lacquer
accumulate	desirable	leisure
achievement	diesel	library
acknowledgment	diphtheria	liaison
acoustic	disastrous	lieutenant
advice/advise	dissension	liquor
all right/already	dissipate	lose/loose

allusion	divide	lonely/loneliness
amateur	eccentric	maintenance
annual	ecstasy	maneuver
argument	eligible	marshal
arraign	embarrass	memento
auxiliary	enforceable	misspell
battalion	exaggerate	necessary
beginning	exhilarate	occasion
believe	existence	occur/occurred/
benefited	exorbitant	occurrence
business	experience	omit/omitted/
capital/capitol	explanation	omission
category	exuberant	pantomime
cemetery	fiery	perennial
chose/choose	fluorescent	personnel
colossal	forcible	Philippines/Filipino
coming	forty/fourteen	prevalent
committee	friend	privilege
commuter	fuchsia	procedure
comparative	fulfill	questionnaire
competition	gauge	quiet/quite
complement/	grammar	recommendation
compliment	height	repetition
connoisseur	hemorrhage	rhythm
conscious/conscience	homogeneous	roommate
consensus	hypocrisy	separate
corollary	independent	similar
council/counsel	influential	skeptical
counterfeit	initiative	sergeant
decision	inoculate	stationery/stationary
definite	irrelevant	villain
deity	irritable	weird

That, Which. *That* defines and restricts:

The car *that* needs repair is in the garage.

In this example, *that* introduces information to define the car being discussed and to restrict the reader's attention to that car. *Which* is nonrestrictive:

The car, *which* has no fenders, will run well if it has a grease job.

In this example, the information after *which* tells more about the car being discussed, but the clause does not attempt to define the car. The information in the *which* clause could have been placed in another sentence:

The car will run well if it has a grease job. It has no fenders.

In contrast, making two sentences of the first sentence above would require:

The car is in the garage. It's the one that needs repair.

In short, making two sentences that carry the same sense forces a definition. *That* is appropriately used much more often than *which*. (See also *Commas.*)

The fact that. It is not possible to purge writing of this phrase. But every writer should use it sparingly.

Total of. Except when "a *total of*" is used to begin a sentence to avoid beginning with a numeral, *total of* is usually redundant.

Toward, Towards. Although either may be used, *toward* is preferred American usage.

Try and. Use *"try to."*

Type. Use *type* cautiously and remember these points:

1. Like *kind of* and *sort of*, *type of* should not be used to mean "somewhat" or "rather." Instead, *type of* refers to a member of a class.

2. Many uses of *type* can be deleted to make crisper sentences. Change "He was a strong *type of* leader" to "He was a strong leader."

3. Never use *type* without *of* before a noun:

> It was a different *type* examination.

> That *type* beauty doesn't attract me.

> It's hard to describe their *type* operation.

Of is needed in all these examples.

4. Use *type* as part of a compound adjective only in writing on technical subjects.

> "I have B-type blood" is acceptable.

> "He is a Kennedy-type candidate" is colloquial.

Uninterested. See *Disinterested.*

Unique. Use *unique* only to refer to anything that is one of a kind. Nothing is "a bit *unique*," "fairly *unique*," or "very *unique*." It is *unique* or it is not. In most instances, "unusual" is meant.

Unknown. This is often misused for "undisclosed" and "unidentified," as in:

> The president's destination is *unknown*.

> What she thinks of him is *unknown*.

The president's destination is known to him. Her thoughts, if she knows her own mind, are known to her. In each example, "undisclosed" is the meaning. In the case of the "Unknown Soldier," "unidentified" would be more precise.

Use, Utilize. Utilize and utilization seldom have any value that is not better expressed by *use*.

> He *utilized* all the garden tools.

He *used* all the garden tools.

They were unhappy with our *utilization* of stringed instruments.

They were unhappy with our *use* of stringed instruments.

Many sentences containing *use of* can be better written without it:

Gardening is improved with the *use of* the right tools.

Using the right tools improves gardening.

Will. See *Shall*.

Would. See *Shall*.

Verbs, Voice. *Verb* comes from the Latin word meaning "word," which suggests the importance of verbs. Their value is pointed up in so many passages in this book that it is necessary here to mention only the property of verbs known as "voice."

1. Active voice: "Susan *wrote* the paper."

2. Passive voice: "The paper *was written* by Susan."

3. In nearly all instances, the active is preferred because it *is* active, and thus lends vigor to writing. The passive is better only when the focus is on what was acted upon.

Verbals. Gerunds, participles, and infinitives are derived from verbs and are known as verbals:

1. Gerunds end in *ing* and are used as nouns: "*Dancing* is fun."

2. Participles are used as adjectives: "This *driving* manual is dull."

3. Infinitives, which are made up of *to* and a verb, are used primarily as nouns, occasionally as adjectives or adverbs: "We began *to sweat* after an hour."

Like most verbs, most verbals lend vigor.

When, Where. Resist the temptation to use these to introduce definitions:

Passing a law is *when* the legislature votes in favor of a bill and the governor signs it.

Making good in this society is *where* you're able to buy many things.

Whether or not. Use *or not* only to give equal emphasis to the alternative. In most instances, *whether* does all the needed work.

Which. See *That*.

While. Use *while* to indicate time, not as a substitute for "although," "even though," "but," and "and." "*While* she was working, he made dinner."

Who, Whom. Although *whom* is seemingly disappearing in speech, it is still useful in writing when it is used appropriately, as an object. *Who* is always a subject. *Whom* is always an object.

-wise. Like *-ize, -wise* is being married to words it dislikes: *gradewise, pricewise, saleswise.* It is comfortable with *otherwise* and *clockwise.* Let it rest there.

Would. See *Shall.*

APPENDIX C
American Society of Journalists and Authors Code of Ethics and Fair Practices

Preamble

Over the years, an unwritten code governing editor-writer relationships has arisen. The American Society of Journalists and Authors has compiled the major principles and practices of that code that are generally recognized as fair and equitable.

The ASJA has also established a Committee on Editor-Writer Relations to investigate and mediate disagreements brought before it, either by members or by editors. In its activity this committee shall rely on the following guidelines.

1. Truthfulness, Accuracy, Editing

The writer shall at all times perform professionally and to the best of his or her ability, assuming primary responsibility for truth and accuracy. No writer shall deliberately write into an article a dishonest, distorted, or inaccurate statement.

Editors may correct or delete copy for purposes of style, grammar, conciseness, or arrangement, but may not change the intent or sense without the writer's permission.

2. Sources

A writer shall be prepared to support all statements made in his or her manuscripts, if requested. It is understood, however, that the publisher shall respect any and all promises of confidentiality made by the writer in obtaining information.

3. Ideas

An idea shall be defined not as a subject alone but as a subject combined with an approach. A writer shall be considered to have a proprietary right to an idea suggested to an editor and to have priority in the development of it.

4. Acceptance of an Assignment

A request from an editor that the writer proceed with an idea, however worded and whether oral or written, shall be considered an assignment: (The word "assignment" here is understood to mean a definite order for an article.) It shall be the obligation of the writer to proceed as rapidly as possible toward the completion of an assignment, to meet a deadline mutually agreed upon, and not to agree to unreasonable deadlines.

5. Report on Assignment

If in the course of research or during the writing of the article, the writer concludes that the assignment will not result in a satisfactory article, he or she shall be obliged to so inform the editor.

6. Withdrawal

Should a disagreement arise between the editor and writer as to the merit or handling of an assignment, the editor may remove the writer on payment of mutually satisfactory compensation for the effort already expended, or the writer may withdraw without compensation and, if the idea for the assignment originated with the writer, may take the idea elsewhere without penalty.

7. Agreements

The practice of written confirmation of all agreements between editors and writers is strongly recommended, and such confirmation may originate with the editor, the writer, or an agent. Such a memorandum of confirmation should list all aspects of the assignment including subject, approach, length, special instructions, payments, deadline, and kill fee (if any). Failing prompt contradictory response to such a memorandum, both parties are entitled to assume that the terms set forth therein are binding.

8. Rewriting

No writer's work shall be rewritten without his or her advance consent. If an editor requests a writer to rewrite a manuscript, the writer shall be obliged to do so but shall alternatively be entitled to withdraw the manuscript and offer it elsewhere.

9. Bylines

Lacking any stipulation to the contrary, a byline is the author's unquestioned right. All advertisements of the article should also carry the author's name. If an author's byline is omitted from a published article, no matter what the cause or reason, the publisher shall be liable to compensate the author financially for the omission.

10. Updating

If delay in publication necessitates extensive updating of an article, such updating shall be done by the author, to whom additional compensation shall be paid.

11. Reversion of Rights

A writer is not paid by money alone. Part of the writer's compensation is the intangible value of timely publication. Consequently, if after six months the publisher has not scheduled an article for publication, or within twelve months has not published an article, the manuscript and all rights therein should revert to the author without penalty or cost to the author.

12. Payment for Assignments

An assignment presumes an obligation upon the publisher to pay for the writer's work upon satisfactory completion of the assignment, according to the agreed terms. Should a manuscript that has been accepted, orally or in writing, by a publisher or any representative or employee of the publisher, later be deemed unacceptable, the publisher shall nevertheless be obliged to pay the writer in full according to the agreed terms.

If an editor withdraws or terminates an assignment, due to no fault of the writer, after work has begun but prior to completion of the manuscript, the writer is entitled to compensation for work already put in; such compensation shall be negotiated between editor and author and shall be commensurate with the amount of work already completed. If a completed assignment is not acceptable, due to no fault of the writer, the writer is nevertheless entitled to payment; such payment, in common practice, has varied from half the agreed-upon price to the full amount of that price.

13. Time of Payments

The writer is entitled to payment for an accepted article within ten days of delivery. No article payment should ever be subject to publication.

14. Expenses

Unless otherwise stipulated by the editor at the time of an assignment, a writer shall assume that normal, out-of-pocket expenses will be reimbursed by the publisher. Any extraordinary expenses anticipated by the writer shall be discussed with the editor prior to incurring them.

15. Insurance

A magazine that gives a writer an assignment involving any extraordinary hazard shall insure the writer against death or disability during the course of travel or the hazard, or, failing that, shall honor the cost of such temporary insurance as an expense account item.

16. Loss of Personal Belongings

If, as a result of circumstances or events directly connected with a perilous assignment and due to no fault of the writer, a writer suffers loss of personal belongings or professional equipment or incurs bodily injury, the publisher shall compensate the writer in full.

17. Copyright, Additional Rights

It shall be understood, unless otherwise stipulated in writing, that sale of an article manuscript entitles the purchaser to first North American publication rights only, and that all other rights are retained by the author. Under no circumstances shall an independent writer be required to sign a so-called "all rights transferred" or "work made for hire" agreement as a condition of assignment, of payment, or of publication.

18. Reprints

All revenues from reprints shall revert to the author exclusively, and it is incumbent upon a publication to refer all requests for reprint to the author. The author has a right to charge for such reprints and must request that the original publication be credited.

19. Agents

According to the Society of Authors' Representatives, the accepted fee for an agent's services has long been ten percent of the writer's receipts, except for foreign rights representation. An agent may not represent editors or publishers. In the absence of any agreement to the contrary, a writer shall not be obliged to pay an agent a fee on work negotiated, accomplished, and paid for without the assistance of the agent.

20. TV and Radio Promotion

The writer is entitled to be paid for personal participation in TV or radio programs promoting periodicals in which the writer's work appears.

21. Indemnity

No writer should be obliged to indemnify any magazine or book publisher against any claim, actions, or proceedings arising from an article or book.

22. Proofs

The editor shall submit edited proofs of the author's work to the author for approval, sufficiently in advance of publication that any errors may be brought to the editor's attention. If for any reason a publication is unable to so deliver or transmit proofs to the author, the author is entitled to review the proofs in the publication's office.

ON "WORK MADE FOR HIRE": A STATEMENT OF POSITION

ANNOUNCED APRIL 28, 1978

It has long been the established practice for responsible periodicals, in commissioning articles by free-lance writers, to purchase only one-time publication rights—commonly known as "first North American rights"—to such articles, the author retaining all other rights exclusively and all revenues received from the subsequent sale of other rights reverting to the author.

This practice is affirmed by the Code of Ethics and Fair Practices of the American Society of Journalists and Authors (ASJA), the national organization of independent nonfiction writers. The philosophy underlying this tradition has been further reaffirmed by the Copyright Law of 1976, which took effect in January of 1978 and states explicitly that copyright is vested in the author of a work and commences at the moment of creation of that work. "Copyright" is, literally, the "right to copy"—i.e., to publish in any form; that right is the author's, transferable only by written agreement and only to the degree, and under the terms, specified by such agreement.

It has come to the attention of the ASJA that certain periodical publishers have recently sought to circumvent the clear intent of the law by requiring independent writers, as a condition of arti-

---

cle assignment, to sign so-called "all rights transferred" or "work made for hire" agreements. "All rights transferred" signifies that the author, the recognized copyright owner, transfers that ownership—and the right to all future revenues that may accrue therefrom—to the publisher. A "work made for hire" agreement specifically relegates the independent writer, so far as the article under consideration is concerned, to the status of an employee and creates a mythical—but nonetheless presumably legally binding—relationship in which the author agrees to function as a hired hand, while the publisher assumes the mantle of "creator" of the work, with all the rights of ownership vested in the creator under the law.

Both types of agreement clearly presume that the work being produced has an inherent value beyond one-time publication. Both the law and the ASJA Code of Ethics recognize that presumption, and it is the intent of both documents that the transfer of any rights beyond one-time publication take place only as the result of negotiation that assigns a monetary value to each such specific right a publisher seeks to acquire. Both types of agreement described above deny the author's basic role as owner and creator and seek to wrest from the writer, even before work has been produced, all future interest in revenues that may derive from that work.

This effort, subverting the intent of the law and contrary to ethical publishing trade practices, is condemned by the American Society of Journalists and Authors. The demand for blanket assignment of all future right and interest in the article or other creative work simply *will not be met* by responsible independent writers. Publishers who persist in issuing such inequitable agreements in connection with commissioned works will find that they have done so at the certain risk of losing a healthy flow of superior professional material. The result, for those periodicals, is likely to be a sharp and inevitable decline in editorial quality—an erosion and debasement of the standards on which periodicals must rely in order to attract readers and maintain their own reputations.

SUGGESTED LETTER OF AGREEMENT

Originating with the writer (to be used when publication does not issue written confirmation of assignment).

EDITOR'S NAME & TITLE   DATE
PUBLICATION
ADDRESS

Dear EDITOR'S NAME:

This will confirm our agreement that I will research and write an article of approximately NUMBER words on the subject of BRIEF DESCRIPTION, in accord with our discussion of DATE.

The deadline for delivery of this article to you is DATE.

It is understood that my fee for this article shall be $ AMOUNT, payable on acceptance, for which sum PUBLICATION shall be entitled to first North American publication rights in the article.[1] If this assignment does not work out after I have submitted a completed manuscript, a kill fee of $ AMOUNT shall be paid to me.

It is further understood that you shall reimburse me for routine expenses incurred in the researching and writing of the article, including long-distance telephone calls, and that extraordinary expenses, should any such be anticipated, will be discussed with you before they are incurred.[2]

It is also agreed that you will submit proofs of the article for my examination, sufficiently in advance of publication to permit correction of errors.

This letter is intended to cover the main points of our agreement. Should any disagreement arise on these or other matters, we agree to rely upon the guidelines set forth in the Code of Ethics and Fair Practices of the American Society of Journalists and Authors.

Please confirm our mutual understanding by signing the copy of this agreement and returning it to me.

Sincerely,

(signed)

WRITER'S NAME

PUBLICATION

by _____
         NAME AND TITLE

Date _____

NOTES

[1]If discussion included sale of other rights, this clause should specify basic fee for first North American rights, additional fees and express rights each covers, and total amount.

[2]Any other conditions agreed upon, such as inclusion of travel expenses or a maximum dollar amount for which the writer will be compensated, should also be specified.

AMERICAN SOCIETY OF JOURNALISTS AND AUTHORS, INC.
1501 BROADWAY, SUITE 1907, NEW YORK NY 10036 • (212) 997-0947

APPENDIX D
Glossary of Newspaper and Magazine Terms

NEWSPAPER TERMS

Ad   An advertisement.

Advance   A news story about an event to occur in the future.

AM   Morning newspaper.

Angle   A slant or special aspect of a story.

AP   Associated Press.

Art   General term for all newspaper illustrations, including photographs.

Backroom, or Backshop   Mechanical section of a small newspaper plant.

Banner   A headline stretching across a page; also known as a streamer, a line.

Beat   An exclusive news story; also, a reporter's regular run, as "City Hall beat."

BF   An abbreviation for bold face or black face type.

Body type   The small type, usually 8-point, in which most news stories are printed.

Box   News material enclosed by line rules.

Break   To become available for publication.

Bull dog   The earliest edition of the newspaper.

Bulletin   An urgent last-minute news brief.

By-line   Signature of a reporter preceding a story.

Caps   Capital letters.

Caption   Cutline; explanatory material that accompanies art.

CLC   Capital and lower-case letters, as in headlines.

Clip   A newspaper clipping.

Cold type   Characters set through a photographic or computerized process without use of Linotype machine or metal type.

Color story   A feature story that plays up the descriptive elements of a news event.

Copy   All news manuscript.

Copy desk   The desk where copy is edited and headlines are written.

Copy reader   A newsroom employee who reads and corrects copy and prepares heads.

Correspondent   An out-of-town reporter.

Cover   To get all the available news about an event.

CRT   Cathode Ray Terminal, also Video Display Terminal (VDT), on which an editor may view and edit copy entered into a computer by a reporter or wire-service machine.

Cut   Metal plate bearing a newspaper illustration.

Dateline   The line preceding an out-of-town story giving the date and place of origin.

Deadline   The last moment to get copy in for an edition.

Deck   A section of a headline.

Dummy   A drawing or layout of a newspaper page.

Ears   Small boxes or type on either side of the newspaper nameplate (flag) on page one.

Edition   All copies of a newspaper printed during one run of the presses.

Editorialize   To inject the writer's opinion into a news story.

Engraving   Same as *Cut*.

Exclusive   A story printed by only one paper; a scoop.

Extra   An edition other than those regularly published.

Feature   (1) To give special prominence to a story; (2) the most important or interesting fact in a story; (3) also, human interest or magazine type of story.

File   To send a story by wire.

Filler   A short, minor story to fill space where needed.

Flag   Front-page title of a newspaper; also known as nameplate.

Fold   The point at which the front page is folded in half.

Follow-up   A story presenting new developments of one previously printed; also known as a second-day story.

Fotog   Photographer.

Galley   A shallow metal tray for holding type as it comes from composing machine.

Graph (or Graf)   Paragraph.

Guideline   A slug or title given each news story as a guide to both copy editor and printer.

Handout   Piece of publicity material.

Head   Headline.

Hold for release (HFR)   News not to be printed until a specified time or under specified circumstances.

How-to-do-it   A story that explains in minute detail how to perform some activity.

HTK   Head to come; endorsed on copy indicating the headline will follow.

Human interest   Emotional appeal in stories; a story with emotional appeal as contrasted with straight news.

Insert   New material inserted in the body of a story already written.

Italic   Type in which letters and characters slant to the right.

Jump   To continue a story from one page to another.

Jump head   Headline carried over continued portion of jumped story.

Kicker   A small, short overline over the headline.

Kill   To strike out or discard part or all of a story.

LC   Abbreviation for lower case.

Lead   (1) Introductory sentence or paragraph of a story; a tip that may lead to a story. (2) Thin metal strips used to space out lines of type; the process of spacing out.

Leg man   Reporter who gathers information and telephones it in to a rewrite man at the office.

Linotype   A keyboard-operated machine that sets type in the form of a metal slug.

Localize   To stress the local angle of a story.

Makeup   Arrangement of news matter and pictures on a newspaper page.

Masthead   An editorial page box giving information about the paper.

ME   Managing editor.

More   Word put at the bottom of a page of copy meaning "more to come."

Morgue   Newspaper library for clippings, photos, and reference material.

Must   Designation on copy ordering that it be used without fail.

New lead   A new or rewritten item replacing a lead already prepared; new lead usually contains new developments.

News feature   Tied to a news event, the story is approximately halfway between the straight news story and the feature story.

Obituary   Obit; a death story or a biography of a dead person.

OCR   Optical Character Recognition or Reader. A device that interprets typewritten copy for a computer or typesetting machine.

Overline   Same as *Kicker*.

Pad   To make a story long by padding it out with words.

Personal   News brief about one or more persons; local item.

Personality sketch   A feature story that portrays a person, generally designed for emotional appeal.

Pix   Pictures.

Play up   To give prominence to.

PM   Afternoon paper.

Policy   Story written to suit the publisher's point of view.

PR   Public relations.

Privilege Right granted press by the Constitution to print with immunity news that might otherwise be libelous.

Proof An impression of type taken on paper on which to make corrections.

Quote Quotation.

Rewrite man Staff member who rewrites but does not cover news.

Rim Outer edge of a copy desk where copy readers work.

Roundup Comprehensive story from several sources.

Running story Fast-breaking story written in sections or takes.

Scoop An exclusive.

Seasonal story A feature pegged to the occurrence of an annual event, often a holiday.

Sidebar Usually a feature story that is subordinate to the main news story.

Slant To emphasize a phase of a story.

Slot The inside of a copy desk where the chief sits.

Slug A guideline set in type; notation placed on a story to identify it or specify disposal.

Straight news A plain recital of new facts written in standard style and form.

Sub Substitute.

Subhead A small head inserted in the body of a news story to break up long stretches of type.

Summary lead A lead summarizing high points, usually including "who, what, where, when, and why."

Suspended interest News story with climax at end.

Take A portion of copy in a running story, often one page.

Teletypesetter (TTS) Trademark applied to a machine that transmits and sets news into type automatically.

Thirty (30) The end; placed at the last of the copy to signify end.

Tie-in Tie-back; information previously printed and included in a story to refresh the reader's memory.

Tip Information that may lead to a story.

UPI United Press International.

MAGAZINE TERMS

Analysis An article that is a critical examination, usually designed to explain an event.

Angle An aspect or emphasis played up by a writer, as in "woman's angle": emphasizing elements that will interest women.

Art Any illustration.

Assignment A writing or editing task.

Back of the book   Last section of a magazine, usually made up of materials that appear after the main editorial section.

Blackite   Black and white pictures.

Bleed   Running a picture to the edge of a page.

Blurb   A short, appreciative description of a story or article.

Book   Generally, a synonym for magazine.

Caption   Synonymous with *Cutline*.

Center spread   The two facing pages printed on a single sheet.

Color   (1) To enliven writing; (2) to exaggerate and falsify.

Copy   Any written material intended for publication.

Copy reader   One who edits and otherwise processes copy.

Cover   (1) To gather facts; (2) the outer pages of a magazine. The outside front is the first cover; the inside is the second cover; the inside back is the third cover; the outside back is the fourth cover.

Cover plug   Special emphasis on the first cover for one or more stories.

CTC   Copy to come.

CTG   Copy to go.

Cut   (1) An engraving; (2) to shorten copy.

Cutline   The text accompanying art.

Dateline   Printing of date on any page.

Deadline   Last minute for turning in copy or art.

Department   A regular column or page.

Descriptive   The article given to describing, usually a place.

Dirty copy   Written material heavy with errors or corrections.

Double-page spread   Two facing pages of text or pictures or both.

Double truck   An editorial or advertising layout covering two pages made up as a single unit.

Dress   The appearance of a magazine.

Dummy   The draft of a magazine showing positions of elements. A diagram dummy is careful and complete. A hand dummy is roughly drawn. A paste-up dummy is made up of proofs of elements pasted in their positions. A positive blue dummy shows blueprints in roto-gravure form.

Duotone   Art in two colors.

Edition   All identical copies.

Ed page   Editorial page.

Essay-review   A feature article that reviews a book, a movie, a play, etc. within the larger context of the subject of the book, movie, or play.

Fat   (1) Oversize copy; (2) type that is too wide.

Feature   (1) To play up or emphasize; (2) an article, usually human interest, related to news but not necessarily news.

Filler   Copy set in type for use in emergencies.

Format   The size, shape, and appearance of a magazine.

Free-lance   An unattached writer or artist.

Front of the book   The main editorial section.

Galley proof   An impression of type that is held in a shallow metal tray, or galley.

Ghost writer   One who writes for others without receiving public credit.

Gutter   The space between left- and right-hand pages.

Hack   A writer who will work on any assignment for any publication.

Handout   Publicity release.

Head   Name, headline, title of a story.

Headnote   Short text accompanying the head and carrying information on the story, the author, or both.

Hokum   Overly sentimental copy or art.

Hold   Not to be published without release; HFR, or "hold for release."

House ad   An advertisement for the magazine in which it appears or for another issued by the same publisher.

House magazine   (also known as house organ or company magazine) Internal house publications are issued for employees; external house publications may go only to company-related persons (customers, stockholders, and dealers) or to the public.

HTK   Head to come: a note to the printer that the headline is not accompanying the copy, but will be supplied later.

Human interest   Feature material designed to appeal to the emotions. Also called personality sketch.

Impure pages   Those carrying commercial *puffs*.

Indicia   Mailing information data required by the post office.

Informative   A feature article that informs readers, normally about a place or a process.

Island   Position of an advertisement surrounded by reading matter.

Jump   (1) Running a story from one page to another; (2) the portion jumped.

Jump head   The title or headline over the jumped portion.

Jump lines   Short text matter explaining the destination or course of the continued text.

Jump the gutter   Titles or illustrations that continue from a left- to a right-hand page.

Layout   Positioning of text and art on layout sheets.

Legend   Explanation of an illustration.

Make-up   Planning or placing elements on a page or a group of pages.

Markup   A proof on which changes are indicated.

Masthead   Information, usually on the editorial page, on publishing, company officers, subscription rates, and the like.

Must   Copy or art that must appear.

Name plate   (also known as flag) The publication's name on the cover.

Narrative   A feature article that is story-telling in that the events are tightly transitional.

Outline   The gist of an article.

Pad   To increase length.

Page-and-turner   Text running more than a page.

Page proof   An impression of type that makes up a page.

Personal experience   A first-person feature article that relates the writer's experience.

Pic   Picture.

Piece   A synonym for story.

Pix   Pictures.

Play up   To emphasize.

Policy   A magazine's viewpoint.

Position   Where elements of a magazine appear.

Profile   A feature article that describes a person.

Puff   Praising publicity release.

Pulps   Magazines printed on coarse paper stock.

Punch   Vigor in writing or editing.

Query   A letter summarizing an article idea and asking whether the manuscript might be considered for publication.

Rejection slip   A printed form accompanying a manuscript returned to its author and rejected for publication.

Reprint   (1) To print a story that has appeared in another publication; (2) a separate printing of an article after publication.

Review   A magazine carrying literary stories, critical articles, and commentary.

Running foot   Identifying information (magazine title, date, and so forth) appearing in the bottom margins in some magazines.

Running head   Same as the *running foot* except that it appears in the top margins.

Shelter books   Magazines that focus on housing or related subjects.

Slant   Generally, synonymous with *Angle*.

Slicks   Magazines printed on glossy paper and having large (usually mass) circulation.

Slug   Word or words placed on copy as a guide to the printer.

Slushpile   The mass of unsolicited manuscripts received by magazines.

Spread   A long story, often with many illustrations.

Standing head   A title regularly used.

Tail-piece   A small drawing at the end of a story.

Tight   An issue with little space left for additional material.

Trim   To shorten.

Typo   A typographical error.

Vignette   A very short sketch or story.

When room   Copy or art that can be used at any time.

Wide open   An issue with plenty of room for additional material.

INDEX

NOTE: Boldface items are in the appendixes.